United States Cryptologic History
Series IV: World War II
Volume X

West Wind Clear:
Cryptology and the Winds
Message Controversy-
A Documentary History

Robert J. Hanyok
and
David P. Mowry

Center for Cryptologic History
National Security Agency
2008

Table of Contents

Preface and Acknowledgments vii

Foreword. xxi

Chapter 1: Background: Interwar U.S. - Japan Relations and Cryptology. 1
    United States-Japan Relations, 1919-1940
    (Japanese Diplomatic and Naval Cryptology and American Codebreaking between the Wars)
    United States - Japan Relations Worsen, 1940-1941

Chapter 2: Intercepted Japanese Diplomatic Messages Reveal a Warning System, 19 November-28 November 1941. 15
    The Cryptography of the J-19 System
        Japan Fields a New Diplomatic Manual Cryptographic System
    The Americans Solve the New Manual System
    November 19: Japanese Message #2353 – The First Winds Instruction Message
    November 19: Japanese Message #2354 – The Second Winds Instruction Message

Chapter 3: The Hunt for the Winds Execute Message, 28 November – 7 December 1941 31
    The Search Begins – 28 November 1941
    Tokyo Sends More Instructions about Destroying Cryptographic Material
        The Hidden Word Message – A Complement to the Winds Messages
        Tokyo Sends Even More Instructions, 28 November-6 December
        7 December 1941: The Hidden Word Message Is Sent
        7 December 1941: The Winds Execute Message Is Sent

Chapter 4: The Winds Controversy: Myth and Reality. 53
    Captain Laurance Safford – In the Eye of the Controversy
    Safford Searches for the Missing Winds Execute Message
    Safford's Detailed Claim about the Winds Execute Message – February 1946
    Examining Safford's Version(s) of Events
        The Intercept of the Winds Execute Message

  Actions Taken in the Aftermath of the Winds Execute Message
  Who Saw the Winds Execute Intercept or Translation?
  The Matter of Missing or Destroyed Records
  Some Observations on Captain Laurance Safford
 The Case of Captain Alwin Kramer's Changing Testimony
 What the Japanese Said about the Winds Execute Message
 What the British and Dutch Radio Monitors Heard
 The Winds Controversy Resurfaces – Ralph Briggs' Claim
 The Winds Execute: The Final Casting

Afterword: The Winds Message, American Cryptology and History 95
 The Impact and Intelligence Value of the Winds Messages
  What the Winds Messages Tell Us about Prewar American Cryptology
  The Winds Messages and the Historical Process

Exhibits (Nos. 1 to 55) 103
1. Recovered Decode Chart of Text for J-19 Transposition System
2. Japanese J-19 Transposition Matrix or Stencil
3. Intercept copy of Japanese Diplomatic Message No. 2353
4. Intercept copy of Japanese Diplomatic Message No. 2354
5. K-10/J-19 Indicator Groups and Transposition Key for November 1941
6. Message No. 2353 translation worksheet
7. Kana texts of Japanese diplomatic messages Nos. 2353 and 2354
8. U.S. Navy translation of message No. 2353 (SIS #25432/JD-1: 6875)
9. Revision of translation of No. 2353 (26 September 1944)
10. True form or matrix (stencil) for message No. 2354
11. Translation worksheet of message No. 2354
12. U.S. Navy translation of message No. 2354 (SIS #25392/JD-1:6850)
13. Revision of translation of message No. 2354 (26 September 1944)
14. Transcription of Morse (Kana) Japanese news broadcast 8 December 1941
15. Message from Commander-in-Chief Asiatic Fleet to Washington re: British intercept of Winds instructions, 28 November 1941
16. Intercepted version of "Stop" message No. 2409 27 November 1941

17. Stencils of decrypted version of message No. 2409
18. Translation worksheets for message No. 2409
19. Translation of Japanese diplomatic message No. 2409
20. Example of telegram from Japanese Consulate, Honolulu, encrypted in J-19
21. Translation of Japanese diplomatic message No. 118, 28 November 1941
22. FCC documents related to monitoring Japanese broadcasts, 18 August 1944
23. FCC translation worksheets for Japanese "weather" broadcasts on 4, 5, and 8 December 1941
24. FCC, Radio Intelligence Division logs, 28 November - 8 December 1941
25. Translation of Japanese diplomatic message No. 2444, 1 December 1941
26. Translations of Japanese diplomatic message Nos. 2445 and 2447, 2 December 1941
27. Translation of Japanese diplomatic message No. 867, 2 December 1941
28. Translation of Japanese diplomatic message No. 2461, 3 December 1941
29. Listing of HARUNA messages from Japanese diplomatic facilities
30. WDGS G-2 message to Hawaii Department regarding contact with Commander Joseph Rochefort, 5 December 1941
31. Translation of 8 December 1941 Broadcast with Winds message - "West Wind Clear"
32. Intercepted "hidden word" or "Stop" message No. 2494, 7 December 1941
33. Corrected translation of 7 December 1941 "hidden-word" message
34. War Department message to monitoring stations requesting copies of all Japanese clear messages with "Stop"
35. U.S. Navy Technical Mission to Japan interrogation No. 11 – Mr. Shinroku Tanomogi, 30 November 1945
36. U.S. State Department message to London, United Kingdom, Canberra, Australia, and The Hague, Netherlands, requesting information on monitoring for Japanese Winds message, 6 November 1945
37. Message from American legation, Canberra, Australia, 16 November 1945
38. Messages from American embassy, The Hague, Netherlands, 5, 6 December 1945 and 26 January 1946
39. Messages from American embassy, London, United Kingdom,

  4, 15 December 1945 and 31 January 1946
40. Captain Laurance Safford's statement before the Joint Congressional Committee, 25 January 1946
41. Letter from Captain Safford to Commander Alwin Kramer, 22 December 1943
42. Letter in response, Kramer to Safford, 28 December 1943
43. Safford's coded letter to Kramer, 22 January 1944 (with code listing)
44. Letter, Admiral Husband Kimmel to Admiral William Halsey, 18 March 1944
45. Memorandum, Subject: "JD-7001, Special Studies Covering." 8 November 1945
46. Morio Tateno interview, 30 June 1961
47. Memorandum to Carter W. Clarke from William F. Friedman, plus handwritten notes, 19 September 194.
48. Operator log for Station "M," 2 December 1941, with notation by Ralph Briggs
49. Message describing destruction of Cheltenham facility records, 3 November 1945
50. Operator log for Station "M" without notation by Ralph Briggs
51. Message from COIS, Singapore, received in London 8 December 1941
52. Cable from S.I.S. representative in Manila to S.I.S. representative in Honolulu, 3 December 1941
53. British response (GC&CS #11279), 31 August 1945 to Colonel Clausen inquiry
54. Multinational Diplomatic Translation #25783
55. Telegram from Walter Foote, U.S. Consulate General
56. True form or matrix (stencil) for message No. 2353

Glossary of Terms and Abbreviations 317

Sources and Selected Bibliography 319

Index 323

Preface and Acknowledgments

"There is nothing makes a man suspect much, More than to know a little." – Francis Bacon

In the seemingly never-ending debate over the 7 December 1941 Japanese attack on Pearl Harbor, one of the significant topics of contention pressed by some revisionist and conspiracy writers, historians, and critics of the conventional view of the attack and the Roosevelt administration's role in it has been the phenomenon of the so-called "Winds Message" (hereafter referred to as Winds message). In the years after World War II, several writers and scholars and a few politicians espoused the position that this message was a clear warning that the Japanese were going to attack the U.S. fleet at Pearl Harbor. They have also argued that, beyond the simple fact of the occurrence of the Winds message, the contents and importance of this message had been revealed to senior American civilian and military leaders. They have contended further that the failure by Washington to warn the army and naval commands at Pearl Harbor, even though the former had intercepted the warning, made the ensuing calamitous attack inevitable. After the attack, the claims continue, high-level government officials participated in, or oversaw, a destruction of the evidence that such a warning had been received. The two commanders in Hawaii at the time, Admiral Husband Kimmel and Lieutenant General Walter Short, both claimed in later statements during their testimony before the Joint Congressional Committee reviewing the attack that if they had had knowledge of the Winds message they could have prepared for an attack.[1] To some adherents of this claim, the Winds message had acquired a near mythic status within the larger controversy over Pearl Harbor.[2]

During and after the war, the Japanese surprise attack on Pearl Harbor was subjected to a number of investigations by the United States government. In fact, the attack was the subject of eight separate investigations from late 1941 through mid-1946. Among them, three were conducted by the Navy Department, three by the War Department, and one was chaired by Associate Supreme Court Justice Owen Roberts that began within weeks of the attack. The final and most comprehensive was the postwar hearings by the Joint Congressional Committee under the chairmanship of Senator Alben Barkley (D-KY), which, among other things, incorporated all of the evidence, testimony, exhibits, and findings of the previous seven inquiries.[3]

With the exception of the Roberts Commission, which met in late December 1941 and limited its review of decrypted Japanese diplomatic messages,

---

The Eight Investigations of the Pearl Harbor Attack:

The Roberts Commission, 18 December 1941 – 23 January 1942
The Hart Inquiry, 12 February – 15 June 1944
The Army Pearl Harbor Board, 20 July – 19 October 1944
The Navy Court of Inquiry, 24 July – 19 October 1944
The Clarke Investigation, 14-16 September 1944, 13 July – 4 August 1945
The Clausen Investigation, 23 November 1944 – 12 September 1945
The Hewitt Inquiry, 14 May – 11 July 1945
The Joint Congressional Committee, 15 November 1945 – 31 May 1946

all of the other investigations considered in detail testimony and evidence regarding the Winds message in the two weeks prior to 7 December. Two of the seven Pearl Harbor inquiries prior to the Joint Congressional Committee Hearings of 1945-1946, The Army Pearl Harbor Board (20 July – 19 October 1944) and the Navy Pearl Harbor Court of Inquiry (24 July - 20 October 1944), heard testimony that a "Winds Execute" (hereafter referred to as the "Execute message") had been sent before 7 December. Both investigations concluded that the Execute message had been intercepted sometime on 4 December and that the substance of it indicated war between the United States and Japan and warned of the attack on Pearl Harbor. Both bodies also concluded that knowledge of the Execute message had reached the intelligence staffs of both the Navy and War Departments.[4]

Pearl Harbor Naval Board of Inquiry, July – October 1944

On the surface, these findings appeared to have some merit because there was a smattering of supportive evidence. The Winds message, that is the warning or alert that was known to some in prewar U.S. intelligence as the "Execute" message, had been intended by the Japanese Foreign Ministry (*Gaimusho*) as an emergency method to warn its diplomatic posts of a downturn in relations between Japan and the United States, Great Britain, or the Soviet Union. Tokyo expected that, in the time of crisis prior to any hostilities, its diplomats would have to destroy classified papers, as well as their manual codes and ciphers and any cipher machines in their facilities. Tokyo also expected that in such a time of crisis a host country would limit direct communications between Japanese diplomats and the Foreign Ministry, or even totally cut off such links.

To get around this potential severance of communications, the Japanese Foreign Ministry, near the middle of November 1941, had sent special instructions to its diplomats in the United States and Latin America directing them how they were to be kept informed of the status of relations between Japan and the United States, Great Britain, and the Soviet Union. One method involved the placement of innocuous phrases about the weather in shortwave voice news programs transmitted overseas by Japanese government radio stations. This method of sending secret messages is referred to as an "open code." These phrases indicated with which country relations with Japan were in trouble:

East Wind Rain – United States
North Wind Cloudy – Union of Soviet Socialist Republics
West Wind Clear – Great Britain

Based upon the evidence and testimony gathered by the various Pearl Harbor inquests, as well as later additional claims made by certain U.S. navy personnel, some scholars and writers from the postwar years advanced revisionist or conspiracist theories about the attack on Pearl Harbor and further claimed that such an Execute message had been sent and intercepted as many as three or four days before the Japanese strike. They also contended that the U.S. government had conspired to suppress this knowledge about the possession of the warning message. According to their version of events, high government officials had ordered the destruction of critical records, doctored other official papers, and badgered potential witnesses into silence or forced them to make scripted and mendacious testimony.

The primary, and almost exclusive, source fueling these claims of a conspiracy surrounding the Winds message was Captain Laurance Frye Safford, the founder and first commander of the U.S. Navy's code-breaking unit, OP-20-G. Safford had started the Navy's cryptologic section in the 1920s and commanded it until 1942. Safford first publicized his version of events concerning the Winds message in early 1944 when he testified before the Hart Inquiry. He later repeated variations of his initial story before the Army Board and the Navy Board of Inquiry later that same year. It was largely because of Captain Safford's high reputation within the cryptologic and intelligence communities that his charges were taken seriously by the various hearings before which he testified at the time.[5]

Captain Laurance F. Safford

Today, a substantial portion of the public still subscribes to this conspiracy view of the Winds message. This group could very well have grown over the years thanks to the proliferation of websites on the Internet about Pearl Harbor that contain entries about the Winds message. Many of these sites circulate the same charges and evidence that were first raised in the written literature of the last decades.[6]

Of course, there are many scholars and researchers who are skeptical or critical of the various revisionist and conspiracist claims revolving around the Winds message. Most of these researchers and scholars point to the serious technical and contextual shortcomings in the evidence put forward by those who see conspiracy behind the handling of the Winds message. Others suggest that the conspiracy claims are based on a selective reading of the testimony and evidence that surfaced during the Pearl Harbor hearings and in later years.[7]

Scholars and writers who have written about the Winds message from both sides of the controversy have been confronted with a mass of evidence, mostly in the form of detailed and difficult testimony during the seven hearings that addressed this issue. On top of this considerable body of evidence, there are several thousands of pages of documents to peruse as well. Generally, scholars have restricted their examination of the sources to a limited number of basic documents, usually a small number of translations of related Japanese diplomatic messages, selected excerpts from testimony given at the several Pearl Harbor hearings, and short, apt quotes from individual pieces of correspondence of the principal personalities. Yet, even the more detailed narratives of events still leave questions unanswered about how the story that the execute message might have been intercepted, the context of the original instructions, or "setup message," and the timing and origins of Captain Safford's version of events.

The reason for the shortcoming is that the available evidence consists of more than the documents gathered by the various hearings and published as exhibits. The U.S. government's departments, agencies, and commissions collected far more material than was ever used as exhibits. Then, again, there is some additional relevant material that has existed outside of the many hearings, and this latter material has seldom been invoked in the literature of the Winds message controversy. The existence of all of these sources suggested that it may be possible to examine important aspects of the Winds message story in a deeper fashion than before.

To the authors of this history, it seemed that at least two critical areas of interest in the Winds message controversy needed better explanations. The first concerns both the substance and circumstances of the Japanese warning system supposedly centered on the Winds message. As we shall see later, the Japanese Foreign Ministry was very specific when it set up the text, format, and procedures in its instruction message to its diplomats. At the same time, the Japanese also issued further, and in some cases, parallel instructions for similar systems that mandated code destruction, as well as other ways to inform its diplomats of the state of relations with the United States. The existence of these other systems will be told as well.

An important element related to the Japanese warning system is how the United States radio intelligence apparatus reacted to the knowledge of the instructions from Tokyo intercepted in late November 1941. Obviously, at the heart of the controversy is whether or not the Winds Execute message was ever heard. The answer to this issue is contingent on understanding the actions of the various elements of the U.S. government involved in the story: the U. S. Army's Signal Intelligence Service, the U.S. Navy's OP-20-G, and the Federal Communications Commission.

The second area of interest concerns the evidence for the various claims put forward by Captain Safford. In early 1946, Safford offered the Joint Congressional Committee a written and detailed memorandum of his allegations. Usually, it is this document to which reference is made regarding his allegations that the Execute message was intercepted and that knowledge of this event was suppressed. But Safford had been making similar charges for the better part of two years. And what he stated initially before the Hart Inquiry regarding the Winds message differed from what he asserted in early 1946. At the same time, there is important documentary information from before the hearings that point to the origins of his thinking and his search for what he believed was the evidence of the missing Winds execute message.

It is clear that only a deeper review of the documentary sources could resolve the many questions surrounding the Winds controversy.

This history, then, intends to present the story of the Winds message with an emphasis on selected documentary evidence, that is, with attached images of relevant and important documents. While a handful of the documents presented here have been seen either as images or in transcribed form, such as can be found in the several volumes of exhibits of the Pearl Harbor hearings, this single volume contains all of the standard, critical documents. This history also includes many documents that have not been seen before, such as the U.S. Navy's translation and cryptanalytic worksheets of the 19 November 1941 Japanese Winds instruction messages, and the translation worksheets of the Federal Communications Commission from early December 1941.

After reviewing the documents and discussing their context within the chronology of the Winds message controversy, this history should answer the following questions: (1) What was the cryptology behind the Winds message? That is, what were the communications and cryptography used by the Japanese to set up the Winds warning system and then what, if any, warnings were actually sent? At the same time, how did the American radio intelligence and code-breaking agencies intercept, decrypt, and interpret the Japanese messages, and how did the Americans react to the information about the Winds warning system? (2) What were the origins of the controversy that encompassed the Winds message? What claims were put forward regarding the intercept of the Winds execute message, as well as claims for a purported cover-up?

Two further questions are suggested by an examination of the documents. The first is this: Was there any way in which the warnings contained in the Winds message, which were aimed at Japanese diplomats, could have been construed as a specific warning of an attack on Pearl Harbor? As we shall see, a few of the major characters in the controversy believed this connection existed and some scholars in later years have repeated the claim. The second question is, what effect did the Winds message have upon the effectiveness of the operations of prewar American cryptology? There is no doubt that the Americans reacted to the knowledge of the possibility of a Winds execute warning message being sent. So how did the knowledge of the potential warning message affect American cryptology? Did the American reconfigure their operations, and, if so, how and to what effect on their overall workings?

Why a Documentary Approach?

One of the by-products of the eight hearings on the attack on Pearl Harbor was the retention of the documents that ordinarily would have been destroyed as part of the legally prescribed records disposition process employed by the military services and other agencies of the federal government at the time. Also, many personal records, especially those of individuals important to the events of late 1941, were retained as evidence gathered by the hearings, or for use in later memoirs or histories. This tide of source material has allowed scholars the opportunity to examine all aspects of the attack in a detail seldom replicated.

Even the most highly classified intelligence of the time – the decrypts and translations of Japanese diplomatic messages, including those encrypted in the cipher machine known to the Americans as Purple, were available to the various hearings. The intelligence from all such decrypts and translations was categorized under the title of "Magic." During the various investigations, many of these translations were entered into the record as exhibits and were sometimes discussed in great detail at the hearings. Along with the diplomatic translations, army and navy personnel associated with cryptology often discussed at length other aspects of radio intelligence, including such arcane disciplines as direction finding and traffic analysis. This exposure allowed later scholars and writers to discuss in detail these elements of codebreaking and radio intelligence in their works.

Yet, the abundance of source material did not always lead to a clear understanding of what constituted the Winds message or the context around it. The Winds message phenomenon often fell victim to the claims and counterclaims about the content, format, timing, and meaning of the warnings contained within the actual text. To the authors of this history, many of the arguments, both pro and con, regarding the questions of whether a Winds Execute message was intercepted prior to 7 December and whether there was a cover-up or a conspiracy to suppress evidence of the intercept, appeared to be disconnected from the available documentary evidence. Often, the explanations and descriptions about the execute message seemed to be talking about something not at all like what Japanese diplomats had been instructed to listen for on their shortwave radios. At the same time, these discussions often paid little attention to the context of all of the diplomatic messages during the crisis period before 7 December; it was, at times, as if the Winds message existed in a separate reality.

It appeared that if we were to enter the fray over the Winds message, it was necessary to bring along as much of the documentary evidence as we could retrieve. So this history, really a documentary history of the controversy, is intended to make available to all sides the basic sources: the worksheets and the translations of the pertinent Japanese diplomatic correspondence, the logs and chronologies of events, the pertinent correspondence amongst the major players, and associated memorandum and notes. With these papers available readily to everyone with an interest in the Winds story, it is hoped that we can achieve a resolution to the controversy.

The Sources and Nature of the Documents

The publicly available archival sources of the documents used in this collection were legion.

Foremost among the collections is the evidence contained in the Joint Congressional Committee Hearings on Pearl Harbor (1945-1946). The congressional hearings incorporated the evidence and testimony from the previous seven hearings and boards into its report. The Committee's Hearings included thirty-nine volumes of testimony and documentary evidence along with its Final Report.

Joint Congressional Committee, November 1945 - May 1946

Interestingly, the enormous number of pages of material – estimated by some at about 15,000 pages of testimony and 9,000 pages of documentary exhibits – do not reside in only one archival location. As several U.S. cabinet departments, agencies, boards, and commissions contributed material to the various investigations, the resulting documentation can be found among several Record Groups in the National Archives, at both the Archives in Washington, D.C., and at Archives II in College Park, Maryland.

There are a number Records Groups (RG) that hold documents of interest and relevance: RG 59, Records of the U.S. Department of State; RG 80, Records of the Secretary of the Navy, Records of the Pearl Harbor Liaison Office Files; RG 128.3, Records of the Joint Committees, 51st – 98th Congresses; RG 165, Records of the War Department; RG 38, The Records of the Chief of Naval Operations (CNO), Chief Naval Security Group; RG 457, the Records of the National Security Agency/Central Security Service (NSA/CSS); and RG 173, the Records of the Federal Communications Commission (FCC).

During the research we also consulted smaller collections of records such as the Laurance F. Safford Collection maintained by the National Cryptologic Museum Foundation, Fort George G. Meade, Maryland, and the David Kahn Collection also accessible from the National Cryptologic Museum Library. A further useful set of material regarding the Winds controversy is found in the collection of papers of Admiral Husband E. Kimmel, located in the archives of the American Heritage Center at the University of Wyoming, Laramie, Wyoming.

There is another minor source for this work that merits a special mention: the working papers of the late former NSA Historian Henry F. Schorreck. During his twenty-one-year tenure as the NSA Historian, Henry, or "Hank" as everyone called him, assiduously gathered or saved important caches of cryptologic records, especially those from the many decades preceding the establishment of the National Security Agency. Among his papers were copies of the encoded versions of the original Japanese instructions to the Winds message, the cryptanalytic and translation worksheets, and final translations. All of these documents are copies of the originals, which can be found in Record Groups 38, 80, and 457. It was the discovery of these worksheets that inspired the authors to proceed with this book.

The primary criterion for including a document in this history as an exhibit was its relevance, interest, or importance to either the cryptology of the Winds message or the ensuing controversy over whether an execute message had been sent and intercepted. While an estimated few hundred documents and scores of pages of testimony were generated by the seven hearings and inquiries that considered the question of the Winds message, a much smaller portion of the material actually passed muster when it came to relevance, insight, and importance. Those we did not include fell to the side for reasons of redundancy, prior publication, or because they simply did not add anything of value to the story. Interestingly, about forty percent of the exhibits that are contained in this history originally were not featured as exhibits from any of the eight Pearl Harbor hearings. These rather unique documents were discovered during research into the Pearl Harbor holdings of the many record groups and collections the authors reviewed for this history.

This volume finally came to contain fifty-six exhibits of the most interesting and relevant documents on the Winds message controversy. They have come from many sources and represent many of the episodes of the narrative of the Winds message. It is possible that some readers may dispute our choices or press for other items. But we believe that we have selected the documents that best tell the story.

Sometimes a version of a document was just too unique to pass up, and, therefore, we felt it should be included as an exhibit. During our research, we encountered copies of the translations of Winds instruction messages with substantial handwritten marginalia by William F. Friedman, the putative doyen of early American military cryptology. Friedman was a minor character in the ensuing controversy, having discussed aspects of the cryptologic context of the Winds message with Captain Safford. Friedman's notes on the translations are useful comments on Safford's claims, and to the authors appeared more useful (and insightful) than unannotated versions, both of which are available at the National Archives.[8]

For those who have researched any portion of the enormous cache of records related to Pearl Harbor, it soon becomes obvious that, while the hearings by Joint Congressional Committee and the other boards and courts conducted a complete as possible and exhaustive task of identifying pertinent records, the documents available in the various record groups are not originals, but versions or copies – whether they be photocopies, transcriptions, or paraphrases. This is not unexpected or unusual. The original records belonged to the various U.S. government departments and commissions, so making copies for the purpose of the hearings and investigations was the proper procedure.

Sometimes making a copy made good sense from the standpoint of preservation or usefulness. Some records consisted of handwritten notes, logs, or letters on paper that would have never stood up to the handling required during an investigation. At the same time, some of these same records were handwritten and for them to be easily referred to required that the text be transcribed. Therefore, many of the records of the various hearings available in the national Archives are, in reality, transcribed versions of the originals.

In some cases, records were entered as hearing exhibits marked as "paraphrases" of the original. This usually occurred when documents that were to be cited as exhibits could not be declassified in their entirety In these cases, the paraphrase was made when certain technical aspects of a message, such as communications or cryptographic details about the correspondence, or when information regarding sources or intelligence methods required protection. Examples of paraphrasing can be found in some of the October 1945 messages from General Douglas MacArthur's Headquarters in Tokyo to the War Department regarding interviews with Japanese nationals relating to Pearl Harbor.[9]

The Terminology Used in This History

Beginning with the initial revelations of the World War II Ultra success by the Allies in the early to mid-1970s, notably F.W. Winterbotham's *The Ultra Secret*, the public has been exposed to numerous arcane terms associated with the business of intercepting messages and the making or breaking of codes and ciphers. Unfortunately, from the early literature on the Ultra story through today, there still exists among many scholarly and popular writers the tendency to confuse or incorrectly mix these terms. This misuse of terms often has led to inaccuracies such as describing the German Enigma device as a "code machine," or confusing the term Purple – the covername given to the analog device used to decrypt Japanese high-level machine cipher messages – with the solution of the Imperial Japanese navy's main operational code, known as JN-25. Such mistakes in the terminology invariably lead to error-prone narratives and some incorrect conclusions about the role and importance of codebreaking to the outcome of World War II. For the reader's ease, many of the relevant terms used in this history will be explained below.

COMINT is the acronym for **communications intelligence** and can be defined as measures taken to intercept, analyze, and report intelligence derived from all forms of communications. This definition describes broadly and most accurately the entire American communications intelligence structure and process in late 1941 that existed to exploit Japan's and other nations' communications. This structure included the principal American code-breaking centers in Washington, D.C. It also includes the monitoring stations manned by American soldiers, sailors, marines, and civilians who listened in on the world's communications. It further encompasses the work of the analysts who decrypted, translated, and reported the contents of the intercepted messages, as well as those who passed this intelligence to the national command authorities in the White House, the Departments of State, War, and the Navy, and the service chiefs of staff for the armed services. It also refers to the theater sites, known as Communications Intelligence Units, and staffs who reported directly to the Commanders of the Pacific and Asiatic Fleets. The structure also connects, as well, to collaborating Allied agencies such as British Government Code and Cypher School (GC&CS) and its subordinate stations, especially the component in Singapore that was part of the Far East Combined Bureau (FECB). A closely related term is **radio intelligence**, which was more commonly used during the period before Pearl Harbor. Radio intelligence usually referred to intelligence gathered from radio transmissions short of actual decoding or decryption of messages, but often was synonymous with communications intelligence.

A similar term, **signals intelligence**, or **SIGINT** also is often used synonymously with COMINT. Signals intelligence, though, includes a broader range of emissions as targets. SIGINT includes the intercept, processing, and reporting of intelligence derived from noncommunications signals such as radar and navigational beacons. In late 1941, the idea of deriving usable intelligence from such signals was relatively new. At that time, the main use the of such intelligence, now referred to as **electronic intelligence (ELINT)**, was to develop so-called countermeasures to such signals, exemplified best by the use of the famous British "window" or chaff – strips of aluminum that reflected German radar signals and obscured their tracking of Allied bombing missions over Europe.

Another general term, **cryptology**, is defined as the study of the making and breaking of codes and ciphers. **Cryptography** is the study of the making of codes and ciphers. Cryptography is often used to describe both the entire inventory of such items for a country or some discrete element within it, such as "Japanese diplomatic or naval cryptography." A **code** is defined as a method in which arbitrary, and often fixed, groups of letters, numbers, phrases, or other symbols replace plaintext letters, words, numbers, or phrases for the purposes of concealment or brevity. To **encode** is to transform plaintext into a coded form. To **decode** is the break the code back to its underlying plaintext. A variation of a code is known as an **"open code"** or **codeword**. This occurs when a seemingly innocuous or ordinary word, words, phrase or number is used in a message or transmission to convey certain information or initiate an action previously agreed upon by the sending and receiving entities. The true meaning of an open code or codeword, as opposed to its literal or accepted meaning or connotation is supposed to be denied to anyone else who might be listening other than the intended recipient. As will be seen, this type of code plays a significant part in the Winds story.

Before World War II, codes came in the forms of pages, tables, or a book. On each page of a **codebook** or table, a plaintext word or phrase is aligned opposite its code unit or **code group** equivalent. Codebooks were arranged alphabetically or numerically in order of the plaintext, making it easier to encode a message. To facilitate decoding by the intended recipient, a second codebook was used that was arranged alphabetically or numerically by the code group. This procedure of using two separate books, known as a **two-part code**, was intended to complicate the cryptanalytic recovery of the codebook, a process known as **"bookbreaking."**

A **cipher** is a method of concealing plaintext by transposing its letters or numbers or by substituting other letters or numbers according to a **key**. A key is a set of instructions, usually in the form of letters or numbers, which controls the sequence of the encryption of the text or the decryption of the cipher back to the original plaintext. A cipher that results from transposing text is known as a **transposition cipher**. A cipher resulting from substitution is known as a **substitution cipher**. Transforming plaintext into cipher is called **encryption**. Breaking cipher back to plaintext is called **decryption**.

Two examples of famous ciphers from World War II are the Axis cipher machines, the German Enigma and the Japanese device, codenamed Purple by the Americans, but known to the Japanese as the *97-shiki O-bun In-ji-ki*, or Alphabet Typewriter '97. Both machines substituted letters for plaintext elements according to daily key settings for each device. Ironically, though, most ciphers used by all sides during World War II overwhelmingly were manual in nature. That is, they used paper charts, tables, and key.

Many countries used various ciphers to further secure codes they employed. This entailed applying any one of a number of encryption techniques to the code groups, thereby additionally concealing the "true" code groups. One encryption method was to add random groups of number, or digital, key to codes that employed numeric code groups. The resulting new, or cipher, group was then transmitted. This was the technique used by the Japanese navy to encrypt JN-25 operational code group. Japanese diplomats used a transposition cipher, namely, scrambling or breaking up the sequence of the true code groups, usually composed of letters. This method of additional encryption, sometimes called **super-encryption** or **super-encipherment**, made decoding even more difficult: before a codebreaker could recover the plaintext value associated with a code group, he or she had to first recover the true code group.

Cryptanalysis is the analytic method whereby code or cipher text is broken back to its underlying plaintext. **Traffic analysis** is the analytic method or methods whereby intelligence is derived from the study of the communications activity and the elements of messages short of actual cryptanalysis. The difference between cryptanalysis and traffic analysis can be explained through an analogy of a piece of mail. Traffic analysis can be compared to the study all of the external information on a letter's envelope and even an analysis of the characteristics of the envelope, such as its weight. Cryptanalysis is the reading of the contents of the letter.

Nations like Japan used a number of cryptographic systems within a single service or department like the navy or the foreign ministry. These services often used ciphers and codes of increasing complexity depending upon the nature and sensitivity of the information that was to be protected. Any station, whether an army unit, ship, or diplomatic facility, often had in its possession the cryptographic materials necessary to send and receive messages that involved a number of separate codes or ciphers. In order to distinguish between cryptographic systems used for various messages, and to further conceal what system was being used, cryptographers resorted to the use of a **discriminant** or **indicator**. This item was a group or some other combination of letters and numbers that identified to the recipient of the message what cryptographic system was used to encode or encrypt that particular text. Some indicators appeared in the message text, others in the message's header. Sometimes an indicator also identified a particular recipient or larger audience of the message. Just as likely, foreign cryptanalysts who had gained a working familiarity with a particular code or cipher easily could recognize such indicators, which, in turn, could facilitate the effort to solve the system.

To make reading easier, as well as to avoid clumsy repetition of terms, we will use terms like "cryptology," "communications intelligence," "COMINT," "signals intelligence," "SIGINT," and "radio intelligence" interchangeably either as adjectives or as nouns by which to describe the overall American intelligence system to exploit Japanese communications and cryptography. Using these terms as general descriptors will not sacrifice accuracy and will make the text more readable. Any other special or one-use terms from cryptology will be identified when they are encountered in the text.

Organization of the History and Exhibits

In this history we will refer to a particular documentary exhibit at the point in the text as necessary. The reference will be contained within brackets "[ ]" with the appropriate exhibit number. The exhibits are listed in the Table of Contents and are attachments at the end of this volume.

In the first chapter we will provide a short background sketch of the political and strategic situation in the Pacific and East Asia, especially paying attention to the diplomatic confrontation between the United States and Japan over the issue of Tokyo's invasion of China. In this same chapter, there will also be a discussion of the early cryptologic operations of the United States against the communications and cryptography of Japan's military, navy, and foreign ministry.

The second chapter will recount the cryptologic background to the Winds instruction messages, which includes the intercept, analysis, processing, and reaction to them. The background to the specific cryptographic system used by Japan to secure the instructions, as well as the American solution to this system also will be discussed in some length. The next chapter will consider the reaction by United States military and naval intelligence to the instructions in the Winds messages. Specifically, we will consider the measures taken for further monitoring and the subsequent intercepts that were made, including purported and actual Winds message. Following this, in chapter four, we will discuss the controversy surrounding the Winds message and examine the chronology and substance of the claim put forward by Captain Laurance Safford before the various Pearl Harbor hearings that a Winds execute message indeed had been sent and intercepted by the United States government prior to the Japanese attack of 7 December 1941.

This book concludes with a chapter that considers the Winds message story as a way of measuring the effectiveness of the prewar U.S. cryptologic system in handling the apparent warning that it appeared to be at the time. We will also briefly consider how the controversy played out within the context of the story of Pearl Harbor.

A few comments on citations used in this book are necessary. Throughout this work, when a reference is made to material from the thirty-nine-volume set of the Joint Congressional Hearings and the single volume Final report, the citation will be for the specific volume, or "Part," and the page number of the volume. For example, "PHH, Part 8: 555," refers to page 555 of Volume Eight of the Hearings. This definition is important because the forty volumes of the various inquiries, boards, and committees carry a dual system of page notations for the transcripts and exhibits. Whenever speakers in the various hearings refer to a page of previous testimony, it is to the particular hearing or inquiry *transcript* page number of its testimony. The transcript page number can be found imbedded in the transcript of testimony within a set of brackets, "[ ]." This method of reference can be confusing to first-time researchers using the Pearl Harbor Hearings volumes. The natural inclination is to go to the volume page number, but it can mean the transcript page number. For our purpose, though, we will refer to the volume page number.

Acknowledgments

As in many other endeavors, this work could not have been done without the help of many others. The authors gratefully acknowledge the following people and their contributions.

Sadly, though, this section must begin with a statement about one of the authors, David Mowry, who passed away in July 2005. When David and I began this manuscript in 2004, we originally envisioned a short tutorial on cryptanalytic and translation techniques of the pre-World War II era aimed specifically at professional cryptologists. As we progressed through the material, especially those papers concerning the postwar hearings, we both agreed that there was a need for a history of the Winds controversy. But this work should not be just a narrative. Rather, it had to be a documentary history that would bring the source material to the public. Throughout the initial draft of this book, especially with regards to the cryptanalytic part of the story, Dave provided the technical expertise necessary to understand the work of the army and navy codebreakers. He also proved to be a demanding reader of the initial drafts. Dave was a voracious reader, and he possessed a great joy for life and took much pleasure in the intellectual challenge inherent in cryptology. All that was this man will be sorely missed by his colleagues and friends.

"West Winds" represents the initial effort by the Center for Cryptologic History to produce a documentary history. Many people worked on a book whose format and organization were decidedly different than previous productions by the Center. Principal among them were my editor, Stephanie Shea, who accepted each of my changes, additions, and updates to the text and exhibits with a forbearance that was as admirable as it was enduring. Barry Carleen, the chief of the publishing team, took on the challenge to see this project through. We also want to acknowledge the contributions of the members of the CCH, Dave Hatch, John Clabby, and Sharon Maneki, who reviewed the manuscript and offered suggestions and corrections. We also wish to acknowledge the advice from a number of scholars from outside of the NSA. This group included David Kahn, Norm Polmar, Raymond Schmidt, Colin "Brad" Burke, and Betty Koed. At the U.S. National Archives, we would like to thank both Matthew Olsen and Kris Wilhelm for their help in locating documents in the records of the State Department and congressional committees. Overseas, in the United Kingdom, gracious help in locating material about the British communications intelligence effort in the Far East came from Michael (Mick) Smith and the late Peter Freeman. Finally, I wish to acknowledge the technical help from those people whose current duties prohibit them from being thanked publicly.

Notes

1. Roberta Wohlstetter, *Pearl Harbor: Warning and Decision* (Stanford, CA: Stanford University Press, 1962), 388; "Hearings Before the Joint Committee on the Investigation of the Pearl Harbor Attack, Congress of the United States, Seventy-Ninth Congress, Pursuant to Senate Concurrent Resolution No. 27 Authorizing an Investigation of the Attack on Pearl Harbor on December 7, 1941, and Events and Circumstances Relating Thereto." (Washington, D.C.: United States Government Printing Office, 1946). For Kimmel's statement, see Part 6: Pages 2551-2, and for Short's statement see Part 7: Pages 2957, 2960.

2. For the thesis that connects the Winds message with the attack on Pearl Harbor, see, among others, Rear Admiral Robert Theobald, USN, *The Final Secret of Pearl Harbor: The Washington Contribution to the Japanese Attacks* (New York: The Devin-Adair Company, 1954), 134-152; John Costello, *The Pacific*

War, 1941-1945 (New York: Quill Books, 1981), 643-649; and John Toland, *Infamy: Pearl Harbor and its Aftermath* (New York: Berkeley, 1983), 141-144 and 209-217, and George Victor's *The Pearl Harbor Myth: Rethinking the Unthinkable* (Dulles, VA: Potomac Books, 2007), 69-75. Beginning in the latter years of World War II, and especially after the revelations of the Joint Congressional Committee Hearings (1945-46), there has been a bounty of so-called revisionist histories of the attack on Pearl Harbor. In truth, most of these works were largely politically inspired by the anti-Roosevelt sentiments held by a number of scholars such as Charles Tansill, *Back Door to War: The Roosevelt Foreign Policy, 1933-1941* (Chicago: Henry Regnery Company, 1952) and Charles Beard, *President Roosevelt and the Coming of the War*, 1941 (New Haven, CT: Yale University Press, 1948), who saw an FDR plan at work to provoke the Japanese attack. Of the more recent revisionist works, some come from writers whose approach can be characterized as "conspiracist" or "conspiratorialist." This group of writers claims that intelligence about Japan's intentions to attack was available to various individuals at many levels in the United States government and yet this information was withheld from Admiral Kimmel and General Short prior to the attack. Their story continues with the further claim that after the war knowledge of this intelligence was suppressed or destroyed and individuals were warned to keep silent. Robert Stinnett's *Day of Deceit: The Truth about FDR and Pearl Harbor* (New York: The Free Press, 2000) and George Victor's *The Pearl Harbor Myth* are the most recent example of the conspiracy literature about Pearl Harbor. Interestingly, Mr. Stinnett downplays the significance of the Winds message.

There has not been a recent review of the Pearl Harbor literature for some time. A monograph, *What Every Cryptologist Should Know about Pearl Harbor*, is a good, but dated, review (1987) and is available to the public at the National Cryptologic Museum. For a somewhat more dated summary of the various controversies, including the Winds message, see Hans Trefousse's *Pearl Harbor: The Continuing Controversy* (Malabar, FL: Robert E. Krieger Publishing Co., 1982).

3. "Hearings Before the Joint Committee on the Investigation of the Pearl Harbor Attack, Congress of the United States, Seventy-Ninth Congress, Pursuant to Senate Concurrent Resolution No. 27 Authorizing an Investigation of the Attack on Pearl Harbor on December 7, 1941, and Events and Circumstances Relating Thereto." (Washington: United States Government Printing Office, 1946), Thirty-Nine volumes. Hereafter referred to as "PHH." A final committee report was issued with the title "Report of the Joint Committee... etc." This volume is hereafter referred to as "PHR." For a limited but useful index to the hearings, see Stanley H. Smith, *Investigations of the Attack on Pearl Harbor* (New York: Greenwood Press, 1990).

4. For a summary by the Congressional Committee on the findings about the Winds message by the Naval Court of Inquiry and the Army Pearl Harbor Board, see PHH, Part 16:2314-16. Also see PHH, Part 39: 224-226, for the Army Pearl Harbor Board finding on the Winds message and 324-325 for the finding of the Naval Court of Inquiry.

5. Safford's statement to Congress and subsequent testimonies can be found in the various hearings: Hart Inquiry, Part 26:388-395; Army Pearl Harbor Board, Part 29: 2366-2378; Hewitt Inquiry, Part 36: 66-77, and the Joint Congressional Committee Hearings, Part 8:3577-3893. For an evaluation of Safford's role, see Gordon Prange's synopsis in *Pearl Harbor: the Verdict of History* (New York: McGraw-Hill, 1986), 317-330; Also see PHH, Part 16:2316-19, for the congressional committee's summary of Safford's role in the Winds controversy.

6. For example, a search for "winds message," with Pearl Harbor, returns hundreds of websites, many of which subscribe to the claim that the Execute message was sent prior to the attack and that the message was a clear warning of the attack on Pearl Harbor. Examples of such sites – www.geocities.com/PENTAGON/6315/pearl. html, or www.carpenoctem.tc/cons/pearl/html, and www.thenewamerican.com/tna/2001/06-04-2001/vol17no12_fact.html

7. A short list of these writers includes Gordon Prange, *Pearl Harbor: the Verdict of History, 312-330;* Roberta Wohlstetter, *Pearl Harbor: Warning and Decision* (Stanford, CA: Stanford University Press, 1962), 50-53; Ronald Lewin, *The American Magic* (New York: Farrar, Strauss, and Giroux, 1982), 70-76; and David Kahn, *The Codebreakers: The Story of Secret Writing* (New York: MacMillan Company, 1967), 32-47.

8. For an unmarked version of this translation, see SIS Translations 25432 and 25392, both from Tokyo to Washington, 19 November 1941, located in National Archives, College Park (NARACP) RG 457, Entry 9032, Box 301, Multinational Diplomatic Translations (MNDT).

9. PHH, Part 13:394

Foreword

For historians and many members of the informed public, the Japanese attack on Hawaii provoked "the never-ending story." Multiple official investigations and private historical inquiries into the attack and its background have generated enormous stocks of information about both the American and Japanese sides. It may well be that we know as much about December 7, 1941, as we do about any event in the last century, the Kennedy assassination possibly excepted.

However, even with this virtual mountain chain of data, information gaps still exist, and many important questions remain under discussion or debate.

The discussions and debates are not simply the province of conspiracy buffs. Academics and other researchers interested in World War II have a serious stake in settling the issues of the U.S.-Japan conflict; definite answers to many of the controversies would either confirm or refute theories of the war's origins and its meaning.

Robert Hanyok and the late David Mowry from the Center for Cryptologic History have made a significant contribution to our knowledge and understanding of two of the event's controversies, the Winds Message and the state of U.S. communications intelligence prior to the Hawaiian attack.

This assemblage of documents, supplemented by the authors' clear guide to their meaning, places the reader, as it were, right in the middle of the behind-the-scenes events and helps the scholar and researcher to follow them closely.

For further reading, I suggest Fred Parker's *Pearl Harbor Revisited: United States Navy Communications Intelligence, 1924-1941* and Robert L. Benson's *A History of U.S. Communications Intelligence during WWII: Policy and Administration,* both published by the Center for Cryptologic History.

This was the final publication for the CCH by Robert Hanyok before his retirement from a long career in government service. I also second Bob's comments about David Mowry in the acknowledgments: he was a remarkable man. Both Bob and Dave will be missed.

DAVID A. HATCH
NSA Historian
Center for Cryptologic History

Chapter 1

Background: Interwar U.S. – Japan Relations and Cryptology

In the Pacific, the years between the end of the First World War and the attack on Pearl Harbor saw the growth of the strategic rivalry between the United States and Japan in East Asia, especially centered on events in China. Japan had occupied and detached China's industrial north, Manchuria, and created the puppet state of Manchukuo in 1932. In 1937, in response to an incident outside of Beijing, Japan invaded China from the north and east. Tokyo's hopes for a quick campaign faded in the face of Chinese resistance and the sheer territorial enormity of China. Japanese forces could not force a military solution and were mired down. The war absorbed Japan's economic and military resources. Japan's efforts to force a solution to the "China incident" led to the occupation of French Indochina. This action precipitated U.S. (and British and Dutch) embargoes in trade, oil, and the freezing of Japan's assets in 1941. Vulnerable, Japan plunged into planning to seize the resource-rich regions of Southeast Asia and the Netherlands East Indies.

Beginning in 1919, the American Black Chamber focused on exploiting Japanese diplomatic messages. Initial successes in the early 1920s soon vanished. In the mid-1930s, a resurgent U.S. Army mission, the Signals Intelligence Service, began exploiting a number of Japanese diplomatic messages encrypted in manual and machine cipher systems. American cryptanalysis' crowning achievement occurred in September 1940 when it penetrated Japan's primary diplomatic cipher machine, codenamed Purple. As the relations between the two countries deteriorated, Washington's leadership leaned more heavily on the intelligence from its code-breaking organizations for clues to Japan's aims and plans.

United States-Japan Relations, 1919 – 1940

At the end of World War I, the strategic situation in the Pacific and East Asian regions was dominated by the two powers at either far shore – the United States and Japan. Because of the costs of the First World War, the preponderant European colonial powers in East Asia – France, Great Britain, and the Netherlands – were far weaker militarily in the area than before 1914. France and Great Britain, though victorious over Germany, had absorbed extraordinary manpower and economic losses. London and Paris could not afford to maintain extensive military, naval, and security forces on station in their Asian colonies. The Netherlands, while not a combatant in the war, could barely afford much more than a "shadow" naval presence. While adequate security and military forces were on hand to suppress and control indigenous independence movements, primarily in French Indochina, British India, and the Netherlands East Indies, these forces could not match the military and naval forces of any power like Japan intent on seizing these lands. Nor could they match the naval forces of a relatively friendly power like the United States Pacific Fleet. Great Britain especially realized the potential threat from Japan after the Anglo-Japanese Naval Treaty was abrogated as part of the 1922 Washington Naval Agreement. It moved, albeit slowly, to increase its military presence in the Far East by building a major naval base and bastion at Singapore.

Both the U.S. and Japan had emerged from the First World War in much stronger positions in the Pacific and East Asia. Japan had scooped up most of the German island possessions in the Central Pacific. (Australia had grabbed German colonies in the southwest Pacific.) These island groups, such as the Marshalls, the Marianas (less Guam), and the Carolines would become known to Americans in later years when so many paid with their lives to seize them. While the terms of the Washington Naval Treaty prohibited the Japanese from initially fortifying these islands, they began a rapid construction of military facilities and fortifications just prior to the war.

Although the United States gained no territory as a result of the war, its financial position as the preeminent creditor nation made it the dominant economic and financial power in the world. The major U.S. colony in the western Pacific was the Philippine archipelago. The islands had been liberated from Spanish control in 1898. The U.S. then spent five years pacifying a nationalist insurrection among the Filipinos who resisted the American occupation. The Philippines was to be granted independence in 1946. Various American pre-World War II war plans had recognized the vulnerability of the Philippines and recommended several measures to increase its defenses.

In the post-World War I years, the U.S. and Japan watched each other with the cool eyes of strategic rivals in the high stakes game of Pacific dominance. This competition had its roots back to the turn of the twentieth century. In the immediate wake of the Russo-Japanese War of 1905, Japanese naval leaders cast the United States as the most likely new threat.[1] In postwar plans and exercises, Japanese military and naval planners continued this view of the United States as its primary potential enemy in the Pacific.[2] Some observers speculated that the two countries were going to struggle for dominance in the Pacific basin. Whether this conflict was inevitable or not, there did exist a number of points of contention between the two countries that conceivably might lead to a future war.

Foremost among them was the situation in China. The United States had declared an "Open Door" policy in 1900 claiming free and equal international access to markets within China. During World War I, Japan undermined this commercial access with its "Twenty-One Demands" on China in early 1915 that reserved certain economic activities exclusively for Tokyo. With the Lansing-Ishii Agreement in 1917, the United States had recognized Japan's special position in Manchuria and on the Shantung Peninsula. In the decades after the war, Japan continued to seize Chinese territory – actually a continuation of conflicts that dated to the late nineteenth century. It seized control of Manchuria in 1931 and later created the puppet state of Manchukuo. A moderate plan put forward by the League of Nations would have returned Manchuria to China and promised "considerations" for Japanese interests. Japan refused the plan and withdrew from the League of Nations.

The United States had tried diplomatic and economic measures to restrict Japan's expansion into China. In 1930 it had unsuccessfully lobbied the League of Nations for effective international sanctions against Japanese aggression. Negotiations would continue through the decade, but the plight of China, pressed by a highly vocal China lobby of politicians and writers played on the sympathies of the American population.

However, with the full effects of the Great Depression at its worst in the early 1930s, American active interest in China took second place to domestic economic and foreign trade priorities. President Roosevelt refused to take an activist policy in the region, and therefore left the U.S. State Department under Cordell Hull and his Far East expert, Stanley Hornbeck, to respond to Japanese encroachments with statements about adhering to treaties and maintaining "good behavior."[3]

In 1937, after a questionable "incident" outside of Beijing, Japan invaded China from the north and east. Japanese forces could not force a

Chinese surrender, despite an overwhelming military superiority and the use of terror tactics like the aerial bombing of Chinese cities and the massacres in Nanking. The war, referred by Tokyo as the "China Incident," absorbed an increasingly larger portion of Japanese military and economic resources. It also led to local incidents between Japanese and American forces, such as the attack on the U.S. Navy gunboat *Panay* in December 1937. Frustrated by the interminable war, Tokyo began to seek a solution by expanding the conflict to the periphery of China. The Japanese believed that China's resistance depended upon the flow of arms and other aid from the West that came over the Burmese border and through northern French Indochina. Beginning in 1939, Tokyo moved to shut off these routes through political and military pressure.

For the United States and Japan, the effective spearpoints of each country's strategic power in the Pacific and East Asia were their respective navies. Both the Japanese and American fleets dwarfed the squadrons of the other powers in the region; the table was theirs alone to play. In the postwar period, the world's major naval powers had tried with the Washington Naval Conference (1922) and the London Naval Conference (1930) to limit the size and number of their capital ships. Eventually, Japan, feeling threatened by the combination of American and European fleets in the Pacific, and certain that the restrictions were part of a plan to deny its preeminent place in Asia, set off on its own and initiated a massive naval construction program. The United States belatedly started its own building program in the late 1930s that culminated in the Two-Ocean Naval Expansion Act of June 1940, which called for the construction of 200 ships, including eighteen fleet carriers by 1946. Under this act, there were two appropriations in May and July 1940, for the fiscal year 1941. It was this construction program that built the U.S. fleet that fought and won the naval war in the Pacific.

Both countries' naval planning staffs also continued to devise strategic maritime plans for a campaign against the other's fleet. Ironically, both countries achieved a near congruence of plans: both called for "decisive engagements" in the mid-Pacific region near the Mariana or Marshall Islands. Japan sought to lure the American Pacific Fleet into a major ambush and destroy it. The United States, realizing the fundamental vulnerability of the Philippines to Japanese attack, devised a war plan that called for its relief that would be spearheaded by a thrust to the central Pacific by its fleet against the "Orange" power, Japan.[4]

Events in the world, though, later forced a change in strategic emphasis for U.S. war planning in the Pacific that affected related activities such as intelligence gathering. Beginning in 1940, the Nazi victories in the west against France and the Low Countries, and the near isolation of Great Britain by German U-boats, caused the United States to reorder its priority in war planning. This change first appeared in the American-British Commonwealth Staff Agreement (ABC-1) concluded in March 1941. The Agreement recognized that the principal threat was Nazi Germany and that the United States would reorient its major military effort against Hitler.[5] New war plans that were derived from the ABC-1, known as Rainbow 4 and 5, emphasized offensive action in the Atlantic while the Pacific became a secondary theater, one relegated to a "strictly defensive" posture. These plans overturned Washington's previous strategy, War Plan (WPL) 13, which projected the offensive priority in the Pacific against Japan.

The only concession to the perceived Japanese threat in the Pacific and East Asia was the permanent stationing of the Pacific Fleet in Pearl Harbor after the completion of a major exercise in June 1940. (Prior to mid-1940, the Pacific Fleet's main base was San Diego, California. Pearl Harbor, at the time, was a forward base that lacked many fleet maintenance and fuel facilities that existed in California.) This move, ordered by President Roosevelt, who may have seen the Fleet as a deterrent, was made despite the objections of the then Commander, Pacific Fleet, Admiral James Richardson, who argued that Pearl Harbor was both vulnerable to attack and at the end of a tenuous supply line from the west coast of the United States. In February 1941, Richardson was relieved because of his opposition and replaced by Admiral Husband Kimmel.

In 1940, as Japanese and American naval staffs spelled out their plans and the diplomats maneuvered over the issue of China, a secret war of sorts between the two countries already was two decades old – the struggle between the cryptologists of the two nations.

Japanese Diplomatic and Naval Cryptography and American Codebreaking between the Wars[6]

It was during World War I that Japan first began to encrypt and encode its diplomatic, military, and naval message traffic. Tokyo's Foreign Ministry, the *Gaimusho*, started securing its diplomatic messages towards the end of the war. In the decades leading up to the outbreak of general war in the Pacific in late 1941, Japan's diplomats used a variety of manual codes and cipher systems often simultaneously or for overlapping periods. Initially, Japan's diplomatic cryptography emphasized codes over ciphers. The code groups themselves were composed of polygraphic combinations of two, three, four, or five vowels and consonants. These codes often were supplements with so-called "auxiliary" or, more accurately, adjunct systems, such as speller tables for words, notations, and expressions in Western languages, geographic place-names, reference number tables (message serial numbers), and transposition or substitution cipher schemes by which to encrypt code messages (more below on this).

The first Japanese diplomatic cryptographic system, designated "JA" by the Americans, appeared in December 1917 and was replaced in early 1923. It was a code that used digraph (double letter) code groups without any method of encryption to further disguise the groups. JA consisted of two tables of codes, one of vowel-consonant combinations and the other of consonant-vowel. American cryptanalysts quickly broke this system largely because the constant repetition of code groups allowed for the recovery of the underlying plaintext. A number of successors to the JA, albeit with tetragraph (four letter) code groups, continued to be fielded by Tokyo's diplomats until the late 1930s. A variant of this multiple "table" approach was the LA system introduced in 1925. This system used four tables of code groups composed of digraphs. The user would switch among the four tables. Generally, most of these early systems were replaced fairly regularly with the basic differences from one to the next being that succeeding systems essentially consisted of rearranged tables of code and corresponding plaintext values.

In late 1932 Japanese diplomatic cryptography took a major step forward with the introduction of its first cipher machine known to the Americans by its covername Red. The machine used two sets of cipher wheels and an elementary plug board, not unlike some of the early cipher machines such as the Kryha device.[7] The Japanese machine encrypted messages between Tokyo and its important diplomatic missions. It was phased out over the span of two years from 1939 to 1940.

Along with the appearance of the Red machine, but less well known, the Japanese instituted a major advance in the security of their manual codes with the introduction of an encryption method known as transposition. This method of encryption required the sender of a message to scramble the code groups in a message according to a preset arrangement so that the "true" code groups and their sequence were broken up. The recipients of the message used the same dictated arrangement, or "key," to reconstitute the original makeup of the code groups and their sequence. (This method is explained in more detail in chapter 2, pages 20-22.) The transposition method increased the complexity of the cryptanalytic problem for enemy codebreakers and was used to encrypt virtually all Japanese manual diplomatic codes up to the beginning of the war in 1941.

In 1939 the Japanese began replacing the Red machine with a new device that the American codebreakers referred to as Purple, but the Japanese title was 97-shiki O-bun In-ji-ki, or Alphabet Typewriter '97. The Japanese also called the device the HINOKI system. An encryption device, Purple secured diplomatic traffic between Tokyo and major world capitals from its introduction in early 1939 throughout the entire Second World War and came to symbolize, whether correctly or not, the zenith of Japanese cryptography.

Japanese naval cryptography followed much the same path as its diplomatic counterpart. In 1913, a one-part, Roman-letter code was introduced for use by the navy's technical and logistics bureaus. In 1918 a substitution cipher disc system was initiated for Navy Ministry messages.[8] These systems were quite primitive and ironically used Roman letters for the elements of code groups and the cipher. They were quickly replaced with a series of codes that used a transposition cipher to gain further security.

The first such system was known as the Red Code (later notated B-Code by the U.S. Navy), which appeared in 1925. This code consisted of three kana character groups that were transposed using a key. The "B-Code" was designated an administrative code by the Japanese, to differentiate it from exercise codes used by all shore and command elements and ships of the IJN. This code was replaced in 1930 by the Blue or "A-Code." The Japanese navy also used a cipher machine, known as the IKA System, as early as the end of 1931. This machine was used by shore activities and naval bureaus, but was replaced in 1933.[9]

During the 1930s, the Japanese navy created a number of codes and ciphers to handle various aspects of its operations and administration. There were codes and ciphers for reporting ship movement, activities in naval yards, intelligence, direction-finding results, aircraft communications, hydrographic reports, and auxiliary ship messages. There were special codes and ciphers for units fighting in China and stationed in Manchukuo. There also was a special variant of the diplomats' Red machine, the M-1 cipher machine (codenamed Orange by the Americans) for naval attachés and liaison officers.

In November 1938 the Blue Code was replaced by the "A-D" Code, also called the Black Code by the Americans, which was used for administrative traffic. In June 1939 Tokyo introduced a new administrative code, known initially to the Americans as the "AN Code," or by its first title as "Administrative and Ship Movement Code." This new system represented a radical departure for Japanese naval cryptography that for years had emphasized transposition of polygraphic code groups much like those used by Tokyo's diplomats. The new system consisted of a book filled with five-number or -digit code groups that corresponded to plain text. These code groups were further encrypted by a method known as "false addition." A Japanese communicator or code clerk would consult another book, its pages filled with five-digit groups, known as cipher or key. He then would add the digits of this cipher group to the digits of a code group. The method of addition had no carryover values to the next place. The resulting new group of digits, that is, the "sum" of the code and key, was known as the cipher text. It was this group and similarly derived groups of the message that were transmitted by radio to the recipient. At the receiving site, the code clerk would "subtract" the same groups of key from the cipher text, in which the digits assumed a "tens value" when the individual number was smaller. The basic method is quickly illustrated below:

Code groups:	75381	90564	27801
Cipher or key:	+34795	42389	16528
Cipher Text:	09076	32843	33329
Check by subtraction:	- 34795	42389	16528
Original code groups:	75381	90564	27801

Encryption of digital code groups

This new system, eventually designated as "JN-25" in July 1942 by the U.S. Navy, would carry the brunt of the Japanese navy's message traffic. Prior to the attack on Pearl Harbor, the code-book itself would be replaced by two new editions, while the books of key would be changed at three- or six-month intervals for a total of eight editions.

• •

During this interwar period, the United States actively worked against the encrypted messages of other countries, including Japan. The first organized attack was by the American Black Chamber formed and headed by a former U.S. State Department code clerk and War Department cryptanalyst, Herbert O. Yardley. The Black Chamber was an office jointly funded by the U.S. Departments of State and War.

Herbert O. Yardley

Situated in New York City, Yardley's team attacked the encrypted diplomatic and commercial messages of several countries. One of his team's primary targets was the encoded diplomatic traffic of Japan.

The Black Chamber's greatest success came during the Washington Naval Conference of 1922. The conference had been convened in late 1921 by the major naval powers of the world to try to reduce the number of capital ships in each navy to a fixed ratio of relative strengths. This ratio would be achieved through a combination of a construction moratorium and the scrapping of excess ships. The United States and Great Britain pressed Japan and the other attendees to acquiesce to a ratio of capital ships among themselves of 5:5:3 with the US and Britain at 5 and Japan at 3. The Japanese, on instructions from Tokyo, held out for a slightly higher ratio of 3.5 to the ships of the American and British navies. Yardley's team, working out of their New York office, acquired copies of the encoded Japanese diplomatic cables from the cable companies. Yardley managed to decode the instructions between Tokyo to its delegation in Washington. The Japanese relied on two codes, designated JO and JP by the Americans, used to encode the messages, as well as the auxiliary system (JE), which contained English speller and vocabulary tables. These systems were straight codes with no additional encryption. Therefore, one of Yardley's cryptanalytic techniques for solving the code involved "cribbing," that is, the substitution of certain common phrases by which to recover some of the text.

The American delegation, headed by former Supreme Court justice Charles Evan Hughes, believed that the Japanese ultimately would accept a lower ratio and that by holding steady to the demand for the lower ratio of 5:5:3, the Japanese would accede. Part of this confidence was built on the knowledge of a Japanese message on 28 November, decrypted by Yardley's team, which indicated that Tokyo would consent to the lower ratio. The Americans held to their position, and by 12 December the Japanese gave in. Yardley's work had enabled the American delegation to hold firm with a reasonable expectation that they would prevail, which was based on earlier intelligence and bolstered by the information from the decrypted messages.[10]

The American Black Chamber was closed in 1929. While the output and quality of work of Yardley's team had declined to a fraction of its product since 1921, the principal reason for its closure lay in the attitude of then Secretary of State Henry L. Stimson. Some accounts of the shutting down of the Black Chamber have caricatured Stimson as naïve in the ways of *realpolitik* – since countries do not "read each others' mail." But Stimson, a highly principled man, believed that the relations between states should be governed by mutual respect and trust. He thought the idea of the State Department decoding messages of other governments was unethical. However, he did not discount codebreaking; he felt it was better suited to the War or Navy Departments.[11]

As the days of the Black Chamber ground to zero, the U.S. Army reorganized its cryptologic activities to accommodate the assumption of the Chamber's code-breaking mission. The Army combined under one shingle within the Signal Intelligence Service (SIS) of the Signal Corps the previously disparate production of codes, the solution of foreign cryptographic systems, and the intercept of foreign messages. Ostensibly under the command of a signal officer, the true heart and brain of the SIS was William F. Friedman. Friedman was born in 1891 in Kishinev, Russia. His parents immigrated to the United States in 1892. Friedman, a dapper man with an inquisitive personality, had graduated from Cornell with a degree in genetics. Employed by a businessman, George Fabyan, to work at an early version of a "think tank," Friedman soon found himself drawn into the business of codes and ciphers. During World War I, he had written manuals on code-breaking and later joined the staff of the American Expeditionary Force in France attacking German cryptographic systems.

William F. Friedman

After the war, Friedman eventually headed the Code and Cipher Compilation unit of the Signal Corps. In 1929 he was selected to run the SIS. While his own ability to solve cryptographic systems was excellent, Friedman's real contribution to early American cryptology was to organize it around sound, practical training with an emphasis on a scientific-technical approach to solving systems and the accumulation of technical references and literature on all aspects of cryptology. In 1930 he hired the nucleus of the team that would go on to crucial interwar and wartime successes: Abraham Sinkov, Solomon Kullback, John Hurt, and Frank B. Rowlett. For a few years this team did not break codes, but spent its time learning how to construct such systems. It was not until around 1932 that the SIS began to attack foreign codes and ciphers.

Even at that, the SIS was limited at what systems to try to solve, mainly diplomatic traffic. The major problem was that the Army still lacked a substantial intercept element to collect the messages. An early provisional unit at Fort Monmouth, New Jersey, began to monitor and copy some diplomatic and commercial messages in the mid-1930s, and these, by default, became the main target of SIS cryptanalysts. Early successes followed against Japanese manual systems like the early syllabary codes. In 1934, after a few months of effort and help from the U.S. Navy's cryptologists, the SIS solved the Japanese diplomatic cipher machine known as Red.

It would be a mistake to assume that from the very beginning of the SIS success against the Red machine that there was an audience for its product. In fact, for some time, the interest in the codebreaking success of the SIS remained largely within the confined circles of army and navy intelligence. It would take time and circumstances before the translations of the SIS decrypts would travel to the White House.[12] Yet, ironically, it was what the Red cipher device revealed in Europe that clinched the interest in what the SIS was doing. In 1937 the Red decrypts revealed Italy's interest in joining the German-Japanese anti-Comintern pact from the previous year. While American diplomats had reported on the negotiations among Berlin, Rome, and Tokyo, the Red decrypts provided direct information on the participants. For the first time, the leadership in the White House and the Departments of War, State, and the Navy took a major interest in the diplomatic decrypts from SIS.[13]

The greatest achievement of the SIS, and the one most known to the public, occurred in September 1940. After eighteen months of sustained effort, the Japanese diplomatic cipher machine, the "B-machine," or what the Americans would call Purple, was solved. A team of cryptologists under Frank Rowlett, a former high school science and math teacher from Virginia who displayed a near virtuosity in solving Japanese ciphers and codes, worked at solving the device. Help from some navy codebreakers, some inspired cryptanalysis, and an engineering insight from other team members led to the machine's solution in September 1940. The team reconstructed an *analog* of the Japanese machine, a point often misunderstood by many writers on the subject. The Purple device was really an analog, that is, a machine that simulated the workings of the actual Japanese cipher device. In essence, then, the Americans had their own version of the Japanese machine.

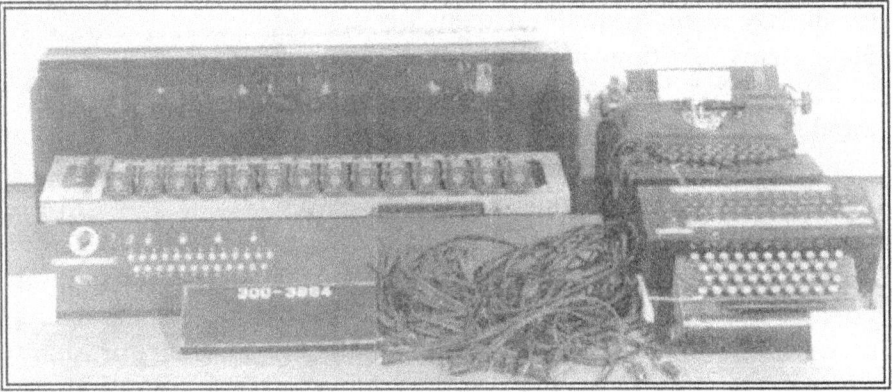

Purple analog device

It was the product of this success, the translations of diplomatic messages between Tokyo and its diplomatic missions around the world, which set American cryptology on the road to its permanently important position within the government. Combined with the solution of several other Japanese manual diplomatic systems and their auxiliaries, SIS now had a window into another country's diplomatic correspondence perhaps seldom equaled in the history of codebreaking.

However, the accomplishment carried its own problems. The demand from the Washington leadership for current translations of Purple intercepts, as well as other messages, taxed the small workforce of the SIS' Japanese section. Help was asked for and received from OP-20-G. A division of effort was agreed upon in which the Navy worked all Japanese diplomatic intercepts from odd days, while the Army worked messages intercepted on even days. But this arrangement also forced the American cryptologists to prioritize the work on intercepted Japanese diplomatic messages. Purple traffic trumped all others. This meant that some traffic would wait days, even weeks, before it was decrypted and translated.

During the same decades, the U.S. Navy's cryptologic unit, OP-20-G, had developed an ability to exploit a substantial portion of the Japanese navy's communications and cryptography. Through a concerted effort at codebreaking and traffic analysis, the U.S. Navy had achieved a significant degree of understanding about Japanese naval planning, doctrine, tactics, and organization.[14] Beginning in the mid-1920s, the head of OP-20-G, Commander Laurance Safford, established a regular codebreaking effort within the organization, known as the Research Desk, charged with solving Japanese naval cryptography. Staffed with early luminaries such as Agnes Meyer, and later supplemented with the likes of Joseph Rochefort, Japanese naval codes such as the Red, Black, and Blue Operational Codes succumbed to the Americans.

However, the navy success would end in June 1939, when the IJN replaced the old systems with two new codes: the Flag Officers Code and a new general-purpose system, known as the "AN–Code," the Administrative and Ship Movement Code, or by the shorthand nicknames given it by the OP-20-G cryptanalysts, the "Five-numeral" or "Five-num." The Fleet Officers Code would be worked unsuccessfully for two years before it was dropped. The AN-Code was another matter. Initially, it was believed also to be a code for Ship Movement. So, it was used more extensively than the earlier administrative systems.[15] But it was the cryptography of the system that was different from all previous systems used by the Imperial Japanese Navy. As described earlier in this section, the AN-Code used five numeral or digit groups to encipher further the basic numeric code groups from the codebook. This was the first time American naval cryptanalysts had seen such an enciphering method, and it took them several months before they could strip the cipher away and attack the underlying code groups.

The system, named JN-25 in July 1942, contained over 30,000 entries. Washington's naval codebreakers could make only the most limited progress in recovering the underlying plaintext values. And whatever progress would be made was negated since the Japanese replaced the basic codebook one time before the attack on Pearl Harbor, while the cipher system used to encrypt the code groups would be superseded eight times during the same period. By the time of the attack on Pearl Harbor, OP-20-G codebreakers had recovered the underlying plaintext values of about ten percent of the code groups.

It would be a mistake to believe that this ten percent figure meant that ten percent of all messages or ten percent of each message encrypted in the AN-Code could be deciphered. In reality, the situation for the analysts of OP-20-G was analogous to trying to translate a tract in a foreign language with only a random ten percent of the entries in a dictionary being available. For the U.S. Navy, the major intelligence fallout was that naval cryptologists had to rely almost exclusively on traffic analysis and related techniques rather than cryptanalysis in order to keep tabs on Tokyo's fleet.[16]

There was an important influence in late 1940 that affected the Navy's overall priority of cryptologic targets. Washington's previous plan for military and naval operations in the Pacific in case of war, War Plan 13 (WPL13), which had called for an offensive campaign directed against Japan, was dropped. In its place, WPL46, derived from Rainbow Plan 5, the joint army-navy plan for military support to Britain and France, called for a shift in priority to the Atlantic. The effect of this shift was that by December 1940, of thirty-five cryptanalytic officers assigned to the OP-20-G headquarters in Washington, only two to five could be spared at any time to work on JN-25. A year later, of all naval officer-cryptanalysts, civilian analysts, and code clerks in OP-20-G, most were assigned to European/Atlantic targets, as well as to supplement the exploitation of Purple.[17] Many of the reassigned analysts concentrated on the analytic attack against the German naval Enigma, a project that would prove to be unproductive and a serious drain on personnel.[18]

By the late 1930s, both the Army and Navy had established a number of monitoring sites in the Pacific region that could intercept all types of Japanese communications.[19] The army sites, located on the U.S. west coast, Hawaii, and the Philippines, concentrated on Japanese diplomatic communications. U.S. Navy sites, located also on the west coast, Hawaii, Guam, and the Philippines targeted Japanese naval communications. The facility at Bainbridge, Washington, collected diplomatic traffic from Tokyo.[20]

A final note on the intercept and decryption of Japanese communications in the Far East should be added. The United States was not alone in this enterprise. Two other countries maintained units in the region intercepting and analyzing Japanese transmissions: the Netherlands and Great Britain. The Dutch had a small intercept and code-breaking element stationed in the Netherlands East Indies known as *Kamer* (Room) 14. The organization was located at the Technical College in Bandung (or Bandeong) on the island of Java and was commanded by a retired Dutch army officer. The Dutch had made considerable progress in solving Japanese manual diplomatic systems, but had made little headway with machine ciphers such as Purple, or Japanese military or naval cryptographic systems. The Dutch had an exchange program with the British in Singapore, but it was restricted. The British sent diplomatic intercept to Bandung, while the Dutch sent copies of all their intercept, including Japanese military and naval messages to Singapore. The Dutch, on occasion, did pass some translations of intercepted Japanese diplomatic messages to the American military attaché office in the East Indies.[21]

The Far East Combined Bureau (FECB) controlled British COMINT activity in the Far East. This was a joint services – Army, Royal Air Force, Royal Navy, and Government Code & Cypher School – intelligence and communications intelligence center located in the bastion of Singapore. The FECB had been relocated from Hong Kong to Singapore in 1939 for greater security. By 1941 there were about ninety cryptologists at the FECB, including thirty Women's Royal Navy Service (W.R.N.S.) monitors and twenty civilian radio operators (Civilian Shore Wireless Service and Foreign Office, or C.S.W.S. and F.O.). The Bureau was composed of two sections: an intelligence section that translated decoded messages and a special section (or "S.I.") from the GC&CS that performed codebreaking. The intercept site was located at Kranji about four miles from the FECB complex. The FECB also controlled three monitoring and direction finding (D/F) stations on Stonecutters Island in the colony of Hong Kong, Kuching in northern Borneo, and Penang on the west coast of Malaya.[22]

In late 1940, the Bureau began exchanging technical COMINT with the OP-20-G at Station "C" (or CAST) in the Philippines in late 1940. Of particular interest to the two organizations were the recovery of the Japanese navy's AN-Code, as well as the decrypts and translations of Japanese diplomatic messages.[23]

United States - Japan Relations Worsen, 1940 - 1941

From the middle of 1940 to late 1941, the already uneasy relations between Japan and the United States deteriorated even more. Japan's invasion of China remained the major issue between Tokyo and Washington. However, it was Tokyo's two-stage occupation of French Indochina, begun in September 1940 and completed in July 1941, which set off the train of events that led to war in East Asia and the Pacific.

France had been defeated by Germany in June 1940. That summer, mired in the fighting in China that drained manpower and resources, Japan looked for ways to break the deadlock. Since 1939 Tokyo had believed that western military and economic support had kept China in the fight. One of the major supply lines ran along a rail line through northern Indochina across the border into southern China. If this line was closed, then China's resistance might collapse. So with Vichy France's acquiescence, Japanese forces moved into Indochina and shut down the border.

In response, Washington embargoed aviation fuel and scrap iron exports to Japan. Tokyo further aggravated the situation by signing the Tripartite Pact with Fascist Italy and Nazi Germany, the provisions of which appeared aimed at deterring American involvement in the fighting in Europe or Asia. In July 1941 Japan occupied the rest of Indochina and proclaimed it a protectorate. Japanese naval ships were now anchored in Cam Ranh Bay. Japanese combat aircraft were based at airfields as far south as Saigon – well within range to strike at British air bases in northern Malaya. In response, President Roosevelt froze all Japanese assets in the United States and enforced even stiffer terms of a trade embargo that essentially foreclosed commerce between the two nations. More importantly, the Netherlands and Great Britain took similar measures, including the cutting off of all oil exports to Japan.

Japan now faced a strategic crisis and the clock was running out. Always hostage to its lack of natural resources, Japan and its naval leaders now calculated that the IJN had less than a year of oil reserves on hand, even if it conducted no major operations.[24] Japanese leaders believed that their country had three choices: abandon its ambitions to dominate eastern Asia, work out some sort of compromise with the United States, or attack Dutch, British, and American possessions in Southeast Asia and gain control of the resources they held. The Japanese Army favored war. The Japanese Navy command and staff planned a quick campaign that supported the army's plan to assault Malaya, the Philippines, and other places in the region. It also planned to seize Pacific islands and create a defensive barrier that the U.S. would have to pierce.

A part of this plan was a surprise carrier air strike on the United States Pacific Fleet stationed at Pearl Harbor. The navy's commander-in-chief, Admiral Isoroku Yamamoto, realized that the only major obstacle to any Japanese advance was the American fleet in Pearl Harbor. After its destruction, and with the establishment of a barrier of fortified island bases, he believed that any campaign to retake the territory captured by Japan would be too costly for the Americans and that they would settle for terms that recognized Japan's preeminent position in the western Pacific and Southeast Asia.

The Japanese premier, Fumimaro Konoye, favored some compromise with America. He offered Washington the proposal that Japan would withdraw from Indochina after the "incident" with China was settled. As part of the proposed Japanese agreement, the United States would restore trade with Japan and release its assets. The Roosevelt administration rejected Konoye's proposal, as well as a further suggestion for a later meeting between the two countries' leaders. The United States demanded both a clarification from Japan of its intent in signing the Tripartite Agreement and concrete plans to withdraw from China and Indochina.

In October 1941 Konoye's cabinet collapsed and the minister of war, General Hideki Tojo succeeded him as premier. In early November the Imperial and Navy General Staffs issued orders to prepare for hostilities. Military and naval plans were put into motion while a strategy of talking with Washington continued. Meanwhile, the carrier pilots of the Japanese First Air Fleet, the mailed fist of the Pearl Harbor Striking Force (*Kido Butai*) practiced torpedo and bomb attacks against simulated facilities and target ships in Kagoshima Bay and elsewhere in the southern part of the Japanese Home Islands.

At the same time, American codebreakers and radio intelligence analysts sifted through Japanese diplomatic and naval communications for any clue to Japan's intentions. By mid-November 1941, some diplomatic messages from Tokyo carried references to deadlines. Japanese naval radio traffic indicated that the various fleets of the Imperial Japanese Navy were reorganizing for a major effort to the south. U.S. and British observers in the region verified this latter intelligence. Then, on 19 November, a diplomatic message was intercepted that, once it was decrypted, seemed to offer the promise a clear warning to the start of Japanese actions throughout the Pacific.

Notes

1. David C. Evans and Mark R. Peattie, *Kaigun: Strategy, Tactics, and Technology in the Imperial Japanese Navy, 1887-1941* (Annapolis, MD: Naval Institute Press, 1997), 187-191

2. Evans and Peattie, 197-8; Saburo Hayashi, *Kogun: The Japanese Army in the Pacific War.* (Westport, CT: Greenwood Press, 1978) Reprint of Marine Corps Association edition, 2-3, 7-8

3. Robert Dallek, *Franklin Roosevelt and American Foreign Policy, 1932-1945* (New York: Oxford University Press Paperback, 1981), 75-77

4. The United States military and navy assigned color codes to other nations. "Black" was Germany. France was notated "Gold," while Italy was "Silver." Great Britain was referred to as "Red."

5. PHH, Part 15: 1485-1550

6. Japanese army cryptography is excluded from this discussion since it has no relevance to the Winds message story. Briefly, Japanese army cryptography after the First World War largely used substitution ciphers and codes, not unlike the navy. The process for generating such cryptographic material resided with a section of the Imperial General Staff in the mid-1920s, but that function appears later to have been decentralized to individual armies. It is not until the formation of the Imperial General headquarters in 1937 that the responsibility for designing and producing cryptosystems once more was centralized. The Japanese army considered using a codebook (*Rikugun Angoosho*) with four- and five-letter code groups with a system of additive groups in the early 1930s. But it was not until the China Incident in 1937 that the Imperial General Staff dictated the general use of such a system.

The Signal Intelligence Service had only a sporadic effort against the communications and cryptography of the Japanese army during most of the 1930s. A major reason for this was the lack of monitoring stations that could even intercept Japanese army communications. Tokyo's army used low-power transmissions on HF and medium frequencies for its traffic, which were almost impossible to hear from the closest monitoring site in the Philippines. The British had sites in Hong Kong and India from where they could hear these transmissions and therefore had a stronger technical base from which to attack Japanese army systems at the beginning of the war in the Pacific.

In 1940 the Army's Signal Intelligence Service lacked much technical information about Japanese army cryptography. The few available early intercepts posed problems for the SIS in terms of categorizing them by cryptographic system. Ironically, the SIS had to go to Herbert O. Yardley, recently back from China after directing Chiang Kai-Shek's cryptanalytic effort, for information. Frank Rowlett was dispatched to Yardley's apartment for a series of debriefs about Japanese army cryptography. Yardley also produced a two-hundred-page report. For all this Yardley was paid

4,000 dollars. See Kahn, *The Reader of Gentlemen's Mail*, 199-201.

7. The Kryha mechanical cipher device used a single disk, which appeared to offer security through irregular stepping, but actually was little more than a single polyalphabetic cipher. See Kahn, *The Codebreakers*, 825

8. RIP-84A, "JN Recognition Data Book." 30 November 1943. 60-2,3. NARA RG 457, Entry 9032, Box 1138, Folder 3673

9. RIP-32, "Japanese Naval Cryptographic Systems." 1 January 1936 with Changes 1-8. Section 6-1. RG 457, Entry 9032, Box 1377, Folder 4347

10. David Kahn, *The Reader of Gentlemen's Mail: Herbert O. Yardley and the Birth of American Codebreaking* (New Haven, CT: Yale University Press, 2004), 75 - 80

11. David Alvarez, *Secret Messages: Codebreaking and American Diplomacy, 1930-1945* (Lawrence, KS: University Press of Kansas, 2000), 14-16; David Kahn, *Reader of Gentlemen's Mail*, 97 - 100

12. Alvarez, 42-3

13. Frank B. Rowlett, *The Story of Magic, Memoirs of an American Cryptologic Pioneer* (Laguna Hills, CA: Aegean Park Press, 1997), 251

14. For examples of some of these analyses, see SRH-222, "OP-20 Report on Japanese Grand Fleet Maneuvers, 1930." (Fort George G. Meade, MD: NSA, 1983) and SRH-225, "Various Reports on Japanese Grand Fleet Maneuvers, July – September 1935." (NSA: 1983)

15. RIP-32, Section 25-1 to 25-3

16. PHH, Part 36:14

17. Frederick D. Parker, *Pearl Harbor Revisited: United States Navy Communications Intelligence, 1924-1941* (Fort George G. Meade, MD: Center for Cryptologic History, National Security Agency, 1994), 20, 29-30

18. Jim Debrose and Colin Burke, *The Secret in Building 26. The Untold Story of America's Ultra War against the U-Boat Enigma Code* (New York: Random House, 2004), 44-49

19. The SIS sites included MS-1, Fort Monmouth, New Jersey; MS-2, The Presidio, San Francisco, California; MS-3, Fort Sam Houston, Texas; MS-4 Corozal, the Canal Zone; MS-5, Fort Shafter, Territory of Hawaii; MS-6, Fort McKinley, Philippine Islands; and, MS-7, Fort Hunt, Virginia.

20. The OP-20-G sites included Station "A," Shanghai, China (disestablished in October 1940); Station "B," Guam; Station "C," Corregidor (formerly Cavite), Philippine Islands; Station "G," Amagansett, New York; Station "H," Heeia, Territory of Hawaii; Station "J," Jupiter, Florida; Station "M," Cheltenham, Maryland; Station "O," San Juan, Puerto Rico; Station "S," Bainbridge, Washington; Station "W," Winter Harbor, Maine; and Station "U," Toro Point (formerly Balboa) Canal Zone.

21. Captain H.L Shaw, *History of HMS Anderson*, 24 May 1946, Part II, 1-2. HW 4/25. Public Record Office (PRO), Kew, UK.

22. Shaw, I, 1-4

23. The U.S. Navy was not the only cryptologic unit stymied by the AN Code. The British code-breaking unit in the Far East, the Far East Combined Bureau, located in Singapore, also was having problems solving the system. In February 1941 the British and American cryptologists from Singapore and Cavite, Philippines, began conferring on Japanese naval systems. Yet even this combined effort could make only marginally better inroads into the then current JN-25 version, "B," prior to the Japanese attacks on 7 December 1941. The basic cryptanalytic problem of JN-25B that the British and Americans faced was the recovery of the plaintext values underlying the code groups, of which there were some 35,000 five-digit code groups. These represented plaintext such as dictionary words, ship names, numerals, etc. Some plaintext had multiple code groups for enhanced security that upped the group count to about 50,000. The Americans and British had made substantial progress in recovering the tables of "additives," five-digit groups added to the code groups which produced a new set of groups known as cipher text. However, the recovery of the plaintext values of the code groups was slow. At the time of Pearl Harbor, perhaps some 3,000 to 5,000 groups (estimates vary) were recovered at the time. For a summary of the Anglo-American cryptologic exchanges prior to the war, see Robert L. Benson, *A History of U.S. Communications Intelligence during World War II: Policy and Administration* (Fort George G. Meade, MD: Center for Cryptologic History,

National Security Agency, 1997), 14-22. For the British side of this exchange, see H.L. Shaw, *History of HMS Anderson*, 24 May 1946. Section III, 2-4, and Michael Smith, *The Emperor's Codes* (London: Transworld Publishers, 2000), 78-90.

24. For a detailed description of Japan's vulnerable strategic economic situation in 1941, see H.P. Willmott's *Empires in Balance: Japanese and Allied Pacific Strategies to April 1942*. (Annapolis, MD: Naval Institute press, 1982), 67-78

Chapter 2
Intercepted Japanese Diplomatic Messages Reveal a Warning System, 19 November – 28 November 1941

At about quarter after five in the morning of 19 November 1941, a Navy intercept operator at the naval field station at Bainbridge Island, Washington (Station "S"), monitoring 9160 kilocycles, plucked out of the air an eighty-one group message from Foreign Minister Shigenori Togo in Tokyo to the Japanese embassy in Washington, D.C. The operator noted that the message contained an indicator – a reference to the type of key used to encipher the message – that marked the message as intended for a global audience, that is all Japanese diplomatic stations around the world. This indicator was a five-letter group at the beginning of the cipher text – BUTWJ.

Not all of Tokyo's diplomats would have heard this particular transmission of the message. Due to reception conditions caused by the time of day and local weather, as well as the fact that many Japanese minor diplomatic stations lacked their own radios by which to hear these messages, some designated stations were responsible for retransmitting the message to other regions. The embassy in Washington, D.C., often was charged to relay messages to stations in Latin America. Other stations received a version of the same message via commercial landline telegraph or cablegram operated by the large communications companies such as Radio Corporation of America or Western Union.

The personnel at Bainbridge recognized the nature of the message and the cryptographic system that was used to encrypt it. Since Navy standard intercept procedure used two separate operators, one to copy the actual message and another to copy the accompanying Japanese radio operator procedural communications (or "chatter"), it was relatively simple to prepare the intercepted message for transmission to the OP-20-G operations center in Washington, D.C., where it would be decrypted. The operator typed up the encrypted message text along with the message heading – message number, group count, date and time – on a paper tape. He then contacted Washington and when the connection was made over landline, he fed the tape into his teletype machine. It spewed out on another machine in Room 1649 in the Navy Department Building on Constitution Avenue.

In that building, the message was scanned by someone familiar with Japanese cryptographic systems. He recognized from the indicator "BUTWJ" and other aspects of the message that this message was encrypted in a manual system known to the American codebreakers as "J-19" and marked it so by pencil. The message carried Japanese Foreign Minister Togo's name as the signatory. Since the intercepted message was not as high a priority for decryption as was Purple message traffic, the page with the encrypted message probably was placed in an in-basket to be worked later by a cryptanalyst with some free time.

About six and a half hours later, Bainbridge intercepted another message from Tokyo to Washington, this time forty-eight groups long, that carried the same indicator "BUTWJ" and also was signed by Minister Togo. The message also carried instructions the *Gaimusho* to relay it to Rio De Janeiro, Brazil, Mexico City, Mexico, and the consulate in San Francisco. Bainbridge processed this intercept as it had the other message and sent it along to the OP-20-G watch center. The second intercepted message was tagged also as being encrypted in J-19. As in the first message, these bits of information were identified and noted in pencil on the copy when the message was first scanned at the watch center in Washington. And, like the first message, it was put into the in-basket to be worked later.

U.S. Navy Monitoring Station "S" – Bainbridge Island, 1940

When finally processed, the contents of the messages would form the heart of the controversy known as the "Winds Message." However, before that story can be told, it is necessary to explain the cryptography of the Japanese manual system known as J-19 and how the system played in the drama of American diplomatic codebreaking before Pearl Harbor.

The Cryptography of the J-19 System

As mentioned in the previous chapter, like many countries, Japan relied on a mix of ciphers and codes to secure its diplomatic traffic. Also, Japan was one of the earliest countries to rely on cipher machines to encrypt some of its more sensitive or important communications. However, these machines were expensive to make, maintain, and protect. In the summer of 1940, only about ten diplomatic missions held Red and Purple cipher machines, though more were scheduled to receive the machines.[1] Also, these devices could be available only at missions whose physical facilities were considered secure from physical compromise to the intelligence services of host countries. The physical security status of Japan's overseas diplomatic facilities was heavy on the minds of Tokyo's diplomats. In April and December 1940, the Foreign Ministry queried its overseas facilities about physical security. The results might not have encouraged Tokyo about security at many of the sites such as the embassy in Bogota, Colombia, and the consulate in New Orleans in the United States where the sensitive material was stored in rooms below the consul's bedroom with no sentry save the diplomat sleeping upstairs.[2] In late December 1940, Tokyo informed its embassy in Washington that it was shipping a metal safe that was about two meters high, a little over a meter wide and one meter deep. In this safe would go all cryptographic material, including the embassy's HINOKI (Purple) machines and all manual codes and ciphers.[3] However, the security measures for Washington would not work at most of the other facilities because of a lack of space and insufficient Japanese personnel to maintain security.

The problem for Tokyo in 1940 was that if an important or top-secret message needed to be sent to all stations – a "circular" – encrypting it with either the Purple or Red machine was no solution. The vast majority of Japanese missions did not have either device. A further cryptographic system was needed to supplement the machine systems; yet it had to be secure to the point where sensitive and secret traffic to all diplomatic sites could be encrypted by it. The solution was to field a new manual code with a particularly complex encryption system.

Japan Fields a New Diplomatic Manual Cryptographic System

In mid-June 1940, the Japanese Foreign Office informed all of its overseas stations that a new supplementary manual cryptographic system would soon be put into effect and that they would receive the appropriate code books and auxiliary systems associated with it.[4] The system was called MATSU (Pine). It consisted of two code tables with digraph and tetragraph values for Japanese Kana (phonetic

Japanese syllabary) along with two auxiliary encryption systems, a substitution table and a transposition cipher, designated K-5, by which resulting code text messages would be encrypted for greater security. Both the tables and the auxiliary transposition encryption system were substantial advances in size and complexity over the immediately preceding diplomatic cryptographic systems, notably J-11 through J-15.

About every three months thereafter, this new manual code and cipher system would undergo major upgrade, that is, a new code table and auxiliary system would be introduced, with a total of three changes completed through mid-1941. MATSU was labeled J-16 by the Americans. The final system in this series progression would be designated J-19 by the Americans. The J-19 system would be an important part of the Winds controversy. At the same time, the story of its changes and the American solutions reveals much of the situation of American cryptanalysis against systems other than Purple.

Below is a list of the system designators, reading from the left, the American designator, the auxiliary transposition cipher designator ("K"), the Japanese covername and the effective dates:

J-16	K-5	MATSU (pine)	15 August 1940 – 30 November 1940
J-17	K-6	HAGI (shrub)	1 December 1940 – 28 February 1941
J-17	K-7	Not available	1 March 1941 – 21 June 1941 (London Embassy)
J-18	K-8	SAKURA (cherry)	1 March 1941 - June 1941 (Special use)
"X"	K-9	Not Available	11 March 1941 – 25 April 1941 (Moscow Embassy)
J-19	K-10	FUJI (wisteria)	21 June 1941 – 15 August 1943

Fig. 2 . MATSU code successor systems

The code tables for MATSU were designated J-16 by the Americans soon after they recognized the initial intercepted messages were encoded in groups substantially different from the current code, J-15. MATSU and its successors were considerably more complex than the systems that preceded them. MATSU, with its code structure and the auxiliary systems, in fact, was a quantum leap in size, scope, and sophistication over the previous manual systems used by Tokyo's diplomats. The MATSU code charts were twice as large as those tables for the immediate predecessors J-11 through J-15. These earlier systems, which were in effect from 1939 through mid-1940, carried about 400 to 800 total code group entries consisting of plain text syllables with the corresponding digraphs, tetragraphs, and even the occasional trigraph (three-letter) code group. MATSU carried nearly double the number of code group entries – a total of almost 1,600 code groups. In the final version of MATSU, the J-19 system (with the Japanese cover name of FUJI), for example, the digraph LW represented the kana syllable SHI, and the two-letter group KP represented the syllable HA, and so on. These digraphs formed one code table that contained 676 code-for-text values. The American codebreakers would reconstruct this table in an analog fashion by creating a decrypt chart, being far easier to use for the decryption of messages. [See **Exhibit #1**][5]

Punctuation and format requirements in messages, such as periods, commas, parentheses, line feeds, and new paragraphs were represented with separate and specific two-letter code groups. For example, the digraph "NC" corresponded to the start of a new paragraph in the message.

An accompanying second code chart contained four-letter code groups, which were used for items of text that were too difficult or clumsy to encode by syllable or letter substitution from the two-letter chart. These items included common foreign words, usually of a technical nature, proper names, geographic locations, months of the year, etc. There were 900 such four-letter code-for-text values on this second chart. These code groups were nested in the regular two-letter code text, segregated in the text by the two-letter code groups for special characters, such as HL for the open "[" (open brackets) character. This latter digraph was one of the special two-letter code groups used to alert the Japanese code clerk who was either decoding or encoding the message to refer to the chart of four-letter code groups.

There were two auxiliary cipher systems that were to be used to encrypt the coded messages: the Q-1 substitution system and the K-5 transposition system. The Q-1 process involved a complicated process of adding randomly selected letters to single letters in a coded message text, which were then replaced, or substituted with random two-letter groups from either of two substitution tables. Either of two five-letter indicators – CIFOL and VEVAZ – would appear as the first group of a message and pointed to one of two deciphering tables for the code clerk to use. However, this complicated auxiliary system seems to have been used only rarely.[6]

The auxiliary transposition system, designated K-5, was used almost always to encrypt a message encoded with J-16 and its successors. At its basic level, a transposition cipher mixes the order of the elements of a message's text, whether plaintext or coded text. Generally, the plaintext or coded/cipher text is inscribed horizontally into a matrix, or "cage," of columns and rows of a dimension specified by the length of the message. The cipher text is created when the text is transcribed vertically (or "read out") from the columns of the cage in a specified order, which is established by a "key." A simplified version is given in the example below:

Step 1. The message plaintext, **TOMORROW ALL UNITS ATTACK THE TOWN AT DAWN,** *is inscribed in a 6X6 matrix horizontally:*

1	2	3	4	5	6
T	O	M	O	R	R
O	W	A	L	L	U
N	I	T	S	A	T
T	A	C	K	T	H
E	T	O	W	N	A
T	D	A	W	N	--

Step 2. The "key" for this message is 3-1-6-2-5-4. The text is now transcribed (or "read out") vertically in the order set by the key.

The transposed text now reads (The cipher text is arranged in groups of five for easier transmission. Extra letters or spaces were often filled with "dummy" characters to achieve a complete 5-letter group.):

MATCO   ATONT   ETRUT   HAOWI ATDRL   ATNNO   LSKWW

To decipher the message, the recipient reverses the process and inscribes the enciphered text into the matrix in the order set by the "key" and then reads out the text horizontally.

The K-5 transposition system, and all of its follow-on systems, naturally was far more sophisticated than the above example. In fact, the K-5 system was a major advance over previous transposition systems. Earlier ones that were implemented in 1939, notably K-1 through K-4, used an unfilled matrix for transcribing the coded text. Matrices or cages varied in width, namely, the number of vertical columns, from six to fourteen. The systems also used sets of five keys for transcribing text out of the matrix that were effective for a month. These keys were used on designated days in the month, usually six days picked at random or in a specified sequence of days, such as 1-6-11-16-21-26-31, 2-7-12-17-22-27, etc.

The K-5 transposition system was a major step forward for Japanese diplomatic cryptography because of two innovations. The first was that the parameters for the matrix into which the code groups were inscribed had advanced significantly in both complexity and size. This more sophisticated matrix was the hallmark characteristic of the new transposition system and appears to have been the foundation for the K-5 auxiliary system and all of its successors through K-10. The second innovation involved the use of more frequently changed key settings for the transposition sequence. The K-5 system used one hundred keys for three months as a daily-changing key. The key also varied more in length, being as long as twenty-five elements instead of the old maximum of fourteen. As the Japanese superseded the basic code charts in J-16, the associated transposition system simultaneously would be replaced.

The K-10 auxiliary transposition system associated with the J-19 code merits a detailed description. The K-10 cipher operated in continuous, nonrepeating, ten-day periods for each month, divided by the numbered days of the month 1-10, 11-20, and day 21 to the end of the month. Each ten-day period used a separate transposition matrix or cage, which the American codebreakers would refer to as a "form." A form was a cage at its largest twenty-five columns wide (horizontally) and up to thirty-five rows deep (vertical). The significant aspect of the form was the presence of randomly placed filled spaces in the cage, actually called "blanks," which resembled the nulls in a crossword puzzle. The appearance of blanks had the effect of breaking the flow of the coded text and created irregular lengths for each column of text. This was intended to make the system more secure through irregular segments of the complete text. The Japanese numbered the forms sequentially and each had a unique arrangement of blanks. The Americans called this type of form with embedded blanks a "stencil." [**Exhibit # 2**][7] The Americans designed the blanks for their stencils used for decrypting J-19 messages either as inscribed dark spaces or with punch-outs, much like a grill.

As for the key, in K-10 system, the Japanese used a daily-changing key for the stencil. This key, which defined the number of columns used in a form, was a string of digits from 1 to 25, which varied in length daily from nineteen to twenty-five positions. The predecessors of the K-10 used different sets of key, or "banks." The first one, K-5, associated with J-16, used one hundred separate keys with lengths from fifteen to twenty-five positions. The next variant, K-6 (associated with J-17), merely reused the same one hundred keys, though with different indicators, that is, code groups that pointed to the key to be used for that period. The K-10 key took the process a further step by increasing by nearly a factor of four the possible key values. It is quite possible that the Japanese had generated all possible key settings for all possible key lengths and then randomly selected a number of them for use. By mid-1942, the Japanese may have exhausted this key library, for they began to reuse old 1941 key for messages encoded in J-19. However, they did not just reuse old key, but devised a method for relocating elements in the key string according an algorithm 1-3-5-7...10-8-6-4-2. A second method was devised in which old key strips were added "falsely" together, that is, dropping the resulting tens-position digit.[8]

As mentioned above, the forms were potentially twenty-five columns wide, but a shorter key defined a "thinner" form, diminished from the right-hand side sliding to the left. The final width of the ten-day form was determined daily by the length of that day's key. The height or depth of the form was determined by the length of the message being encrypted: the longer the message, the higher or deeper the form.

An indicator, a group of five letters placed in the first position of the beginning of the message's cipher text, designated the key to be used on that particular day. The Japanese attempted to complicate further the solution of messages encoded in J-19 by establishing separate indicators (or "channels") for four distinct groupings of diplomatic stations: a general, worldwide audience, one for stations in Europe (which included diplomatic facilities in North Africa and the Middle East), another for those in both Americas (which included the United States), and one for stations in Asia. But American cryptologists had readily identified the indicator. This was the group that personnel at Bainbridge Island monitoring station recognized and therefore they were able to identify the J-19 cryptographic system used for the two messages of 19 November.

This allocation of audiences resulted in the situation whereby on any given day there were four additional sets of daily key in addition to the layout of the form that had to be recovered by the Americans. This process of recovering the key added to the difficulty required for the complete exploitation of messages encrypted in J-19 and its auxiliary transposition systems daily.[9] Recovery of keys and the form often took well over a week. For example, the keys and form for messages of 18 November 1941 were not recovered until 3 December. By one estimate, at least ten to fifteen percent of J-19 key during the period leading up to Pearl Harbor was not recovered.[10]

The Americans Solve the New Manual System

Shortly after the Japanese introduced the new manual code in mid-summer 1940, an Army code-breaking team headed by Frank Rowlett managed to isolate it in the intercepted diplomatic traffic. Frank Byron Rowlett was one of the first persons hired in 1930 by William Friedman for the newly hatched Signals Intelligence Service. Rowlett was born in southwest Virginia in 1908. After graduating from college, he took a job as a high school math and science teacher. In 1930 Friedman offered Rowlett a job as a "junior cryptanalyst," a position that was a mystery to him until he arrived at SIS. Rowlett demonstrated an ability to beat machine cryptography, solving the Japanese Red machine in 1935 and later supervised the team that broke Purple in September 1940. He also designed the major U.S. machine system known as Sigaba, a system that defied all Axis efforts to solve.

There is some confusion, though, with the story of the solution to J-16 and that is in the vagueness of the chronology of the breakthrough. Rowlett, in his memoirs, relates that the new diplomatic system, which eventually would be labeled J-16, appeared about the time that the processing of Purple intercepts had gotten down to "a routine procedure." The first "Magic" translations were produced on 27 September 1940, but this "first" was achieved only because the two translations were of messages that used the same key. However, it would be about another three or four weeks before translations would be produced daily. The production had to await both the recovery of the Japanese method of key generation for Purple, as well as the construction of an analog device that performed all of the functions of the HINOKI machine.[11] This would place the "routine" production of Magic sometime in the latter part of October.

However, available translations of Japanese diplomatic messages encrypted in MATSU indicate that the SIS team was exploiting the J-16K5 system well before the Purple breakthrough. While fragmentary, the dates of translations suggest the following chronology. As of late August 1940, a number of Japanese diplomatic facilities had begun to use J-16, notably the consulates in Seattle, Washington, and Honolulu, Territory of Hawaii. On 28 August the Japanese embassy in Geneva was informed that, as of the receipt of that day's message number #79, it was to begin using MAT[S]U. It also mentioned that eight other cities, including Washington, D.C., had

Frank B. Rowlett

already switched to MATSU.[12] Within a week, a number of other stations were using MATSU or J-16, though some stations, such as Rome, were still using J-14 as late as 12 September.

Interestingly, the SIS was producing translations of messages in the new J-16 system as early as 7 September 1940, some three weeks before the first Purple machine translations were completed and several weeks before "Magic" translation production became a routine procedure. So, Rowlett's narrative, even as vague as it is, differs from the records. If, by late August, the Japanese were already using J-16 in eight cities, it could not have come "on-line" much earlier than that month. This means that Rowlett and his codebreakers did not have much time to analyze the new system and then solve it; in fact, it was only a few weeks.[13] How did they solve it so quickly?

When the diplomatic traffic encrypted in the new system was studied, Rowlett noticed that the groups of characters in the new system differed in composition and frequency from those seen in the Japanese machine ciphers systems. He suspected a new manual system. Diagnostic tests that could derive clues to the system were applied to the groups in the intercepted text. The results suggested that a code was being transposed, but with a greater effectiveness than the predecessor systems like J-14.

Rowlett initially suspected that the Japanese were using a variation of a World War I German military field cryptographic systems known as "ADFGVX." The German Army implemented this field cipher as it prepared for the massive offensives of March 1918 that almost broke the Allied armies defending Paris. It effectively prevented the Allies from reading German radio traffic for several weeks until it was broken by the French in early June in time to stop the German onslaught. This was a system in which a plaintext message was encrypted with a digraph substitution cipher that used only the referenced six letters – hence the eponymous title. The message was inscribed into a form or *tableau*, but with nulls, that resembled something not unlike a checkerboard. The horizontal and vertical values, that is, the placement of the six letters, were scrambled every day. To further complicate the issue, the cipher text then was superencrypted using a transposition scheme. This last step had the effect of fracturing the original cipher text digraphs, thereby destroying the frequency of their incidence within a message – the best method for exploiting and solving the cipher, the frequency of certain digraphs, had been removed.[14]

Rowlett reported that his team worked with an OP-20-G team on the effort against the new system, but that little progress had been achieved by either group. Then, about a month after the system had been in effect, probably late August 1940, Rowlett was invited by the Navy cryptanalysts in OP-20-G to visit them in their nearby offices. They revealed to him that naval intelligence (OP-16) had recently burglarized an unspecified Japanese diplomatic facility in the U.S. They had opened the code clerk's safe and photographed the codebooks, key, and other material. The haul included snapshots of the most recent J-16 codebooks, ten-day forms, and some of the key for the new auxiliary transposition system. From the pictures the Navy had taken, Rowlett now knew how the new J-16 cryptographic system functioned. He realized that the Japanese were encoding the plaintext and then transposing the resulting text. This technique broke up the code's digraphs and made solving it extremely difficult. Now, armed with copies of the documents photographed by the Navy, the solution and exploitation of the system, soon to have the J16K5 designator, would be much easier. This acquisition of the J-16 material explains how the first published translations of messages encrypted in J-16 were available in the second week of September.

The United States Navy's Office of Naval Intelligence (ONI) had compiled a long history of break-ins of diplomatic facilities and residences in various U.S. cities in order to obtain copies of cryptographic materials and other classified documents. Between the end of the First World War and 1941, Naval Intelligence carried out a number of these "black bag jobs." In the early 1920s, ONI had purloined the main Japanese naval code book to which the covername "Red" (not to be confused with the Red diplomatic cipher machine) was given. In 1935 the apartment of the Japanese naval attaché in Washington was burglarized, though nothing of value was found. Later, in May 1941, in one of the most brazen efforts, a team of navy and customs personnel boarded the Japanese merchant ship *Nichi Shin Maru* of the Pacific Whaling Steamship Company at Port Costa near San Francisco. They planted some drugs in the captain's cabin and in the ensuing confusion confiscated his copy of the current merchant (*Maru*) code and several other documents dealing with communications. When the Japanese consulate intervened and requested the documents' return, U.S. Customs replied they would give the documents back when the investigation was completed; presumably they meant the drug issue. The Japanese consulate informed Tokyo by cable of the situation. It also suggested to Tokyo that if any other Japanese vessels were boarded in the future, then the cryptographic material that was on hand should be destroyed lest it fall into American hands.[15] The SIS, which had already broken that code, was angry that the Navy's stunt would alert the Japanese to American interest in their codes.[16]

Despite the bounty, Rowlett was uneasy with the implications of the Navy's burglary and rightly so. While their photographic snatch had helped immeasurably in reducing the time needed to recover the new diplomatic code and its auxiliary transposition cipher system, Rowlett was worried about the long-term potential for compromise these actions posed for current and future Army cryptanalytic projects. If the Japanese ever suspected that their facilities had been entered and their cryptography had been compromised, they would change whatever systems were operational and, therefore, place him and his codebreakers back to the beginning. Moreover, if the Japanese became truly concerned over the scope of the compromise of their cryptographic systems, they might even go further and replace the Red and Purple cipher machines that had taken Rowlett and his codebreakers so long to exploit.[17]

Rowlett went to the Army brass with his concerns about the Navy's break-ins. He saw Brigadier General Joseph Mauborgne, who was the Chief Signal Officer, head of the Army's Signal Corps, under which the SIS operated. General Mauborgne was an accomplished cryptanalyst and a long-time proponent of communications intelligence, going back to the early 1930s when he sat alone listening to his radio for foreign radio traffic while he was stationed in the army base in the Presidio in San Francisco, California. Mauborgne had been promoted to the position of the Chief Signal Officer in 1938 and had pressed for expansion of all parts of the army's COMINT program.

Mauborgne agreed with Rowlett's fears about the navy's second-story jobs. He wanted these clandestine forays into foreign diplomatic missions to end before a major compromise happened. He told Rowlett that he would "take it to the White House" if the navy refused to desist.[18] However, Mauborgne, who was a technically gifted codebreaker in his own right, also had reservations regarding the Rowlett's ability to solve the new Japanese system without recourse to the Navy's "lifted material." In this, William Friedman, who headed up the SIS, seconded the general's doubts. Friedman believed that the new transposition cipher could not be broken by pure cryptanalysis.[19] Still, the Army codebreakers went to the Navy Building next door to their offices in the Munitions Building on Constitution Avenue in Washington, and convinced the head of OP-20-G, Commander Laurance Safford, to get naval intelligence to agree to hold off for a while and to inform the Army about any future break-ins.

Mauborgne and Friedman's pessimism about the effectiveness of pure cryptanalysis against J-16 became a red flag waved in front of Rowlett. He was determined to prove the system could be recovered through pure cryptanalysis. He won a concession from both the Navy and Army cryptologic staffs for time to allow him to attempt to recover any changes to the new system without any covert acquisitions. He banked upon the Japanese tendency to regularly replace current systems. He did not have to wait long. At the end of November, the Japanese replaced the auxiliary transposition system, K-5, with a new version, labeled K-6, as well as the basic code, which was known as HAGI (Shrub), which the Americans later labeled J-17. After two weeks, the Japanese slipped up. A message encrypted in K-6 was sent as a circular. A circular message is one that is sent to more than one station; in the case of this system, it probably meant that the message was sent to all of the stations in one of the four audiences. However, one station in this group received a version of the circular message with about fifty extra letters of text. This additional text allowed Rowlett to solve K-6. As it turned out, the K-6 transposition system merely reversed the indicators from the K-5 system and also inscribed text into the form beginning from the extreme right column instead of the left.[20]

Over the next year, as each new variant to the original MATSU system was activated by Tokyo, the Army cryptanalysts were able to solve it. The code structure remained the same with plaintext values merely being reshuffled to new code groups. The auxiliary cipher systems were a variant of the preceding system. At the same time, independently of the Americans, the British and Dutch codebreakers in Singapore and Bandung were also exploiting the new manual system and its successors.

By August 1941 the *Gaimusho* cryptographers were ready to activate the latest variant. Rowlett and his team were tipped to the new system by a message from Tokyo to Washington on 22 June 1941. In the text Tokyo announced that the current code, SAKURA, known as J-18 to the Americans, would be replaced by the new version called FUJI.[21] The first two messages in the new FUJI system were discovered to have been literally double superenciphered with the Purple machine. After the Purple cipher had been stripped away, the transposed code text was exposed. Rowlett analyzed the code groups after they had been transposed back to the original four-letter groups. Upon inspection of these groups, he recognized some curious combinations that led him to suspect that the groups were not from a table like the three earlier systems, but were derived from some other source. His suspicions centered on a letter count of the messages, which revealed that forty-eight percent of the text consisted of vowels. This did not square with the percentages from the previous system, J-18 or SAKURA.[22]

Rowlett recognized that the coding system used in the FUJI appeared to be a derivative of a code known as "CA," which had been in use since 1936. The system had stopped using a cipher in 1937. Its use was often indicated by the appearance of the digraph "CA" in the first group. The system also had an auxiliary English speller table with twenty-six digraphs substituted for the letters of the English alphabet. This auxiliary system usually carried the indicator "AQ." This was another point of recognition that Rowlett may have locked onto during his analysis of the cipher. However, the first efforts to transpose the messages back to the original code groups failed.

Rowlett tried another approach, which was to recover the key and forms used in the messages. From these he derived the 1,600 digraphs of untransposed code. Then he developed an index for the recovery of the tetragraphs. By analyzing the new system in this manner, Rowlett looked first for the tetragraphs that would have indicated dates or foreign names. He found the tetragraphs in question; in fact, they were groups from the J-

18 table which had been reversed. He broke the new system within a day.[23]

However, solving FUJI, or J-19K10 as the code and its auxiliary transposition cipher were now titled by the American codebreakers, did not necessarily mean that exploitation of the traffic encoded in that system was easy. In fact, exploiting messages in J-19 remained a difficult proposition at best. Captain Safford estimated that the Americans failed to recover about ten to fifteen percent of J-19 key whereas only two to three percent of Purple key was not recovered.[24] Actually, the key recovery rate was much lower. According to an OP-20-G cryptanalytic report from October 1941, as of the end of the previous month only twenty-one percent of the J-19K10 key had been recovered.[25] The problem, of course, was that each day's key had to be recovered, while three times during a month the form or stencil was replaced. Estimates of time needed to exploit a message encoded in J-19 ranged from about a half day to as many as five, but individual messages could take anywhere from ten to fifteen days to decrypt.[26] The irony was that, while the J-19 system was far easier to solve, it remained a considerably more difficult system to exploit daily. Purple took eighteen months to solve, but its exploitation was far easier – usually the decryption and translation of a Purple message were completed within one day of receipt of the original intercept, thanks in large part to the recovery by the navy cryptanalyst Frank Raven of the Purple daily key generating scheme.

The tradeoffs in the relative security of cryptographic systems sometimes belie their ultimate importance, as well as their vulnerability. The relative importance the Americans assigned to the exploitation of J-19 and Purple suggests that J-19 traffic was not considered as important to complete as was that for Purple. Precisely why is not clear. It is possible that the ease of solution for J-19 might have biased American codebreakers into believing that, in terms of importance, it was a secondary system relative to Purple. Also, that Purple machines generally were distributed to major capitals or cities might have led the Americans to consider the machine a far more valuable intelligence source. Whatever the reason or mix of reasons, Purple became and remained the priority Japanese diplomatic target for the army and navy codebreakers up to and beyond Pearl Harbor.

The resulting joint effort against Purple continued to consume the major portion of time and analytic resources available to both services. After Purple, the two services worked J-19, PA-K2, and the LA systems, followed by plaintext traffic and broadcasts. The efforts against messages in systems other than Purple suffered by comparison because of this prioritization. This deficit can be measured in terms of messages translated, the penultimate step in processing any intercept. For example, from 1 November to 7 December 1941, American cryptologists decrypted and translated about two-thirds of all intercepted Purple messages. During the same period, only sixteen percent of all intercepted messages encoded in J-19 were translated.[27] Essentially, even if a message had been decrypted quickly, it could sit in an in-basket awaiting translation. There was, in the words of Captain Safford, "no urgency" attached to exploiting messages encrypted in J-19.[28]

November 19: Japanese Message #2353 – The First Winds Instruction Message

The first message intercepted by the monitoring site at Bainbridge Island, Washington, Japanese message number 2353 [**Exhibit #3**],[29] was not completely processed until 26 November. It is not certain when it was decrypted, but there is some evidence that the British FECB in Singapore recovered the key to that day's J-19 cipher and relayed it to Washington via London on 24 November.[30] The recovered key sequence [**Exhibit #5**][31] used to transcribe the coded text into the columns read: 3-17-12-4-5-18-2-10-19-7-11-9-14-1-6-16-13-15-8. The indicator BUTWJ designated the message for a global audience and that form (or stencil) #8 was to be used for the transposition cipher.

Since the message was intercepted on an odd-numbered day, it was OP-20-G's job to process it. The analyst's first step was to inscribe the code text into the correct Form, number 8. [**Exhibit #56**][32] The next step was to correctly read out the code digraphs on a worksheet. But this required the daily key, which was not available until 24 November. On this sheet the analyst would write the Japanese kana plain text value under the code groups. [**Exhibit #6**][33] After this, a Navy linguist produced the kana text version of the message to translate. [**Exhibit #7**][34] A translation was finally published and released on 28 November. The translation carried two serial numbers representing the split/double duty by the two services. There was the Army SIS number, "25432," and the Navy JD-1 (Japanese Diplomatic Translation, 1941), "6875."[35] [**Exhibit #8**][36]

The main points of message number 2353 were these:

*The "execute" message phrase was to be sent in case diplomatic relations between Japan and one of the three named countries were "in danger."

*There were three phrases, each unique and signifying the state of relations with one of the three countries:

– HIGASHI NO KAZE AME (East Wind Rain) if Japan – United States relations were in danger,
– KITA NO KAZE KUMORI (North Wind Cloudy) if Japan – Soviet Union relations were in danger, and
– NISHI NO KAZE HARE (West Wind Clear) if Japan – Great Britain relations were in danger.

*Each phrase would be repeated as a special weather bulletin, **twice in the middle** and **twice at the end** of the daily Japanese language short wave voice news broadcast.

*When the message was heard, each diplomatic facility was to destroy all codes and important papers.

Interestingly, the SIS revised this translation in September 1944. This was done at the request of William F. Friedman, who, at the time, was preparing to testify before the first round of hearings of the Clarke Investigation into the attack on Pearl Harbor. Three Army linguists worked on the new translation, including John Hurt, who had been hired by Friedman in 1930 as part of his original staff. The translation added some of the personal tone of the message missing in the original. The revised version differed little in the text except for one point. In terms of relations with Great Britain, it added that the situation also could include an occupation of Thailand, the invasion of the Netherlands East Indies, and the invasion of Malaya. [**Exhibit #9**][37] No one knows why these three additional scenarios were kept out of the original translation issued on 28 November 1941, especially since the reference to the Netherlands is obvious in the kana text.

November 19: Japanese Message #2354 – The Second Winds Instruction Message

The second Winds message, number 2354 [**Exhibit #4**][38], was decrypted and translated by 26 November, seven days after it had been intercepted. The message's encoded text was inscribed into Form #8. [**Exhibit #10**][39] As with message #2353, the analyst recovered the true code text only after receiving the key from the British site in Singapore on 24 November. The analyst then produced the worksheet of the original code text with the plaintext kana values written underneath each digraph code group. [**Exhibit #11**][40] The translation was then produced, reviewed, and issued on 26 November. Like its predecessor, the final translation of message #2354 carried two translation serial numbers representing the split/double duty performed by both services. There was the SIS number,

"23592," and the OP-20-G serial, JD-1 "6850." **[Exhibit #12]**[41]

The lower serial numbers by both services indicates that message #2354 was completely processed and released before #2353. Why this occurred is not totally clear, though the fact that the second message was about forty groups shorter may have been a factor. Also, like the first message, in September 1944 a revised version was done at the request of William Friedman. The revised version, though, differed little in substance from the original. **[Exhibit #13]**[42]

The main points to message #2354 were these:

*The warning was to be sent if relations were in danger of breaking down – "mortally strained" was how the 1944 version translated the expression.

*Three single words were listed as the alert codewords. These words happened to be the same first word of the three code phrases contained in #2353:

– HIGASHI (East) if it related to U.S.-Japan relations;
– KITA (North) if it concerned Japan-USSR relations; and
– NISHI (West) if it concerned Japan-Great Britain relations, which included the situation in Thailand, Malaya, and the Netherlands East Indies.

*Each word would be repeated five times both at the beginning and end of the General Intelligence, or News Broadcast [IPPA JOHO]. In the 1944 version of the translation, the instructions stated that the words would be inserted in the General News Broadcast, which was a Japanese overseas news broadcast transmitted in Morse code. For an example of a transcription of this type of news broadcast. **[Exhibit #14]**[43]

The Americans were not the only ones to intercept and process these two messages. Cryptologists for Australia and Great Britain also collected, decrypted, and translated the same messages. They produced slightly different texts, as would be expected. For example, for message #2353, Eric Nave, a Royal Australian Navy linguist, translated the introductory paragraph this way:

> **Owing to the pressure of the international situation, we must be faced with a generally bad situation. In that event, the communication between Japan and the countries opposing her would be severed immediately. Therefore, should we be on the verge of an international crisis we will broadcast twice....**[44]

On 28 November the Commander-in-Chief of the U.S. Asiatic Fleet (CINCAF), Admiral Thomas C. Hart, who later headed an inquiry into Pearl Harbor from February to June 1944, relayed the news to Washington and Honolulu that the British at the FECB in Singapore had intercepted the same two Winds messages. The message added that the British and the U.S. Navy monitoring station at Cavite, Philippines (known as "Cast"), would be listening for the two broadcasts as outlined in the messages. The message noted that the intercepted messages contained warnings that were to be broadcast if relations between Japan and any of the three other countries were "on the verge of being severed." **[Exhibit #15]**[45]

The Dutch intercept station in the Netherlands East Indies, *Kamer* 14, also intercepted and decoded the same two messages as the British and the Americans. The first, Japanese serial #2353, was transmitted from Tokyo to diplomatic stations in the Far East. The second, serial #2354, was relayed from the Japanese embassy in Bangkok to their consulate in Batavia on the island of Java. The Dutch authorities passed along the contents of the Japanese messages to both the American military and naval attachés in Batavia. Both attachés cabled the War and Navy Departments of the Dutch intercept. The State Department also was alerted to the messages by its representative in Batavia, Consul General Walter Foote. **[Exhibit #55]**[46] Foote reported the two Dutch translations, though he stated that the coded phrases meant "war" with either of the three named nations. Yet, in the same message to Washington, Foote added that the second message from Bangkok to Batavia carried the expression "threat of crises." Foote, however, was skeptical of the importance of the information from the Dutch. He noted in his report that since 1936 such warnings of impending Japanese hostilities in the region "had been common."[47]

It is worth emphasizing that the Japanese Foreign Ministry established two distinct, though related, ways of notifying its diplomats of a change in relations that warranted the destruction of vital papers and cryptography. The *Gaimusho* intended to set up a warning mechanism that accomplished three things. First, it would be effective even if traditional lines of communications were cut off. Tokyo's diplomats could listen over any shortwave radio for the broadcasts. Secondly, it was a mechanism that was unique for its intended audience. The scenarios spelled out in the Winds instruction messages, in which the open code (or codeword) phrases or words would be passed, were distinct from any situation in which a phrase or word about the weather could be misconstrued, i.e., a regular weather report or broadcast.

Finally, that anyone else might hear the open code phrase or word was not important. The meanings of the Winds codewords or phrases were innocuous to anyone else who might be monitoring the overseas broadcast out of Tokyo. The security of the mechanism was that the knowledge of the true meaning of the Winds code was restricted to the Japanese Foreign Ministry and its diplomats. The sense of security was heightened by the fact that the Japanese were certain that FUJI (J-19) could not be exploited.

However, in their certainty, the Japanese diplomats were gravely mistaken. Although the code phrases and words were difficult to exploit quickly, the Americans (and British and Dutch) within a week knew in detail the instructions contained in the Winds phrases and words. With this information in their hands, the Americans now had a way of measuring any change in the relations between Japan and the United States. A Japanese news broadcast that contained the Winds code phrases and words signified an increase in "danger" in relations between the two nations. The Americans knew that the next step was for Tokyo's diplomats to destroy all of the classified material and equipment held in its facilities. What could be a clearer warning than that?

What remained to be done was for the SIS and OP-20-G to task their respective monitoring sites to listen for the Winds message(s) and then await their transmission. Yet what was apparently simple would, over the next ten days, become complicated and confusing.

Notes

1. Frank B. Rowlett, *The Story of Magic* (Laguna Hills, CA: Aegean Park Press, 1998), 174; Multinational Diplomatic translation (MNDT) #9719, Tokyo to Washington, 13 August 1940. RG 457, Entry 9032, Box 291.

2. MNDT # 6938, Bogota to Tokyo, 24 April 1940 and #6906, New Orleans to Tokyo, 24 April 1940. RG 457, Entry 9032, Box 288.

3. Department of Defense, *The "Magic" Background of Pearl Harbor* (Hereafter "Magic" Background), Vol. I (February 14, 1941 – May 12, 1941) (Washington, D.C.: USGPO, 1977), A-101 to 104

4. It is not clear how Tokyo first informed its diplomatic facilities of the change of the codes to J-16 (MATSU). Frank Rowlett says that a circular message sometime in June encoded in an old system tipped off the SIS to the change. But a review of SIS translations from the period (Entry 9032, boxes 287-289) does not

uncover such a message. There are some scattered messages from Tokyo instructing stations to begin using the MATSU system, but these are dated from late August and early September 1940.

5. "Japanese Diplomatic Network and Crypto Systems, Pre-During (sic) the War." RG 457, Entry 9032, Box 992, Folder 3015.

6. "Auxiliary Diplomatic Systems." R.I.P.-37B, 15 September 1940, 9-1. RG 457 Entry 9032, Box 1137, Folder 3671

7. "Change No. 4 to R.I.P. 37B, "K10 Transposition System." 1 April 1944. RG 457, Entry 9032, Box 1137, Folder 3672, 7-119

8. Ibid., 7-58 to 7-59

9. "J-19 System Description (Draft)." RG 457, Entry 9032, Box 992, Folder 3015, "Jap Diplomatic Network Cryptosystems; Pre and During WWII." 2-3

10. Wohlstetter, 175

11. For a description of this process, see Alvarez, 80-82 and Stephen Budiansky, *Battle of Wits*. (New York: The Free Press, 2000), 164-168. Almost all narratives of this event draw heavily from William Friedman's "Preliminary Historical Report on the Solution of the B Machine," 14 October 1940, "History of Japanese Cipher machines," RG 457, Entry 9032, Box 808

12. MND Translation #10437, Tokyo to Geneva, 28 August 1940. RG 457, Entry 9032, Box 291

13. Rowlett, 175.

14. For a more detailed narrative about the solution and exploitation of the ADFGVX cipher, see Kahn, 341-345; Also War Department, Office of the Chief Signal Officer, Washington, *General Solution for the ADFGVX Cipher System: Technical Paper*. (Washington, U.S. Government Printing Office, 1934). For information about the diagnostic analysis and solution of transposition ciphers, see Lambros D. Callimahos and William F. Friedman, *Military Cryptanlaytics, Part II* (Fort George G. Meade, MD: National Security Agency, Office of Training Services, 1959), 415-434.

15. MND Translation #18037, San Francisco to Tokyo, 28 May 1941. RG 457, Entry 9032, Box 738, Folder 1812, "Jap Suspicions that U.S. [and] Allies Reading Codes, (1940-42)"

16. For more on the Navy's program of stealing or copying codes, see Stephen Budiansky, *Battle of Wits*, 84; Rear Admiral Edwin T. Layton with Captain Roger Pinneau and John Costello, *And I Was There: Pearl Harbor and Midway – Breaking the Secrets* (New York: William Morrow and Company Inc., 1985), 109-110; Frederick Parker, *Pearl Harbor Revisited: The United States Navy Communications Intelligence, 1924-1944* (Fort George G. Meade, MD: NSA, Center for Cryptologic History, 1994), 4-5; and Ellis Zacharias, *Secret Missions: The Story of an Intelligence Officer* (New York: G.P. Putnam's Sons, 1946), 178-82

17. Rowlett, 180-1

18. Ibid., 183

19. Ibid., 182-3

20. R.I.P. 37B, 7-33

21. MND Translation, Tokyo to Washington, Circular #1295, 22 June 1941. RG 457, Entry 9032, Box 992, Folder 3015, "Jap Diplomatic Network Cryptosystems; Pre- and During WWII."

22. "J-19," Ibid. Frank Rowlett's Notebook, also in Box 992.

23. "J-19," Ibid. For more on the CA system, see R.I.P 37A, "General Characteristics of Japanese Diplomatic Systems," Part I, Section 5-25. RG 457, Entry 9032, Box 1137, Folder 3670.

24. PHH Part 36:314; also in Wohlstetter, 175

25. "Monthly Progress Report for September 1941," RG 38, Entry 1040, Box 115, Folder 5750/198, "GYP-1 History"

26. Ibid.; Kahn, *Codebreakers*, 16-18

27. PHH, Part 37:1081-83

28. "Friedman notes of meeting with Captain Safford," page 11. RG 457, Entry 9032, Box 1360, Folder 4217. "Pearl Harbor Investigation and Miscellaneous Material."

29. CCH Series XII.S, Box 22 and "Jap Msgs, oct-Dec 1941," RG 38, CNSG Library, Box 156, Pages 3803-4.

30. CCH Series XII. S, Box 22. SIS #23542, 28 November 1941. William Friedman Marginalia: "Key furnished by British (Navy says Singapore to London to Washington 24 Nov[ember] [19]41). F[riedman]

31. R.I.P. 37b, 7-83

32. NARA, RG 80, PHLO, Entry 167A, "Office Reference ("Subject") Files, 1932-1946." Winds Code, Station "W" to Witnesses. Folder: Winds Code - Misc Material.

33. Center for Cryptologic History, Series XII.S, Box 22 and NARA, RG 80, PHLO, Entry 167A, "Office

Reference ("Subject") Files, 1932-1946." Winds Code, Station "W" to Witnesses. Folder: Winds Code - Misc Material. A copy of the same worksheet also is available at NARA, RG 457, Entry 9032, Box 1360, Folder 4217, "Pearl Harbor Investigation and Miscellaneous Material."

34. GSB 180, 6 November 1941[5]. RG 38. CNSG Library, Box 166, Folder 5830/69, "Winds Msgs."

35. The Army SIS used a simple one-up serialization scheme for its diplomatic translations beginning in 1939. The SIS also included a prefix to this numbering system. During the war, the prefix changed three times – "SSA" to "SSD" to "H" – but the numbering system continued. The Navy's OP-20-G used a more complicated system for diplomatic translations. The serial consisted of a trigraph indicating the country and element, in this case "JD" for Japanese diplomatic messages. The third element in the trigraph was a single digit representing the last digit in the year that the message was translated. So "JD-1" indicated that the translation was of a Japanese diplomatic message completed in 1941. This digit changed with each year, so "JD-2" indicated a Japanese diplomatic translation completed in 1942 and so on through 1945. The serial number after the trigraph was the serial of that translation. The Navy would reset the serial number to "0001" on 1 January of the new year. Translations of Japanese naval messages used the same method – "JN-2" indicated a translation completed in 1942.

After the war, OP-20-G decrypted and translated Japanese naval messages it had intercepted prior to the start of the war, emphasizing those relevant to Pearl Harbor. These messages all bear serials with the trigraphs of "JN-5" or "JN-6" meaning they were completed in 1945 or 1946.

36. CCH Series XII.S, Box 22

37. Ibid.

38. Ibid., and NARA, RG 80, PHLO, Entry 167A, "Office Reference ("Subject") Files, 1932-1946." Winds Code, Station "W" to Witnesses. Folder: Winds Code - Misc Material.

39. CCH Series XII.S, Box 22 and "Jap Msgs, Oct-Dec 1941." RG 38 CNSG Library, Box 156, page 3798.

40. Ibid.

41. Ibid. A copy of this translation, without Friedman's inscribed comments, can be found in the Multi-National Diplomatic Translation collection, SIS # 23592, Tokyo to Washington, 19 November 1941. RG 457, Entry 9032, Box 301.

42. Ibid.

43. Japanese News Broadcast by station "JVJ," 8 December 1941. NARA, RG 38, CNSG Library, Box 167, Folder 5830/69 (3 of 3), "Pearl Harbor Investigations: Winds Msgs."

44. James Rusbridger and Eric Nave, *Betrayal at Pearl Harbor: How Churchill Lured Roosevelt into Wordl War II* (New York: Summit Books, 1991), 135-6. This example of differing translations points to an issue raised in a book by Keiichiro Komatsu, *The Origins of the Pacific War and the Importance of 'Magic'* (New York: St. Martin's Press, 1999). Professor Komatsu claims that the translations produced by the American cryptologists often exaggerated, mistranslated, or misconstrued the original Japanese text, thereby misleading American leaders as to the true intent of Tokyo, which, as he claims, was for a negotiated way out of the confrontation.

Yet, the Roosevelt administration in Washington had problems assessing Japan's ultimate intent in the Far East. There were many causes, including the technical difficulties in rendering subtle Japanese diplomatic text into an English version that was faithful to the original and conveyed that same meaning to the Americans. But the effect of Japanese actions were more important. The civilian government in Tokyo failed adequately to control the Imperial Japanese Army's actions in China. As a result, Tokyo's policy often appeared to the Roosevelt administration as erratic, deceptive, or at cross-purposes. Also, it must be understood that American policymakers were reacting to nearly ten years of overt Japanese aggression in Manchuria and China. Likewise, the two-stage takeover of French Indochina by Japan (1940-41), and the American economic sanction in response, which came to be the probable major immediate *casus belli* for the Pacific War, could only be interpreted within the same context of previous Japanese aggression in China. The cause of the Pacific War was far more than a matter of how intercepted Japanese diplomatic dispatches were being translated. Rather, it was the aggressive Japanese policy of aggrandizement throughout East Asia that lay at the heart of the dispute between Washington and Tokyo and ultimately led to hostilities.

45. CINCAF Intelligence Report, 281430, 28 November 1941. PHH, Part 17:2660

46 ALUSNA, Batavia CR0222, 031030 December 1941. NARA, Washington D.C. RG 128.3, Exhibit 142, Box 334; also in RG 38, CNSG Library, Box 166, Folder 5830/69.

47. Batavia to Secretary of State, Washington, DC, 4 December 1941. NARA, RG 38, CNSG Library, Box 166, Folder 5830/69. Interestingly, in an article in 1986, James Rusbridger claimed that the British and Dutch had both intercepted the Winds Execute message on 4 December. However, Rusbridger then stated that the message, which was sent in two parts, was transmitted to Washington by the British monitoring station in Singapore and that the Dutch had passed their intercept to the U.S. consul-general, who, in turn, relayed the intercept to the War Department. Aside from the misconceptions about the flow of information, that is, Singapore would have sent the information to London and/or the US Navy site at Cavite, Philippines, and not directly to Washington, Rusbridger has confused the two messages intercepted on 19 November with the alleged Execute message. In fact, in his description of the exchanges between the Americans, British, and Dutch actually is that of the exchanges of the two Winds instruction messages. See "Brit Researcher Confirms Briggs' Winds Execute Intercept." *NCVA Cryptolog*, (Volume 8, Number 1, Fall 1986), 1-2, 21.

Chapter 3
The Hunt for the Winds Execute Message,
28 November – 7 December 1941

As soon as both translations of the instructions that set up the two Winds Execute messages were available to Army and Navy cryptologists and intelligence officers, they went about tasking monitoring stations to search and intercept them. The search for these messages, more precisely the appearance of the code phrases and words within either a voice or Manual morse Japanese news broadcast, was conducted against a background of increasing diplomatic and political tension between the United States and Japan. While at the time it might have been presumptive to predict the certain outbreak of war between the two nations, in the last weeks of November and into December 1941, translations of Purple traffic between Tokyo and its two negotiators, Saburo Kurusu and Kichisaburo Nomura, indicated that the current impasse might be coming to a head.

On 26 November a liaison conference of Japanese military and civilian leaders had met and decided not to use an American proposal as a basis for negotiations. Moderates, though, won another day of delay to see what Ambassador Nomura could gain in a meeting with President Roosevelt and Secretary of State Cordell Hull. But the meeting on 27 November failed to achieve any agreement. The United States still suspected Japan's intentions based on its continued adherence to the Tripartite Pact signed with Nazi Germany and Italy.[1] The growing Japanese troop strength in French Indochina could not be accepted as "defensive." In a message of 28 November (and translated by the Americans the same day), Tokyo informed its two representatives that the "negotiations will be *de facto* ruptured. This is inevitable." The message also instructed the two emissaries not to "give the impression" that negotiations will be broken off. Rather, they should simply say that they were awaiting further guidance from Tokyo.[2] Four days later, on 1 December, Tokyo cabled the two diplomats in Washington and told them "The date set in my message #812 *(November 29th for the absolute deadline to complete negotiations)* [my italics] has come and gone, and the situation continues to be increasingly critical."[3]

That same day, President Roosevelt met with his War Council, Secretaries Hull, Knox, and Stimson, Chief of Staff General George Marshall, and Chief of Naval Operations Admiral Harold Stark. At this meeting, Hull stated that there seemed to be no chance of an agreement with Japan and that a "surprise attack" [not specified] might be part of the Japanese plan. The council was aware of Japanese troop convoys sailing south, but the administration could not decide on a specific action. Still, not all in the administration believed the clock was running out. The Joint Board, a consultative body composed of the Chief of Staff and the Chief of Naval Operations and their division chiefs, had written that time might still exist to build up defenses in the Philippines, which might ultimately deter Japanese aggression to the south. Some members of the State Department suggested that Japan would hold off until the next year to attack.[4]

It was into this roiling cauldron that the translations of the two Winds instructional messages arrived. With the just published translations of the *Gaimusho's* instructions to its diplomats for the Winds Execute code phrases and words, the Americans believed they held at least one key that might tip off when the Japanese might initiate hostilities. The next step was to organize and stage a monitoring effort to intercept the Winds execute message. But in the next ten days leading up to the surprise attack on Pearl Harbor,

American cryptologists would find that the Japanese sent out additional instructions that weaved a more complicated warning system. Inevitably, there were errors in identifying Winds Execute messages, while precious cryptologic resources, especially radio intercept operators, radio receivers, and linguists, were tied up collecting and processing plaintext broadcasts that might contain the coded Winds phrases or words.

The Search Begins – 28 November 1941

By 28 November, with the two translations of the Japanese *Gaimusho* messages setting up the Winds code phrases and words, along with the message from the Commander-in-Chief Asiatic Fleet, Admiral Thomas Hart, which reported the British exploitation of the same two messages, American naval intelligence was ready to act. The Director of Naval Intelligence (ONI), Rear Admiral Theodore Wilkinson, passed a request through the Director of Naval Communications (DNC), Rear Admiral Leigh Noyes, that the communications intelligence arm of DNC was to make every attempt to intercept any Winds Execute message. Noyes seconded the request to Captain Safford, adding that it was to be construed as an order.[5]

The first thing the American cryptologists had to do before any tasking could be set for monitoring for the Winds Execute messages was to draw up a list of Japanese commercial radio stations that might transmit the phrases or words, along with their operating frequencies and broadcast schedules. Fortunately, in the preceding months, the Americans had translated a number of Japanese diplomatic messages that dealt with the ability of Tokyo's embassies and consulates around the world to hear these broadcasts stations. The diplomats had reported back to Tokyo both on the strength of the transmissions and their clarity. In many cases, the diplomats reported any problems with regional atmospherics or interference from local transmitters. These reports included the voice programs on the high frequency band (3 to 30 MHz), as well as those voice and Morse code transmissions on the medium frequency band (300 kHz to 3 MHz) and even lower.[6] The Americans, then, already had a good sense of the capabilities of Japanese overseas broadcasts.

On 27 November Tokyo sent a message to the Washington embassy that included a set of broadcast schedules and frequencies for four Japanese news broadcast stations to various parts of East Asia, the Pacific coast of the United States, and Europe.[7] The contents of the message were available to the Americans the next day:

Station	Frequency (KHz)	Schedule	Reception Area
JVJ	12275	6:00 PM	Pacific Coast
JUO	9430	6:30 PM	Western Hemisphere
JVJ	12275	6:30 PM	Western Hemisphere
JVJ	12275	7:00 PM	Coast (not further identified)
JHL	5160	8:00 PM	Coast (not further identified)
JHL	5160	9:00 PM	Coast (not further identified)
JHL	5160	2[1]0:00 PM	Coast (not further identified)
JHP	11980	10:30 PM	Europe

Captain Safford took the schedule from this message and made it the main part of a technical message that the CNO staff (OPNAV) sent out to a number of navy commands the very next day. In sending out this message, he had acted quickly, he said later, because "it would be a feather in our cap if the navy got it [the Winds Execute message] and our sister service did not."[8] The message was sent at priority precedence to naval intercept and analytic elements in the Philippines and Hawaii. But it seems that Safford may have acted a bit precipitously in sending out this information. Some of the data in the OPNAV message was incomplete, incorrect, and not current. Safford also had failed to take into consideration what broadcasts the various navy field sites could hear due to propagation and local reception conditions.

More importantly, the OPNAV message as sent had not tasked any navy site to listen for the Winds code phrases or words. The sole correspondence that had mentioned any monitoring activity was the 28 November message from Admiral Hart's Asian Fleet command notifying Hawaii and Washington that his command and the British at Singapore would be listening for the Winds code words or phrases. But this message from the Far East was not followed up by one from OP-20-G, ONI, or the DNC that detailed any further tasking for navy intercept sites. Instead, the OPNAV message contained only the technical information on Japanese broadcast schedules that Safford had compiled from the translation of the Japanese message with the schedules.

In the technical message to Hawaii and the Philippines, Safford departed a bit from the information in the Japanese listing. For one thing, he assumed that all the broadcast times were in Tokyo time. Secondly, he presumed that the broadcast schedule times for station "JVJ" at 6:00 and 7:00 PM were for the Pacific coast. While possibly valid, these assumptions were not necessarily correct, either. Recall that the broadcast schedule had been sent only to the embassy in Washington. The question implicit in the message from Tokyo was whether or not these broadcasts could be heard by the embassy.

On 27 November the Japanese embassy in Washington had responded to the broadcast schedule message. In it, the embassy noted that it could only poorly receive the broadcasts from stations JUO and JVJ and that Tokyo had to replace those stations with broadcasts from stations JAV (27.327 MHz) and JUP (13605 KHz). Also, Washington wanted the frequency for JHL changed to 13605 KHz from 5160 KHz. Yet Safford did not mention these modifications in his 28 November message. Nor did he note in the OPNAV message that stations JUO and JVJ, as well as their replacements, JAV and JUP broadcast in Morse code, while JHL was a voice program, the *Domei* news broadcast.[9] The importance of this distinction was that for a monitoring site to copy a voice broadcast required the presence of individuals qualified in the Japanese language.

These differences took on importance when, on 28 November, OP-20-GX, the element in OP-20-G that was responsible for tasking the navy's monitoring stations, sent the same text of Safford's message via TWX (teleprinter exchange via leased cable lines) to Stations "M" at Cheltenham, Maryland, and "S" at Bainbridge, Washington. Again, as in the earlier message, no mention was made of any Winds code phrases. When the message was received at the station, the personnel there requested a clarification of the times of the broadcasts – specifically were these Greenwich Civil Time (GCT) or Pacific Standard Time (PST)? OP-20-GX told Bainbridge that the time zones were uncertain and unverifiable. On their own initiative, the personnel at Bainbridge recalculated the frequencies and times of the stations they could hear. The resulting schedule, though, was quite different from the list from Washington.[10] At Bainbridge there were no Japanese linguists qualified to monitor voice transmissions, so it could only record the broadcasts made by voice.[11]

In the Philippines at the navy's communication intercept station on Corregidor Island in Manila Bay, known as "C" or "Cast," coverage of the broadcasts was assigned to two receivers, one for the voice and one for the manual Morse broadcast. A Japanese-qualified linguist was assigned to monitor the voice transmissions, while all intercept copied from both receivers was reviewed by another linguist for any sign of the Winds code phrases or words.[12]

In Hawaii, the chief of naval intelligence for the Fourteenth Naval District, Captain I.H. Mayfield, acting possibly in conjunction with instructions from Admiral Kimmel's command, ordered two language-qualified officers to monitor Japanese language programs broadcast by the local commercial radio stations KGU and KGMB. Both officers were instructed what phrases and words to listen for during their monitoring. Both were further told that if any such phrases were heard, then they were to report the information to Mayfield, Commander Edward Layton, Pacific Fleet Intelligence Officer, or Commander Joseph Rochefort, the commander of the Communications Intelligence Unit (CIU) subordinate to the 14th Naval District, otherwise known as Station HYPO or "H." Oddly, since there was no information about broadcasts of the Winds Execute phrases or words appearing on local U.S. stations, precisely why the District Intelligence Officer ordered this monitoring is unclear.[13] It is possible that Mayfield misunderstood the instructions and believed that the phrases or words would appear on the local Japanese language programs. It is also possible that the navy believed that instructions to the local Japanese population to commit sabotage might be passed on these same programs in the same code.[14]

Also in Hawaii, four Japanese language-qualified naval officers were transferred from the Rochefort's code-breaking center in Pearl Harbor and stationed in Heeia on the northern side of Oahu. They were ordered to maintain a twenty-four-hour watch on overseas Japanese language broadcasts. These four officers were briefed on the three phrases to listen for and their meaning. They were further told to inform Commander Rochefort if they heard such phrases.[15] The officers listened to the Japanese news broadcasts and paid particular attention to the programs on the hour and half-hour when weather forecasts were more likely to be sent.[16]

On 28 November the SIS head of intercept operations, Captain Robert Schukraft, after consulting with Colonel Otis Sadtler, contacted, via teletype, the Army's Monitoring Station No. 2 at the Presidio in San Francisco and instructed them to listen to the Japanese general intelligence broadcast. He also drove to Monitoring Station No. 7 at Fort Hunt, Virginia, and personally delivered intercept instructions.[17] Some five days later, the Army's SIS tasked several of its monitoring stations located in the Philippines, the Panama Canal Zone, the Presidio in San Francisco, Fort Sam Houston, and the Signal School at Fort Monmouth, New Jersey, to "copy all Japanese plain text in addition to code text diplomatic traffic. Stop. This traffic will be forwarded with regular traffic."[18] The army's message is peculiar in two ways. First, it was sent out some five days after the translations of the Winds instruction messages were available. Secondly, the tasking message never mentions the Winds Execute phrases or words, simply to copy all Japanese plaintext, which could result in the collection of a high volume of traffic with no sense of exactly what was being sought by SIS headquarters.

Late on the afternoon of 28 November, a Colonel Wesley Guest from the staff of the Army's Chief Signal Officer called the chief of the Radio Intelligence Division (RID) of the Federal Communications Commission, George Sterling, and asked that the Commission alert its numerous radio monitoring stations to listen for the Winds Execute phrases. The FCC was an independent agency in the federal government charged with management of the radio spectrum in the United States, as well as the enforcement of regulations for radio licensing and operations. As part of its charter, the FCC also listened for illegal or illicit communications. It also monitored foreign broadcasts and delivered full transcripts or summaries to departments of the government such as the Department of State. Sterling, a field engineer with experience in radio communications going back to the First World War, had organized a special division of the FCC, the Radio Intelligence Division, to copy military, naval, and illicit (agent) communications, using the FCC's almost four dozen monitoring stations located throughout the continental United States and overseas territories like Hawaii. The FCC also had worked with the FBI in targeting Axis communications from Latin America beginning in 1940.

The Army's instructions, though, limited the FCC to listening for the three phrases that were to be sent over the Japanese voice broadcasts. Guest further asked that if any of the three phrases were heard the FCC watch center should notify Colonel Rufus Bratton, the chief of the Army's Far East Intelligence Section of G-2. Bratton gave the FCC watch office his work and home phone numbers and told them to contact him anytime they heard the phrases. The Army failed to pass along to the FCC important technical information such as broadcast schedules, call letters of the suspected Japanese broadcast stations, or their operating frequencies. While Sterling accepted the Army's request, he disagreed with the Army's projection (based on the Navy's data) that the Japanese broadcast might be heard by the FCC's monitoring stations on the U.S. east coast like the one at Laurel, Maryland. Instead, he assigned primary coverage to the FCC station in Portland, Oregon.[19]

George Sterling, Chief, Radio Intelligence Division, FCC

If the servicemen and the FCC monitors were to have any chance to hear the critical words or phrases, they were going to have to listen to a number of Japanese broadcasts, both in the Morse code and voice. Navy analysts and radio intercept operators were given index cards with the relevant phrases in *Kana*, the Japanese phonetic syllabary script adapted for Morse code, as a means of quick reference to check intercept. Some officers carried the cards around while on duty and a few even took them home for reference in case they were called by phone with a possible intercept. Hawaii and Station "Cast" in Corregidor screened Japanese broadcasts for the next several days until the war started, dutifully copying down *Kana* news broadcasts and turning them over to a linguist to review.

A major drawback to this close coverage of Japanese radio broadcasts was that it forced major changes to current target lists and operations of the affected field sites. All of the tasked army and navy monitoring sites already had significant numbers of Japanese communications links as their primary and secondary targets. Now, these field sites had to amend standing intercept target lists to accommodate coverage of these broadcasts. These sites had a limited number of receivers and intercept operators to cover the new intercept targets. While the highest priority, usually high-level diplomatic or naval communications links, would not be affected, site coverage of Japanese and other nations' communications stations considered nonpriority would be displaced. On 4 December the Director of Naval Communications, Admiral Leigh Noyes, in whose organization the OP-20-G resided, complained to Admiral Wilkinson at ONI about the assigned broadcast coverage. He pointed out to Wilkinson that the Federal Communications Commission had over 450 radio receivers to monitor overseas broadcast. He suggested that in Hawaii, for example, the Navy could not duplicate the work of the local FCC component.[20] In 1941 the Navy had barely a third of the receivers that the FCC had for its global coverage. Of these, about sixty in the Pacific were available for the Winds coverage, that is, at the stations at Bainbridge, Hawaii, and the Philippines, but most of these already were tasked with priority monitoring of Japanese naval, merchant ship, and diplomatic radio terminals.[21]

The British attached much the same importance to the possible Winds Execute message as had the Americans and accordingly set up means to intercept it. The British in Singapore had intercepted the two "setup" messages, as had their partners the Americans and Dutch. The FECB had shared this information with their station in Hong Kong and the Americans at Corregidor. The Bureau in Singapore instructed the listening post in Hong Kong on Stonecutters Island to monitor Japanese commercial broadcasts for the Execute message. At the S.I. section in Singapore a special receiving set was installed and a watch schedule of Japanese language officers was started. This special arrangement was necessary because the nearby intercept site at Kranji was staffed entirely by Morse intercept operators who were not able to listen to Japanese language broadcasts – a predicament similar to that at American listening stations, where, as in the case at Hawaii, a number of linguists had to be detailed to review the intercept of the broadcasts every day.[22]

Meanwhile, Army and Navy analysts and linguists were literally buried under the new intercept they had to review. One estimate was that the weekly normal intercept received at OP-20-G by teletype increased from about three to four feet of copy per week to as much as *200 feet per day!*[23] Then Lieutenant Alwin Kramer, an ONI Japanese language-qualified officer on loan to OP-20-G, recalled later that there were only three linguists available to translate all of the copy and that the volume of it was "simply tremendous, swamping."[24] The Army's analytic personnel were similarly beleaguered with the demands of the new priority coverage.[25]

Considering the varying degrees of expertise in the Japanese language and broadcasts, as well as the partial or vague tasking to the Navy, Army, and FCC sites, it should have come as no surprise that there were instances of mistaken intercept, false alarms, and confusion of the Winds Execute message with regular Japanese weather reports. In the week preceding Pearl Harbor, a number of such mistakes or false alarms occurred.

The first incident occurred on 1 December. The navy intercept station at Corregidor informed both Hawaii and Washington that a Japanese broadcast station, JVJ, one of the stations listed on the technical message from OP-20-G on 28 November, had stated on its afternoon program that "all listeners be sure and listen in at 0700 tomorrow morning since there may be some important news." According to the Pacific Fleet Intelligence officer in Hawaii, Commander Edwin Layton, the "impression" at that time was that the Winds Execute message would be broadcast then. The officers monitoring the voice broadcasts and the Morse news programs were ordered to listen for the important news, but no such message or notice was heard on JVJ or any other station.[26]

Meanwhile, the FCC monitoring site in Portland, Oregon, which had begun its monitoring on 28 November, started to pick up a number of broadcasts that contained weather phrases that appeared to resemble the Execute message. As instructed, the FCC watch officer dutifully called Colonel Bratton with what was believed to be Winds Execute phrases. On 1 December he called Bratton at 5:45 PM (EST) and on 3 December again called him, probably at home, at 7:35 PM (EST). The watch officer also called George Sterling to apprise him of the intercepted broadcasts. But as Colonel Bratton would recall later, these FCC intercepts were mistaken or false alarms. Bratton also said he notified naval intelligence officials, in this case Captain McCollum and Lt. Alwin Kramer, of the FCC intercept reports.[27]

One of the more significant erroneous intercepts occurred at 1700 hours EST (5:00 PM) on 4 December when the FCC monitoring station in Portland, Oregon, overheard a weather broadcast by Tokyo station JVW3 (not on the OPNAV or the Japanese lists by the way) that appeared, at first, to fit the Winds format. [**Exhibit #22**, page 2[28] and **Exhibit 23**, page 1[29]] The phrase "North Wind Cloudy" was heard, which indicated a break in relations with the Soviet Union. Within three hours of Portland, reporting the phrase, the FCC watch officer in Washington, unable to contact Colonel Bratton or his assistant, reported the intercept to the OP-20-GY watch officer, Lt. Francis M. Brotherhood, USN, at about 8:45 PM (EST). After checking with his superiors, Brotherhood called the FCC back at 9:00 PM and wrote down what the FCC site had intercepted. Lt. Brotherhood recalled that the message seemed to be "missing" something from what he had been led to expect. He probably checked his instructions and realized that there was no mention of the phrase relating to relations with America, HIGASHI NO KAZEAME.

Brotherhood then called Admiral Noyes at his office on a special (probably secure) telephone. Brotherhood repeated to Noyes the phrase from the broadcast the FCC had heard. Brotherhood recalled that Noyes had said something to the effect that the "wind was blowing from the wrong direction."[30] More to the point, the FCC had heard the "North Wind Cloudy" phrase only once in the broadcast, instead of the required two times in the middle and end of the news program. Also, the same broadcast carried the phrase "North Wind Slightly Stronger May become Cloudy,' as well as the phrase "North Wind Clear." It was obvious this was not the Winds Execute message. At 9:30 PM, Brotherhood did call back to the FCC to check if any there were any other references to the weather in the program, but was told there were none. [**Exhibit #24**, page 4][31]

This report of an erroneous winds report echoed into the following Friday morning, 5 December. At about 9:00 AM, Colonel Bratton was called to a meeting in the office of the Army's G-2, Major General Sherman Miles. Lieutenant Colonel Otis Sadtler, a Signal Corps officer attached to G-2, told Bratton that Admiral Noyes, the Director of Naval Communications (OP-20), had called him and said that the "weather" message was in. Bratton referred to his card with the

Lieutenant Colonel Otis K. Sadtler

code phrases and words and asked Sadtler what the message said and whether it was in either English or Japanese. Sadtler was not certain and said that the report might be a false alarm. Interestingly, he said that Noyes had indicated that the message referred to Great Britain and Japan.[32]

According to Bratton, he told Sadtler to call Noyes, confirm the intercept and to get a copy of it for the army. Sadtler contacted Noyes over a secure telephone between G-2 and the DNC. Noyes, Sadtler reported to Bratton, told him again that it was the phrase that referred to relations between Great Britain and Japan, but that he did not have the Japanese text. Bratton still wanted confirmation and told Sadtler to get the text. Bratton never saw Sadtler again that day. Meanwhile, Bratton called naval intelligence and spoke either to Captain McCollum or Lt. Kramer who told him that they had not received any Winds message. Bratton also called the SIS office and was told that no Winds message had come in.

The SIS had seen a copy of this mistaken Winds message. Colonel Sadtler had obtained a copy of the FCC teletype and showed it to Captain Robert Schukraft. He saw about two lines of text and immediately realized it was not the correct format and therefore not the expected execute message.[33] Unfortunately, word of the intercept, though not verified, continued to be spread around the navy and army offices. Sadtler had told Major General Leonard Gerow, chief of the War Department's Planning Division, and Colonel Walter Smith, assistant of General George Marshall, that the "Winds was in." Later in the day, Noyes informed Admiral Richard Turner, chief of the Navy's War Plans Division (OP-12), that a weather message was in, but that it referred to the Russians and that it seemed "wrong."[34]

Another mistaken Winds Execute message was heard on the evening of 5 December. The same station, JVW3, at 9:30 PM (Tokyo time) broadcast a weather report that read "TODAY NORTH WIND MORNING CLOUDY AFTERNOON CLEAR BEGIN CLOUDY EVENING. TOMORROW NORTH WIND AND LATER FROM SOUTH." [**Exhibit #22**, page 167[35] and **Exhibit 23**, page 172[36]] This report was repeated three times. A half hour later, the FCC monitors in Portland heard the same station send a timing signal. and then an announcer came on the air and said, "I will now give the weather report," but then halted.

The Portland monitoring site watch officer called George Sterling with a report of this transmission. Sterling then called Colonel Bratton and read him the text. Bratton realized that the format of the transmission was not as specified in the original Japanese instructions. The phrase did not appear in the middle or end of the news program. Also the phrase was not exact – "North Wind Morning Cloudy" – and was stated only the one time.[37] Still, Bratton told Sterling, "he was encouraged by the reporting," and that "we have that much more time." [**Exhibit 24**, pages 177 and 181][38] This last comment suggests that Bratton believed that with the continued absence of the Winds Execute phrases and words that an anticipated Japanese deadline in United States-Japan relations had not yet been reached. Interestingly, when Sterling asked Bratton if he should inform the Portland site that the weather phrases would appear in the middle and end of a news program, Bratton said that he would get back to Sterling on that issue.[39]

While the Americans struggled with processing the increased broadcast intercept and encountered a number of "false alarms," the Japanese already had begun to add new instructions for their diplomats about the destruction of classified material.

Tokyo Sends More Orders about Destroying Cryptographic Material

Almost within a week of the transmission of the two Winds instructions messages, Tokyo began to send out more instructions to its diplomatic stations around the world concerning the destruction of cryptographic holdings and other sensitive papers. These new instructions, which were not all available to the Americans in a timely fashion due to the already slow processing of traffic using cryptographic systems like J-19 and PA-K2, in some instances appeared to contradict prior orders, while, in other cases, seemed to ignore the Winds directives.

The Hidden Word Message – A Complement to the Winds Messages

It now seems that the Japanese were not satisfied with just the open code Winds message by which to warn its diplomats of the status of relations with the United States, Great Britain, or the Soviet Union. They provided their diplomatic stations with another method to warn them of an impending break in relations. On 27 November, Tokyo transmitted a quite long, four-part message, Tokyo Serial No. 2409, encrypted in J-19K10, to a number of embassies and consulates located in North and South America, as well as East Asia. The Navy monitoring station "S" at Bainbridge Island intercepted this message. The complete intercepted version was sent via teletypewriter to OP-20-GY in Washington for decryption and translation. Station "S" copied the message that was sent to the Japanese consulate in San Francisco. The operators noted in the intercept log that the same cipher text, except for two groups at the end of part three, also was sent to Washington. [**Exhibit #16**][40]

The Navy had the responsibility for processing this message since it was intercepted on an odd-numbered day. Because the message was sent in four parts, the decryption of the transposed text required four copies of the stencil, or form, from the ten-day period of 21 to 30 November. The indicator in the message was the group BYHBD, which meant that the message was intended for a general or worldwide audience. The navy analysts still had to recover the encryption key for the day. [**Exhibit 17**][41] The transcribed code text was then divided into the coded digraphs that were then decoded by a navy analyst prior to being translated. [**Exhibit 18**][42] A translation of this message (SIS #25609, OP-20-G JD-1 #6985) was issued on 2 December 1941. [**Exhibit #19**][43]

ed above is a chart of the message parts placed in correct order. It illustrates the "analytic chain" used to rearrange the message parts in the correct sequence from intercept to decryption to translation worksheet.

When the Americans viewed the message, it was clear that it carried instructions for another warning system for Japanese diplomats in certain parts of the world.[44] It instructed them in the use of a "hidden word" (INGO DENPO) or open code word system. The new system operated in the following manner. In a crisis, the Japanese intended to send telegrams over commercial radio or telegraph links to the affected diplomatic missions. The warning message would be disguised, with certain "hidden words" placed within seemingly innocuous plain text.

These "hidden words" were found on a table of code words that were transmitted along with the instructions. It consisted of two columns. The left-hand side contained the code words and the right-hand side listed their plain text meaning.

Intercepted Message	>>>>	**Decryption Stencil**	>>>>	**Translator W.S.**
Nr. 511 – "UUTDY"	>>>>	"UUTDY"/"XEICN"	>>>>	818 – "XEICN"
Nr. 518 – "RFOCJ"	>>>>	"RFOCJ"/"LZNCW"	>>>>	819 – "LZNCW"
Nr. 523 – "FLVAN"	>>>>	"FLVAN/"PPOGU"	>>>>	820 – "PPOGU"
Nr. 520 – "NBQNC"	>>>>	"NBQNC"/"POUIM"	>>>>	821 – "POUIM"

Fig. 3. Sequence of processing of the "Stop" message parts. [See Exhibits 16-17-18]

This chart consists of three columns that represent the "analytic chain," that is, the method used to arrange the intercepted parts in the proper sequence: the transmitted message number and the first five-letter code group from the intercepted message; the decryption stencil with the first encrypted code group inscribed in the vertical column under '1" (listed as "/" or "1" in Kanji) along with the first five letters in the horizontal position from the stencil; and the page number of the translator's worksheets and the first five letters from that worksheet.

Curiously, the Japanese sent the message in four parts, and in the transmission of it, sent part four prior to part three. This out of sequence transmission had no effect on the decryption or translation of the message. However, the order of the intercept may confuse the reader. So provid-

The list contained several words and phrases that covered a broad gradation of relationships between Japan and other countries. There were separate expressions to indicate "severed relations," "not in accordance," "military forces clashing," and for "general war." For example, the codeword message for a general war between the United States and Japan would read "HOSINO MINAMI." In another case, the codeword "ASKURA" meant that Tokyo "will communicate by radio broadcast, you are to directed to listen carefully."[45]

A further distinguishing characteristic of this method of codeword message was the use of the English word "STOP" at the end of a message as an indicator that this was a "hidden word" message instead of a non-code commercial cable, which would use the Japanese word "OWARI," literally "end [of message]." American cryptologists would come to refer to this warning system either as the so-called "hidden word" message or the "STOP message."

Tokyo sent three updates to the list and instructions. Two of the updates, Japanese serial Nos. 2431 and 2432, were transmitted from Tokyo to its embassy in Rio de Janeiro for "special use in your area." The new list consisted of codewords for Latin American capitals and statements about continued passage of Japanese merchant shipping in the territorial waters of these countries. The embassy in Rio, and later the one in Mexico City, was ordered to pass along these updates to all stations in Latin and Central America.[46] On the same day, Tokyo sent another version of the "hidden word" instructions to the Japanese representative in Singapore, which was unique to "the particular needs of your localities to supplement for the already given list."[47]

The Americans apparently interpreted the "hidden word" warning system as a supplement to the two Winds coded methods seen earlier in November. Many, if not all, of the same stations that had received the instructions about the Winds codewords and phrases Japanese serials No. 2353 and No. 2354, also received No. 2409. The reason for these complementary warning systems may have been the technical limitations of the existing Japanese global diplomatic communications network. Some Japanese diplomatic missions, especially small consulates, lacked transceiver radio sets with which to communicate directly with the Foreign Ministry in Tokyo. Even if a station had the radio receivers to monitor shortwave (high frequency band) Japanese news broadcasts, there was no guarantee these programs could be heard due to the physical properties of the propagation of radio signals, especially those in the broadcast bands between 300 kHz to 3 MHz and those in the high frequency band (3-30 MHz). Reception of broadcasts transmitted from Tokyo depended upon factors such as the frequency of the broadcast, the time of day, weather along the propagation path, and background signals in the reception area. A broadcast at a certain time and frequency could not be heard by all of Tokyo's diplomats. This fact of radio propagation meant that a warning message could not be transmitted to all stations at the same time with any assurance that all recipients "got the message."

The Japanese used two communications methods to ensure that all diplomatic stations received all relevant circular, or large or general audience messages. In the first, Tokyo designated some diplomatic stations as "radio relays," that is, they retransmitted important messages to other diplomatic facilities in the same or adjacent geographic region. For example, Berlin would retransmit messages to Lisbon, Portugal, Helsinki, Finland, Budapest, Hungary, and Vienna, Austria. The Japanese embassy in Berne, Switzerland, would send along messages to Vichy, France, Ankara, Turkey, Madrid, Spain, and Lisbon. In Southeast Asia, Bangkok would pass along circular messages to Hanoi and Saigon. While this method overcame many of the problems of local reception, it still was not a complete guarantee that messages intended for a large or general audience would receive them in a timely manner.

A second method for communication between Tokyo and its foreign diplomatic missions was to send telegrams or cables over commercial radio or cable systems, or through national Post Telegraph and Telephone agencies (PT&T). In the United States, Japanese diplomatic messages destined for its embassy or consulates, or messages that were intended for other countries and that transited the US cable system, were handled by American communications firms such as the Radio Corporation of America (RCA), Western Union, or Mackay Wireless. A courier would deliver the cable from the telegraph office in a city to the Japanese consulate or embassy. The Japanese diplomats would deliver their cable, usually encrypted or encoded, to the cable company office for transmission to Tokyo. Very often, an important message would go by radio and cable, or even over multiple company cable lines. (In fact, the famous fourteen-part final message from Tokyo to Washington that was delivered to Secretary of State Hull the afternoon of 7 December was sent simultaneously over both the Mackay Wireless and RCA cable networks.)

The danger of any cable system was that it was subject to control by the host country. Because of censorship regulations in effect in 1941, American commercial communications firms provided the War and Navy Departments, and later the U.S. Office of Censorship, with copies of all Japanese diplomatic cable traffic, encrypted or plain text, sent through U.S. cable terminals. [See **Exhibit #20** for an example of a cable passed to the Censorship Office.][48]

Tokyo Sends Even More Instructions, 28 November – 6 December

Even after the "hidden word" message had been sent on 27 November, Tokyo continued to pass more instructions to its diplomats about the destruction of sensitive material, including cryptographic material like codes and cipher devices, to its diplomats around the world.

The first of these was a message, encrypted in J-19K10 that was sent to the Japanese consulate in Honolulu on 28 November. This message, which was not decrypted and translated until 7 December, and therefore not available to American intelligence offices during this critical period, contained important new provisions regarding the use of the special warning messages, in particular those in the "hidden word" instructions. Tokyo told its consul in Honolulu "these broadcasts are intended to serve as a means of informing its diplomats in the country concerned of that situation without the use of the usual telegraphic channels. *Do not destroy the codes without regard to the actual situation in your locality* [our italics] but retain them as long as the situation there (*sic*) permits and until the final stage is entered into." [**Exhibit #21**][49]

The provision in this instruction about retaining codes seemed to contradict the earlier orders that called for the destruction of all codes upon the receipt of the Winds code phrases or words. These new prescriptions suggested that Japanese diplomats could retain all or some of their cryptographic material for as long as they felt they could securely and safely do so. These new instructions also implied that the Winds execute codes did not necessarily mean that a final break in relations between the United States and Japan was about to occur.

Three days later, Tokyo began to transmit another series of messages to its diplomats around the world that outlined more provisions for the destruction of cryptographic material that they held. One of the first was from Tokyo to Washington, Japanese serial No. 2444, sent on 1 December (and translated the same day by OP-20-G). The message informed the Washington embassy that the diplomatic missions in London, Hong Kong, Singapore, and Manila had been instructed to destroy their "code machines." The cipher machine (Purple) in the consulate in Batavia, Netherlands East Indies, had been returned to Tokyo. The Washington embassy was ordered to hold onto its machines and "machine codes."[**Exhibit #25**][50]

On 1 December, the Japanese embassy in London received separate instructions for its destruction measures. The embassy was to send the single word SETUJU ("receipt" or "received") to acknowledge that it had received the instructions and then to transmit the word HASSO ("forwarding") when the destruction was complete.[51]

Another circular message from Tokyo, Japanese serial No. 2445, was sent the next day, 2 December (but not translated by the SIS until 8 December) to all diplomatic stations. It ordered them to destroy all codes except for a copy of the OITE (PA-K2 code) and the LA systems. This order included all codes for the military and naval attachés as well. The diplomats were further told that as soon as they completed the destruction of this material, they were to send a one-word message to Tokyo – HARUNA (an active volcano located in the Gunma Prefecture in Japan).[52] Tokyo also instructed the missions to destroy all of their confidential papers, but to do so in such a way as to avoid attention or suspicion. A second version of this circular message, Japanese serial No. 2447, which was sent on the same day (but translated by the SIS on 6 December) carried much the same information. To assure its reception, Tokyo had some of its diplomatic facilities relay the message to diplomatic missions in Europe, the Middle East, and Latin America. [**Exhibit #26**][53]

On 2 December, the Japanese embassy in Washington received additional instructions about the disposition of its cryptographic holdings. The SIS translation of this message, Japanese serial No. 867, was available the next day. The embassy was told to retain a copy of both the PA-K2 and LA code systems and to burn all of the rest. In addition, Washington was ordered to destroy one of its cipher machines (Purple). When all of this destruction was completed, the embassy was instructed to send the codeword HARUNA. All other classified papers were to be destroyed at "your discretion."[**Exhibit #27**][44] This message, except for the reference to the disposal of the embassy's extra machine cipher devices, was the same as the circular messages (Nos. 2445 and 2447) sent the same day, but not translated until 8 December.

The next day, 3 December, the Japanese Foreign Ministry sent another circular message, Japanese serial No. 2461, to all of its stations. This instruction, translated by OP-20-G on 6 December, reminded all stations to keep the "hidden word" list and the broadcast (Winds) codes until the "last moment." Tokyo added that if any stations accidentally had destroyed these papers, the *Gaimusho* would retransmit the pertinent instructions. This message added that "it," the Winds code words and phrases and the "hidden word" code word lists, was a "precaution." [**Exhibit #28**][55] While this message appeared to reinforce the penultimate importance of both warning systems – the "hidden word" and Winds code – the references in the message to holding until the "last moment" and the description of the codes as a "precaution" suggest that even these methods might become irrelevant or circumvented by events.

Within that first week of December, right up to 7 December, many of Japan's diplomatic posts around the world reported that they had destroyed their cryptographic holdings and classified files. The codeword HARUNA was seen on many cable and radio circuits. On 2 December the consulates in New York City, Vancouver, British Columbia, and Hollywood, California, reported that they had completed the destruction. The next day, diplomatic facilities in the Netherlands East Indies and Portland, Oregon, did the same. The U.S. Navy liaison in Wellington, New Zealand, reported that the Japanese consul there had received special orders to destroy his codes. The embassy in Mexico City, Mexico, reported the completion of the destruction on 7 December. During this six-day period, the Americans monitored as many as twenty Japanese diplomatic facilities sending the codeword HARUNA to Tokyo. The intercept of most of these transmissions was available to army and naval intelligence in Washington within a two-to-four-day period; most intercepts were sent to Washington by airmail, though a few still arrived after 7 December. [**Exhibit #29**]⁵⁶

However, this flurry of Japanese code destruction presented a dilemma to the Americans. Army and navy intelligence officials had come to construe the destruction of cryptographic holdings by diplomats to be a good indicator of an impending break in relations. Tokyo's numerous instructions to its diplomats and the continuous reports of completed code destruction strongly indicated that a break with Tokyo might be near, but the cryptologists and others might have wondered when exactly the rupture might occur and under what circumstances. The early December flurry of code disposal instructions and the belated, nearly week-long, staggered responses from diplomatic posts around the world complicated any American calculation of a "deadline," as well as clouded understanding of Japanese intentions.

The orders in the instructions to both the "hidden word" and Winds code warning systems had specified that all cryptographic material and important papers were to be destroyed upon receipt of the correct phrases or codewords. On the other hand, the messages of 1 and 2 December from Tokyo had ordered Japanese diplomats to destroy all codes but two (while Washington and presumably other major embassies maintained their cipher machines). The 3 December message had reminded the diplomats to hold on to their copies of the "hidden word" (STOP) and Winds codes until the last moment, or as a "precaution."

Yet it must be recalled that the Americans did not have all of these messages available as translations prior to 7 December. Because of the sometimes-tardy exploitation of these messages, intelligence officers in the army and navy knew only parts of the complete program. It is possible that they viewed the Japanese actions as ominous, but also contradictory and perhaps even confusing. More importantly, though, the binge of code destruction was occurring without the transmittal of the Winds Execute message. How could the American cryptologists account for this?

It could be argued that the instruction of 1 and 2 December amplified those in the Winds and STOP messages of late November. The December directives had exempted the PA-K2 and LA codes from destruction. But these messages contained no references to the instructions in the Winds or STOP messages. And those orders had specifically mentioned the destruction of "all codes." It is possible, though unlikely, that there were other messages that "bridged" the difference between the November and December transmissions, but there is no evidence for this. Another possibility is that the 1 and 2 December messages were not related at all to the Winds and STOP instructions, though it is not clear why such a distinction would have been made in the first place. Then there is the 3 December message that reminded its recipients to hold onto the Winds and STOP codes until the last moment. This last message might have refined the instructions in the 19 and 27 November messages.

For all of the new instructions and the destruction activity, the point is the Winds instructions were still in place and had to be viewed as at least one of Tokyo's primary methods of warning its diplomats of the situation between Japan, the United States, Great Britain, and the Soviet Union.

This flurry of destruction had not gone unnoticed and it was acted upon. On 2 December, the United States Navy ordered some of its facilities in the Pacific to begin destroying their cryptographic material and report completion with the single code word of "Boomerang."⁵⁷ Colonel Bratton, after seeing the messages from Tokyo that ordered the code destruction, approached General Sherman Miles, the Assistant Chief of Staff for Intelligence and Major General Leonard Gerow and asked that an additional warning message be sent to the Army Pacific commands. Both generals demurred on this point and claimed that enough warnings had been sent. Undeterred, Bratton contacted his opposite in naval intelligence, Commander Arthur McCollum, for help. He suggested to Bratton that Commander Joseph Rochefort in Hawaii was the most knowledgeable person on Japanese communications and that his Communications Intelligence Unit (known as Station "H" or HYPO) had been tasked to listen for the Winds Execute message. So Bratton drafted a message signed by Miles to the head of military intelligence in the Hawaii Department, Brigadier General Kendall Fielder, and sent it on 5 December. [**Exhibit #30**][58]

It read, "Contact Commander Rochefort immediately through the Commandant Fourteen Naval District regarding broadcasts from Tokyo reference weather." There was a problem in that General Fielder did not have access to Magic material and therefore had no prior interaction with the navy in Hawaii concerning communications intelligence. In testimony after the war, he recalled not seeing the cable from Washington. However, Fielder's deputy, Lieutenant Colonel George W. Bicknell, did see it and later contacted Rochefort, who assured Bicknell that the navy was listening for the message.[59]

Perhaps not unexpectedly, in light of the new instructions from Tokyo about code destruction, some officers in army and navy intelligence began to question the ultimate importance of the Winds Execute message. During the Joint Congressional Committee hearings after the war, a number of senior naval officers testified that they had begun to doubt the importance of the Winds Execute message during the final week before Pearl Harbor. Admiral Noyes stated that the new instructions received at the beginning of December lessened the significance of the Winds method. Maybe, he suggested, the messages were still important enough to monitor for, but their role as an indicator or warning of war had been considerably reduced.[60]

Admiral Royal Ingersoll, the Assistant Chief of Naval Operations (ACNO) at the time, weighed in that even if a Winds code message had been heard, the "most it could have done was to have confirmed what we had already sent out [the earlier War Warning message sent from the CNO to Admiral Kimmel on 27 November] and it [a possible Winds message] was not as positive [a sign] that war was coming as we had sent out."[61] Captain McCollum noted that the Winds message was only one of several messages instructing Japanese diplomats what to do with their sensitive papers and codes.[62] And even Colonel Bratton, who urged the Army brass to send out another warning message on 5 December, admitted in testimony after the war that, in light of the 2 December instructions to Japanese diplomats to destroy their codes, "any Winds Execute message received after that would simply just be another straw in the wind confirming what we already knew."[63]

The questioning of the usefulness of the Winds Execute message as a warning or indicator of Japanese intentions for the Americans has merit. The vague reference in the instructions to "relations in danger" could encompass a multitude of situations. Therefore, it would be hard to define exactly what level of rupture in relations constituted a "danger." On the other hand, the STOP/"hidden word" message carried a number of more detailed possibilities, to include beginning of hostilities. This system seemed to be a more discrete indicator of what Japan was planning. Still, despite the obtuseness of the Winds warning, and whatever doubts about the usefulness of the warning carried in the coded phrase or words, the military and FCC monitoring stations continued to listen for the messages.

7 December 1941: The Hidden Word Message Is Sent

Shortly after 4:00 AM (Eastern Time) on the morning of 7 December 1941, the navy monitoring site at Bainbridge island intercepted a message from the Japanese Foreign Ministry in Tokyo to twelve diplomatic stations, including San Francisco, Panama, Honolulu, New York, Seattle, and Ottawa, Canada. The Japanese radio station "JAH" transmitted the message on the frequency 7630 kHz. [**Exhibit #32**][64] Bainbridge noted that the message, Japanese serial No. 2494, was addressed to "KOSHI [Minister] Washington" and that the Tokyo operator had sent a service message note to the radio operator in San Francisco that this particular message, along with another copy of the message marked urgent for "KOSHI, Panama," was very important.[65] The other addressees were consuls (RIYOJI, or RYOUJI)). To further ensure reception of the messages, Tokyo had transmitted on both the RCA and MRT (Mackay Radio & Telegraph Company) commercial radio circuits. The message, in Kana, read as follows:

*KOYANAGI RIJIYORI SEIRINOTUGOO ARUNITUKI **HATTORI MINAMI** KINEN-BUNKO SETURITU KIKINO KYOKAINGKAU SIKYUU DENPOO ARITASI*

STOP – TOGO

The inclusion of the word "STOP" at the end of the message marked it as a "hidden word or STOP message. Bainbridge sent the intercepted text to OP-20-G headquarters in Washington by leased teletype. The trick for the navy analysts in Washington was to translate the text and then place the correct values to the three hidden codewords (shown in darkened lettering).

The literal translation of the message read thus:

*"Please have director **Koyanagi** send a wire stating the sum which has been decided to be spent on the **South Hattori** memorial Library. Stop - Togo"*

In Washington, Lt. Alwin Kramer hurriedly put together a translation of the codewords he saw in the text, SIS # 25856 and JD-1 #7148.[66] It originally read: "Relations between Japan and England are not in accordance with expectations." "KOYANAGI" was the codeword for "England," while "HATTORI" meant "Relations between Japan and ...(blank)... are not in accordance with expectations." A translation was published that same morning and was ready for a 10:00 AM meeting in Washington of the secretaries of state, war, and the navy. It was slipped into the same folder that contained the translation of the first thirteen parts of the awaited fourteen-part message that Japan had transmitted the day before.

However, Kramer's initial translation was incorrect. He had missed the significance of the word "MINAMI," which ordinarily meant "south," but in the INGO DENPO code really meant the "United States." So the message should have read, "Relations between Japan and United States and England are not in accordance with expectations." Kramer soon realized his error and later that morning phoned in the change to the recipients of the translation who were meeting at the State Department. [**Exhibit #33**][67]

The "hidden word" message, if considered alone, arguably might be regarded as some sort of indicator of an impending break in relations between Japan and the United States and Great Britain. As mentioned above, the code system for the STOP message had several codewords that referred to a number of possible situations between Japan and other countries, including outright hostilities. Yet the message that arrived in Washington and the rest of North America carried the word for relations "not in accordance with expectations" and not an open codeword that would alert the Americans that the opening of hostilities was mere hours away.

Was there a chance that a STOP message that indicated that war was going to start had been sent to some other Japanese diplomatic station(s)? On 7 December, the War Department's

G-2 sent a priority message to all of the army intercept sites in the Pacific region with the order to scour all of their files for any STOP messages since 27 November. [**Exhibit #34**][68] There is no record that any other field site had intercepted any other version of a STOP message.

The STOP message from Tokyo had arrived on 7 December as American cryptologists were completing work on the decryption and translation of the last part of the fourteen-part message, Japanese serial #902, which had arrived earlier that morning. This was the final part of the Japanese statement of its position to an earlier United States diplomatic statement, the so-called *modus vivendi*, which offered several points for the Japanese to accede to if talks were to continue.[69] Shortly after this message arrived, another was received from Tokyo, Japanese serial No. 907, which instructed the Japanese representatives Kursuru and Nomura to deliver the entire fourteen-part message to Secretary of State Cordell Hull at 1:00 PM (EST).[70]

At about 10:00 AM, Lieutenant Kramer delivered to the secretaries a folder that contained the translations of the STOP message, part 14 of message No. 902, and message No. 907 that specified the 1:00 PM delivery time. Kramer pointed out the time of delivery to the secretaries. The interest of the Roosevelt administration leaders was directed at the final installment of the fourteen-part message. The STOP message, with its incorrect translation did not add or detract anything from the understanding of the Japanese position, except to suggest problematic relations between Japan and Great Britain – no surprise to Roosevelt's cabinet secretaries. Intelligence reports from the previous day had reached American commands in Washington and the Pacific, which reported Japanese troop transports had been sighted steaming from bases in French Indochina towards the coast of British Malaya.[71]

In fact, it was the time of delivery mentioned in message No. 907 (Japanese serial) and not the text of the "hidden word" message that convinced Colonel Bratton that morning to have General George C. Marshall send an additional warning message to the various military commands in the Pacific region. The story of the failed effort has been recounted elsewhere. The message was delayed in transmission and delivery through a series of technical mishaps.[72]

There is little to suggest that even a correct translation of the "hidden word" message that referred to relations to the United States being not in "expectations" would have influenced the already pessimistic American assessment of the situation. In any event, that particular set of words would have made much less impact than the important last sentence of the fourteen-part message: "The Japanese Government regrets to have to notify the American Government that…it cannot but consider that it is impossible to reach an agreement through further negotiations."[73]

Despite the timing of the "hidden word" message, there was nothing in its contents that would have warned the Americans of the attack on Pearl Harbor.

7 December 1941: The Winds Execute Message Is Sent

It had been almost three weeks since Tokyo had sent out instructions to its diplomats for the Winds codeword or phrase warning system. Since 28 November, American, British, and Dutch radio operators had been monitoring Japanese voice and manual Morse news broadcasts for any of the three code phrases or words sent in the specified format during a news program. Late on 7 December, Tokyo finally sent the Winds Execute message. But the message that was transmitted would be anticlimactic in its timing and content.

The morning of 7 December was a busy one for the staff of the Japanese embassy in Washington. Aside from message No. 902, which came in fourteen parts, and the further instructions to deliver it at 1:00 PM, Washington time, the staff was burdened with further problems of getting message 902 ready to deliver because of difficulties in decoding the last part and a late start on typing it up to present to Secretary Hull. Another message, Japanese serial No. 910, arrived shortly after the other messages telling the staff to begin destroying the last cipher machine. To this, the embassy replied that once the previous day's long messages had been decoded, it would comply with the latest instructions.[74]

Nomura and Kurusu arrived at Secretary Hull's office shortly after 2:00 PM. At the time the envoys were delivering the long message to Hull, the first wave of Japanese aircraft were in the midst of their attack (almost 9:00 AM, Honolulu Time) on the ships of the Pacific Fleet. In a cold fury, Hull received the message from the two diplomats and then brusquely dismissed them noting that "In all my fifty years of public service I have never seen a document that was more crowded with falsehoods and distortions – infamous falsehoods and distortions on a scale too huge that I never imagined until today that any Government on this planet was capable of uttering them."[75]

Later that night, shortly after 7:02 PM Eastern Time (0002, 8 December, Greenwich Mean Time), FCC monitors at the Portland, Oregon, monitoring station tuned in to the news programs on two Japanese broadcast stations. For the next thirty-five minutes, these two stations, JLG4 on 17376 and 15105 kHz and JZJ on 11800 kHz, made the same news broadcasts. About halfway through the program, the announcer was heard to make this statement, as translated into English: "This is the middle of the news, but today, specifically at this point, I will give the weather forecast: 'West Wind Clear'." The phrase was repeated twice in the middle and then at the end of the broadcast.[76]

The FCC watch office called Colonel Carlisle C. Dusenberg, the assistant to Colonel Bratton, with the news of the intercept. Dusenberg told the Commission watch officer "the information was received too late." He then thanked the FCC for its work and added that no more monitoring for these broadcasts was necessary. Colonel Bratton was reached later and when told of the broadcast asked that the information be forwarded to the U.S. Service Corps that same hour.[77]

At about the same time in Hawaii, 1:32 PM, Honolulu Time, some five and one-half hours after the Japanese attack had begun, personnel at the FCC field monitoring station "HA-P" were listening to the Japanese language news broadcast of station JZI, Tokyo, on 9535 kHz. For the next half hour, the news anchor read a long program that recounted the day's actions as Japanese forces struck at numerous points across the Western Pacific and Southeast Asia.

After a near breathless report that boasted of a "death defying attack" upon the American naval and air forces in the Hawaiian area, the announcer interrupted the news narrative to state: "Allow me to especially make a weather broadcast at this time, 'West Wind Clear'." He then repeated the phrase. [**Exhibit #31**][78] At the end of the news program, the announcer made this statement: "At this time, let me again make a weather forecast: 'West Wind Clear'," which was then repeated. This was the only phrase heard during the news program. After the phrase was repeated, and the news program was over, the announcer then went on to read a statement to overseas Japanese citizens written by a General Yoshizumi from the 2nd Directorate of the Information Bureau.

In a memorandum attached to the transcript, it was noted that the translator from naval intelligence that in the broadcast "Here a weather forecast was made – as far as I recollect, no such weather forecast has ever been made before. The ONI translator also suggested that since these broadcasts could also be heard by the Japanese Navy it also might be some sort of code." The memorandum also mentioned that the same broadcast was made again later on 8 December, but it appears that no transcript of it was made.

There are two obvious points about this broadcast, as well as the one heard by the FCC station in Portland at about the same time. The first is that the warning phrase that was sent was the one that referred to relations with the British, their colonies in the Far East, and the Netherlands East Indies. *The code phrase referring to relations with the United States was absent from these broadcasts.*

The second point is that the coded phrase had been sent over six hours after the attack on Pearl Harbor, the Japanese landings in Malaya, air raids on the colony's air bases, and air strikes against the Philippines, Hong Kong, and Wake Island. The Japanese offensive across Asia and the Pacific had been going on for several hours when the code phrase was broadcast. Considering that the original intent of the Winds Execute message was to warn Japanese diplomats of a danger to relations, the timing of the broadcast from Tokyo seems almost absurdly anticlimactic or irrelevant. Japanese diplomats in the United States and Great Britain (and its Commonwealth) certainly were not being forewarned through the Winds warning broadcast mechanism. The expectations held by American naval and army cryptologists and intelligence officers of the value of intercepting the broadcast(s) simply went by the boards in the light of what was sent and when.

Events had demonstrated that the "hidden word" message was too little to make a difference; the Winds execute message was too late to matter.

● ●

The smoke had barely cleared from the wreckage of the ships and facilities around the Hawaiian Islands when calls were heard in congress for an investigation of the debacle. Within weeks a commission under Supreme Court Justice Owen Roberts went to Pearl Harbor to investigate what happened. In the aftermath of that investigation and those that were to follow in the next four years, the Winds message story should have been a very minor point. After all, it had proven to be a dead end as far as intelligence was concerned and of no value as a warning of Japanese intentions.

Yet within two years of Pearl Harbor, the issue of the Winds message and all of the implications in its story became a major issue in the investigation of the disaster at Pearl Harbor. Seemingly once done away with, the issue would return in the decades after the war. New players would emerge and stir up old controversies.

Notes

1. "Magic," Vol. IV, Appendix A111-113, Washington to Tokyo, Four Parts, 27 November 1941, #1206.

2. "Magic" Volume IV, Appendix A-118, Tokyo to Washington, 28 November 1941, #844. Also located in RG 457, Entry 9032, Box 301, Multi-National Diplomatic Translations, SIS # 25445.

3. Ibid., Also see A-120, Tokyo to Washington, 1 December 1941, #865. Also MND Translation, SIS #25605. NARA, RG 457, Entry 9032, Box 301.

4. PHH, Part 14: 1082-4; Part 20:4487; PHR, p. 394

5. "Safford Statement ," 2. PHH, Part 8:3579-3581

6. For example, see Washington (Nomura) to Tokyo, 5 November 1941, Japanese number #1039 that discusses the hearibility of station JLG. "Magic," Volume IV, Appendix, A-188 and Tokyo (Togo) to Washington, 24 October 1941, Japanese #2222, A-286.

7. MND Translation, Tokyo to Washington, 27 November 1941, SIS #25446. RG 457, Entry 9032, Box 301

8. "Statement Regarding Winds Message," by Captain L.F. Safford before the Joint Committee on the Investigation of the Pearl Harbor Attack, 1 February 1946. PHH, Part 8:3580. (The entire statement is included from pages 3578 to 3590.) Captain Safford's statement also is available at NARA RG 38,

Entry 1040 (CNSG Library), Box 166, Folder 5830/69 [See Exhibit 31]

9. "Magic" Volume IV, Appendix A-210, Washington to Tokyo, 27 November 1941, Japanese serial #1197.

10. "Radio Intelligence Report for the Month ending 30 November 1940, Station "S." NARA – Seattle Records Center. RG 181, "Naval Districts and Shore Establishments – 13th Naval District – Seattle, Box 7392 – Folder A81.

11. "Statement Regarding Winds Message," 4

12. PHH, Part 36:50

13. FBI Memorandum, Pearl Harbor Inquiry," from Robert L. Moore, Special Agent in Charge, to Director FBI. November 27, 1945. RG 457, Entry 9032, Box 1127, Pearl Harbor Investigation.

14. On 3 December, an espionage message from the Japanese consul Kita in Honolulu was sent to Tokyo.(MND Translation, SIS #26145 (JD-1 7370), translated 11 December 1941. In it were specifications that set up, among other items, a series of open code messages that took the form of seemingly innocuous radio ads, which reported the type and number of ships in Pearl Harbor, and which were to be broadcast over the two local radio stations. It was later believed that these ads would be heard by the Japanese task force sailing east to attack Pearl Harbor. There is no evidence that any such ads were placed and sent over the airwaves. See PHH, part 12:637-9.

15. Baird, Forrest R., "Sometimes They Forgot to Notice..." *NCVA Cryptolog* (Vol. 10, No. 2, Winter 1989), 2-3. It is not clear if these same four officers included the two that Captain Mayfield assigned to monitor the Japanese language programs on the local Hawaiian radio stations.

16. PHH, Part 35:83

17. PHH, Part 10: 4914-15

18. Message, OCSigO, December 2, 1941. CC H Series XII.S, Box 22. The SIS monitoring station at Fort Shafter, TH, was notified the same day by a separate message.

19. Memorandum to the Chief Engineer, FCC, from George Sterling, 5 July 1943. NARA, RG 173, Entry 180, Box 5, "Papers of George Sterling." Also see PHH. Part 18:3305

20. Memorandum, Director of Naval Communications, Subject: Japanese Radio Stations, broadcasts from." 4 December 1941. NSA Release 10-20-2004 (DOCID: 2015818)

21. "United States Navy Monitoring Stations as of 1941. RG 38, Entry 1040, Box 118, Folder 5750/208, "OP-20-GX/G-3 War Diary"

22. Shaw, 10-12

23. Wohlstetter, 218.

24. PHH, Part 36:81

25. Edwin T. Layton, 264-5; SRH-252, John B. Hurt, "A Version of the Japanese Problem in the Signal Intelligence Service (Later Signal Security Agency) 1930-1945." (Fort George G. Meade, MD: National Security Agency, 1983) 26-29; Gordon Prange (with Donald Goldstein and Katherine V. Dillon), *Pearl Harbor: The Verdict of History*, 315.

26. PHH, Part 36:130-131

27. PHH, Part 33: 840-1

28. NARA CP, RG 80, Pearl Harbor Liaison Office (PHLO), Entry 167EE, Box 122, Exhibit #142, Item 3 (5 pages). Also PHH, Part 18:3305-6

29. NARA, RG 173, Entry 180, Box 5, "Personal Papers of George Sterling

30. PHH, Part 33, 840

31. NARA CP, RG 80 (PHLO), Entry 167EE, Box 122, Exhibit 142A, "FCC Logs." Also, PHH Part 18: 3320-1

32. PHH, Part 9:4520 and Part10: 4629

33. PHH, Part 10: 4916-17

34. PHH, Part 10: 4630, Part 9:4520-21, Part 10:4733-34, and Part 4: 1968-9

35. NARA CP, RG 80 (PHLO), Entry 167EE, Box 122, Exhibit 142.

36. NARA CP, RG 173, Entry 180, Box 5, "Personal Papers of George Sterling."

37. PHH, part 37:662

38. "FCC Logs, Radio Intelligence Division, Night Watch Log 28 November – 8 December 1941." RG 80 (PHLO), Entry 167EE, Box 122, Exhibit 142A.

39. PHH, Part 34: 173-4, Exhibit 12

40. RG 38, Entry 1040, Box 156, pages 4506-4514 and 4522-4524, "Diplomatic Intercept."

41. R.I.P. 37B, page 7-83. The key was: 12-14-7-13-9-1-19-6-8-17-2-16-11-3-15-18-4-10-5. Also, CCH Series XII.S, Box 22

42. Ibid.

43. MND Translation, Tokyo to Washington, 27 November 1941, SIS #25609. NARA RG 457, Entry 9032, Box 301.

44. The addressees included Rangoon (Burma), Colombo (Ceylon), Singapore (British Malaya), Batavia (Netherlands East Indies), Rio de Janeiro (Brazil), Santiago (Chile), Mexico City (Mexico), Bogota (Colombia), Caracas (Venezuela), Panama, Havana (Cuba), San Francisco, New York City, New Orleans, and Washington, D.C. See RG 38, Entry 1040 (CNSG Library), Box 156, "Diplomatic Intercept." Also see PHH, part 12:186-8.

45. MND Translation, Tokyo to Washington, 27 November 1941, SIS #25609. NARA RG 457, Entry 9032, Box 301.

46. PHH, Part 12:219-221; also located in NARA, RG 457, Entry 9032, Box 301, "Multi-national Diplomatic Translations."

47. PHH, Part 12: 216-9

48. Honolulu (Kita) to Tokyo, 13 November 1941. NARA, RG 38, Entry 1040, Box 167, Folder 5830/69, "Pearl Harbor Investigation: Winds msgs." (3 of 3)

49. MND Translation #25869, Tokyo to Honolulu, 28 November 1941 (translated 7 December 1941). NARA, RG 457, Entry 9032, Box 301. Also see PHH, Part 37:668

50. MND Translation #225606, Tokyo to Washington, 1 December 1941. NARA, RG 457, Entry 9032, Box 301.

51. "Magic," Vol. IV, A-321, Tokyo to London, 1 December 1941, Japanese serial #2443.

52. MND Translation #25879, Tokyo to Havana, 2 December 1941. NARA, RG 457, Entry 9032, Box 301

53. MND Translation #25837, Bern to Ankara, 2 December 1941. NARA, RG 457, Entry 9032, Box 301

54. MND Translation, #25640, Tokyo to Circular, 2 December 1941. NARA, RG 457, Entry 9032, Box 301

55. MND Translation, #25855, Tokyo to Circular, 3 December 1941. NARA, RG 457, Entry 9032, Box 301

56. SRH-415, "HARUNA messages from Various Japanese Offices Abroad Signalling (*sic*) Destruction of Codes, December 1941." (Fort Meade, MD: National Security Agency, 1993), 3. It is likely that the destruction of codes and important papers carried out by the Japanese consulate in Honolulu on 6 December was part of this process.

57. PHH, Part 14:1407-09

58. NARA, RG 457, Entry 9032, Box 1369, Folder 4217, "Pearl Harbor Investigation and Miscellaneous Material."

59. PHR, 474; PHH, Part 35: 144-5

60. PHH, Part 10: 4729-31

61. PHH, Part 9:4226

62. PHH, Part 36:28; SRH-081, "Information from Captain George W. Linn USNR Ret." 1

63. PHH, Part 9:4522

64. "Jap Msgs, October – December 1941." NARA, RG 38, Entry 1030 (CNSG Library, Box 156; PHH, Part 37:729

65. "Jap Msgs, October – December 1941." NARA, RG 38, Entry 1030 (CNSG Library), Box 164, Folder 5830/50, "PH Investigations: Ops Logs Stations H, M, S, J; 24 Nov – 6 Dec 1941"

66. MND Translation, #25856 (JD-1, #7148), Tokyo to Circular, 7 December 1941. RG 457, Entry 9032, Box 301. See "Magic" Vol. V, 55-57, for a discussion of the message and Kramer's translation error. Also see PHH, Part 36:355-7. Kahn, *The Codebreakers,* 56-7

67. NARA CP, RG 80 (PHLO), Entry 167EE, Box 120, Exhibit 142; PHH, Part 37:3321

68. Center for Cryptologic History Series XII. S. Box 22. One author made a kind of "categorical" connection between the "hidden word" message and the "execute" version of the Winds message. Ladislas Farago in *The Broken Seal* states at one point that the "hidden word" message sent out early in the morning of 7 December was a sort of "execute message" (*sic*) itself. There was never any connection between the two systems in the Japanese instructions (New York: Random House, 1967), fn. 326, fn. 328

69. MND Translation, #25843 (JD-1 #7143), Tokyo to Washington, 6-7 December 1941. NARA, RG 457, Entry 9032, Box 301

70. MND Translation, #25850 (JD-1 #7145), Tokyo to Washington, 7 December 1941. NARA, RG 457, Entry 9032, Box 301

71. PHH, Part 14:1246. Exhibit 12, State Department Cable, London to Washington, #5918, 6

December 1941; also CINCAF to OPNAV, CR 0151, 06155 December 1941. PHH, Part 15:1680

72. Michael Gannon, *Pearl Harbor Betrayed* (New York: Henry Holt, 2001), 219-224

73. "Magic," Vol. IV – Appendix, A-134, Tokyo to Washington, 7 December 1941, Japanese serial #902.

74. MND Translations, #25854 (JD-1 #7147), Tokyo to Washington, 7 December 1941 and #26047, Washington to Tokyo, 7 December 1941 (Translated 11 December 1941). NARA, RG 457, Entry 9032, Box 301.

75. Cordell Hull, *The Memoirs of Cordell Hull,* Vol. II (New York: The MacMillan Company, 1948), 1096

76. Pearl Harbor Exhibit 142D, page 5, Federal Communications Commission, NARA, RG 80 (PHLO), Entry 167EE, Box 120; also see PHH, Part 18:3325-3329.

77. "Memorandum to the Chief Engineer [FCC], 9 February 1944." RG 128, Records of the Joint Committees, 51st – 98th Congresses. Pearl Harbor Hearings, Box 334, Folder 112.

78. "Pearl Harbor Exhibit 142D, Federal Communications Commission." NARA, RG 80 (PHLO), Entry 167EE, Box 120; also in PHH, Part 18:3325-3329

Chapter 4
The Winds Controversy: Myth and Reality

Beginning in late 1943, and continuing into the time of the Joint Congressional Committee Hearings on Pearl Harbor (November 1945 – May 1946), a controversy ensued over the allegation that a Winds Execute message had been intercepted by American naval radio intelligence, processed and passed to the leadership in the Roosevelt administration at least three days prior to the Japanese attack on 7 December.

As we shall see, the initial source for this claim and the supporting evidence that, days prior to Pearl Harbor, a Winds Execute message had been sent by Tokyo to its diplomatic facilities and had been intercepted by the U.S. Navy, was Captain Laurance F. Safford. He made this claim during several hearings, culminating in a session before the Joint Congressional Committee's hearings in early February 1946. In response to his allegations, the government made a massive search of its records, but nothing could be found to support Safford's position. Safford's claims were shown to be completely mistaken during cross-examination of his testimony before the Congressional Committee. His evidence was revealed as little more than a farrago of fabrication, speculation, poor memory, rumor gathering, and plain error-filled opinion. Yet certain historians and other researchers sympathetic to Safford have charged that the American government went through enormous lengths to discredit his claims about the handling of the purported Winds Execute message.[1] Meanwhile, evidence from Japanese, British, and Dutch sources supported events, as they were known to have occurred – that the Winds Execute was sent only after the attack on Pearl Harbor.

Captain Laurance F. Safford – In the Eye of the Controversy

At the center of the Winds message controversy – in fact its primary and almost exclusive source – was Captain Laurance Frye Safford. Safford had played a critical role in the founding and operation of modern American naval cryptology. He had been put in command of the fledgling cryptanalytic section of the U.S. Navy in 1924 – the (Cryptanalytic) Research Desk within the Code and Signal Section of the Navy's Division of Naval Communications (OP-20-G). He had overseen the recruitment, training, and formation of the corps of radio intercept operators who manned the Navy's monitoring sites around the world and in the United States. Safford played a role in the establishment of the navy's constellation of monitoring and direction finding (DF) sites in the Pacific region from the mid- to late 1930s. He had also recruited and staffed the research Desk of the Code and Signal Section with such notables of naval cryptanalysis as Agnes Meyer Driscoll, Joseph Rochefort, and Thomas Dyer. Safford had set up a program of training in cryptanalysis of selected naval and marine officers, rotating them into the Research Desk for periods of on-the-job training before they returned to positions in the fleet. Safford also had allowed, albeit reluctantly, the early experimental use of machine aids in cryptanalysis – among them early IBM punch card sorters to tabulate and inventory code groups and specialized typewriters modified to copy Japanese Kana characters sent via Morse code.[2]

Safford had nurtured OP-20-G through the hard and lean interwar years and, at the rank of Commander, was in charge of the entire section in late 1941. He was highly respected by other cryptologic and intelligence officers from both the navy and the army. From a technical standpoint, Safford was a talented officer, though his true ability lay in the collection, forwarding, and processing – the "front end" of cryptology – and not in the analysis of the intercept or dissemination of communications intelligence. Sometimes he simply misunderstood the analytic process, especially the technical background to major cryptanalytic breakthroughs and the fact that major systems were changed, or superseded, and required substantial efforts to recover them. This was illustrated in a short history of prewar communications intelligence he authored in late 1943, "The Undeclared War," in which he made two glaringly incorrect assertions. First, he claimed that the "Navy had solved the primary Japanese Fleet System (JN-25) to a partially readable extent."[3] This statement greatly overstated the actual progress that was limited to less than ten percent of the AN-1 codebook (later notated as JN-25B). In fact, he may have referred to the predecessor variant, AN (later notated as JN-25A), but it is unclear from his writing which system he meant – a vagueness that has confused some researchers in the decades since. Secondly, he attributed the S.I.S. solution of the Purple cipher machine to the fact that the "Army had acquired a model of the Japanese Diplomatic machine and the original set of cipher keys used with it." To this comment, William F. Friedman, in 1952, greatly objected and wrote an emphatic note in the margin of this section: "This is not true. Army acquired it the hard way – cryptanalytically!"[4]

While Safford had fostered the development of OP-20-G and in 1936 had become its first permanently assigned commander, by the time of Pearl Harbor he probably had come to be overmatched by the enormous demands in time and resources made upon his organization.[5] The rapidly multiplying targets and the simultaneously growing workforce of OP-20-G – the worldwide mission included some 500 people – overwhelmed the prewar structure he had built. As mentioned earlier, the OP-20-G mission was stretched globally, with two centers of interest, the ongoing U-boat struggle in the Atlantic and the Pacific crisis that vied for the scarce resources of the section. The multiple demands may have simply outstripped Safford's ability to effectively manage OP-20-G.

Symptomatic of the problem was his approach to solve the German U-boat Enigma device in the eighteen months prior to Pearl Harbor. In 1940 Safford set up a small team dedicated to solving enciphered German U-boat traffic. At the time, OP-20-G did not know that this cipher traffic was generated by a more advanced naval version of the commercial Enigma cipher machine, a copy of which the navy possessed. The cryptanalytic effort was small, perhaps fewer than ten people, but it represented a diversion of scarce resources. In the months prior to Pearl Harbor, he resisted efforts to coordinate work with the British in OP-20-G's attack on the traffic. When he finally allowed cooperation, he often ignored their experienced technical advice in favor of that from his own analysts like Agnes Driscoll that proved ultimately to be an analytic dead end. The navy's attack on Enigma proved to be unproductive for the first two years.[6]

Safford's actions at OP-20-G in the months before Pearl Harbor were erratic: at times he controlled activities completely; at other times, as we shall see later in this section, he seemed to let parts of the mission slip. In testimony before various hearings that in the weeks leading up to the attack on Pearl Harbor, he stated he had worked longer than normal hours. He said that he was deeply involved in all aspects of the section's operations. And he was. In all probability, though, he tried to do everything, and as a result, many problems developed, especially in the administration of daily activities. In fact, many officers in naval intelligence and cryptology were working almost twelve- to fourteen-hour days. *Yet, on 7 December, Safford stayed out of his office the entire day*, only to return the following Monday morning.[7]

Curiously, in early 1942 Safford had suggested to the CNO staff that, as part of a recommended reorganization of OP-20, he be replaced as head of OP-20-G. By the spring of 1942, Safford was gone as the commander of the code-breaking element and was placed in charge of the office supervising the not unimportant job of developing and fielding of cryptographic systems for the U.S. Navy – OP-20-Q.[8]

Safford Searches for the Missing Winds Execute Message

The story of Safford's search for the missing Winds Execute message begins about two years after the attack on Pearl Harbor. We do not know with much detail what he initially did to locate records, how he went about the search, to whom he first spoke, and when he searched. The exact date of origin and source of his belief that such the message had been sent cannot be precisely placed. What we do know is that sometime in mid- to late 1943, Captain Safford had begun writing a short history of American naval radio intelligence called "The Undeclared War."[9] It was completed on 15 November 1943. Interestingly, the last section of the monograph concerned the intercept and handling of the Winds Message instructions, Japanese serial Nos. 2353 and 2354. The section ends on 28 November 1941 with the transmission of the technical message to Hawaii and the Philippines that contained the Japanese broadcast schedule. Next to Safford's signature is a comment: "Not written smooth beyond this point."[10] Ordinarily, this comment would be interpreted simply as a comment about the unfinished nature of the history. But in the light of events to come, it now appears to have been an omen.

According to Safford in later testimony, at about the time of his abrupt termination of the history project, he was reading the transcript of the Roberts Commission (18 December 1941 – 23 January 1942) that investigated the Pearl Harbor attack, when he realized that a warning message to Admiral Kimmel from naval intelligence, drafted by Commander Arthur McCollum on either 4 or 5 December, which Safford previously understood had been sent to Pearl Harbor, in fact, had never been transmitted.[11] According to Safford, this proposed warning message to Kimmel had resulted from the intercept of a Winds Execute message on the morning of 4 December.

Concerned that no warning message had been sent, Safford undertook his own private investigation to find the translation of the Winds Execute intercept and discover what had happened to McCollum's warning message. His first step was to recover the original Winds intercept and translation: the yellow TWX paper from the intercept station that had copied it and all of the copies of the translation (anywhere from six to over ten) that he believed had been distributed to the S.I.S. and various offices within the Navy. Unable to locate any copies of the documents within the navy, he later informally asked personnel in the Army's S.I.S. and G-2 "on several occasions" to send him a copy of the translation, but he was advised that the document could not be located, though Safford would testify later that he believed that it "was common knowledge [in the Army]" that the translation existed.[12] During the search through OP-20-G files that had come up empty, Safford stumbled across a reference to a cancelled navy serial number, JD-1 #7001, which he believed was the serial number OP-20-G had assigned to the translation of the Winds Execute message for which he was searching.[13]

No doubt Safford became frustrated over his inability to recover the missing intercept or the translation. He also tried to locate the intercept logs of the East Coast navy monitoring stations he believed had copied the Winds message. But he struck out here, as well. The station logs could not be found. A further inquiry turned up information that at least one station, Winter Harbor,

Maine, had destroyed all the logs in mid-1942 with the approval of the Navy.[14]

During this time Safford widened his search for evidence and wrote a letter on 22 December 1943 to the one person he believed knew about the Winds Execute message, Commander Alwin Kramer. **[Exhibit #41]**[15] In the letter Safford posed a series of vaguely worded and leading questions about the intercept of Japanese diplomatic messages during the week prior to the attack on Pearl Harbor. One question, number 18, concerned the Winds message. "We cannot find

Captain Alwin D. Kramer

the original "Weather Report" (Sent Dec. 5th) and its translation. What became of it?"[16]

Kramer's response, which took some time to arrive since he was stationed at the Joint Intelligence Center, Pacific Ocean Areas, Hawaii, came in a letter of 28 December. It did not help Safford's cause. **[Exhibit #42]**[17] In his letter, Kramer noted that "The first (*sic*) one of the '" "' was not as indicated in parentheses..." It was, as Kramer added, really one of the file of translations turned over at the meeting, which Hull, Stimson, and Knox attended on the morning of 7 December. The folder included the Part 14 of message serial No. 902, the STOP message, and the instructions from Tokyo to the embassy in Washington to deliver the message by 1:00 PM, the latter of which Kramer refers to as "Item 11 (first one) on how the hour tied with the sun, and moves in progress, elsewhere." Kramer then added that he believed that the translations were available in the sections of OP-20-G that handled either collateral intelligence, "GL," or translations and code recovery, "GZ."

This was not the answer Safford expected (or wanted), and he told Kramer so in the next letter he mailed on 22 January 1944. **[Exhibit #43]**[18] This letter becomes critical to the story of Safford's later claims for two reasons. First, Safford created a "condensation code" of names, places, dates, and objects that ran two pages. **[Exhibit #43, pages 266-7]** This code list he appended to the letter. Why he chose to create a "code" for his correspondence was revealed in the letter. He perceived an effort by people in the staff of the CNO to "frame-up" Admiral Kimmel. This leads to the second point in that this letter becomes Safford's initial statement regarding the nature, scope, and gravity of an apparent conspiracy that covered up the record of the events surrounding the Winds Execute message as he recalled them.

Safford began with a warning to Kramer (with the text in place of Safford's code values):

> **Be prudent and be patient...No one in OPNAV [The Chief of Naval Operations' Staff] can be trusted. Premature action would only tip off the people who framed Admiral Kimmel and General Short. Tell Halsey [Admiral William "Bull" Halsey] that I knew Adm[iral] Kimmel was a scapegoat from the start, but did not suspect that he was a victim of a frameup until about 15 November 1943, and did not have absolute proof until about 18 January 1944. Safford [here he refers to himself in the third person] has overwhelming proof of the guilt of OPNAV**

and [Army] General Staff, plus a list of about fifteen reliable witnesses.[19]

Safford then followed with more questions for Kramer. Then he added a "Comment" section in which he first laid out some of the details of the incident concerning the Winds Execute message and the suppressed follow-up warning message from McCollum:

> With regard to the quotes of my item 18 (about the Weather Report") and your items 18 and 10(c) [from Safford's first letter and Kramer's response] you were describing Circular #2492 – the "hidden word" message, of which we have copies of the original and the translation in the GZ files...I was asking about the General Intelligence Broadcast containing [the] false "Weather Report" which was Broadcast at 0430 (EST) on December 4, 1941 or December 5. (Not sure of exact date.) It was heard by "M" [Cheltenham, Maryland] and "W" [Winter Harbor, Maine] and sent in by teletype. It was unheard by "S"....who listened for it. (I have this from the Station "S" files, plus statements of [Lt. Lesley A.] Wright and [Captain Redfield] Mason.) This message (in Morse) included the words – 'Higashi no kazeame.' Nishi no kaze hare (Negative form of kita no kaze kumori.)" The warning was not sent in the manner prescribed by Circular #2353 or #2354, but was a mixture. The [OP-20] GY watch officer was not sure of it so he called you and you came in early and verified it. [Lt. Allan] Murray [a GY watch officer] recalls it so do I. Either you or Brotherhood [another GY watch officer, Lt. Francis.M.] (?) were waiting in my office when I came in that morning and said "Here it is!..."
>
> As a result of the General Broadcast, McCollum [then Commander Arthur] prepared a message – which was a very long message ending up with a translation and significance of the warning in the General Intelligence Broadcast. I read the message in Admiral Noyes' office and was witness to the discussion of it between Noyes and Admiral Wilkinson. I took for granted that the message would be sent and did not know otherwise until 2 December 1943. I believe that I told you about this message and stated that it had been sent. Anyway, I was living in a fool's paradise from 4 December to December 7, 1941. I learned from Wright [Commander Wesley A] that McCollum knew that the message had not been sent (Wright had been informed by McCollum at Pearl Harbor).[20]

In the early part of the letter, Safford notes that he did not have "absolute proof" of the "frameup" until about 18 January 1944. Safford does not state explicitly what the source of the proof was, or its nature, but information that came out later that year points probably to one or more conversations he had with William F. Friedman of the S.I.S. as the critical point of origin.

That Safford and Friedman should cross paths in early 1944 was not a surprise. Both had once run their respective services' communications intelligence sections, but had been replaced shortly after the war started. They were familiar with each other's role in establishing the original COMINT programs for both the army and navy. On occasion, they had cooperated by sharing information on code-breaking projects of mutual interest, as with the joint effort against the Japanese Purple machine cipher device. Both now were engaged in issues relating to communications security for the army and navy. The two happened to meet a number of times during 1944.

The discussion of interest was at one of these meetings. When this particular discussion occurred is not clear – perhaps as early as January 1944, but the scant evidence available also suggests sometime later in the year. Friedman remained vague about

William F. Friedman

the exact date and believed it occurred sometime in the eighteen months prior to his testimony before the Clarke Investigations in mid-July 1945, which would place the meeting of interest in the first three months of 1944. Safford in later testimony would not give a date. During the meeting, Safford related to Friedman what he had found so far about the Winds Execute message that he believed had been sent on 4 December and how the intercept subsequently was handled. He also repeated his information about the disappearance from the files of any trace of the translation of the Winds Execute message. Perhaps because he was caught up in the moment of Safford's story, or because he was not aware of the direction or intent of Safford's search, Friedman related a story he had heard regarding the Winds translation. Earlier that year, he had met with Colonel Otis Sadtler, who had served as a communications officer with G-2 at the time of Pearl Harbor. Friedman asked Sadtler if he knew of a Winds Execute message that had been intercepted before 7 December 1941. Sadtler said that he was told that the material had been destroyed. Shocked, Friedman asked who ordered the destruction. Sadtler replied that General George C. Marshall had ordered it. Friedman then told Safford that Sadtler had learned this story from Colonel Isaac (Ike) Spalding, who was head of G-1 Staff (Personnel) at the time. Friedman later testified that he did not give much credence to the story and was surprised that Safford bought into it.[21]

The subject – General Marshall's order to destroy the Winds material – would surface later, first during the Hewitt Inquiry, then the Clarke Investigation, and finally during the Joint Congressional Committee hearings. As for Safford and Friedman, they continued to talk about the missing Winds Execute translation. On one occasion, 17 September 1944, Friedman made notes of an exchange with Safford. [**Exhibit #47**][22] Many of the points that Safford made to Kramer in his letters from nine months earlier were repeated in these notes, notably when the Winds Execute was heard, which station intercepted it, how it was processed and then turned over to ONI for action. Absent, though, were the claims of destruction of intelligence material held by the War Department and that this action had been ordered by General Marshall.

Safford's Detailed Claim about the Winds Execute Message – February 1946

While Safford was conducting his search for what he believed to be were the missing papers related to the intercept of the Winds Execute message, pressure mounted for a review of the attack on Pearl Harbor. There was much criticism, especially from the Republican Party and critics of President Roosevelt, over the administration's handling of the prewar negotiations with Japan, as well as the findings of the Roberts Commission, which essentially placed the blame for the debacle completely on the shoulders of Admiral Kimmel and General Short. These two were accused of "dereliction of duty" for failing to consult with one another and a lack of proper responsibility in carrying the requirements of their respective commands.[23] Pressure from administration political opponents generated demands for new hearings. Both the War and Navy Departments initiated a total of five new hearings on Pearl Harbor during 1944. Safford would testify and offer evidence of his claims about the Winds message at three of them – the Hart Inquiry, the Army Pearl Harbor Board, and the Navy Board of Inquiry. Interestingly, in the other two investigations carried out by the War Department, the Clarke Investigation and the Clausen Investigation, the Winds Execute issue, and Safford's role in it, would emerge as an important topic for consideration. Two more investigations would start in 1945, the Hewitt Inquiry and the Joint Congressional Committee hearings, the latter of which would continue into 1946. Safford would appear at both and give testimony. (Interestingly, the six hearings prior to the congressional one were closed to the public at the time, while some contained classified annexes.)

We do not intend to examine in detail Safford's testimony and evidence delivered to each of the six Pearl Harbor hearings prior to the Joint Congressional Committee hearings. The main reason for not relating the allegations made to the other hearings is that such a recounting easily becomes difficult to follow simply because Safford often offered different evidence or narratives of events concerning the Winds Execute message to all of the hearings at which he testified. In addition, these narratives, in general, differed significantly from the first chronology of events concerning the Winds message he described to Alwin Kramer in the letter of January 1944. The best way to describe Safford's claim is through an examination of his most complete and finished version of events about the Winds Execute message. This is contained in his memorandum to the Congressional Committee delivered on 1 February 1946.

However, we cannot ignore completely Safford's testimony and the reaction to it from each investigative board. So, before we examine his statement to the Joint Congressional Committee, we will briefly describe how each hearing handled the information Safford had provided them, as well how they judged the evidence he offered. How the previous hearings reacted to Safford's allegation(s) provides an important context in which to understand the conclusion the Congressional Committee reached about the Winds Execute message.

The first hearing that took Safford's testimony regarding the Winds message was the Hart Inquiry. It was charged to examine those naval officers knowledgeable about the attack, take their testimony, assemble exhibits, and submit the material to the secretary of the navy, at the time Frank Knox. Admiral Thomas Hart, who had been the commander-in-chief of the Asiatic Fleet in December 1941, chaired the inquiry. There was no final report as such, as were produced by many of the other hearings. Safford appeared as a witness on 29 April 1944. After questioning about code-breaking efforts prior to hostilities, the examining officer asked Safford if he wanted to make any further statement. Safford responded by making a four-page statement regarding the Winds message. Among other items in his statement, Safford named fifteen individuals who he claimed had some knowledge of the message. The inquiry board asked him no questions regarding his statement and adjourned for the day.[24]

On 13 June 1944, Congress passed a Joint Resolution directing the secretaries of war and the navy to conduct investigations of Pearl Harbor. In response, both the Army Pearl Harbor Board and the Naval Court of Inquiry were established. Safford gave testimony first to the Army Pearl Harbor Board. Safford testified before this hearing, though his testimony, as that of Colonel Otis Sadtler, was considered "Top Secret" because of its content, that is, it contained details of code-breaking against Japanese diplomatic communications. Safford's testimony can be found in the Top Secret annex to the Board's hearings. The transcript indicates that the Army Board did not press Safford on his evidence. On the other hand, it did question many army officers from G-2 and S.I.S. regarding the existence of a Winds Execute message. The Board completed its hearings and issued a report on 20 October 1944. The Army attached a Top Secret Memorandum, which dealt with the "Magic" aspects of the case. Its finding on the Winds Execute was somewhat ambiguous. It said, "It is this message [Winds execute] which the Army witnesses testified was never received by the Army. It was a clear indication to the United States as early as December 4. The vital nature of this message can be realized."[25]

A year later, on 14 September 1945, the Army's judge advocate general wrote a memorandum to the secretary of war regarding the most recent evidence and their effect on the Board's findings. It contained the following statement:

> **Captain Safford had testified before the Board that on 4 December he saw a Navy intercept which contained the execute message to the Japanese "Winds Code," and that two copies were sent to the Army. Colonel Clausen's investigation discloses no evidence that the Army ever received any such copies and I understand the testimony of Captain Safford has been qualified considerably by testimony of himself and other Navy personnel before Admiral Hewitt.**[26]

Concurrently with the Army Board, the Navy Department conducted its own Court of Inquiry from 24 July to 19 October 1944 when its report was issued. Safford testified before the Court of Inquiry. His assertions about the existence and handling of the Winds Execute message were accepted by the Court. The Court asked him few questions about his evidence. The Court did ask him about whether his memory of events was direct or hearsay. But he was not challenged to produce any concrete evidence to support details of his allegations.[27]

Like its Army counterpart, the Navy Inquiry included an addendum to its report to deal with "certain other important information" meaning the testimony and evidence related to the breaking of Japanese diplomatic codes.[28] The Inquiry reported that on 4 December an intercepted Japanese broadcast employing the Winds code was received in the Navy Department. While the message was subject to two interpretations, the information from the broadcast was not transmitted to Admiral Kimmel or any other fleet commanders. Furthermore, the Inquiry noted that, while the Pacific and Asiatic Fleets were monitoring the airwaves for these broadcasts, no attempt was made to verify they had heard it. The report finally noted that the [Winds] message in question could not be located in the Navy Department.[29]

The Navy added a number of endorsements, official approbations, to the Inquiry's final report. The Second Endorsement of 6 November 1944 noted that while no copy of the suspect message could be found, there was "considerable testimony in the record as to what was done with the 'Winds message.'"[30] The Third Endorsement repeated that the intercepted broadcasts had been transmitted to the Chief of Naval Operations, Admiral Harold Stark, and the Director of Naval Communications, Admiral Noyes, but that neither man could recall receiving it.[31]

Between 14 and 23 September 1944 and from 13 July to 4 August 1945, the Army conducted an investigation into the handling of Top Secret documents related to Pearl Harbor. Colonel Carter W. Clarke, who was Deputy Chief of the Military Intelligence Section of the General Staff at the time, headed up the study. In 1941 he had been in charge of the Safeguarding Military Information section of the Military Intelligence Division prior to the war. Though these hearings did not take testimony from Captain Safford, the issue of the Winds Execute message was part of the investigation.

The initial investigation had lasted just nine days in September 1944. A number of Army officers involved in the processing and distribution of "Magic" translations of Japanese diplomatic messages were questioned. Regarding the Winds message, the bottom line from all of the testimony was that no Army monitoring site ever heard the message, nor did the War Department receive any such message or translation of it from its navy counterparts.[32] The Clarke hearings did not issue a formal report at this time.

However, in July 1945, after William Friedman had testified to the Hewitt Inquiry on 5 July 1945 (see below), Clarke reconvened his hearings to investigate statements made by Friedman. During his testimony before the Admiral Hewitt Inquiry, Friedman had repeated the story that he had told Safford about the statement from Colonel Sadtler that alleged General Marshall had ordered the destruction of material concerned with the Winds Execute message.[33] So on 13 July Friedman was questioned about this statement. In turn, those named by Friedman who knew of the story – Colonel Otis Sadtler, Brigadier General Isaac Spalding, and Brigadier General John Bissell – also were queried. Clarke reported a month later that he could find no evidence that any such material had been destroyed, or that such an order had been given, and he repeated the initial finding that no such "Winds Code" message was ever received by the Army or to have been destroyed.[34] The story about General Marshall's order to destroy all copies of the Winds Execute message would resurface during the Congressional Committee hearings and will be dealt with in depth later in this chapter.

On 23 November 1944, Secretary of War Stimson directed Major Henry C. Clausen from the Judge Advocate General Department to conduct an investigation into "a number of unexplored leads" which appeared during the Army Pearl Harbor Board hearings. Clausen was given extraordinary access to personnel and records, even Top Secret material. Clausen's far-reaching franchise was extended to the Navy Department when the new secretary of the navy, James Forrestal, agreed to Clausen's access to naval personnel and records that directly connected to army matters.

Although Clausen never directly interviewed Safford, the latter's claim about the Winds Execute message being transmitted and intercepted on 4 December would shadow Clausen's investigation. Eventually it would lead him to suspect that the British may have heard such a message (see pages 83-4). Clausen interviewed some navy and numerous army personnel, including General Douglas MacArthur and his staff. His approach, unlike the various boards and inquiries, was to obtain written affidavits from everyone – a legal approach that he seemed more at home with since he was a lawyer.

Clausen kept the War Department informed of his investigation through a series of memoranda from February through August 1945. His memorandum of 23 May 1945 stated that he could find no evidence that a Winds message, as described, was ever sent.[35] He added that "the evidence to date of the existence of such an implementation [message] depends primarily on the recollection of certain Navy witnesses among whom there is a conflict. He would reiterate this position, though in a much stronger tone in his memoirs.[36]

The last hearings before the Joint Congressional Committee was the Navy's Hewitt Inquiry, which held hearings from 14 May to 11 July 1945. This inquiry was established by order of the secretary of the navy on 2 May and was charged to examine all previous investigations and to conduct any further study deemed necessary. It was noted that previous inquiries and investigations had disclosed, "matters of importance, principally concerning intelligence, [which] had not been investigated thoroughly."[37] There were eleven items of interest to review. Among them was Item (G), the Winds message.

Admiral H. Kent Hewitt's mandate for this inquiry read: "to determine whether or not there was a 'winds code' message relating to the United States. In connection with the 'Winds code' message, it should be noted that according to Captain Safford the last time he saw the message was when it was sent to the Roberts Commission. It should be determined whether or not the message was there or is there now."[38]

The Hewitt Inquiry took testimony from Safford on three separate occasions, the latter two dealt with issues not related to the Winds message. In its final report, the Hewitt Inquiry reviewed the evidence and made two pronouncements on the issue. The first was that the "winds code" message would have conveyed no intelligence of significance which the CNO, Admiral Stark, or Admiral Kimmel did not already have. The second conclusion was that there was no evidence from any source other than Captain Safford that a Winds Execute message had been intercepted. The Inquiry noted that even Captain Alwin Kramer, in previous testimony, had confused the "hidden word message" with the "winds code." The Hewitt Inquiry finding concluded that the findings from the earlier Army Pearl Harbor Board and the Naval Court of Inquiry that a Winds message had been sent prior to 7 December were based primarily on the testimony of Safford and Kramer. It was noted that every other person questioned by the various inquiries had denied any direct knowledge of the message as Safford had described, while others stated they knew of it by hearsay only.

It is important to note that these six hearings had been closed to the public. There emerged much bipartisan political pressure for open hearings on Pearl Harbor. Within days of Japan's surrender, both the Senate and House passed a Concurrent Resolution calling for such hearings. Four months later, on 15 November 1945, the Joint Congressional Committee would begin its hearings into Pearl Harbor. The Committee, chaired by Senator Alben W. Barkley (D-Kentucky), had issues almost from the moment the first gavel was struck.

Senator Homer Ferguson (R-Michigan) raised an objection that the minority members of the committee had just received thousands of pages of material released under the order by President Harry Truman to the Executive Department and they needed time to review the papers.[39]

The background to this dispute was that on 28 August 1945 President Truman had issued a memorandum to seven cabinet and office secretaries and directors that ordered them to take such steps as necessary to prevent release of any information regarding "past or present status, technique or procedures, degree of success attained or any specific results of any cryptanalytic unit acting under the authority of the United States Government or any department thereof."[40] This was a blanket directive meant to protect all aspects of wartime cryptanalysis from compromise and not to hide Pearl Harbor records. Two months later, on 23 October, Truman issued another memorandum, which specifically exempted the congressional hearings from his earlier order and directed the State, War, and Navy Departments to make available all material to the committee, as well as authorize any employee or

Senator Alben Barkley. Courtesy U.S. Senate Historical Office

member of the armed forces whose testimony was desired to appear before the committee.[41]

Safford Tells His Story

Captain Safford appeared before the Joint Congressional Committee on 1 February 1946. He introduced his position by entering into the records of the hearings a prepared statement, which represented his most articulate narrative of his version of events. It detailed his assertion that the Winds execute message had been intercepted and reported to the government. [**Exhibit #40**][42] It began with these short, dramatic sentences: "There was a Winds message. It meant War – and we knew it meant War."

Safford's version of the intercept and handling of the Winds Execute can be summarized as follows. On 28 November 1941, OP-20-G had tasked numerous navy monitoring stations in the continental United States and its possessions in Hawaii and the Philippines to listen for the Winds Execute message. Safford expected that if such a message was to be heard by the navy sites, that it would be heard on a Morse code not voice news broadcast.

Shortly before 9:00 AM (EST) on 4 December 1941, a teletype message (TWX) from the intercept site at Cheltenham, Maryland (Station "M" in correspondence), arrived at the operations center of the Navy's code-breaking and translations section, OP-20-GY. It was a transcription of a news broadcast, in Morse, by station JAP (Tokyo) transmitted on frequency 11980 kilohertz. The broadcast had been heard at Cheltenham at about 8:00 AM and forwarded over the wire to OP-20-GY some thirty to forty-five minutes later. The intercept, on yellow TWX (teletype) paper, was about two hundred words long. According to Safford, all three of the expected Winds code phrases appeared in the middle of the text. Safford said these phrases equated to "War with England," "War with the United States," and "Peace with Russia." In the last case, he claimed that the coded phrase for Russia, which translates as "North Wind Cloudy" was in "the negative form," though Safford did not elaborate on how he reached that conclusion.

Safford reported that then Lt. Alwin Kramer and the GY duty watch officer, unnamed in his statement, had brought him the TWX. When he entered the office, Kramer told Safford that "This is it." Safford says he interpreted Kramer's exclamation to mean that the intercept indeed was the Winds Execute message that everyone had been listening for and that it was the "tip-off that would prevent the U.S. Pacific Fleet being surprised at Pearl Harbor the way the Russians had been surprised at Port Arthur."[43] Safford noted in his prepared statement that Kramer had underlined all three phrases in the text and had penciled (or crayoned) in the translations. He added that he was not certain of the order and perhaps the phrase for England appeared first and maybe there was written "No War" for Russia.[44]

Safford continued his story and said that he next made sure that the " 'original' of the Winds Message (*sic*)" was sent to Rear Admiral Noyes, the Director of Naval Communications. (Recall that OP-20-G was part of the Naval Communications (OP-20), not the Office of Naval Intelligence or ONI). Safford ordered an unnamed officer to deliver the paper to Noyes in person. He was to "track down" Noyes and not to take "no" for an answer. In due course, Safford said he received a confirmation that Noyes had the message. After that, he recalled that Noyes had telephoned the "substance" of the message to the War Department, to the "Magic" distribution list in the Navy Department, and to the Naval Aide to President Roosevelt. Six or seven copies of the message/translation were "rushed" over to the War Department as soon as possible. Here, he says, the navy's responsibility ended. He added that the "smooth" or final translations (presumably with both army and navy serial numbers like all other such translations) were distributed at noon that same day to the authorized Navy

Department officials and to the White House. Safford added that he had no reason to suspect that the Army would not make a prompt distribution of the translations of the Winds message.[45]

In earlier testimony to the Hewitt Inquiry, Safford maintained that the intercept from the morning of 4 December was not to be confused with the FCC intercept of the "false" or mistaken Winds intercept from the evening of 4 December. The FCC had phoned in a report of this broadcast to the OP-20-GY watch center about 9:00 PM (EST) on 4 December. Safford added that on the morning of 5 December, Kramer had been shown this particular FCC intercept. When he read it, Safford observed, he knew it was not the Execute message. He crumbled up the paper and "threw it in the waste basket."[46]

Safford went on to aver that more proof of the existence of the Winds Execute Message came on 15 December when he, along with Kramer, viewed the contents of a folder of "Magic" material that Admiral Noyes was to present to the Roberts Commission, which included the same Winds translation. He said that he and Kramer had checked over the contents of the folder for completeness. Safford reported that Kramer had discussed "these messages" with then Assistant Secretary of the Navy James Forrestal for some two hours around 10 December while Secretary Knox was at Pearl Harbor. Safford wrote in his statement that he believed that the translation of the Winds Execute message had been given the Navy serial number JD-1 #7001, because this serial number was missing from the files of correspondence and translations for that period. Safford's last comment on the matter of the distribution of the translation was that it was the responsibility of the Office of Naval Intelligence. He made the odd statement that he, Safford, had no responsibility in the matter after he forwarded the original message to Admiral Noyes and later made sure that Kramer's "folder" had the translations and that they were in order.[47]

Safford then added a new twist to the story that upped the ante for the importance of the Winds Execute message as a warning mechanism for U.S. intelligence. He stated that the message also served as a "Signal of Execute" of some sort. He believed this "theory" was confirmed when the Japanese navy had changed the cipher system of the General Purpose Fleet Code system – notated as AN-1 at the time – on 4 December some seven and one-half hours *before* [our italics] the Winds execute was transmitted. Safford added that there was only one station JAP broadcast for the European region that day and that it coincided with change.[48]

Safford claimed that, as a result of the intercept of the Winds Execute message, a number of messages were sent out late on 4 December to various U.S. naval facilities ordering them to destroy excess cryptographic material. [**Exhibit #40, page 244**] In later testimony before the Congressional Committee, he also stated that Captain Arthur McCollum from ONI had drafted a multipage warning message for CNO to send out. In this draft was a reference to the warning contained in the intercepted Winds message.[49]

In testimony the next day, Safford expanded his allegation. He offered another memorandum that he had prepared for the Hewitt Inquiry on 14 July 1945, but that he had withdrawn at the "suggestion" that Inquiry's counsel, Lieutenant Commander John Sonnett. In this second memo, Safford claimed that Sonnett had tried to get him to change his testimony to reconcile "all previous discrepancies."[50] Safford's memo added that Admiral Hewitt had told him that there was no evidence of a "Winds Execute" message beyond his unsupported testimony. But Safford believed that Sonnett had "succeeded in pulling the wool over his [Admiral Hewitt] eyes."[51]

This memo contained another inflammatory section: a list of officers "who knew, in December 1941, that the Winds Execute message had been broadcast on (or about) 4 December 1941...

although some of them did not learn about it until after the attack on Pearl Harbor." Among those named were eleven army officers and thirteen navy officers and one navy enlisted man. The list included watch officers, linguists, and cryptanalysts like Lt. Colonel Frank Rowlett, who headed the team that solved the Japanese diplomatic cipher machine known as Purple, as well as senior officers such as Admiral Harold Stark, Chief of Naval Operations at the time, and General George C. Marshall, Chief of Staff, United States Army.

Oddly, Safford restricted his list to officers from the Army and Navy and excluded the civilian leadership from the War or Navy Departments, or the White House. He also left off many individuals who had testified at any of the earlier hearings and who had heard of the Winds Execute message such as William F. Friedman. It did it not include anyone who might have been at the intercept station at Cheltenham where Safford believed the message had been copied. When questioned further, Safford then named

The Twenty-Six Government Officials Named by Captain Safford

Name	Present Rank	Station and Duty on 7 December 1941
George C. Marshall	General of the Army	Chief of Staff, U.S. Army
Leonard T. Gerow	Lt. Gen., USA	Director War Plans Division
Dawson Olmstead	Maj. Gen., USA (ret)	Chief Signal Officer
Sherman Miles	Maj. Gen., USA	Director of Military Intelligence
Clayton Bissell	Maj. Gen., USA	War Plans Division (WDGS)
Otis K. Sadtler	Col., USA	Army Communications, OCSigO
Rufus T. Bratton	Brig. Gen., USA	In charge, Far Eastern Section, MI
Rex W. Minckler	Col. USA	Chief, SIS, OCSigO
Harold Doud	Col. USA	In Charge, Japanese Section, SIS, OCSigO
Robert E. Schukraft	Col. USA	In Charge, Intercept Section, SIS, OCSigO
Frank B. Rowlett	Lt. Col., USA (Reserve)	Principal cryptanalyst, Japanese Section, SIS, OCSigO
Harold R. Stark	Admiral, USN	Chief of Naval Operations
Royal E. Ingersoll	Admiral, USN	Asst., Chief of Navy Operations
Richard K. Turner	Vice Admiral, USN	Director, War Plans Division
T.S. Wilkinson	Vice Admiral, USN	Director, Naval Intelligence
Leigh Noyes	Rear Admiral, USN	Director of Naval Communications
John R. Beardall	Rear Admiral, USN	Naval Aide to the President
John R. Redman	Rear Admiral, USN	Asst. Director of Naval Communications
Frank E. Beatty	Rear Admiral, USN	Aide to the Secretary of the Navy
Laurance F. Safford	Capt., USN	OP-20-G, In Charge Security Section
Arthur H. McCollum	Capt., USN	OP-16-F2, In Charge Far Eastern Section, Naval Intelligence
George W. Welker	Capt., USN	OP-20-GX, In Charge, Intercept and Direction Finding Section
L.W. Parke	Comdr., USN	OP-20-GY, In Charge, Cryptanalytical Section
A.A. Murray	Lt. Comdr., USN	Watch Officer in OP-20-GY
H. L. Bryant	Chief Ship's Clerk, USN	Confidential Yeoman in OP-20-GZ

more individuals who, at the time, were junior navy officers, any one of who he believed might have delivered the Winds translation to Admiral Noyes that morning.⁵²

One more part of Safford's charge surfaced the afternoon of 2 February when he was questioned about what happened to all of the copies of the Winds message translation and the original Japanese text. In response to separate questions about what happened to the copies of the Winds Execute translation and any associated records, Safford stated that material had disappeared. He added that there was the "appearance" of a conspiracy between the Navy and War Departments to destroy all of the copies.³³ As to who issued the order to do so, Safford backed off from his earlier assertion before the Hewitt Inquiry that the destruction was carried out under the direct order of General Marshall. When asked by the congressional inquiry whether he believed that Marshall had ordered the papers destroyed, Safford declined to answer.⁵⁴

Examining Safford's Version(s) of Events

Safford, after two days of testimony and his two memoranda, failed to convince the Joint Congressional Committee that a Winds Execute message had been intercepted and disseminated within the U.S. government prior to Pearl Harbor. He also failed to persuade the committee members that there had been a cover-up of the event. Instead, his story and evidence were shredded during the Committee's cross-examination of the evidence supporting his allegations. When he had testified before the other panels, aside from some queries to seeking more details, Safford had never been questioned critically nor had his evidence been examined with any rigor. Still, as was reported earlier, even with virtually no skeptical questioning, the majority of the prior Pearl Harbor investigations harbored some reservations about Safford's claim – the major issue being that he was the sole source of the allegations about the intercept and subsequent cover-up.

In front of the Joint Congressional Committee, though, Safford's story was subjected to a thorough and skeptical scrutiny. In trying to defend his version of events, Safford proved to be his own worst witness. He certainly was done in by his lack of tangible evidence. But, more importantly, the changing nature of his narrative finally caught up to him, and the congressional investigators would jump on this. Worst of all for Safford, the Committee had access to his original letters to Kramer and the transcripts of his testimony before the preceding Pearl Harbor inquiries and boards.

What this evidentiary trail revealed was that for the past two years Safford had been changing significant details of his narrative of events at each hearing. More importantly, as we shall see, the cross-examination revealed that he had literally fabricated the text of the purported Winds Execute message of 4 December. He revealed that he had taken the code phrases in the original message of 19 November 1941 and then presented those phrases as the text of the purported Execute message. As he was questioned further, more revelations would emerge that would expose his story as a construct of conjectures, assumptions, and misunderstandings.

In recent decades, some writers have alleged that elements of the U.S. government went through enormous efforts, to include a major search of records, as well as "hostile" questioning, in order to discredit Safford's claims about the intercept and handling of the Winds Execute message.⁵⁵ Yet this interpretation is simply wrong for two reasons. First, the congressional hearings gave Safford the best platform from which he could make his case publicly. If he passed the cross-examination, then his case was solid. However, his position withered quickly as his testimony and evidence were challenged and found wanting.

Secondly, the writers miss the point that Safford's standing within the American cryptologic community commanded such respect that when he charged that a Winds Execute had been intercepted, it had to be investigated completely. The cryptologic and intelligence offices of both the Army and Navy took Safford's claim seriously and combed all of the relevant records looking for any substantiating evidence. Safford even received help from other navy officers to conduct his own search prior to the congressional hearings.[56]

Another aspect of this records search, which is often overlooked, is that both the army and navy already had conducted searches for relevant evidence about the Winds Execute *a full year prior* [our italics] to the congressional hearings. In September 1944 the navy conducted a search of its records for any material concerning an "'execute' to the so-called '"Winds" message," but found nothing. This search, by the way, was done in response to a memorandum from Captain Safford.[57]

The S.I.S. conducted its own search; again it was done more than a year before the congressional hearings. That service organized a thorough review of its records beginning in late September through October 1944 by order of then Colonel Carter W. Clarke as part of his review of classified records handled prior to Pearl Harbor. A team of five people combed all records and found nothing to support the contention that a Winds Execute message had been intercepted and processed. An index of pertinent translations of Japanese was drawn up and studied. Like the navy search, nothing could be found to validate Captain Safford's claim.[58]

For this review of Safford's version of what happened, it will be simpler to separate the events into four parts: the intercept of the Winds Execute message; actions taken in the immediate aftermath; who saw the intercept or its translation; and the matter of the missing or destroyed records.

The Intercept of the Winds Execute Message

Before any discussion of whether there was an intercept of the Winds Execute message can begin, there exists the problem with Safford's recollection of which navy monitoring stations had been tasked to listen for the transmissions. In his February 1946 memorandum to the Joint Congressional Committee, Safford stated that he, or Commander George Welker, chief of the section responsible for actual intercept (OP-20-GX), had sent TWX tasking messages to the Navy's monitoring stations at Bainbridge Island, Washington, and Cheltenham, Maryland, to listen for Japanese Morse broadcasts. He added that he might have sent the instructions to other stations, though he does not name any specifically. However, in the same statement, he mentioned that another site, Winter Harbor, Maine, was listening for these broadcasts. He also included citations from those three stations monthly reports as evidence that they were listening to broadcasts. [**Exhibit #40, pages 233-4**]

The problem with Safford's statement is twofold. First of all, in a statement from 4 December 1945 Safford averred that he had sent tasking by TWX to five navy sites, including the earlier mentioned Bainbridge Island and Cheltenham along with Winter Harbor, Jupiter, Florida, and Amagansett, New York. In his testimony before the congressional hearings, he reaffirmed that these five stations were indeed listening for the broadcasts, though in his statement, he mentions only three sites. The contradiction may seem minor, but, within a span of three months, Safford had offered three different lists of stations.

The second, and much graver problem, was that when the monthly reports of the sites were examined, there was no record of any tasking being received from Washington, D.C., except for Cheltenham and Bainbridge Island. Statements from the radiomen in charge of operations at Cheltenham, Winter Harbor, and Jupiter indicate that they never received any tasking for the Winds message.[59] Their position is correct inasmuch as they were never tipped off to the reason for the special tasking – the Winds message. Those monthly reports from the stations at Cheltenham and Jupiter that Safford submitted as evidence of his special tasking, actually reflected the mission tasking of those sites *prior to* 28 November, such as the Japanese merchant marine broadcast (known as MAM) copied at Cheltenham and the Tokyo and Osaka broadcasts to Europe monitored by Winter Harbor.[60] Further, Lieutenant Commander George Welker had told Safford in a letter that he recalled no tasking specific to the Winds message was sent to the stations that OP-20-G controlled.[61]

Safford's statement indicated that the Winds Execute message was intercepted by Cheltenham shortly after 8:00 AM (EST) during a broadcast by Japanese station JAP. The intercept was then quickly sent in by teletype to the OP-20-GY watch section within a half hour. **[Exhibit #40, pages 229-241]** Safford also wrote that an unnamed watch officer first had shown the intercept to Lt. Kramer. According to Safford's account, Kramer underlined the important code phrases – all three were present in the text – and wrote in pencil "free" translations which were "War with England" (including the Netherlands East Indies), "War with the U.S.," and "Peace with Russia." Kramer came into Safford's office and said, "Here it is." **[Exhibit #40, page 240]**

Safford's account of the time of the intercept contradicted virtually every prior statement he made. In his second letter to Kramer, Safford wrote that the "Weather Report" was broadcast at 4:30 AM (EST) on either 4 or 5 December 1941. In front of both the Hart and Hewitt hearings, he indicated that the intercept occurred on the evening of 3 December and had been sent to Washington that evening when Kramer had verified the text.[62] By the time of the congressional hearings, Safford had settled on 8:00 AM, 4 December, as the time of intercept. Why he had done so, as he explained to the Committee, was that just two weeks earlier he had reviewed monthly reports from the sites at Winter Harbor and Cheltenham. He had seen information in the reports which allowed him to postulate when the Winds Execute might have been intercepted and by which station. Safford never detailed what he saw, but information in his statement suggests that he had noted that, according to his calculations, both stations could have heard the Japanese broadcast station with the call letters "JAP," one of the stations he earlier had speculated might broadcast the Winds execute. **[Exhibit #40, page 251]**

Yet this statement only exacerbated Safford's problem because his postulated time of intercept left him with only the *possibility* it was heard by either Winter Harbor or Cheltenham. In his statement of 1 February, he had confidently asserted that Cheltenham had intercepted the Winds Execute. But here the weight of his previous testimony bore down on him. In his January letter to Kramer, Safford had written that the message had been heard by both Cheltenham and Winter Harbor. But, later in his statement to the Hart Inquiry, he left out any mention of the intercept site. (Safford claimed that Admiral Hart thought the information "irrelevant.") Before the Naval Court of Inquiry Safford did not name a station.[63] In front of the Hewitt Inquiry, Safford said he did not know what station actually intercepted the message, but "guessed" that both sites had the better facilities for monitoring for the broadcast.[64]

Yet even Safford's guess could not hold up to scrutiny. In fact, the navy had interviewed the radiomen-in-charge of the Cheltenham and Winter Harbor stations, D.W. Wigle and Max Gunn, and both deposed that their sites had not intercepted such a broadcast as the Winds Execute.[65] Finally, during the congressional hearings, only a day after he presented his statement with the confident assertion that Cheltenham had heard the Winds message, Safford was forced to admit to the Committee counsel that there was no evidence that "Cheltenham got that message."[66] His Cheltenham claim was based solely on a conjecture that Cheltenham theoretically could have heard a broadcast by station JAP.

As for the action inside the OP-20-GY office spaces when the message supposedly arrived, Safford's version of those events came under considerable correction from the very people he had named as participants. In his 1 February statement, Safford did not name the watch officer who brought the intercept to Kramer. However, from as far back as early 1944, Safford had claimed that at least one of the GY watch officers was a witness to the existence of the Winds Execute message. In his January letter to Kramer, Safford insisted that one Lt. Allan Murray recalled the message, while either Kramer or another watch officer, Lt. Francis M. Brotherhood, brought the message to him. In front of the Hart Inquiry, Safford had stated that Brotherhood was on watch on the evening of 3 December when the Winds execute arrived. Before the Naval Court of Inquiry, Safford said that Lt. Murray or "possibly Kramer" had come in with the yellow teletype sheet and said, "Here it is."[67] When the congressional counsel asked Safford about the discrepancy in his story, he stated that he had testified that Brotherhood had brought him the message since that officer had told him the message had come in.[68]

However, when Murray and Brotherhood testified to the Hewitt Inquiry, they denied they had delivered such a message. Brotherhood recalled the FCC mistaken intercept of the evening of 4 December and that he had notified Admiral Noyes that same evening. Murray stated that he was the watch officer for the day shift for both 4 and 5 December. His watch ran from 8:00 AM to 4:00 PM. He told the Inquiry that he would have been aware if any such Winds Execute had arrived at the time described by Captain Safford, but he stated no such message came in.[69]

Alwin Kramer testified before the congressional committee for almost four days. His version of events differed decidedly from Safford's. He recalled that the incident occurred on 5 December. He had been handed a short piece of teletype paper with about two or three lines of Japanese text, not the two hundred words Safford recalled. He could recall the text in detail, but he said that there was only one phrase on it. He never underlined it or translated the phrase. Nor would he have used the word "War," since the instruction messages never used that word, rather the Kana phrase WAGAHOO NO GAIKOO KANKEI KIKEN NI HINSURU [**Exhibit #7**], which was translated as "our foreign relations are approaching danger." He added that he had looked at the paper for only about ten to fifteen seconds. He could not recall whether he had entered Captain Safford's office. He never saw that strip of paper again.[70]

Kramer's testimony leads into the serious question of exactly what the contents were of the Winds Execute message that Safford believed existed. Recall that Safford stated that all three phrases appeared in the message. (Safford in his statement referred once to codewords – a misleading expression. He later referred to code phrases in his statement and always "phrase" in his testimony.) He said that the phrases occurred during a Morse broadcast. Safford maintained that the Winds Execute message did not have to be sent in a Voice broadcast. [**Exhibit #40, page 10**] That was true, but it is not the entire story. According to the instructions in Japanese message No. 2354, the format for the Winds Execute in the General Intelligence (Morse) Broadcast was the repetition of a single codeword – HIGASHI, KITA, or NISHI – five times at the beginning and then at the end of the broadcast. The code phrases were to be used in the *voice broadcast*. Yet, according to Safford, the code phrases, intended for the voice broadcast, appeared in the Morse broadcast. Even more, Safford could not verify if the format was correct and if the phrases had been repeated at the end of the purported broadcast of 4 December.[71]

As far back as his second letter to Kramer, Safford had admitted that the format of the Winds Execute was "not right." Yet he could never explain why, after the Japanese *Gaimusho* had established two discrete formats for warning messages intended for its diplomats, it would then send the warning phrases on the Morse broadcast when it previously had set up a format with single codewords?

Safford also had claimed that the phrase regarding relations with the Soviet Union, KITA NO KAZE KUMORI meant "Peace with Russia" (or "No War"). In testimony to the Congressional Committee, Safford added that it had been believed that " 'no war' would be no mention [of the phrase], but they [the Japanese] gave a positive, specific mention as to Russia, but in a negative sense, which we concluded meant peace, or not war as yet."[72] This interpretation was totally opposite the meaning set out by the Japanese message No. 2353, in which it is stated explicitly that the phrase meant that relations were approaching a dangerous point. The absence of the phrase from the broadcast was the true "negative" meaning, that is, no danger to relations.

Yet Safford's odd interpretation of the phrase KITA NO KAZE KUMORI was not new. Back in his second letter to Alwin Kramer, Safford had stated that there was a "negative form" of the phrase for Russia, KITA NO KAZ KUMORI (North Wind Cloudy). He said that this "form" was the phrase KISHI NO KAZE HARE. But this "negative form" phrase actually was the warning phrase for relations with Great Britain, which translated to "West Wind Clear." In later testimony, he would change his explanation of the format for his so-called "negative form." Before the Hart Inquiry in April 1944, he stated that this "negative form" was KITA NO KAZE KUMORI, which meant, according to Safford, "Neither North Wind or Cloudy."[73] Clearly, this translation of the phrase is not supported by the text. During the June 1945 Hewitt Inquiry, Safford again was challenged on this point, but he managed to avoid a direct answer by just restating that KITA, or "north," was the "negative form."[74]

Safford's confusion over the meaning of the code phrase for Russia revealed the fundamental discrepancy at the heart of his claim. It was this: In early 1944, as Safford began to construct his claim about the Winds Execute message, he realized he could not recall any of the text of the purported Winds Execute message of 4 December, including what open code phrase, or phrases, had appeared in it. In fact, it was in Kana and he could not read it. Therefore he had to reconstruct the entire message, specifically the code phrases. To do so, he simply *appropriated the three phrases from the 19 November message No. 2353 and then misrepresented those phrases to the Hart Inquiry (April 1944) as the actual text of the Winds Execute message.* Exactly what text he recalled and what he added, Safford was unclear. He revealed this ploy before the Army Pearl Harbor Board. On 2 October 1944, during his testimony, this exchange occurred:

> **General Russell. Now let us turn back to the message. From what source did you obtain these Japanese expressions or words which are found in your evidence given to Admiral Hart?**
> **Captain Safford. I got those from the messages setting up the "Winds" code, plus my recollection of the events: that two came exactly as we expected them, that is one for America and for England, and also the negative form of the Japanese for "North Wind Cloudy." I do not know enough about Japanese to be able to give that from memory. I mean, I remember that it was exactly what we expected to get on those two occasions, and garbled up on the Russian business.**

General Russell. Then the memorandum from which you refreshed your recollection at that time you testified before Admiral Hart, as a matter of fact, was the code that you had discovered prior to November 28, 1941, [the release date of the translation of message No. 2353] and that you took that language from that Japanese code and compiled from recollection the message of December 4th and gave that to Admiral Hart as being the message of December 4th; that is the truth?
Captain Safford. That is correct, it being essential or the substance of what we were interested in, because there was a lot more which was just straight Japanese news, and I couldn't make head or tail of it.[75]

This exchange also enlightens the origin of the issue of the "negative form" of "North Wind Cloudy." If Safford insisted that all three phrases appeared in the purported Winds execute, then he had a paradox and that was the fact that Japan did not attack the Soviet Union in 1941. Therefore, according to the Japanese format, the phrase KITA NO KAZE KUMORI should not have appeared. So Safford needed to interpret the phrase for the Soviet Union in a completely different manner than the original Japanese meaning in order for it to have appeared in his "reconstructed" Winds Execute message. From then on, in order to portray his artificial Winds Execute message as valid, Safford had to claim that the KITA phrase meant "peace" not war with Russia, which flew in the face of the meaning the Japanese had assigned to it.

In essence, Safford, being unable to recall the full contents of the Winds message he imagined had been sent, simply appropriated the phrases from the set-up message of 19 November and then presented them as the actual Execute message.

Actions Taken in the Aftermath of the Winds Execute Message

Safford, in his prepared memorandum, stated that he had sent the original intercept of the Winds message to Admiral Noyes (Director of Naval Communications and Safford's superior officer) by a courier. Admiral Noyes' office was one floor up and directly above Safford's office. He told the courier to deliver it to Noyes and not to take "no" for an answer. Within a few minutes, Safford said he had received a report that the message had been delivered. Safford also stated that he was satisfied that Noyes had telephoned the "substance" of the message to the War Department, the "Magic" distribution list in the Navy Department, and the Naval Aide to President Roosevelt. Six or seven copies of the translation were sent to the War Department, though a "smooth" (or finished) translation was made in the Navy at that time. Safford added that he believed the Army had distributed the translation. Eventually, a translation was made with the serial number "JD-1 7001." Safford also added that two urgent messages went out from the CNO staff (OPNAV) to various naval facilities in the Pacific, which, in view of the critical situation, ordered the destruction of certain ciphers. **[Exhibit #40, pages 242-245]**

Again, like much else from Safford's statement, his previous statements and testimony contradicted his testimony before the congressional hearings about the distribution of the translation. In his statement to the Hart Inquiry as well as in testimony to the Naval Court of Inquiry and the Army Pearl Harbor Board, Safford never mentioned sending the intercept to Admiral Noyes. Instead he claimed that OP-20-G, his office, prepared the smooth translations and distributed to the appropriate navy offices such as the CNO, the Director of War Plans, intelligence, communications, etc. Copies were also sent to the State Department, the White House, and the War Department.

Safford stated that this widely disseminated translation had been given the serial of "JD-1, 7001" on 4 December, but when he had tried to locate it he discovered that serial had been cancelled with out any explanation. However, Safford was wrong about the missing serial being assigned to the translation. For one thing, he could not account for the fact that serial numbers subsequent to 7001 had been assigned to messages intercepted prior to 4 December. A list of Navy serial numbers showed, for example, serial number "7017" had been allocated to a Japanese diplomatic message to Washington that was intercepted on 2 December. The translation was issued on *3 December* – a full day before the purported Winds intercept. **[Exhibit # 45]**[76] In fact, when Safford testified to the Army Pearl Harbor Board, he had admitted that he had no direct evidence that JD-7001 was the serialized translation of the 4 December Winds message. At best, he said, there was only "circumstantial evidence." When pressed for a better explanation that serial "7001" had been issued on 3 December, a full day before his purported intercept of the Winds Execute message, Safford could reply only that "things sometimes got a little bit out as far as putting those numbers on was concerned."[77]

As for the flurry of warning messages sent out as a result of the arrival of the Winds Execute, Safford had some part in preparing two messages on 4 December sent out to naval bases in the Pacific that ordered the destruction of extraneous ciphers. What is remarkable about Safford's actions after the intercept of the Winds Execute was that he did nothing else. Yet in all of the retellings of his narrative, as far back as his statement to the Hart Inquiry in mid-1994, through to his memorandum to the Congressional Committee in early 1946, Safford emphasized that the Winds message meant war, or that Japan was committed to war. Before the Hart Inquiry he even went as far as to state "We [persons not further identified, but likely Naval Intelligence and OP-20-G] believed that the Japanese would attack by Saturday (December 6), or by Sunday (December 7) at the latest.[78] This remarkable sentence is echoed loudly in his 1 February 1946 memorandum that the Winds message "meant war."

For all the urgency that Safford evoked four years after the purported intercept, at the time he did nothing that suggested he saw the immediate danger of war. The two cipher destruct messages he referred to as being transmitted in response to the Winds warning, in reality, were drafted originally by Admiral Noyes' office and sent to the CNO for release. What is more telling, though, is that the CNO had sent out similar messages about code and cipher destruction the day before (3 December) and two days later (6 December). In fact, Safford's selected messages are just part of an ongoing effort by the Navy to remove potential compromises of excess cryptographic material.[79] There is no evidence that the alleged Winds Execute had any connection to this series of messages.

As for the warning message that Captain McCollum supposedly was to send to the Pacific commands based on the purported Winds message, the record did not bear out Safford's claim. When the Congressional Committee asked him about the warning message, McCollum explained that on 4 or 5 December, he drafted a message to the Pacific commands that highlighted recent intelligence that suggested, or indicated, that the Japanese might initiate hostilities very soon. He said he took the message to his superior and then on to Admiral Wilkinson, Chief of ONI. Wilkinson said that it had to be approved by Admiral Richmond Turner, the head of the War Plans Division, who was responsible for drawing such conclusions from intelligence. According to McCollum, Turner edited the warning parts of the message and then showed him the warning messages already sent to Admiral Kimmel. McCollum took the edited message back to Wilkinson, who told him to leave it. McCollum added that the message was not sent. But this was not unusual, he added. Many dispatches had gone unsent; that was the prerogative of his senior commanders.[80]

When asked directly whether the draft dispatch was related to the Winds Execute, McCollum stated that Safford was misinformed. He added that Safford's claims that the drafted message had a reference to the Winds message and that McCollum had wanted to avoid another Port Arthur (a reference to the surprise attack by Japan on the Russian Pacific Fleet in 1904) were untrue because there was no such Winds message in the first place. When Safford was confronted with McCollum's denial, he insisted that he had been in Admiral Noyes' office when Wilkinson brought in the message. Safford recalled looking its several pages over and seeing the reference to the Winds execute. When told that McCollum had stated that the draft message was about one-half a page, Safford could only claim he had seen a multipage one.[81] Safford said that he had phoned McCollum late on 3 December and pointedly asked him if he was going to send a warning to the Pacific Fleet.[82] But this exchange occurred a day *before* the purported Winds Execute intercept. Safford also admitted that he had never spoken to McCollum after that time; he had assumed that McCollum had seen the Winds message.[83] Admiral Wilkinson stated that there had been a draft message that both McCollum and Turner had decided it was not necessary to send out. But Wilkinson added one interesting note during his testimony: that another such message was contemplated when word of a Winds message first came in, but was dropped once the report was proven false.[84] This placed the incident on 5 December and tied it in with the mistaken FCC intercept.

While Safford was limited in what messages he could send out, certainly he could have drafted some notice to all involved naval monitoring sites, and to those of the army and FCC as well that the Winds message had been intercepted. Yet in his memorandum he records no other action. In an earlier memorandum to the Hewitt Inquiry, (14 July 1945) Safford stated that this very issue of alerting monitoring stations to the intercept had come up. He added that, after discussions with the head of intercept operations, Lieutenant Commander George Welker, it was decided not to order a cessation of the collection of Japanese broadcast because of the chance that the "hidden word/STOP" message might be sent.[85] Interestingly, though, Safford did not mention this story in his statement to the Congressional Committee. There is a good reason: in a letter to Safford in January 1946, Welker told him that he could recall nothing of a Winds message ever being intercepted or what was done afterwards with it.[86]

Finally, Safford's actions in processing the purported Winds Execute message seem odd in view of the prescribed division of effort between the S.I.S. and OP-20-G. Recall that the S.I.S. had responsibility for processing intercepted messages on even days. Yet on 4 December Safford did not inform the army that the message had been intercepted. In both versions of events that Safford told, whether he informed Admiral Noyes of the intercept or prepared translations of it, in neither case did he pass the intercept to S.I.S. to produce a translation as was required under the standing agreement. He kept it within the Navy offices. This action should be contrasted with that of Alwin Kramer, who, on 6 December, when notified of the arrival of an important Japanese diplomatic message – the fourteen-part message that ended negotiations – proceeded to call back in civilian S.I.S. analysts who had just left to go home for the day, to work on the decryption and translation.

The fact is that Safford, aside from some undetermined role in the preparation of two messages to Pacific installations ordering destruction of cryptomaterial, did nothing else in response when the purported Winds Execute message was intercepted, despite his later claims that he recognized that the appearance of the message "meant war."

Who Saw the Winds Execute Intercept or Translation?

As with all the preceding parts of Safford's story, his various lists of those "who knew" in some way or manner about the Winds Execute was a fluid affair with names on one list disappearing from another, while the nature of an individual's knowledge changed over time.

Safford's most recent list was one he presented to the Congressional Committee on 2 February 1945 that included twenty-six names (see page 65 for list). This list was a copy of the one that had been prepared earlier for the counsel of the Hewitt Inquiry, Commander John Sonnett, on 14 July 1945. He explained that these people "knew in December 1941 that the Winds Execute message had been broadcast from Tokyo on 4 December, although some of them did not learn about it until after the attack on Pearl Harbor."

Yet when the Congressional Committee's counsel pressed Safford for more information about the names, he was less certain about them. For example, during the 2 February 1946 session, immediately after he read the names of the twenty-six people who he claimed knew about the Winds message, Safford was asked who on the list actually saw the message or translation. At first Safford said that the named individuals had "seen or been told about it." A committee member asked him again if he could verify that the people on the list saw the message. Safford backtracked and said that, except for Captain Alwin Kramer, "I have no knowledge that any of these people saw it."[87]

Of the twenty-six individuals named by Safford, twenty-two testified or deposed under oath before the many hearings that they had no knowledge of the Winds Execute message being intercepted before 7 December. (One, Colonel John T. Bissell, was mistakenly identified by Safford as General Clayton T. Bissell.) Some recalled that a mistaken or "false" Winds message had come in the week prior to Pearl Harbor.[88] Many of the witnesses said that they had learned of the Winds message only recently from reading the papers. No wonder, since prior hearings had been held *in camera* and many of these individuals had not been asked to testify. At least one later writer tried to transmute these truthful statements into a lie by implying that the common response about the newspapers appeared to have been scripted.[89] But this aspersion could not hold. If there had been no Winds Execute, how else could these witnesses learn about it but through the papers or hearsay?

As for the four witnesses that the Congressional Committee did not interview, two, Welker and Chief H.L. Bryant, previously had responded by letter to mailed inquiries from Safford in which he asked them about the Winds message. Both Welker and Bryant wrote back to Safford that they never knew of such a message being intercepted.[90] Interestingly, both had replied to Safford before he had supplied their names to the committee. As for Commander Parke, Safford noted before the Hart Inquiry that he had only second-hand knowledge of the message. General Olmstead, at the time the Army's Chief Signal Officer, had been in Panama on an inspection trip from about 2 or 3 December until 20 December.[91]

Two days later, Safford was asked about the claim in his letter to Kramer that there were other unnamed people with knowledge of the Winds message. The line "No one in OPNAV can be trusted," was read to him. A senator asked him to supply the names of those he knew in OPNAV with knowledge of the message. Safford refused, announcing, "I would prefer not to answer." The committee then queried him about the line, "Premature action would only tip off the people who framed Admiral Kimmel and General Short." Safford replied that he did not know who framed the two officers. He added that he was "referring to the War and Navy Departments in general, but not to any specific individual I can identify."[92]

In his letter to Kramer of 22 January, Safford mentioned he had a list of fifteen reliable witnesses. When the committee asked him to name these people, Safford told them that he had given the list to the Hart Inquiry, but at this moment could not recall one name from the same list. Grilled more about this list, Safford admitted that of the fifteen, eleven would no longer "make the same statements as they did two years ago." Only four – Alwin Kramer, Colonel Moses Pettigrew, Colonel Rufus Bratton, and Colonel Otis Sadtler – could give him (Safford) some support if not complete support. As it turned out none gave him support. By the time of the Hewitt Inquiry, Kramer had already substantially reversed his version of events that once had seemingly supported Safford. (See section about Kramer, page 77.) Pettigrew, who was the executive officer of G-2 at the time of Pearl Harbor, recalled that he had been told on 5 December about a "Winds Code" and that subsequent to this, a message had been sent to the Army G-2 in Hawaii to get in touch with Commander Rochefort about the Winds.[93] Bratton and Sadtler testified that they had reacted to the "false" Winds on 5 December. They had received notice of a possible Winds message from Admiral Noyes on the morning of 5 December, but it had turned out to be wrong. Colonel Sadtler could not have known about the purported Winds message until 5 December since was out of his office the day before. He was attending a meeting of the Defense Communications Board.[94]

The Matter of Missing or Destroyed Records

Safford had made the charge of missing or destroyed records an important part of his allegation. It already has been demonstrated previously in this chapter that the so-called missing translation of the Winds execute, "JD-1, 7001," was, in fact, assigned a day before the purported intercept of the broadcast. So it was not, as Safford believed, the serial of the translations of the Winds Execute message. The cancellation of the serial was irrelevant.

Another major charge by Safford, which came out in the Hewitt investigation, was the statement that General George Marshall had ordered the destruction of all records related to the Winds message. Safford maintained that William Friedman sometime before the Hewitt Inquiry had told him this story.[95] When confronted by the Congressional Committee counsel as to who told him and who else might know about Marshall's order, Safford could tell the counsel only that he had never had any conversation with anyone other than Friedman about the alleged order from Marshall. Safford also was unaware of the findings of the Clarke investigation, which had already reviewed the basis for the charge and had found no evidence supporting it.[96]

The Clarke investigation had reviewed this incident in detail and had followed the chain of the hearsay back to its alleged source. When Colonel Clarke asked Friedman from whom he had heard this story, he said Colonel Otis Sadtler had told him this. Sadtler, in his turn before the investigation, said Colonel Ike (Isaac) Spalding, head of Army G-1, or Personnel, at the time had told him[97] Spalding told the investigation that he had been told the story about Marshall's order by Colonel John T. Bissell, head of Army counterintelligence at the time. Bissell had said that certain army intelligence papers or files had been destroyed after Pearl Harbor.[98] When Bissell testified to the Clarke Investigation, he said that this was not true. He had no access to communications intelligence material from the S.I.S. He did recall that the draft version of the message from G-2 to Hawaii about the possibility of sabotage had been destroyed shortly after Pearl Harbor.[99]

As for Safford's claim that all the records of Cheltenham were missing, this, too, was demonstrated to be false. What Safford did not realize was that the navy's standard procedure called for the periodic destruction of outdated or extraneous material at field stations. Far from being the exception, Cheltenham, like all other sites, had burned such records regularly. Cheltenham's records from late 1941 had been destroyed in December 1942. [**Exhibit #49**][100] The copies of intercepted messages, reports, and logs from Cheltenham had been shipped to Washington and were available for review.[101]

In fact, Safford was being disingenuous when he insisted the records had been destroyed. A Lt. George W. Linn, who had been one of the OP-20-G watch officers during that period – in fact, he was the senior officer of the watch and spent daytime working hours in the GY office area and was present on 4 and 5 December – assisted Safford in his search for record evidence to support his contention. As Linn recalled, Captain Safford had decided to search station intercept logs for a copy of the execute message. He believed that some station had heard it and this would be reflected in the logs. As Linn recounted, Safford worked out the possible broadcast times and frequencies and the monitoring stations that might have heard them based on his own estimates of the local propagation conditions. Linn would then retrieve *the microfilm records and check the station intercept logs* [our italics]. He found nothing. Still, Safford believed that Cheltenham had heard the message.[102]

Some Observations on Captain Laurance Safford

With all of the skepticism that greeted Safford's claim about the Winds Execute message at the congressional hearings and the reservations expressed about it by some of the preceding inquiries, as well as his continued inability to produce any supporting evidence after a two-year search, it is probably fair to ask why Safford stubbornly persisted in his claim? One observer, George Linn, noted that Safford was not "pleased" with the lack of progress in convincing the various boards and inquiries of his case.[103]

There is evidence that Safford believed that Admiral Kimmel was being treated unfairly and blamed totally for the Pearl Harbor disaster. Certainly Safford was not alone in his conviction; many fellow officers believed Kimmel was a scapegoat for the failure in the Roosevelt strategy in preventing Japan's attack. Interestingly, Safford admitted to the Congressional Committee on 6 February 1946, initially he was very "bitter" towards Admiral Kimmel for failing to take measures to alert Pearl Harbor to a Japanese attack, even more so since he believed the 4 December warning message from McCollum had been sent out. But after he learned of the unsent message, the object of his bitterness turned, as he said, to the men in the Navy Department and himself. Now he felt it was important for him to do everything he could to help Kimmel.[104] Yet does this turn of heart explain Safford's persistence in the face of continued skepticism or reservations about his allegation or his almost libelous accusation that General Marshall ordered the destruction of relevant records?

Safford's conversion does not explain satisfactorily the lapses in his expertise in areas of radio signal propagation, collection, Japanese communications procedures, and the information available in the Winds "set up" messages. Yet Safford seems to have shrugged off the obvious contradictions and technical errors that permeated his statement and testimony. To those outside the fields of communications and cryptology, Safford's claim may have appeared solid and technically based. Yet when the details of his narrative were examined, many were found to be wrong, or in the case of the "negative form" of the positive phrase for the Soviet Union, to be simply absurd.

It must be pointed out that Safford was not the unambiguously unselfish and solitary hero who struggled alone against a government-wide conspiracy to sacrifice Admiral Kimmel in order to cover up its knowledge of the impending attack on Pearl Harbor. Safford was not above trying to convince other witnesses they were wrong, as in the case of Lieutenant Brotherhood. He may have convinced Kramer against the latter's better judgment that an Execute message had been sent. But when Kramer changed his testimony, Safford portrayed his former colleague as "befuddled."[105] Safford also claimed that individuals, such as Chief Bryant and Commander Welker, knew about the Winds intercept, when, in fact, in private correspondence with him they explicitly had denied knowing anything about the message. Also, Safford readily passed along, without any effort to verify it, the charge that General Marshall had ordered the destruction of records dealing with the Winds message. Before and during the congressional hearings Safford had been in close contact with the minority (Republican) members of the Joint Congressional Committee. Admiral Kimmel's counsel had coached Safford on how to answer the committee members, especially the technique of answering any question without giving more information than for which he had been asked. This latter ploy was obvious during his testimony regarding who had seen the Winds message.[106] When everything about Safford's role in the Winds controversy is considered, he was, according to Henry Clausen, "a strange duck."[107]

The most damaging problem for Safford was that a major portion of his version of events and many of the details of his evidence continued to change over the two and half years from when he began his search in late 1943 through to his testimony before the various hearings on Pearl Harbor from 1944 to 1946. The glaring differences in events and details that marked Safford's testimony at each separate inquiry finally caught up to him when he appeared before the Congressional Committee. The malleable clay that was Safford's evidence was not the stuff upon which a solid case could be built.

In the final analysis, Captain Safford's "evidence" for the existence of a conspiracy to cover up the Winds Execute message simply failed to pass muster. He had not encountered such questioning in any of the previous inquiries or hearings. In those sessions, his testimony and claims were accepted, usually with only queries designed to elicit more detail. Under the cross-examination of the committee's counsels and its members, his case simply disappeared.

After its hearings, and in considering all the evidence from the prior investigations, the Joint Congressional Committee arrived at its conclusion about Safford's story, the existence of a Winds Execute message, and the importance of it all:

> .... it is concluded that no genuine message in execution of the code and applying to the United States, was received in the War or Navy Departments prior to December 7, 1941...it is believed that Captain Safford is honestly mistaken when he insists that an execute message was received prior to December 7, 1941. Considering the period of time that has elapsed, this mistaken impression is understandable.
>
> Granting for purposes of discussion that a genuine execute message applying to the winds code was intercepted before December 7, it is concluded that such fact would have added nothing to what was already known concerning the critical character of our relations with the Empire of Japan.[108]

The Case of Captain Alwin Kramer's Changing Testimony

Here the actions of Captain Alwin Kramer need to be addressed. Kramer's role in the Winds controversy is difficult to assess. Some critics find his recanting of earlier support for Safford a dark indicator of a deep and sinister undercurrent to the entire Pearl Harbor controversy. When Kramer had testified before the Hewitt Inquiry (May - June 1945), he changed the testimony he had given previously to the Naval Court of Inquiry (July – October 1944). Some writers have suggested that Kramer's recanting may have resulted from pressure from the Navy's hierarchy bent on destroying Safford and discrediting his testimony.

Kramer's changing testimony went like this. On 24 July 1944, in front of the Naval Court of Inquiry, Kramer testified that he had been shown a message on teletype paper by the OP-20-GY watch officer, either on 3 or 4 December. The message contained the phrase HIGASHI NO KAZEAME, which referred to the United States. But Kramer could not name the watch officer who had shown him the message. He could not identify what monitoring station had intercepted the broadcast; nor could he recall what Safford did with the copy of the text afterwards, though he assumed it was shown to Admiral Noyes. This vague recollection of events was the sum of Kramer's testimony supporting Safford's position that such a message had been received.[109]

Actually, this statement represented a complete change from his first position regarding the existence of a Winds Execute message. Recall, when Kramer responded initially to Safford's letter in December 1943, he had construed Safford's reference to a "Weather Report" to be, in fact, the "hidden word" or STOP message of the morning of 7 December 1941. He did not recall or refer to any Winds broadcast. In fact, it was not always clear to Safford exactly what Kramer might have seen or known. On 29 April 1944, when Captain Safford testified before the Hart Inquiry, he had not included Kramer's name on a list of officers who "recall having seen and read the 'Winds Message.'" Instead, Kramer's name was on a list of those officers who should have "some recollection of the Winds Message."[110]

When Kramer appeared before the later Hewitt Inquiry on the afternoon of 22 May 1945, he stated that he had had "no recollection" of the Winds message when it was first mentioned to him in early 1944. Here he was referring to Safford's second letter from the correspondence of December 1943 to January 1944. Kramer added that later he was given some details about the message. He never mentioned where these "details" came from, but it seems likely that Safford spoke to him. He recalled that a message had been received at the OP-20-GY operations center a few days before 7 December. He continued that he remembered showing it to Safford. When asked by the investigating counsel what the subject of it was, Kramer replied that it was a "winds code message." He could not recall the wording, though. Kramer added that he was "less positive of that now than I believe I was at the time." He said he could not recall any overt mention of the United States in the message, only maybe Great Britain.[111]

In front of the Congressional Committee on 6 February 1946, Kramer explained that he recalled that on the morning of 5 December 1941, he was shown a short TWX sheet with two or three lines of plaintext Japanese. He said he did not write on the sheet and that he never used the word "war" as a translation of the Japanese text. He said that he and the watch officer entered Safford's office. He testified that he might have said, "Here it is!" but could not remember. At any rate, he said he stayed no more than half a minute, after which Safford departed for Admiral Noyes' office. Kramer noted that subsequently he never saw that message again. In later testimony to the Committee, Kramer asserted that originally, he had confused Safford's reference to the "Weather report" with the "hidden message" when he and Safford had exchanged letters.[112]

As for the story Safford told in which both he and Kramer had reviewed the folder of decrypted messages for the Roberts Commission that contained the translation of the Winds Execute message, Kramer said simply he did not recall it happening that way. Kramer did remember that when such a folder was completed, Captain Arthur McCollum from the Office of Naval Intelligence had asked him about the erroneous first translation of the "hidden word" message. It was included in the folder, and Kramer told McCollum that the words "United States" should have been part of the correct translation.[113]

When the Congressional Committee asked Associate Supreme Court Justice Owen Roberts if he had seen a copy of the Winds message, Roberts denied having received any such thing during his hearings – he actually refused to review the folder of "Magic" material. He later admitted that when he had been queried about the message in a letter from the Committee he had confused that Winds message with a reference to a "wind blowing from the east" contained in the transcript of an intercepted commercial radiotelephone message from Honolulu to Tokyo by a Japanese merchant by the name of Mori who resided in Hawaii.[114]

During the hearings, some newspapers had reported that Kramer had been confined to Bethesda Naval Hospital for health reasons, that he was "beset and beleaguered" by the navy brass, and that he had been not allowed to have any visitors. The newspapers added in loud headlines that prior to the congressional hearings Kramer had "disappeared. As it turned out, though, none of these stories were true. Kramer had been in the hospital prior to the hearings. But, contrary to the press, he had been allowed visitors. He stated that he had received somewhere between six to eight visitors during the weeks he was in the hospital, including committee members Frank Keefe (R-WI) and Bertrand Gearhart (R-CA) who interviewed him about the Winds message.[115]

In addition, Safford had visited Kramer in the hospital, and over chocolates and chess they had discussed numerous topics, but nothing to do with Pearl Harbor or the hearings.[116] As for his supposed "disappearance," Kramer stated that he had been given permission to "subsist," or temporarily check out of the hospital overnight so he could stay with his wife who had arrived to visit him. Kramer noted in his testimony that no one at any time attempted to influence his testimony.[117]

Considering the permutations in his testimony and written record – the letters with Safford – it is obvious that Kramer, far from recanting his testimony, had returned to the same position that he had first stated to Safford in his letter of 28 December 1943. He remembered the "hidden word" message of 7 December (and even the incorrect first translation), but did not recall a Winds message of 4 or 5 December. In his initial response to Safford, Kramer had even corrected his friend, stating that the message was not as indicated – a weather message – but was the "one" he delivered on the morning of 7 December.[118] Whatever Safford later may have thought of the significance of the Winds message, it appears that, at the time of its purported intercept and translation, as well as even two years later, it made no impression on Kramer.

In a twist to this story, Admiral Kimmel, quite possibly tipped off by Safford regarding Kramer's upcoming testimony before the Naval Court of Inquiry in 1944, had written to Admiral William Halsey to have Commander Kramer write an affidavit about the Winds message and send him a copy. **[Exhibit #44]**[119] Kimmel believed that Kramer's statement would help exonerate him. In testimony during the congressional hearings, Kimmel claimed that if he had learned of the 4 December Winds message he "would have gone to sea with the fleet...and been in a good position to intercept the Japanese attack."[120]

However, Kimmel's assertion about his probable reaction to a Winds Execute message is difficult to accept. While he was not oblivious to the building crisis in the Pacific and had instituted some important precautions – prior to 7 December he had ordered a number of security measures in the fleet and had expanded aerial reconnaissance missions – he had failed to act directly to his intelligence staff chief's reports about the unaccounted for Japanese carriers and

Admiral Husband Kimmel

the unexpected communications changes by Tokyo's navy on 1 and 3 December. In fact, he had testified that certain of these actions had not unduly alarmed him.[121] It might be asked of Kimmel that if the Japanese Navy's unusual communications activities had not prompted him to act, why then would he have alerted the Pacific Fleet solely on a vague notice to Tokyo's diplomats of relations in danger?

What the Japanese Said about the Winds Execute Message

Based on the FCC and naval intercept, it is clear that the Japanese broadcast the Winds Execute message, specifically "West Wind Clear," on 7 December (8 December Tokyo time) 1941. Japanese sources, though, contradict one another as to what time that day they actually broadcast the phrase and what coded phrases were sent out over the airwaves. However, it is certain from the evidence that the message was sent only on that day and possibly into the next, considering the time zone difference.

After the war, military investigators for the Advance Headquarters, U.S. Army Forces Pacific, Tokyo, searched the extant records of the Japanese Broadcast Corporation and interviewed its employees regarding the transmission of any Winds messages. The American investigators discovered that most of the records of the corporation, like the records from most of the departments of the Japanese government and the branches of its armed forces, had been destroyed in the two weeks between Tokyo's acceptance of surrender terms and the arrival of the American occupation forces.[122] So the investigators concentrated on interviewing the corporation's employees about the coded Winds messages. They did this without revealing the source of their information – the Winds instructions derived from the decrypted messages Nos. 2353 and 2354 of 19 November 1941.

Initially, the Japanese radio station workers denied knowing anything about the Winds messages. Contrary to some assertions, these denials should come as no surprise. Many Japanese civilian government employees had heard rumors that Americans would execute "war criminals" and were afraid of revealing their participation, no matter how minor or tangential, in any prewar government activities. This fear was common among many Japanese intelligence officials and cryptologists.[123] But when confronted with copies of the 19 November tasking messages, again, without being told their source, the Japanese admitted that such a code phrase was sent, but not until 8 December and that the message was most likely sent on an overseas broadcast sometime after 2:30 AM, 8 December 1941, Tokyo time (7:00 AM, Honolulu and 12:30 PM, Washington).[124]

One employee, who was stationed in Rangoon, Burma, during late 1941, told investigators that he had heard the signal on the voice broadcast on 8 December at 6:30 AM (9:30 AM Tokyo time and 2:00 PM, 7 December, Honolulu). Upon further questioning, he stated that he had heard only one coded phrase, which he could not specifically recall, but he believed it to have applied only to Japan's relations with Great Britain.[125] The broadcast time that he remembered was a little over six hours after the attack on Pearl Harbor. This recollection coincided with the time the FCC monitors heard the two stations broadcast "West Wind Clear" between 12:00 and 1:00 AM, 8 December, GMT (7:00 PM, Washington; 1:30 PM, Honolulu).

During this same period, representatives from the U.S. Navy Technical Mission to Japan interviewed Shinroku Tanomogi, the chief of the Overseas Department of the Japanese Broadcast Corporation. [**Exhibit 35**][126] He told his American questioners that at 4:00 AM on 8 December (8:30 AM, 7 December, Honolulu) he had received a call from the Information Bureau of the cabinet that Japan was at war and therefore scheduled programs would have to be rearranged to handle government communiqués.

When the Americans asked Tanomogi about a Winds weather broadcast being sent at 1500 hours (3:00 PM), he said he had a "vague recollection" that there had been one among the reports being readied for the news program. However, he added that he had not listened to any of the ensuing programs. The Navy report did not specify in what time zone the 3:00 PM reference occurred. If the investigator meant Tokyo time, then the broadcast would have been made six hours after the one heard by the FCC, or sometime around 1:00 AM, 8 December in Washington. If they meant Honolulu time, then the broadcast would have been within an hour of when the FCC station in Hawaii heard "West Wind Clear." But the time zone was not further identified. Tanomogi could not recall for his interlocutors if he had heard any coded Winds message.

In 1960, in an article in the United States Navy Institute *Proceedings*, Takeo Yoshikawa, the Japanese intelligence agent in Honolulu who had sent all of the reports about the Pacific Fleet and air defenses in Pearl Harbor prior to the attack, stated he had heard the Japanese National Broadcast give a special weather report on its program at 0800 (8:00 AM, Honolulu and 3:30 AM, 8 December, Tokyo) 7 December 1941. Yoshikawa said that he had heard the coded phrase "East Wind Rain," which was sent twice in the broadcast. He added, "That this meant that the imperial council in Tokyo had decided for war with the United States."[127]

Another employee of the Japanese Broadcast Corporation, Morio Tateno, though, disputed this version of events. Tateno claimed in an interview that he had read that same news broadcast with the inserted Winds coded phrase that Yoshikawa had heard, except that the phrase he read was not "East Wind Rain," but "West Wind Clear," the warning of a change in relations with Great Britain. [**Exhibit #46**][128]

Tateno asserted that he had been told at 2:00 AM (Tokyo time) to be ready to read a broadcast with a special weather report. However, he was not given the forecast until the 3:00 AM program. He said he read the phrase "West Wind Clear" twice during the 3:00 AM and 4:00 AM newscasts Tateno did not give the call letters of the station that broadcast the program, nor does he mention if any other broadcasts were made at his station or any others during the rest of the day. This lack of information about the broadcast station is important since the broadcast time and frequency would have determined what regions would have heard the transmission of the coded Winds message. While such a broadcast might have been intended for North America, it is just as likely it would have been beamed to Japanese facilities in Southeast Asia.

If Tateno's version of events were correct, then the news programs would have been heard in Honolulu at both 7:30 and 8:30 AM on 7 December. For Yoshikawa to have heard the program at 8:00 AM in Honolulu, it means the broadcast would have been made at 3:30 AM, 8 December in Tokyo. Tateno's version also conflicts with the reports of the Federal Communications Commission whose monitors in Hawaii and Oregon heard the Winds code phrase several hours after the attack, as well as the Navy officers manning the intercept site in Hawaii who heard it hours after the strike.[129] Tateno's version also conflicts with Tanomogi's narrative, which has the special communiqués arriving at the station about 4:00 AM (Tokyo time).

Even conceding that the Japanese might have sent a Winds Execute thirty minutes before the attack does not mean a warning could have been sent out by U.S. intelligence. Recall that there was no direct link from the coded Winds messages to any particular Japanese action or deadline. So the warning value was nil. But even if such a transmission had been heard, if we recall that it took hours before the news of the "mistaken" Winds message of the evening of 4 December reached the OP-20-GY watch center, then any intercept of 7 December would have taken hours to process, and then any warning would have arrived hours after the attack.

Still, regarding the evidence from Japanese sources, while some information was contradictory about the precise timing of the broadcast of the Winds code phrase, they all agree that none occurred before 7 December.

What the British and Dutch Radio Monitors Heard

The Americans had not been alone in scouring the airwaves listening for the Winds Execute message. It was known that the British and Dutch stations in Southeast Asia also had been listening for the Winds code phrases. Did they hear anything? The best evidence provided by the Dutch and the British indicated that neither had heard any transmission of the Winds Execute message prior to the attack on Pearl Harbor. However, two cases appeared that merited further investigation. One incident suggested there was some slight evidence that the British site in Hong Kong may have heard a Winds message at some point on 7 December. In another case, the Clausen investigation mistakenly concluded that such a message might have been sent days before Pearl Harbor.

In early November 1945, the Joint Congressional Committee considered the question of whether the British or Dutch may have heard the Winds execute message. On 5 November the committee requested that the U.S. Department of State query the governments of Great Britain, Australia, and the Netherlands if they had any records of the intercept of such a message. The next day the State Department sent a message to the U.S. embassies in London, England, Canberra, Australia, and the Hague, Netherlands, that the JCC was interested to learn if any of these countries had monitored a Winds Execute message between 19 November and 7 December 1941. The message also laid out the particulars of the Japanese Winds format and the code phrases and words. [**Exhibit #36**][130]

In mid-November the Australian Department of External Affairs reported that it had no record of such a broadcast, though it noted that not all Japanese broadcasts were monitored "verbatim." [**Exhibit #37**][131] Over the next six weeks, the American embassy in the Hague, Netherlands, similarly relayed three messages with the response from the Dutch that their Foreign Office could find no such records of any intercept of any such Winds Execute broadcast, though the note mentioned that the records of the East Indies government had been destroyed shortly after the Japanese attacked the Netherlands East Indies. [**Exhibit #38**][132] Safford pointed out in testimony to the Hewitt Inquiry that, in a private conversation with the former U.S. consul to the Netherlands East Indies, Walter Foote, he had been told that the Dutch radio intelligence unit had listened for, but had not heard, the Winds Execute message.[133]

The British Foreign Office, though, had a different story to tell. In its 4 December response, the British recounted that while no evidence of any such Winds message was received before the attack on Pearl Harbor, it noted that the station in Hong Kong relayed to Singapore a broadcast "by the Japanese that contained messages in code and which was received in Singapore six hours following the attack on Pearl Harbor." [**Exhibit #39**][134] The Foreign Office reported to the American embassy that the text of the "code" currently was unavailable, but could provide it if asked. There is no record that the committee asked for any further information from the British.[135]

The embassy in London did relay two further British responses on the matter. The first, dated 15 December 1945, merely stated that a Foreign Office "Japanese expert" had met with the embassy staff and repeated that no "such [winds] messages" had been heard prior to 8 December, but that the investigation was still ongoing. A final message from 31 January 1946 stated that the Foreign Office had completed its search and had "drawn a complete blank."[136]

What had happened at the British sites in the Far East was this. At about 8:10 PM (GMT or 2010Z; 9:40 AM in Honolulu) on 7 December 1941, the British intercept station in Hong Kong heard a broadcast that it reported as signifying that "[a] severance of Japanese relations? admitted imminent." [**Exhibit #51**][137] While the text of the actual intercepted broadcast is unknown, the vague wording of the Hong Kong report suggests it possibly was based on a Winds Execute code phrase – "West Wind Clear." A later history of the British Far East communications intelligence organization, *The History of HMS Anderson*, stated that it was the Winds broadcast that Hong Kong monitored and that references to both "East" and "West" were heard. (Singapore did not hear it due to "ionospherics.") The problem with this assertion is that this portion of the history was written without recourse to records, which had been destroyed when the FECB was shut down and withdrew from Singapore before its capture by the Japanese.[138] The actual message relayed from Singapore to London carried no statement as to whose relations with the Japanese were being severed. The most reasonable assumption was that this warning referred to Great Britain.

Interestingly, almost three hours earlier, Singapore had notified London of an intercept in which Tokyo had informed "all Consulates that relations between Japan and Great Britain *and United States* are critical." Singapore added that the message was derived from codeword[s] from table for warning telegram." This was a reference to the table of codes for the "hidden word" message.[139]

Singapore relayed the information about the severed relations intercepted by Hong Kong to London at 11:12 PM (GMT or 2312Z) on 7 December 1941. It was received in London at 1:13 AM (GMT or 0113Z) on 8 December 1941. The British had told the Americans at the London embassy in 1946 that the message had been heard six hours after the attack on Pearl Harbor. If we convert the time that London received the message to the time zones of Washington and Honolulu, then the broadcast was sent at 6:12 PM (Washington) and 12:42 PM (Honolulu) on 7 December, well after the attack. This time is within an hour and fifteen minutes of when the FCC heard the "West Wind Clear" code phrase.

But the British report was mistaken. The trouble was that Hong Kong had heard the broadcast at 8:10 PM (GMT or 2010Z). If we take this time as the correct time of the intercepted broadcast, then the concurrent times in Washington and Honolulu would have read 3:10 PM and 9:40 AM, respectively. Still, even with the difference accounted for, the intercept of the possible broadcast of the Winds Execute occurred more than an hour and forty-five minutes after the attack on Pearl Harbor had begun.

There was one more claim that the British may have heard a Winds Execute message prior to 7 December. This one arose during the investigation conducted by Henry C. Clausen, the counsel from the Judge Advocate General Division, for Secretary of War Henry Stimson from 23 November 1944 to 12 September 1945. During his investigation, Clausen had received some material from the British Secret Intelligence Service (S.I.S. or MI-6).

One of the items was a 3 December 1941 message from the S.I.S. representative in Manila, Philippines, Gerald H. Wilkinson, a businessman who worked for Theodore H. Davis & Company, to the S.I.S. agent in Honolulu, Henry Dawson. [**Exhibit #52**][140]

The message consisted mostly of intelligence about military developments within Indochina. Item "C" was the important point which caught Clausen's eye:

> **C. Our considered opinion concludes that Japan invisages (*sic*) early hostilities with Britain and U.S. *Japan does not repeat not intend to attack Russia at present but will act in South.* (our italics)**
>
> **You may inform chiefs of American intelligence and naval intelligence Honolulu.**
> **cc: Col. Bicknell, Mr. Shivers, Capt. Mayfield**[141]

Clausen, who had recently been cleared to view Ultra material as part of his investigations was curious about the source of information behind Item "C," that projected Japanese operations to the south while avoiding any action against Russia. Clausen was familiar with Safford's story, especially that the purported Winds Execute message also meant peace with Russia. Was the British statement based on ULTRA information, possibly either the Winds Execute message or any of Tokyo's orders to destroy codes?[142] The issue remained unresolved for Clausen in late July 1945. In his interim report to Stimson dated 1 August 1945, he had stated that British sources had never intercepted a [Winds] implementation message.[143]

Sometime in early August, Clausen interviewed Gerald Wilkinson and asked him about the source of intelligence in that passage from the 3 December message. Wilkinson had no idea; he merely passed along the information he had received. Clausen then queried the British government about the source. His question produced a response on 31 August from the GC&CS that stated "Colonel C[lausen] anxious to know basic source of Para. C of telegram of December 2nd [3 December in Hawaii], and in particular whether this was in 'special category.' In point of fact Para. C was based on a B.J. Wilkinson was unaware of source..." [**Exhibit #53**][144] A 'B.J.' stood for "Blue Jacket" and was the British shorthand way of referring to translations of decrypted diplomatic messages.

Armed with this reply, Clausen amended his previous interim report which then appeared in the Army's Judge Advocate General's Supplementary Statement of 12 September 1945. It read: "The source of this intelligence was a British intercept of a Japanese diplomatic message *which could have been based* (our italics) upon a Japanese execute message to the 'Winds Code,' or some equivalent message."[145] The Statement later repeated the comment, but referred to Clausen's finding as a "possible inference" that the Winds code would have formed the basis for the British Intelligence Service dispatch from London to Manila and then on to Honolulu.[146]

There was a problem, though, with Clausen's conclusion: the British message occurred well before the date of 4 December, when Safford claimed the Winds Execute had been sent. The Wilkinson message had been sent to Honolulu on 3 December, a full day before Safford's purported Winds Execute was heard. Furthermore, the information from Wilkinson probably originated in London. Either the GC&CS or MI-6 probably composed the message, which means that, at the very least, the intelligence was available no earlier than 2 December. This is what the congressional hearings concluded after reviewing the record of translations. The source of the British information most likely was a 1 December Japanese diplomatic message from Tokyo to Hsinking, China, that read in part, "great care shall be exercised not to antagonize Russia." [**Exhibit #54**][147]

The Winds Controversy Resurfaces: Ralph Briggs' Claim

The Winds controversy virtually disappeared after the conclusion of the Joint Congressional Committee hearings. Some of Safford's supporters kept alive his version, but the general trend for histories of Pearl Harbor written during the next three decades tended to relegate the matter of the Winds message to the role of a curiosity or a mistake on the part of Safford. But this was to change in the late 1970s with the appearance of another source that claimed there had been a Winds Execute message prior to Pearl Harbor, and, furthermore, this source actually had copied it. Within a few years the Winds controversy returned as part of a renewed interest in the charge that the Roosevelt administration conspired to cover up the disaster at Pearl Harbor.

The source behind this new charge about the Winds execute was a former OP-20-G intercept operator by the name of Ralph Briggs. Briggs was a veteran radio intercept operator, one of the first trained to copy Japanese Morse communications as part of the legendary OP-20-G "On The Roof Gang" (OTRG). In December 1941 he was a Morse intercept operator stationed at the navy monitoring station in Cheltenham, Maryland, about fifteen miles east of Washington, D.C. One of the targets he copied was Japanese Morse commercial and merchant marine broadcasts.[148]

In 1977 a navy historian interviewed Briggs. In the interview Briggs said that "On watch on the evening of the mid-shift of 4 December [which means he had begun work late on the evening of 3 December and finished his shift sometime between 4 and 6:00 AM on 4 December.]...I picked up [tuned in on his radio] on schedule the Orange [Japanese] weather BAMS broadcast circuit [merchant ship broadcast]...I soon discovered that I had copied HIGASHI NO KAZEAME, which in Japanese means "East Wind Rain." And also meant a break between the United States and Japan."[149]

Briggs stated that the intercepted message had been forwarded to the operations center (GY) at OP-20-G Headquarters in Washington via leased teletype line (TWX). Briggs added that he had sent the intercept to headquarters after telling his shift supervisor, whom Briggs never identified in his interview but referred to him only as "DW," had agreed to Briggs' decision over the phone.

In a 1986 article in a navy cryptologic veterans newsletter, *Cryptolog*, Briggs embellished his original story from the interview nine years earlier with more telling and provocative details. Briggs claimed that just a few days after he had intercepted the Winds message, Captain Safford had sent a "huge bunch of roses" with an attached note that read "Well Done." Attached to this bouquet was an envelope that contained a classified note from Safford that expressed his appreciation of the station's work.[150]

Briggs stroked the fires of conspiracy by claiming that in 1960, while stationed at the Naval Security Group (a successor organization to OP-20-G) records center in Crane, Indiana, he had reviewed the files of the Cheltenham station. When he checked the files for 4 December, he found they were missing. He said that he wrote a note on the daily intercept log for 4 December that, "all transmissions intercepted by me between 0500 (5:00 AM) and 1300 (1:00 PM) on the above date [of the log sheet for 4 December] are missing from these files & that these intercepts contained the Winds message warning code..." [**Exhibit #48**][151]

Briggs' claim was fresh fodder for the Pearl Harbor conspiracy advocates. When his story was added to Safford's old narrative, the result suggested that perhaps the Winds Execute message had been intercepted, processed, and disseminated throughout the Roosevelt administration. The lack of records could be credited to the conspiratorial cover-up performed by unnamed individuals at the behest of unknown leaders. Whatever gaps existed in the narrative of conspiracy could be filled in with insinuation and questions. It took only a few years for the books to appear with Briggs' story a new feature.

Two books appeared in the early 1980s that featured Briggs' story. These were John Costello's *The Pacific War, 1941-1945* (1981) and John Toland's *Infamy: Pearl Harbor and its Aftermath* (1982).[152] Costello discussed the Winds controversy in an appendix to his book. He averred that Safford's failure to convince people of the cover-up was due largely to his inability to get "backing of powerful [naval] flag officers."[153] Costello also referred to Briggs' statement that he had copied the Winds message in question. In the end, though, Costello backed off from claiming that a full conspiracy existed, adding that there was little evidence that the message had been sent, just the testimony of Safford and Briggs. But Costello left the matter tinted with a hue of suspicion when he wrote that the issue of the purported missing warning message suggests "the lengths most senior level officers in Washington might have been prepared to go to cover up what could be construed as a fatal omission in not passing on vital intelligence."[154] It is not clear if Costello meant the missing "Winds" message or the warning message Admiral Noyes was prepared to send to Kimmel, but did not send.

Toland, in his narrative of events, similarly rehashed all of Safford's charges, cloaking them in the fabric of a massive government-wide conspiracy. Toland added Briggs' dramatic wrinkles to the story, treating them as a major part of his narrative. In Toland's version, Briggs stated that he had been in contact with Safford during the congressional hearings. He had admitted he had copied the Winds message, and then offered to testify to this effect. However, according to Briggs, his commanding officer intervened and ordered him not to get involved. Briggs said that this order had originated from "someone" on the JCC staff.[155]

Seaman Briggs' story simply was too full of holes to hold up to much scrutiny. For one thing, he could not pin down the circumstances of his intercept of the Winds Execute message. In his interview, he said that he had worked the midnight shift from 3 to 4 December. Such a shift would have begun late on the evening of 3 December, probably 9:00 or 10:00 PM, or even as late as midnight. It would have ended around 5:00 or 6:00 AM on the morning of 4 December. Yet a few pages later in his interview, he says that all transmissions copied by him between 5:00 AM and 1:00 PM on 4 December were missing. This statement suggests that he worked sixteen straight hours across two shifts. Now, it was not unusual for navy intercept operators to work two eight-hour shifts in one day, but they were separated by a break of eight hours.[156] In fact, Briggs was working eight-hour shifts at Cheltenham, according to the log he supplied Toland.

Interestingly, for someone who claimed to have copied such an important message, he could recall no details of it. He could not explain at what time he copied the Execute code phrase, how long the transmission was, what station (callsign) sent it, or what frequency he heard it on. Briggs tried to claim that the station was transmitting somewhere between 13 and 15 Megahertz (MHz). Yet this is not near Safford's claimed frequency of 11 MHz and quite far from the 9 MHz on which the FCC heard the actual broadcast.

Briggs did say he heard the weather broadcast on what he called the "Orange" weather BAMS broadcast. BAMS was an acronym for the Broadcast to Allied Merchant Ships, a broadcast message system intended for all Allied merchant ships. What he really meant to describe what he was monitoring was the MAM. The MAM was a term U.S. Navy operators used to describe the Japanese merchant ship broadcast, which was similar in some ways to the "BAMS" system. One of the distinguishing characteristics of the Japanese system was that the trigraph "MAM" was used often as the general callsign for all Japanese merchant ships. The MAM system was a worldwide broadcast for Japanese merchant ships, which carried encrypted traffic, as well as shipping information such as notice to mariners and weather reports.

There may have even been regular transmission of short news programs in Morse sent to the ships.

However, Briggs' intercept story is contradicted by the Winds instruction messages. The code phrases and words were to be sent in a strict format. If they were to be sent in Morse, they would appear on the overseas commercial news broadcasts and only as a single word sent five times at the beginning and end of the broadcast. If the code phrases, such as HIGASHI NO KAZAME, were to be used, they would appear only in the voice broadcast. Most importantly, there was no provision in the instructions for transmission over the merchant shipping broadcast.

In his 1986 article, Briggs claimed that the mysterious "DW" could substantiate his claims. However, "DW" was no mystery man after all. He was D.W. Wigle, who, at the time in December 1941, was Cheltenham's radioman-in-charge of operations at the site. As mentioned previously in regards to Safford's claim that he had sent tasking to Cheltenham, Wigle had contributed a statement to the congressional hearings in which he stated that he had never received any tasking from OP-20-G to monitor for a Winds Execute message and that Cheltenham had no assignment to copy Japanese Morse news broadcast except on an opportunistic basis. Cheltenham's primary missions were German naval and European diplomatic communications. The lowest tasked mission was Japanese merchant marine broadcasts.[157]

The major problem with Briggs' statement was that, since he claimed to have copied just the one phrase, "East Wind Rain," this would have contradicted Safford's claim that *all three phrases* had been part of the broadcast. It would have been difficult to have Briggs testify, as Briggs' claimed Safford wanted him to do, if his story did not match Safford's. As for being ordered not to testify, the truth was that, if the committee had known of his story, it would have subpoenaed him to appear. The Republican members of the committee, especially, would not have let the opportunity slip by. The committee got whomever it wanted to appear. In fact, in one case, a former naval aide to President Roosevelt who was serving at sea aboard the USS *Indiana* at the time of the hearings was subpoenaed. He was flown back to Washington to testify.[158]

Finally, the fact that Briggs discovered that Cheltenham files were gone was not extraordinary at all. Most of the site's papers had been destroyed in 1942 as part of the standard destruction procedures for all noncurrent records.[159] In fact, all navy field sites had performed periodic destruction of noncurrent records during the war. Cheltenham's files from late 1941 had been burned in December 1942 [**Exhibit #49**][160] (Since 1941, the copies of the intercepted messages used in histories and as exhibits for the JCC Hearings have come from files located in OP-20-G headquarters in Washington. These files had been sent to Washington from the field sites. Station logs and other papers that were to be retained were shipped to the Navy's record facility at Crane, Indiana.)

Whatever Briggs had in mind when he came forward with his claim, in the end he could not support it with any concrete evidence. During his interview, he had stated that he had located the Cheltenham intercept log for 4 December at the Crane records facility. He said he had handwritten a statement about the missing files on the log. However, the log sheet he wrote on was the one for *2 December 1941*. That log indicated that he had worked the morning/day shift at Cheltenham from 5:00 AM to 1:00 PM that day. The log noted that he (identified by operator sign "RT") had copied press broadcast for the entire day and not the Japanese MAM broadcast as he had claimed. [**Exhibit #50**][161]

The Winds Execute: The Final Casting

There was a Winds Execute message. But it did not occur, as Captain Safford believed. We have seen that the message and the circumstances surrounding its "intercept" was fabricated. Safford could not recall the text of the illusory message, so he appropriated the three phrases of the Winds instructional message of 19 November and presented them as the authentic text of the Execute message. Of course, this manufactured message left him with a contradiction concerning the coded phrase for the Soviet Union, which he then tried to explain away with a convoluted reading of the original Japanese instructions.

At the same time, his claim that the navy site at Cheltenham, Maryland, intercepted the Execute message was based solely on his conjecture, which, in turn, was based on technical projections of possible propagation paths of these broadcasts and what East Coast station might have heard the transmission from certain Japanese broadcast stations. It has been demonstrated that Cheltenham, and all of the other East Coast sites, never received any tasking to monitor for the Winds Execute message. Nor had they monitored any Execute message, Ralph Briggs' unsupported and contradictory claims notwithstanding.

As for Safford's reaction to the arrival of the Winds Execute message, there was a major gap between what the record showed he did and what he later claimed he did, specifically authoring warning messages, or having seen such messages in draft form. In fact, he did nothing beyond assisting in some fashion with the drafting of messages to outlying U.S. Navy Pacific stations to destroy excess cryptographic material. It has been demonstrated that this series of messages was part of an ongoing set of messages that had begun to go out three days before the purported Winds Execute message was sent. There is nothing in the record, either from Safford himself or from any other person with knowledge of events that suggests such a message arrived and had an effect on subsequent actions.

There is evidence that the sum of the previous week's events had spurred Commander McCollum to draft a warning message to Pacific commands, but this message was not sent. Yet it had nothing to do with Safford's Winds Execute message. At the same time, the claim that Colonel Otis Sadtler drafted a similar message also fails to pass muster. As has been shown, Sadtler was reacting to the mistaken or "false" Winds message of the evening of 4 December. The impetus for Sadtler's message appears to have faded when the 4 December FCC intercept was revealed to have been a mistake.

Safford also claimed that either twenty-six or fifteen people, depending on which one of his lists one consulted, saw or had knowledge of his alleged Execute message. These two lists were largely complementary and did not include other individuals that Safford claimed in later testimony who also might have known of the message. The names on these lists, in fact, were the product of guesswork only, and were not based on direct knowledge of who might have had knowledge of the message, or saw it. His lists were projections based upon the standard distribution of "Magic" translations within the government at the time. Interestingly, individuals who saw the "Magic" translations regularly, such as President Roosevelt and Secretary of State Cordell Hull, were absent from his lists.

A Winds Execute message was sent on 7 December 1941. The weight of the evidence discussed earlier indicates that one coded phrase, "West Wind Clear," was broadcast according to previous instructions some six to seven hours after the attack on Pearl Harbor. At least one Japanese witness claimed the broadcast occurred perhaps a half-hour prior to the attack, but this cannot be verified anywhere else. It is possible that a British site may have heard the broadcast within one to two hours after the attack, but this only substantiates the anticlimactic nature of the broadcast.

In the end, the Winds Code never was the intelligence indicator or warning that it first appeared to the Americans, as well as to the British and Dutch. In the political realm, it added nothing to then current view in Washington (and London) that relations with Tokyo had deteriorated to a dangerous point. From a military standpoint, the Winds coded message contained no actionable intelligence either about the Japanese operations in Southeast Asia and absolutely nothing about Pearl Harbor. In reality, the Japanese broadcast the coded phrase(s) long after hostilities began – useless, in fact, to all who might have heard it.

Notes

1. Costello, 649; Toland, 215-220; Layton, 264-9; Victor, 69-74. See PHH, Part 8:3632-3638 for a sample of the questioning of Safford by the Joint Congressional Committee.

2. Colin Burke, *Information and Secrecy: Vannevar Bush, Ultra, and the Other Memex* (Metuchen, NJ: Scarecrow Press, 1984), 60-62

3. L.F. Safford, SRH-305, "The Undeclared War. History of R.I." (Fort George G. Meade, MD: 1984), 20

4. Ibid.

5. Prior to 1936, officers in OP-20-G, including its commanding officer, rotated regularly "back to the fleet." While this system was necessary for administrative purposes – to qualify for promotion required time in active fleet commands – it hampered technical and operational continuity. OP-20-G had civilian employees, but they rarely appeared in management, unlike in the S.I.S. where the civilians had administrative functions and maintained technical continuity.

6. Debrose and Burke, 46-9

7. PHH, Part 8: 3562-3575, 37111-12, 3717-18; Prange 223, 278-9

8. Benson, 43-44

9. Now SRH-305, see fn. 3. PHH Part 4: 1975, 20029; Part 8:3388-90

10. Ibid., 29

11. PHH, Part 26:393; also Gannon, 146-7. The Roberts Commission, chaired by Associate Justice of the Supreme Court Owen Roberts was given some radio intelligence material as part of its evidentiary search. But the main object of this first investigation was to determine if there had been any dereliction of duty by either the army or navy command. Not surprisingly, both Admiral Kimmel and General Short were criticized while the leadership in Washington received hardly a disparaging word.

12. "Documentary Evidence Re: Winds Execute message." L.F. Safford, 26 September 1944. NARACP, RG 457, Entry 9032, Box 1360, Folder 4217, "Pearl Harbor Miscellaneous Items."

13. PHH, Part 39:225-6

14. RG 80, CNO/Secretary of the Navy Correspondence Files; also CCH Series XII. S. Box22

15. "Safford-Kramer Letter[s]." NARACP, RG 80, Entry 167A, Box 4. Also, see PHH, Part 8:3698

16. Ibid.

17. Ibid.; Also see PHH, Part 8:3699-3700

18. Ibid.; also PHH, Part 8:3700

19. Ibid.

20. Ibid.

21. PHH, Part 34, 80-1

22. NARACP, RG 457, Entry 9032, Box1360, Folder 4217, "Pearl Harbor Investigation and Miscellaneous Material."

23. PHH, Part 39:21

24. PHH, Part 26: 387-95

25. PHH, Part 39: 224-6

26. PHH, Part 39: 291

27. PHH, Part 772-5

28. PHH, Part 39: 323

29. PHH, Part 39: 325

30. PHH, Part 39:341

31. PHH, Part 39: 351

32. PHH, Part 34: 2-71

33. PHH, Part 36:306

34. PHH, Part 34:76

35. PHH, Part 35:120

36. PHH, Part 35:116; Clausen, 70, 447-470

37. PHH, Part 39:403

38. PHH, Part 36:8

39. PHH, Part 1:2-3

40. "Signal intelligence Disclosures in the Pearl Harbor Investigation." SRH-154 (Fort George G. Meade, MD: National Security Agency, 22 February 1982), 39

41. Ibid., 40

42. This statement can be found in many places. NARACP, RG 38, Box 166, "Folders on the Winds Message," Folder 5830/69, "Statement Regarding Winds Message, by Captain L.F. Safford Before the Joint Committee on the Investigation of the Pearl Harbor Attack, 1 February 1946; also PHH, Part 8:3579-3591.

43. "Statement Regarding Winds message," 13; also PHH, Part 8:3586. The Port Arthur reference was to the surprise Japanese attack on the Imperial Russian Pacific

Fleet at Port Arthur, Liaotung Peninsula, in eastern China on 8 February 1904, which initiated the two-year Russo-Japanese War.

44. Ibid., 12
45. Ibid., 14
46. PHH, Part 36:69-70
47. "Statement," 15
48. Ibid., 20; AN-1 would later be notated as JN-25B in July 1942.
49. PHH, Part 8:3668-70
50. PHH, Part 8:3608-9
51. PHH, Part 8:3610
52. PHH, Part 8:3624. They were Lt. William C. Howes, Lt. Cmdr. Robert L. Densford, Lt. Cmdr. Frederick A. Peterson, Commander C.F. Clark and Lt. Cmdr. Paul R.White.
53. PHH, Part 8: 3652-3
54. PHH, Part 8: 3649
55. Costello, 649; Toland, 215-220; James Rushbridger and Eric Nave, *Betrayal at Pearl Harbor* (New York: Summit Books, 1991), 162-167; Victor, 152-157; for a sample of the line of questioning, see PHH, Part 8: 3632-3638
56. SRH-081, 5-7; Memorandum: "Pearl Harbor Investigation – comments on answers furnished by Captain L.F. Safford with his memo of 4 December 1945 to Op-20-4," 14 December 1945. RG 38, Entry 1030, Box 166, Folder 5830/69 (2 of 3) "Pearl Harbor Investigations: Winds Msgs"
57. Memorandum for Major General Clayton Bissell, AC of C, G-2, 28 September 1944. Subject: Pearl Harbor Investigation. NARACP, RG 457, Entry 9032, Box 878, Folder 2609.
58. Memorandum for Colonel Carter W. Clarke, Subject: Evidence re "Winds Execute Message," 30 September 1944. RG 457, Entry 9032, Box 1360, Folder 4217. Also, "The Winds execute Search," by Sam Snyder, T542, June 1981. CCH Series XII, S. Box 22
59. Memorandum: "Pearl Harbor Investigations – comments on answers furnished by furnished by Captain LF Safford with his memo. Of 4 December 1945 to OP-20-4, 14 December 1945. NARACP, RG 38, Entry 1030, Box 166, Folder 5830/69 (2 of 3) Enclosure C, 1; Also see SRH-210, "Collection of Papers Related to the "Winds Execute" Message, U.S. Navy, 1945, 50

60. "Intercept Station Assignments," (1941) RG 38, Entry 1030, Box 165, Folder 5830/62, "Pearl Harbor Investigations" (1 of 3)
61. PHH, Part 9:4009; also Part 8:3696
62. PHH, Part 8:3600; Part 26:394-5
63. PHH, part 8:3630
64. PHH, Part 36:74
65. "DW Wigle's Statement" and Max Gunn's Statement" 11 December 1945. RG 38, Entry 1030, Box 166, Folder 5830/69, "Pearl Harbor Investigations: Winds Msgs" (3 of 3)
66. PHH, Part 8:3630-1
67. PHH, Part 33:771
68. PHH, Part 8:3603
69. PHH, Part 36:87-90, Part 36:258-9
70. PHH, Part 8:3916-3924 and Part 9: 3934-37, 4212-14
71. PHH, Part 8:3604-5
72. PHH, Part 8: 3604
73. PHH, Part 26:394
74. PHH, Part 36:75-6
75. PHH, Part 29:2378
76. Memorandum, Subj: "JD-7001, Special Studies concerning." 8 November 1945. Also see memorandum from J.N. Wenger, Subject: Forwarding of Material Pertinent to Pearl Harbor." NARA CP, RG 38, Entry 1030, Box 166, Folder 5830/69 (2 of 3) "Pearl Harbor Investigations: Winds Msgs." The 8 November 1945 memorandum from Lt. Sally Lightle, who assembled the index, noted that in the JD-series there were a number of other "cancelled" numbers She added that reasons for canceling a message included the presence of duplicates, other parts of the same message with a different serial number, and skipped numbers.
77. PHH, Part 29:2373, 2377
78. PHH, Part 26: 394
79. PHH, Part 14: 1408-09; Part 33:893-895
80. PHH, Part 8:3387-9
81. PHH, Part 8:3669-70
82. Ibid., 3667; PHH, Part 26:392
83. Ibid., 3667
84. PHH, Part 4:1868
85. PHH, Part 8:3613
86. PHH, Part 9:4009; also Part 8:3696
87. PHH, Part 8:3612

88. PHH, Part 36:506-7; Part 16:2319-21; Part 35: 96-102

89. Layton, 269

90. PHH, Part 8:3887-92

91. PHH, Part 34: 83, 87-8

92. Ibid., 3723-4

93. PHH, Part 35:23-4

94. PHH, Part 29:2429-2433; Part 35:97-101, 141-144

95. PHH, Part 35:70-1

96. PHH, Part 8: 3727-9

97. PHH, Part 34:79-82

98. PHH, Part 34:91-2

99. PHH, Part 34:101-2; Prange, 263-5

100. Msg, 082034 November 1945, SUPRADST PT Lyautey to OP-20-G. Also see similar messages about records destruction from Stations "S," "M," and others in RG 38, Entry 1030 (CNSG Library), Box 166, Folder 5830/69, "Pearl Harbor Investigations: Winds Msgs" (Folders 1, 2 of 3)

101. PHH, Part 10:4741-3

102. SRH-081, 5-6; PHH, Part 36:85-7

103. SRH-081, 6

104. PHH, Part 8: 3859-60

105 PHH, Part 8:3606

106. Prange, *Pearl Harbor: The Verdict of History*, 326-8; see PHH, Part 8: 3725-3732

107. Clausen, 306-8

108. PHR: 486

109. PHH, Part 33: 853-4

110. PHH, Part 26:394-5

111. PHH, Part 36:81-2

112. PHH, Part 9:3950

113. PHH, Part 8:3920

114. PHH, Part 7: 3268-9. The *Mori* incident involved the intercept of a transpacific telephone call by the FBI on 5 December from a Japanese dentist in Honolulu to Tokyo that contained references to flowers in bloom and the strong wind blowing. For more see PHH, Part 3: 1456 and Part 10: 5102-8, inter alia, and Layton, 276-7

115. PHH, Part 9:3967

116. Ibid., 3964

117. Ibid., 3965-67

118. Ibid. "Safford – Kramer Letter[s]" 28 December 1943. NARACP, RG 80, Pearl Harbor Liaison Office, Entry 167A, Box 4.

119. Kimmel to Halsey Letter, 18 March 1944, Pearl Harbor Exhibit 150, NARACP, RG 80, Entry 167EE, Box 120; also RG 38, CNSG Library, Box 166, Folder 5830/69, "Pearl Harbor Investigation: Winds Msgs."

120. PHH, Part 6:2551-2

121. Layton, 238 and 242-44; PHH, Part 6:2621-24 *inter alia* for Kimmel's reaction to Layton's intelligence briefing. See Gannon, 164-7, for some of the heightened alert measures ordered by Kimmel.

122. For comments on the size and scope of the destruction, see Ed Drea, editor, *Researching Japanese War Crimes, Introductory Essays*. (Washington, D.C.: NARA Nazi War Crimes and Japanese Imperial Government Records Interagency Working Group, 2006), 9-11 and 23-25

123. Ed Drea, "Reading Each Other's Mail: Japanese Communications Intelligence, 1920-1941." *Journal of Military History* (Vol. 55, No. 2, April 1991), 185-206

124. Message, BSG 210, 211151Z November 1945, Commander-in-Chief, Advance HQ, U.S. Army Forces, Pacific, Tokyo to War Department. "Interrogation of Japanese Concerning Broadcast of 'Winds Execute Message,' October-November 1945." SRH-177 (Fort George G. Meade: MD, National Security Agency, 16 July 1982)

125. SRH-177, Message, BSG 219, Commander-in-Chief, Advance HQ, U.S. Army Forces, Pacific, Tokyo, to War Department, 30 November 1945. Also, see PHH, Part 18: 3308-9

126. U.S. Navy Technical Mission to Japan, Interrogation No. 11; personnel interrogated: Mr. Shinroku Tanomogi, 30 November 1945. NARACP, RG 457, Entry 9032, Box 1369, Folder 4217, "Pearl Harbor Investigation and Miscellaneous Material." Also see PHH, part 18:3310

127. Takeo Yoshikawa and LTC Norman Stanford, USMC, "Top Secret Assignment," *United States Naval Institute Proceedings* (Vol. 86, No. 12, December 1960), 27-29

128. Morio Tateno Interview, 30 June 1961. RG 38, CNSG Library, Box 166, Folder 5830/69, "Winds Msgs."

129. Forrest R. Biard, "The Pacific War Through the Eyes of Forest R. 'Tex' Biard," NCVA *Cryptolog* (Vol. 10, No. 2, Winter 1989), 5

130. NARACP, RG 59, 6 November 1945. 1945-49 Central decimal File, Box 3403, 711.94/11-645

131. NARACP, RG 59, 16 November 1945. 1945-49 Central Decimal File, Box 3403, 711.94/11-1645

132. NARACP, RG 59, 5 and 6 December 1945 and 26 January 1946. 1945-49 Central Decimal File, Box 3402, 711.94/12-545, 711.94/12-645, and 711.94/1-2646

133. PHH, Part 36:318

134. NARACP, RG 59, 4 December 1945. 1945-49 Central Decimal File, Box 3403, 711.94/12-445

135. PHH, Part 18:3312

136. NARACP. RG 59, 15 December 1945, and 31 January 1946. 1945-49 Central Decimal File, Box 3403, 711.94/12-1545 and 711.94/1-3146

137. COIS, Singapore, 2312Z, 7 December 1941. RG 80, Entry 167CC, Box 92, "Exhibit 1, " item "q," Clausen Investigation Exhibits.

138. Shaw, 12-13

139. COIS Singapore, 1746Z, 7 December 1941. RG 80, Entry 167CC, Box 92, "Exhibit 1," item "q," Clausen Investigation Exhibits

140. Manila to Honolulu, 3 December 1941. RG 80, Entry 167CC, Box 92, "Exhibit 1," Clausen Investigation Exhibits.

141. Ibid. Colonel George Bicknell, G-2 Hawaii Department, USA; Mr. Robert Shivers, Chief of FBI Field Office, Territory of Hawaii; and Captain Irving Mayfield, Intelligence Officer, 14th Naval District

142. Clausen, 113

143. PHH, Part 35:203

144. Ultra GOR 632 from GCCS 11279, 31 August 1945. RG 80, Entry 167CC, Box 92, "Exhibit 1," Clausen Investigation Exhibits.

145. PHH, Part 35:135

146. Ibid., 135; also RG 128, Box 334, Folder 114, "Army-Navy Miscellaneous," "Summary of Evidence on the Winds in the Army Proceedings."

147. MND Translation, Tokyo to Hsinking, S.I.S. # 25783, 1 December 1941, Translated 4 December 1941 RG 457, Entry 9032, Box 301.

148. Ralph Briggs was not the only navy intercept operator to claim he had intercepted the Winds Execute message. In 1988 a former OP-20-G officer claimed that in 1962 another sailor, a Lieutenant (j.g.) Thomas Mackie, had told him that, while attached to the Cast monitoring station at Corregidor in the Philippines, he had translated the phrase HIGASHI NO KAZE AME (East Wind Rain) "several days" before Pearl Harbor. However, Mackie stated that the phrase was heard in a "TOO(H) FUU U" format. The format is not further identified in the article, but the TOO FUU U is the phonetic Chinese rendering of the Kanji characters for "East Wind Rain." The expression goes as "East" (TOO) – "Wind" (FUU) – "Rain" (U). Mackie stated that at a meeting of the Cast station officers, all had agreed that since the phrase was not in the correct format, it would not be reported to Washington. See Jim Yandle, "Winds Intercept at Corregidor." NCVA *Cryptolog*, (Vol. 10, No. 1, Fall 1998), 1

149. SRH-051, "Interview with Mr. Ralph T. Briggs by the Historian Naval Security Group (Fort George G. Meade, MD: National Security Agency, 1977), 2

150. Ralph Briggs, "Lost Winds Execute Controversy. Briggs' Own Story." NCVA *Cryptolog*. (Vol. 8, No. 1, Fall 1986), 21

151. SRH-051. This document is also reproduced in John Toland, *Infamy: Pearl Harbor and its Aftermath* (New York: Berkeley, 1983). The original log, with Briggs' handwritten entry in red ink, is located in RG 38, Entry 1030, Box 165, Folder 5830/61, "Pearl Harbor Investigation: Miscellaneous Japanese Intercepts From Stations M, J, and G, November - December 1941."

152. In Toland's book see 203-8 and 337-8. For Costello, see 643-9

153. Costello, 647

154. Ibid., 649

155. Toland, 204-6

156. For example, see "Station 'H' Intercept," RG 38, CNSG Library, Box 159 for the operator logs at this site.

157. "Intercept Station Assignments," from "Statistics on Intercept, Delivery." RG 38, CNSG Library, Box 165, Folder 5830/62, "P.H. Investigations (1 of 3); Also see "Memorandum for Colonel Carter C. Clarke, Listing of Army and Navy Monitoring Stations, Their Locations and Station Directives," June 1942. RG 457, Entry 9032, Box 1374, Folder 4331, "Army-Navy Directive Study."

158. This was Commander Lester Robert Schulz, who at the time of Pearl Harbor was an assistant to

Captain John Beardall, naval aide to President Roosevelt. Schulz was assigned to OP-20-G and was temporarily detailed as an assistant to Beardall at the White House in late 1941. See PHH, Part 10:4660

159. PHH, Part 10:4742-3 and Part 29: 2378-9

160. Msg, 082034 November 1945, SUPRADSTA PT LYAUTEY to OP-20-G. Also see messages from Stations "S," "M," and others in RG 38, CNSG Library, Box 166, Folder 5830/69, "Pearl Harbor Investigations: Winds Msgs" (Folders 1 and 2 of 3)

161. "Station 'M' Operator Log for 2 December 1941, RG 38, CNSG Library, Box 167, Folder 5830/77, "Pearl Harbor Investigations: Info Rqts (*sic*) by Capt Safford, 1946-1947."

Afterword:
The Winds Message, American Cryptology, and History

The Impact and the Intelligence Value of the Winds Messages

Within the tempest of controversy about the nature and amount of available intelligence, especially communications intelligence, and its dissemination prior to the attack on Pearl Harbor, the Winds message imbroglio should have been no more than the smallest eddy. The purpose of the messages, as indicated in the instructions of 19 November, was limited. The alerts were intended merely to warn Tokyo's diplomats that relations between Japan and the United States, Great Britain, or the Soviet Union were "in danger." If such a situation had arisen at the time that warranted an alert, then Japan's diplomats would be warned via specified open code phrases or words sent within voice or Morse news broadcasts. Upon hearing these phrases or words, Japanese diplomats were to destroy their holdings of cryptographic materials and classified or sensitive papers.

In light of the generally poor state of relations between Tokyo and Washington that had existed at least since the late 1930s, whatever information could have been gleaned from the open code phrases or words themselves added nothing concrete to an understanding of the grave situation that existed between both countries. Nor could these phrases or words have provided any clue whatsoever to specific Japanese plans or intentions in the Pacific region. As we have seen, there simply was not one shred of actionable intelligence in any of the messages or transmissions that pointed to the attack on Pearl Harbor, Safford's postwar claim notwithstanding. Finally, as we have seen, further instructions about the destruction of cryptographic material contained in messages sent to Japan's diplomats after 28 November, when the contents of the Winds instructions were known to the Americans, contradicted, or even superseded some, if not all, of the directions found in the two Winds instructional messages of 19 November.

Many American cryptologists and intelligence officers considered the messages as a very important indicator of a possible impending break in U.S.-Japan relations, a sort of "road sign" that pointed to the next move by Tokyo. To give them their due, this view initially was a valid interpretation. The subtleties of diplomatic expressions in the Japanese language were difficult as best; the action of burning cryptographic material and other sensitive papers indicated, at the very least, a crisis in relations was imminent, most likely a break leading to war.

Yet, as we have seen, in the days after 28 November, when the translations of the Winds set of messages became available, the *Gaimusho* sent many new instructions to its diplomats regarding the *immediate* destruction of cryptographic material. While not all of the messages that contained the new directions were decrypted and ready prior to 7 December, enough of them had been exploited to suggest that Tokyo, to some degree, had begun to supersede or contravene the orders contained in the Winds messages. While, in one message, Tokyo reminded stations to hold onto the Winds and "hidden word" codewords and phrases, the case of the HARUNA code message illustrates that the destruction of cryptographic material was underway almost a week prior to the attack on Pearl Harbor. The new destruction proscriptions seem, at the least, to have reduced the singular importance attached by the Americans to the Winds messages. That the Winds execute was sent after hostilities began (or, according to one Japanese source, possibly at the time of the attacks) demonstrated that this method to warn Japanese diplomats clearly was secondary to other warning vehicles, notably the STOP message. For the Americans, the Winds Execute never proved to be the indicator of impending hostilities.

The "hidden word" or STOP message ultimately may have been Tokyo's choice for the covered code warning of its diplomats. The message that contained the instructions and codeword list had been transmitted to Japanese diplomats around the world. Yet, even this method's role may have been overstated in the final accounting of events. While the "hidden word" message was transmitted several hours prior to the attack on Pearl Harbor, the only addressees on the cable intercepted by Station "S" were Japanese diplomatic facilities in North America and Cuba. American cryptologists did not know if similar "hidden word" messages had been sent to Japanese diplomats elsewhere.

The contents of the actual "hidden word" message intercepted by the Americans proved to be no more enlightening than the Winds Execute that was sent hours after the war started. The code list, which was available to the Americans by 2 December, contained coded phrases and words that could be used by the *Gaimusho* to warn its diplomats of specific impending hostilities, such as KASHIWAGI, or "We are commencing military action against..." Yet the code word that Tokyo sent in the STOP message of 7 December was HATTORI, or "Relations between Japan and...are not in accordance with expectations." This plain text phrase added nothing to what already was known in Washington from the Purple decrypts. The "hidden word" message also did not warn of an attack on Pearl Harbor.

What the Winds Messages Tells Us about Pre-War American Cryptology

The Winds messages may not have been useful warnings or intelligence indicators, but the manner in which the American Army and Navy cryptologic agencies handled them, the appreciation of their role and especially the subsequent search for the Winds Execute version, illustrated much about those two organizations and their operations prior to the war. The Japanese messages – circulars No. 2353 and No. 2354 – were like radioactive tracers which a physician tracks to locate problems in a patient's body. The reaction to and subsequent handling of these two messages highlighted some of the inadequacies of the prewar American communications intelligence system.

By December 1941 American cryptology was a system that was stretched to the limit and pushed in too many directions. Conflicting missions left few resources to attack the expanding Japanese cryptologic "problem." Two-thirds of OP-20-G's meager resources, in this case analysts and radio monitors, had been shifted to meet the Roosevelt administration's strategic emphasis on the Axis threat in the Atlantic and European regions as spelled in the various war plans of the time, such as Rainbow 5 and Plan Dog. This left less for Japanese targets, especially to solve the cryptographic systems of the Imperial Japanese Navy. The Army's SIS, as well, was fully engaged in processing diplomatic messages, mostly Japanese. The army site at Fort McKinley in the Philippines (MS-6) once had tried to attack Japanese army communications, but in late 1941 was engaged mostly in decrypting Japanese diplomatic messages. Serious efforts at exploiting Japanese military and air force communications – the main threat to the Philippines – began only under the reality of a Japanese attack on 7 December.

American communications intelligence was organized to attack the Japanese cryptographic problem in a bureaucratic fashion – the mission against Japan, especially its diplomatic traffic, was divided in ways to accommodate the competing ambitions of the two agencies. To demonstrate this, we only need to consider the even-odd day tasking arrangement for intercepting, analyzing, and exploiting Purple and other Japanese diplomatic communications. Also, OP-20-G had divided the attack on the Imperial Japanese Navy's cryptography, especially the important General-Purpose

Code: while the Navy's main analytic center in Washington recovered the previous codebook (AN, later notated in mid-1942 as JN-25A), Corregidor worked the current codebook (AN-1, later notated in mid-1942 as JN-25B) along with the British FECB in Singapore. Meanwhile, the Navy's analytic center in Pearl Harbor (HYPO) worked futilely against another system; it did not receive current technical information on the General-Purpose Code until after 7 December.

Finally, American cryptologists were hostage to the misperception that because the Purple cipher machine was *the* high-level cryptographic system for Japan's diplomatic traffic, therefore it would carry all intelligence of the highest importance about Japan's intentions. But the Purple device was just one diplomatic cryptographic system, and the information it protected did not include any data about the impending operations of the Japan's military and naval forces. The latter exclusion was deliberate; the Japanese War and Navy Ministries effectively restricted knowledge, especially the strike against Pearl Harbor, throughout their own offices and the *Gaimusho*. In fact, even large elements of the Imperial Japanese Navy were unaware of the Hawaii operation (*Hawai sakusen*)!

Any one of the above three conditions would have hampered the ability of American cryptologists to determine Japanese plans and intentions. The confluence of all three contributed to the surprise in Washington, Pearl Harbor, and Manila, at the ensuing successful Japanese attacks at Pearl Harbor and elsewhere across the Pacific on 7 December.

Strictly viewed as a single intelligence issue, the effect of the Winds messages on American cryptology in late 1941 was like one more apple of chaos tossed into an already turbulent crisis. The subsequent tasking set upon army and navy monitoring stations across the Pacific to copy and evaluate Japanese commercial broadcasts further unbalanced priorities and distracted already overloaded analytic centers with literally scores of yards of newly intercepted Japanese text to examine. Many Morse intercept operators and linguists (as in Hawaii) now had to monitor or copy the broadcasts in addition to the current mission. Some personnel were diverted completely from other targets; other analytic personnel had to examine this flood of copy.

Statistically, it is not known for certain the precise impact the intercept of these broadcasts had on intercept and processing rates for Japanese diplomatic traffic. There are no data to measure the impact during the period of the search for the Winds Execute message from 28 November to 7 December. The available data are from the period of 1 November to 7 December 1941. These data suggest that a priority system that already emphasized Purple decryption could only become distorted when it came to exploiting Japanese diplomatic messages encoded or encrypted in other cryptographic systems. During this period, there were 628 Purple messages intercepted and of these 417, or sixty-seven percent, were translated. The Americans intercepted 454 messages exchanged between Tokyo and its embassy in Washington. Of these 268 were translated, a rate of about fifty-nine percent.[1]

In contrast, of the next tier of diplomatic cryptographic systems, intercepted J-19 traffic was translated at a rate of sixteen percent. For another less-known system, J-22, only three percent of intercept was translated. Twenty-five percent of all PA-K2 messages were translated, but only fifty-two messages in that system were intercepted during this period, or about eight percent of the Purple total. As for the LA system, only two percent of those messages were translated.

The result of this skewed emphasis was that many messages encrypted in cryptographic systems other than Purple usually took days, even weeks, to get processed to the point where a translation could be produced. After Pearl Harbor, when American codebreakers got around to decoding and translating some of the pre-attack diplomatic traffic, they discovered that many messages carried important details about the Japanese intentions. For example, on 6 December 1941 Tokyo sent a message to its diplomats in Bangkok that noted that "X-Day," or "Declaration Day," was set for Sunday, 7 December (8 December in Tokyo).[2] That date, the message pointed out, was when the "notice" was to be given. Interestingly, this single detail, the reference (and date), "X-Day," was never mentioned in any Purple traffic to Washington worked by the Americans. This particular message, by the way, was translated on 8 December.

A far more trenchant example on how potentially critical intelligence was missed because of the mistaken priority for processing is illustrated by the espionage messages sent from the Japanese consulate in Honolulu by the covert agent Yoshikawa Takeo and Kita Nagao, the consul. Yoshikawa's observations were Tokyo's primary source of intelligence about the situation in Pearl Harbor, especially what ships were in or out of port. This intelligence, along with that gathered by Japan's own naval radio intelligence effort, was retransmitted by Tokyo on the UTU (Blind) naval broadcast to the Pearl Harbor Striking Force as it steamed in radio silence eastwards to its unsuspecting target.[3] While almost all of Yoshikawa's messages to Tokyo in the ten days prior to the attack were available to American codebreakers – from copies turned over by American cable companies – surprisingly few were translated on a timely basis. Most, fourteen in all, would require anywhere from three days to three weeks to be translated. For example, on 1 December, in message No. 241 (Japanese serial) from Honolulu, it was reported that U.S. battleships usually spent the weekends in port. This message was translated on 10 December.[4] Another message from the consulate sent to Tokyo on 6 December, informed Tokyo that there were no barrage balloons tethered over the harbor and that the ships did not have torpedo nets. Yoshikawa noted in this particular report with a chilling prescience, "There is considerable opportunity left for a surprise attack against these places."[5] This message was translated on 8 December.

There is no certainty, that had these messages been available within a day or two of their intercept, that they would have triggered an alert or defensive action by the Pearl Harbor command which might have altered the outcome on 7 December. But the tardy handling of Japanese intelligence traffic out of Honolulu ensured that even the slimmest opportunity to retrieve the situation from the eventual catastrophe never presented itself. Instead, for example, the 3 December message about signaling the U.S. Pacific Fleet's situation in Pearl Harbor by using lights in a window or advertisements on Honolulu radio station KGMB, literally languished in a junior navy cryptanalyst's in box on 6 December because the supervisor was busy organizing the decryption and translation of another Purple message, the infamous fourteen-part Japanese message that announced the cessation of negotiations. The translation of the message from Honolulu was produced on 11 December.[6]

The Winds Message and the Historical Process

Events had demonstrated that the Winds Execute message had failed to be either a sort of actionable intelligence or a useful war warning. That the actual message was heard several hours after hostilities and applied only to Japan's relations with Great Britain further illustrates that the message was irrelevant. (Even if an Execute message had been sent within a half hour of the attack as one Japanese national radio employee suggested, it would have taken hours to process and disseminate it.) In any subsequent hearings or history of the Pearl Harbor attack, the Winds episode should have warranted nothing more than the briefest reference or a footnote. It did not turn out this way, though.

The Winds issue consumed many hours for each of the inquiries and boards that reviewed it. The Joint Congressional Committee took testimony for *almost three days* from Captains Safford and Kramer just on this one issue. The JCC interviewed another two dozen witnesses about aspects of the

Winds message. The Clarke Investigation was called back for another four days to take testimony to address the claim Safford made before the Hewitt Inquiry that General Marshall had ordered the destruction of papers related to the Winds message.

The Winds incident had been pumped up into a major controversy that fixated a number of the Pearl Harbor investigations and later engaged a number of historians and the public for decades. This phenomenon had nothing to do with the actual events that transpired around the handling of the original message, or the intelligence or warning value of the message itself. Rather, the Winds message became a synthetic incident, significant because of the sinister inferences attached to it by a single individual.

The "conspiratorial" version of the Winds incident was solely the product of Captain Laurance Safford's imagining of events that had occurred prior to Pearl Harbor in the Washington, D.C., offices of naval and army intelligence. Whatever motives existed behind his claims, Captain Safford presented to the various Pearl Harbor inquiries and boards a narrative that ranged so far from the documentary evidence and the memories of all the other participants that it was completely detached from actual events. Safford's charges, though, created a context of alleged government conspiracy around the processing and dissemination of the purported Winds Execute message of 4 December. That his interpretation of events coincided somewhat with similar views about all of the events behind Pearl Harbor which were held by other individuals was unfortunate since they provided Safford with a sympathetic audience that, in turn, gave an unwarranted patina of validity to his claim.

Put to the test, though, Safford's narrative about the Execute message simply failed to stand up to cross-examination. The Joint Congressional Committee shredded Safford's story. The committee reduced it to the collection of unsubstantiated charges that all along had been its foundation. The documentary evidence he said was available simply did not, nor did it ever, exist. In truth, Safford produced nothing upon which any further investigation could proceed. The best (and perhaps kindest) assessment of his actions was that of the Congressional Committee, which said that Safford had been "mistaken." The conclusion stated in the 1946 Pearl Harbor Report regarding the Winds message should have ended that story once and for all.

But this was not to be.

Some thirty-five years after the congressional hearings, the Winds controversy was resurrected. This time, a few private scholars, with the help of at least one apparently "knowledgeable" individual, attempted to resuscitate Safford's allegation of a conspiracy, which surrounded the Winds message. These writers accepted Safford's story as true; as far as they were concerned, the government had not disproved it conclusively. This stand inverted the normal rules of evidentiary argument in which the claimant must produce valid evidence in support of his charges. Instead, these writers insisted that the government had yet to disprove Safford's charges regardless of the fact that he never had produced any evidence to substantiate them thirty-some years earlier.

The scholars and researchers who championed Safford's version of the controversy abandoned the rigorous evidentiary requirements of the historical profession in order to advance their thesis. They based their contentions on excerpts from documents taken out of context and the undocumented statements of Ralph Briggs, who could not even demonstrate his participation (or Safford's) in the events he described. Mostly, though, these writers recited the litany of Safford's "evidence," which included his own previously discredited testimony, unsubstantiated surmises, and nonexistent documents. These scholars hewed closely to the charge that there had been a government conspiracy in the matter of the Winds message. Arguing from this vantage point, they were free to discount creditable contradictory testimony by insinuating that it was scripted lies; they dismissed as fundamentally hostile and biased the skeptical and critical questioning of Safford's assertions; and where the documentary evidence was missing, they charged that the government had destroyed it or continued to withhold it after all these decades.

Ultimately, these writers had to base much, if not all, of their case on Safford's failed evidence and testimony. These failed to withstand scrutiny anew just as Safford's had failed previously in 1946. As we have demonstrated in this history, Safford's case was built on mistaken deductions, reconstructed, nonexistent documents, a mutable version of events, as well as a cast of witnesses that Safford conjured up in his imagination.

In the end, the Winds message controversy was and remains an artificial historical phenomenon. The message's actual impact on events in early December 1941 was limited to aggravating an already overstretched American cryptologic effort against Japan. The Winds message system set up by the Japanese *Gaimusho* on 19 November 1941 proved to be neither a source of actionable intelligence nor a timely warning. What made the message(s) important was the later spin put on it by Captain Safford and a handful of historians and other writers. Their claims created a conspiratorial aura around the purported Execute message that had nothing to do with events as they actually transpired at the time. The conspiratorial version of events they espoused was totally interpretive and subjective.

The artificial controversy that grew around the Winds message never advanced historical knowledge of the events of early December 1941. In fact, the Winds controversy distracted investigations and later historical analyses from far more important issues about the attack on Pearl Harbor, such as the fundamental organizational and operational shortcomings of American cryptology, the arrogant dismissal by American military and naval leaders of a Japanese capability and willingness to conduct such an operation, and the breakdown in the leadership hierarchy that made too many assumptions about the effective operation of the U.S. Pacific command structure in late 1941. That the Winds controversy persisted over the decades is more a result of the misplaced belief by some that history is controlled by conspiracy rather than history being the product of human folly.

Notes

1. "Worksheets for Japanese Diplomatic Traffic, 1941." RG 38, Entry 1030, Box 165, Folder 5830/62, "Pearl Harbor Investigations" (1 of 3). Also see PHH, Part 37:1081-3

2. "Magic," Vol. IV – Appendix, A-542. Tokyo to Bangkok, # 852, 6 December 1941.

3. The issue of the radio silence maintained by the Pearl Harbor Striking Force has been questioned recently by some researchers. Their misperception that the force actually transmitted and gave their position away is caused almost completely by a misunderstanding of the technical aspects of Japanese naval command and control communications and the capabilities of U.S. naval radio monitoring, cryptanalysis, and direction finding capabilities in the Pacific and Washington, D.C. Their errors and speculations notwithstanding, the task force maintained complete radio silence; that is, it did not transmit any radio messages during its passage to Pearl Harbor. The Japanese naval broadcast system supported the task force as it crossed the Pacific. Tokyo transmitted numerous support messages – intelligence updates, weather reports, orders, and morale statements – to the Striking Force (*Kido Butai*) on several frequencies at multiple times. The broadcast method consisted of one-way communications, or "blind" (UTU) sending. Several ships in the force listened to the broadcast and copied the messages. The messages were then repeated to the other ships in the formation by semaphore flag or signal lamp. The Kido Butai did not reply or acknowledge the receipt of any messages; their orders prohibited it. The only element of the force to transmit during the voyage were two reconnaissance aircraft, one each from the cruisers *Tone* and *Chikuma*, sent out on the morning of 7 December to verify the Pacific Fleet's location in Pearl Harbor or at Lahanai anchorage. The planes' reports were sent "in the blind,"

that is, the task force did not acknowledge these messages. The aircraft reports verified an earlier report from the Japanese submarine I-72 from the previous evening that the American fleet was not at the Lahanai anchorage. The submarine sent the report to the Commander of the Japanese 6th Fleet (Submarine Force) located on Kwajalein Island. Kwajalein relayed the message to Tokyo, which, in turn, broadcast it to the Striking Force. See SRN 115367, NARA CP, RG 457, Entry 9014.

 4. MND Translation, SIS # 26053, Honolulu to Tokyo, 1 December 1941. NARA, RG 457, Entry 9032, Box 301.

 5. MND Translation SIS #25877, Honolulu to Tokyo, 6 December 1941. NARA, RG 457, Entry 9032, Box 301

 6. MND Translation SIS #26145, Honolulu to Tokyo, 3 December 1941. NARA RG 457, Entry 9032, Box 301. See PHH, Part 35:303-4

Exhibits

Exhibit #1: Recovered Decode Chart of Text for J-19 Transposition System. From "Japanese Diplomatic Network and Crypto Systems, Pre-During (*sic*) the War."

National Archives and Records Administration (NARA), College Park, MD. RG 457, E9032, Box 992, Folder 3015.

Exhibit #2: Japanese J-19 Transposition Matrix or Stencil.
Stencil is from period 11-21 November 1941.

"Change No. 4 to
R.I.P. 37B, 1 April 1944."

NARA, RG 457,
E9032, Box 1137, Folder 3762, 7-119

TOP SECRET-ULTRA　　　　　　　　　　　CHANGE NO. 4
R.I.P. 37-B　　　　　　　　　　　　　　1 April 1944

K-10 TRANSPOSITION FORMS

FORM #8　　Effective 11-20 November, 1941, inc.

1	2	3	4	5	6	7	8	9	10	11	12	13	14	15	16	17
X	X	X	X			X	X	X	X	X	X			X	X	X
X	X	X	X			X			X							X
X	X	X	X			X										X
X			X	X		X	X	X								X
X			X	X												
			X													
			X													
			X													

etc.

FORM #9　　Effective 21-30 November 1941, inc.

1	2	3	4	5	6	7	8	9	10	11	12	13	14	15	16	17
X			X	X	X			X	X		X				X	X
X					X	X			X		X	X			X	X
X				X					X		X		X	X	X	X
X								X	X			X			X	
X								X							X	
								X								
			X					X								
			X													
			X													

etc.

Exhibit #3: Intercept copy of Japanese Diplomatic Message No. 2353, Tokyo to Washington. Navy Monitoring Station "S" (Bainbridge Island, WA) teletyped to OP-20-G Headquarters, 19 November 1941.

Center for Cryptologic History Series XII.S, Box 22; for unmarked version see "Jap Msgs, Oct-Dec 1941," RG 38, CNSG Library, Box 156, Pages 3803-4.

360 SCDE TOKIO (91) 19 9 40S JG P1/50   38 3

KOSHI WASHINGTONDC

MWZHU BUWTJ NEWZU CNFXA LEKFK OHTZV GONHE WKWWK SXGVB BLNQV
QQPQE MDZXT UTYQD WDPSC QDMCE MXFON VVZOU CGEYK CXDUN KLFDU
XKSXY SQZRL GVQJY MAKFD DBEUY FFUJI ZYYPY OZOAJ GAUMT SWMEJ
AMOGH CWOVB XAGBS CBIEA ZGYMJ UDYDX OCYQX RGKAX SHSZF XNDLO
VKHBH CKDNX IYYVZ IEFEN OGCXB EVZVE GJKYT JGKBL

                                           1312 S RJ
                                           9160

SF DE JAB   S   NOV 41   38 04
P2/360 41W KOS WASHN

KNEWM BLTMV BNJVQ UHIFE UQIPN QLWCM BVXFF MUNFG UAXTC ZJKEX
EXBEW UVBMY NHWSB FGVEX WEMBL MLNCB CZCID KQOFR KWXYX EXPAR
KPUEA SUSKW KSKXL MFBFC VVLGB DDXCL UEZTE WZUYS NEAJT PXTDA
HBENU DXPXM ADCNM MRLYH FXTUJ GNQMT VQRB 84444 BDSHD TAKAO
TOGO

(VQRB) AS SENT   1317 S RJ
                                           9160

Exhibit #4: Intercept copy of Japanese Diplomatic Message No. 2354, Tokyo to Washington. Navy Monitoring Station "S" (Bainbridge Island, WA) teletyped to OP-20-G Headquarters, 19 November 1941.

Center for Cryptologic History Series XII.S, Box 22; also unmarked version, see "Jap Msgs, Oct-Dec 1941," RG 38, CNSG Library Box 156, Page 3798

352 SCDE TOKYO 57 19 811S JG
KOSHI WASHINGTONDC

MWLQU BUWTJ XYJBK SMMTB EQFVD LURHW XEZWO JCRQB YFXYA YCQXL
FSUHX WTEBH EQPUC NMQOL YVZBC XEXUN LZKAR XBKRE LBVLM WNKGK
JQKLK NECHC URUXI EWMUE NZOQG INUSO DCFGM VHTBI SRLGY GXBHT
UXVQG UOQGG XDXWO GLQKN CVUOM XHPBE PGLEO YCVVE CGFZE CCUBQ
OSGLX LMUJS IWWBO CGUCB UJXPM ALLKL MMTNE WCGTK XHPKH BZBZY
48888 CCTKM RGKRV BSIMO

TOGO.

1152 S GL
9160

Exhibit #5: K-10/J-19 Indicator Groups and Transposition Keys for November 1941.

NARA, RG 457, Entry 9032, Box 1137, Folder 3762, R.I.P 37B, Change 4, K-10 Transposition (J-19 Basic system), 7-83.

K-10 INDICATOR GROUPS AND TRANSPOSITION KEYS
(For the month of November, 1941)
GENERAL

Date	Indicator	Key
1	BOWZO	
2		
3		
4	BUBCV	13 17 14 5 12 11 6 19 16 18 4 10 9 2 17 15 8 3
5	BUCDY	
6	BUDEA	
7	BUFFC	16 14 4 10 15 3 9 11 13 2 8 12 17 17 20 6 18 21 19 5
8	BUGGF	3 15 16 9 11 20 19 1 7 18 17 6 14 2 5 12 10 4 13 8
9	BUHHI	
10	BUJIK	
11	BUKJM	12 3 11 9 10 2 8 22 24 13 4 20 7 21 14 15 16 5 18 23 19 17 6 1
12	BULKP	
13	BUMLR	
14	BUNMT	
15	BUPNW	4 23 3 24 22 2 25 9 20 1 8 21 19 5 7 16 18 6 17 13 12 10 15 11 14
16	BUSQC	6 5 7 17 1 16 8 18 4 15 9 2 19 12 14 10 3 20 13 11
17	BUTRE	
18	BUVSH	
19	BUWTJ	3 17 12 4 5 18 2 10 19 7 11 9 14 1 6 16 13 15 8
20	BUXUL	
21	BUZVN	
22	BYBWR	7 12 5 11 6 9 4 8 3 10 2 13 25 1 22 14 24 21 23 20 17 19 15 18 16
23	BYCXT	
24	BYDYV	21 16 7 8 15 6 17 10 5 18 4 14 3 11 13 9 1 12 19 2 20
25	BYFZY	
26	BYGAB	5 18 4 19 17 2 10 8 11 9 1 12 6 15 3 20 14 16 7 13
27	BYHBD	12 14 7 13 9 1 19 6 8 17 2 16 11 3 15 18 4 10 5
28	BYJCF	23 6 16 24 5 15 8 19 4 20 18 3 14 17 7 12 21 2 22 9 11 13 1 10
29	BYKDI	
30	BYLMK	3 15 19 20 16 5 21 7 17 18 6 2 4 1 12 8 13 11 9 14 10

Exhibit #6: Message No. 2353 translation worksheet (W.S.) with code digraph true values inscribed by the translator. (2 pages)

Center for Cryptologic History
Series XII.S, Box 22
and NARA, RG 80,
Pearl Harbor Liaison Office (PHLO),
Entry 167A, "Office Reference ("Subject")
Files, 1932-1946. Winds Code,
Station"W" to Witnesses.
Folder: Winds Code - Misc Material.

STATION S   11/26/41   MC-C (91)

FROM: TOKYO (TOGO)
TO: WASHINGTON (KOSHI)

19 NOVEMBER, 1941
J-19
CIRC #2353 (COMPLETE)
   MWZHU   BUWTJ

XE	TG	NC	ST	WY	NY	KY	ES	NI	CU	KY	MT	AN	WE	UF
DB	TH	ZW	JX	HZ	US	GK	IY	IO	WV	MT	GS	WU	YK	UQ
EQ	XF	UX	KZ	RS	KH	SC	FW	AO	AD	CE	CY	SI	LW	BS
BN	FK	XF	ZW	LU	GS	XE	YM	LZ	FF	US	TR	CD	UQ	EQ
XG	FH	EK	FG	XJ	KC	KY	PE	IY	ZT	VE	FJ	NX	VA	IX
ZW	MS	ZP	KR	DB	NX	AE	NE	LZ	LJ	XJ	CT	NC	LA	BO
TM	WD	XE	YM	KY	UQ	EQ	XG	HL	GU	OM	LW	KY	FE	XD
DW	LD	VB	NC	JG	BO	EF	PB	XE	YM	ZW	UQ	EQ	XG	HL
VM	KY	FE	XD	CU	CN	JM	VB	NC	TK	BO	OC	XP	XE	YM
KY	UQ	EQ	WM	HL	HZ	VB	AO	MS	BL	MD	QV	MO	VB	MT
OV	ER	CX	NV	FA	XP	ZT	VB	HL	ZA	LW	KY	FE	XD	KP
QV	VB	NC	NV	JG	UP	QO	AF	UF	XE	EQ	XJ	KC	GG	BV

| UX | NJ | FX | DM | MG | RA | VD | BO | AD | BE | RV | TM | KD | AD | JB |
| GQ | NC | NU | DM | AG | VP | US | BD | ZK | FB | UX | ZH | M |

Exhibit #7: KANA texts of Japanese diplomatic messages 2353 and 2354. GSB 180, 6 November 1941[5].

RG 38, CNSG Library, Box 166, Folder 5830/69, "Winds Msgs."

6 November 1941

GSB 180

From: War Department

To : Commander-in-Chief
      Advance Hq. US Army Forces
      Pacific, Tokyo

Supplementing GSB 168 there follows full Japanese text of two circulars from Tokyo Foreign Office dated 19 Nov 1941:

    Circular 2353. Kanchoo fugoo atsukai kokusai jigyoo no hippaku no kekka itsu saiaku no jitai ni tachi itaru kamo hakararezaru tokoro kakaru baai wagahoo to aitekoku tono tsuushin wa tadachi ni teishi serarubeki wo motte wagahoo no gaikoo kankei kiken ni hinsuru baai ni wa waga kaigai hoosoo no kakuchi muke nihohoo news no chuukan oyobi saigo ni oite tenki yohoo to shite. 1. Nichibei kankei no baai ni wa "higashi no kaze ame". 2. Nichiso kankei no baai ni wa "kita no kaze kumori". 3. Nichiei kankei no baai ("tai" shinchuu "maree" Netherlands E.I. kooryoku oboe fukumu ("nishi no kaze hare". 02 do zutsu kurikaeshi hoosoo seshimeru koto to seru wo motte migi ni yori angoo, shorui too tekitoo shobun aritashi. Nao migi wa gen ni gokuhi atsukai to seraretashi.

    Circular 2354: Gokuhi. Wagahoo no gaikoo kankei kiken ni hinsen to suru baai ni wa ippah joohoo hoosoo no bootoo oyobi matsubi ni: 1. Nichibei kankei hippaku no baai ni wa "higashi". 2. Nichiso kankei no baai niwa "kita". 3. Nichei kankei ("tai" shin chuu "maree" Netherlands E.I. kooryoku oboe fukumu (no baai mi wa "nishi". Narugo 05 do ate soonyuu subeki ni tsuki goryoochi aritashi.

Both messages sent in _____ * Believe broadcasts mentioned for signalling in circular 2353 were voice broadcasts and those in 2354 were Morse code.

Exhibit #8: US Navy (OP-20-GY) translation of message No. 2353, published on 28 November 1941.

SIS #25432 and JD-1: 6875.

Center for Cryptologic History
Series XII.S, Box 22

From: Tokyo
To : Washington
19 November 1941
(J19)

Circular #2353

        Regarding the broadcast of a special message in an emergency.

        In case of emergency (danger of cutting off our diplomatic relations), and the cutting off of international communications, the following warning will be added in the middle of the daily Japanese language short wave news broadcast.

(1) In case of a Japan-U.S. relations in danger: HIGASHI NO KAZEAME.*

(2) Japan-U.S.S.R. relations: KITANOKAZE KUMORI.**

(3) Japan-British relations: NISHI NO KAZE HARE.***

        This signal will be given in the middle and at the end as a weather forecast and each sentence will be repeated twice. When this is heard please destroy all code papers, etc. This is as yet to be a completely secret arrangement.

        Forward as urgent intelligence.

*East wind rain.
**North wind cloudy.
***West wind clear.

SIS 25432

JD-1: 6875   (Y) Navy Trans. 11-28-41 (S-TT)

Exhibit #9: Revision of translation of No. 2353 issued on 26 September 1944.

Handwritten text, probably by William F. Friedman, reads: Upper right – "(by Hurt);" lower left – *"This for Voice Broadcast – "Twice in middle and twice at end" There is good evidence that "Nishi no Kazehare" was really transmitted in this way."*

See Doc No. 4 of FCC Statement."

Center for Cryptologic History Series XII.S, Box 22

SECRET

From: Tokyo
To : Washington
19 November 1941
(J19)

TRANSLATION REVISED 26 Sept. 44.

(by Hurt)

Circular #2353

Office Chief's Code.

I do not know but what, as a result of the terrible strain in our operations, we have at length come to stand amid the ultimate evil circumstances, and if this be so, our communications with the country (ies) we are dealing with will be cut. And in the event that our foreign relations fringe on catastrophe, then in the <u>middle and at the end</u> of our universal broadcasts, the form of weather predictions, we will repeat and broadcast twice each the following:

    (1)   In the case of Japanese-American relations (HIGASHI NO KAZEAME).

    (2)   In the case of Japanese-Soviet relations (KITA NO KAZEKUMORI).

    (3)   In the case of Japanese-British relations (including their implications in Thai along with Malaya and the Netherlands East Indies), (NISHI NO KAZEHARE).

Hence you will know that you are suitably to destroy codes documents, etc.

You will please guard this in strictest secrecy.

This for Voice Broadcast —
"Twice in middle and twice at end"

There is good evidence that "Nishi no kagehare" was really transmitted in this way. See Doc N° 4 of FCC Statement.

Exhibit #10: True Form or Matrix (Stencil) for message No. 2354 (reverse image).

Center for Cryptologic History
Series XII.S, Box 22

and NARA, RG 80, PHLO, Entry 167A, "Office Reference ("Subject") Files, 1932-1946." Winds Code, Staion "W" to Witnesses. Folder: Winds Code - Misc Material.

B					D	N	C					X				K								1
Y					L	U		S	X	E	Y		M	L	Z									2
F					U	S	T		R	L	P	J	E	U	Q	E								3
X		G	X		K			L	E	D	J	X	J	R	C	K								4
Y		U	W		H	O	A	K	S	N	L	K	U	S	N	C	L							5
A	B	C	T	N	W	D	X	E	Y	M	E		N	I	C	U	K							6
Y	U	Q	E	G	X	G	H	L	G	U	O	T	L	W	V	B	N							7
C	J	G	B	O	E	F	P	B	X	E	Y	M	Z	H	J	Q	E							8
Q	X	G	H	L	L	Z	S	K	V	L	N	C	T	K	B	O	O	C						9
X	P	X	E	Y	M	N	M	H	L	H	Z	V	D	A	O	M	S	H						10
L	M	D	Q	V	M	O	V	N	T	O	V	R	C	X	G	C								11
F	A	X	P	Z	T	J	H	Z	N	U	Q	E	G	X	G	H	L	U						12
S	L	W	U	B	N	C	T	B	N	X	G	C	F	B	U	P	X	K						13
U	L	O	C	C	E	R	B	Z	K	V	I	G	V	K	C	B	L	U						14
H	K	G	N	X	W	Q	I	Y	S	Q														15

DATE 19 Nov 1941   MSG. NO. Circ 2854
FROM Tokyo   TO Washington
K-10 Form   Period 11-20 November 1941   Good for 0 columns

Exhibit #11: Message No. 2354 translation worksheet with code digraph true values inscribed by the translator.

Center for Cryptologic History
Series XII.S, Box 22

and NARA, RG 80, PHLO, Entry 167A, "Office Reference ("Subject") Files, 1932-1946." Winds Code, Station "W" to Witnesses.
Folder: Winds Code - Misc Material.

STATION S   11/26/41 MC-C (57)

FROM: TOKYO (TOGO)
TO: WASHINGTON (KOSHI)

19 NOVEMBER, 1941

J-19

CIRC #2354 (COMPLETE)

MWLQU BUWTJ

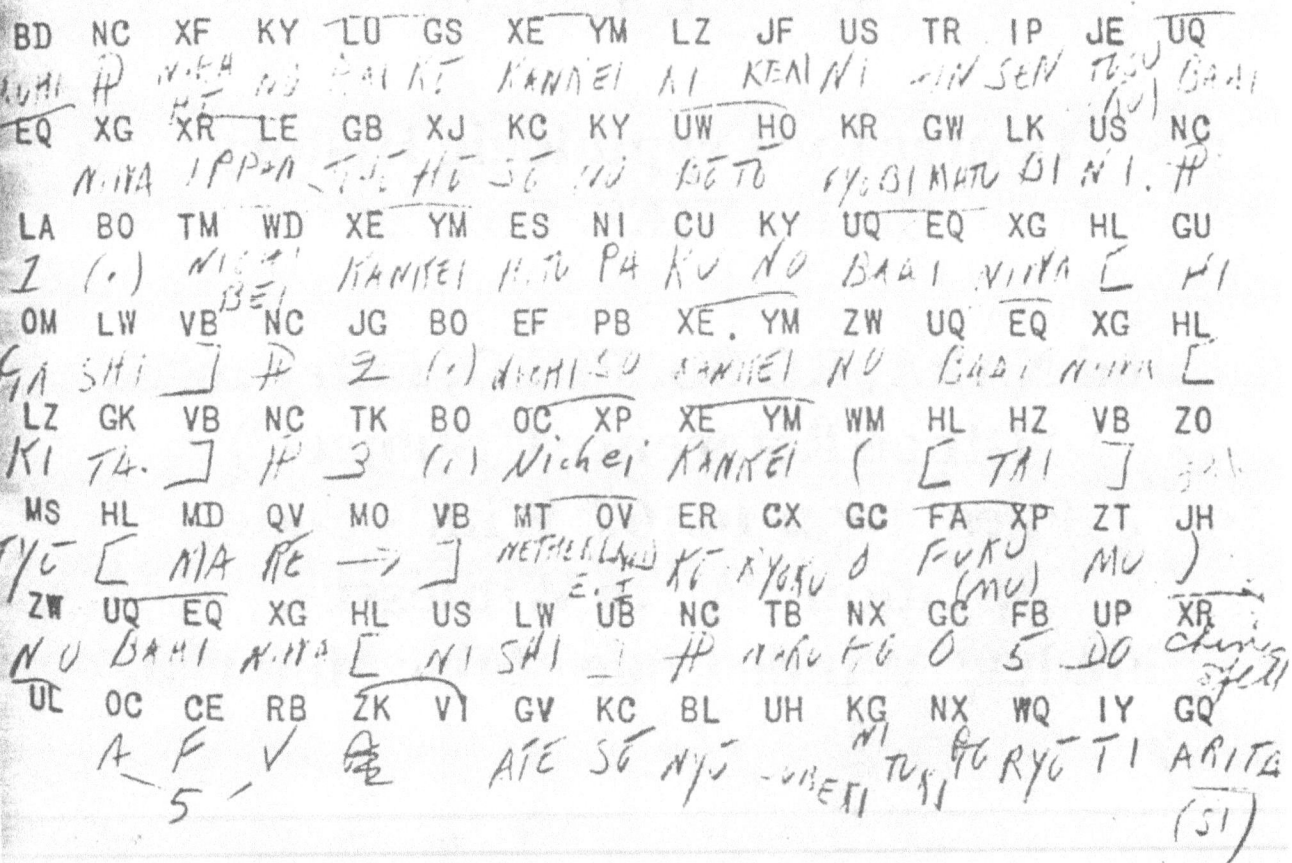

Exhibit #12: Translation, by US Navy (OP-20-GY) of message No. 2354, published on 28 November 1941. SIS #25392 and JD-1: 6850. Handwritten note, probably penned by William F. Friedman, left side reads - *"This for Morse broadcast of News."* Right hand side reads – *"Safford told me (in 1944) the "winds execute" msge [sic] came in on night 3-4 Dec & he saw it about 0800 on 4 Dec. It had a negative KITA, positive HIGASHI, positive NISHI. Msge [sic] was in Morse. If so, it meant break in relations between Japan & U.S., Japan & Great Britain; no break between Japan & Russia. F[riedman]"*

Center for Cryptologic History Series XII.S, Box 22. This translation, without the inscribed comments can be found in Multi-national Diplomatic Translation, SIS # 25392, Tokyo to Washington, 19 November 1941. RG 457, Entry 9032, Box 300

From: Tokyo
To : Washington
19 November 1941
(J19)

Circular #2354

When our diplomatic relations are becoming dangerous, we will add the following at the beginning and end of our general intelligence broadcasts:

    (1) If it is Japan-U.S. relations, "HIGASHI". *[East]*

    (2) Japan-Russia relations, "KITA". *[North]*

    (3) Japan-British relations, (including Thai, Malaya and N.E.I.), "NISHI". *[West]*

The above will be repeated five times and included at beginning and end.

Relay to Rio de Janeiro, Buenos Aires, Mexico City, San Francisco.

[handwritten: File for Morse Broadcasts + news]

[handwritten: From copy in ___ ___ M-J;]
Key furnished by British (Navy says Singapore to London to Wash. on 24 Nov 41) Signed F.

[handwritten: (in 1944) Safford told me, the "winds execute" msge came in on night 3-4 Dec + he saw it about 0800 on 4 Dec. It had a negative KITA, positive HIGASHI, positive NISHI. Msge was in Morse. If so, it meant break in relations between Japan + U.S.; Japan + Great Britain; no break between Japan + Russia.]

SIS 25392

JD-1: 6850

(Y) Navy Trans. 11-26-41 (S)

SECRET

Exhibit #13: Revision of translation No. 2354 issued on 26 September 1944.

Center for Cryptologic History, Series XII.S, Box 22.

Note Kanji characters in parenthesis are "strained."

From: Tokyo.
To : Washington
19 November 1941
(J19)

RETRANSLATION 26 Sept. 44.

Circular #2354

Strictly Secret:

In the event that our side's foreign relations are about to roll up to the shores of calamity, will you note that we will insert 5 times at the beginning and end of General News Broadcasts the following words:

(1) In case Japanese-American relations become mortally strained (必追), HIGASHI;

(2) In the case of Japanese Soviet relations KITA;

(3) Japanese-British relations (including their implications in Thai together with Malaya and the Netherlands East Indies), NISHI.

Exhibit #14: Transcription of a Morse (Kana) Japanese news broadcast, Station "JVJ," intercepted at 1030 (Tokyo Time) and 0130 GMT by Bainbridge Island (3 pages). Japanese News Broadcast by Station "JVJ," 8 December 1941.

NARA, RG 38, Box 167, Folder 5830/69 (3 of 3), "Pearl Harbor Investigations: Winds Msgs." Interestingly, this news broadcast was made about one hour after the overseas voice news program monitored by the FCC in which appeared the phrase NISHI NO KAZE HARE (West Wind Clear). However, none of the three words indicating a change in relations - "Nishi," "Kita," or "Higashi" - appears in the transcript. The first paragraphs describe the attacks in Hawaii and the Philippines.

CQ DE JVJ   (0130 SKED)   S 8 DEC 41

PRESS DE JVJ
HR NW BC AT 1030 DEC 8TH

DOMEI 014 HONORURUNANA NIHONKAIGUN KOOKUTAI BAKUGEKIKI
DAIHENTAIWA HAWAIJIKAN NANAHI GOZENNANAJI SANJUUGOFUN
(NIHONJIKAN HATIHIGOZEN SANJIGOFUN) HONORURUNI HATUKUUSHUUO
KAISISITA
015 WASINTONNANA MOKUZAIO MANSAISITE TAIHEIYOOWO KOOKOOCHUU-
NO BEIRIKUGUN YUSOOSENWA SANFURANSISUKOWO SARU SENSANBYAKU
MAIRUNO SUIIKIDE GYORAI KOOGEKIOUKETA
016 SHANHAIHATIHI SINAHOOMEN KANTAIHOODOOBU JUNIGATUHATIHI
GOZENKUJI HAPPYOO KOGA SINAHOOMEN KANTAI SIREICHOOKANWA
HONHATIHI NIHONWA EIBEI RYOOKOKUTO SENSOOJOOTAINI HAIRERUOMO-
TTE GOZENGOJI NIJUPPUN BAKURYOOWO GUNSITOSITE SOREZORE
SHANHAIZAIKOO IGIRISU PETERERU AMERIKA HOUEEKU RYOOHOOKANNI
HAKEN SHANHAIHOOMENNI OKERU ANNENIIJINOTAME KOOFUKU KANKOKU-
BUNWO KOOFU SESIMETARUNI EIKANWA KOREO KYOZETUSERUO MOTTE
YAMUOEZU KOREOGEKITINSERI BEIK__WA OODAKUSERUO MOTTE HOKAKUS-
ERI
017 MANIRANANAHI HAATO BEIAJIAKANTAI SIREIKANWA NANAHI TUGI
OGOTOKU HAPPYOOSITA BEIKOKUWA NIHONTO SENSOOJOOTAINI ARU
BEIKAIGUNWA JITAINI SOKUOOSITA BANPANNOBOTIO TORITUTUARU
018 TOOGOOGAISHOOWA GUNJIKOODOONO KAISINISAKIDATI HATIHIMIMEI
SANDAI TENNOOHEIKANI HAIETU OOSETUKERARE BEIEINITAISURU
 SAIGONO GAIKOOSOTINI KANSI IKYOKUSOOJOO GOZENWO TAIGENONOTI
GOZENSANJI ZENYAYORI SHUSHOO KANTEINI TAIKISITEITA TOOJOOSHU-
SHOOWO HOOMON YOODANNONOTI KINKYUUKAKUGINI NOZONDA
019 NYUUYOOKUNANA HONORURUYORINO ENU-BIISI HOOSOONIYOREBA
NIHONGUNNO HONORURU BAKUGEKIWA MOORETUO KIWAMETERU SIKASI
BEIKOKU RIKUKAIGUNWA IMANAO SEIKAIKUUKENWO NIGITTERUTO
NIHONGUNNO KUUSHUUWA SANJIKAN TIKAKU KEIZOKUSITERUTO TUTAERA-
RERU
020 NYUUYOOKUNANA HONORURUYORINO YUUPIIDENNI YOREBA SINJUWAN
SEIHOONO BAABAA POINTO OKINI NIHONGUNWO SEKISAISERU YUSOOSEN-
NOKAGEGA MITOMERARETATO
021 (ZENBINTUZUKU) YOTTU JUITIGATU JUNANAHIIRAI NOMURATAISIWA
KURUSUTAISITO TOMONI DAITOORYOO OYOBI KOKUMUCHOOKANTO
KAIKENWOKASANE KOOSHOO KYUUSOKU DAKETUNO YOOARUKOTOWO RIKISE-
TUSERU TOKORO DAITOORYOOWA SINAMONDAINI TUITEWA NISSIKAN
WAHEINO SHOOKAISHA TARUNO YOOIARITONOBE MATA KOKUMUCHOOKANWA
TEIKOKUGA DOITUTO TEIKEISI CRUKAGIRI NITIBEI KOOSHOOWA
SINANARUO MOTTEMAZU KONOKONPONTEKI KONNANWOJOKYO SURUHITUYOO
ARUMUNEO KYOOCHOOSI RYOOSANKAINI WATARIRONGIO KASANETARUMO
NANKANWA IZENTOSITE SANGOKUJOOYAKU KOKUSAITUUSHOO MUSABETUTA-
IGUU MONDAIOYOBI SINAMONDAINI ARUKOTO AKIRAKATO NARERUOMOTTE
TEIKOKUSEIFUWA RYOOKOKU KOKUKOONO HATANWOKAIHI SURUTAME
SAIZENNO DORYOKUO TUKUSANTOSURU KOORYONI MOTOZUKI SUUYOOKATU
KINKYUUNO MONDAINITUKI KOOSEINARU DAKETUO HAKURUTAME JUITIGA-
TUNIJUHI SANOSINTEIANWO TEISHUTUSERI (ITI) NITIBEI RYOOKOKU
SEIFUWA IZUREMO FUTUINYIGAINO NANTOOAJIA OYOBI MINAMITAIHEIYO
O TEIKINI BURYOKUTEKI SINSHUTUO OKONAWAZARU KOTOWO KAKUYAKUSU
(NI) NITIBEI RYOOKOKUSEIFUWA RANRYOOINDONI OITE SONOHITUYOO
TOSURUBUSSINO KAKUTOKUGA HOSHOO SERARURU YOOSOOGONI KYOORYOKU
SURUMONOTOSURU (SAN) NITIBEI RYOOKOKU SEIFUWASOOGONI TUUSHOO
KANKEIO SISANTOOKETU MAENOJOOTAINI FUKUKISUBESI BEIKOKUSEIFU-

JVJ 0130 SKED - PAGE 2   3 DEC 41   5720

TOP SECRET-ULTRA

WA SHOYOONO SEKIYUNO TAINITI KYOOKYUUOYAKUSU (YON)
BEIKOKUSEIFUWA NISSI RYOOKOKUNO WAHEINIKANSURU DORYOKUNI
SISHOOWO ATAURUGA GOTOKI KOODOONI IDEZARUBESI (GO) NIHON
KOKUMINSEIFUWA NISSIKANWAHEI SEIRITUSURUKA MATAWA TAIHEIYOO
TIIKINIOKERU KOOSEINARU HEIWAKAKURITU SURUWUOAGENNI FUTURYOO
INDOSINANI HAKENSERAREORU NIHONGUNTAIO TETTAISUBEKI MUNEOYAKU-
-SU NIHONKOKU SEIFUWA HONRYOOKAI SEIRITUSEBA GENNI NANBUFUTU-
RYOO INDOSINANI CHUUTONCHUUNO NIHONGUNWA KOREO HOKUBUFUTURYOO
INDOSINANI ICHUUSURUNO YOOIARUKOTOWO SENMEISU MIGINITAISI
KOKUMUCHOOKANWA TEIKOKUGA SANGOKU JOOYAKUTONO KANKEIO AKIRAK-
ANISI HEIWASEISAKU SAIYOOWO KAKUGENSURUNI ARAZAREBA MICI
DAIYONKOOWO JUDAKUSI ENSHOOKOOIO TEISISURUKOTO FUKANOONARITO
YUIMATA DAITOORYOONO IWAKYURU NISSIKANWAHEINO SHOOKAISHA
TARANTONO TEIANMO NIHONNOHEIWA SEISAKU SAIYOOWOZENTEI
TOSURUMONO NARUMUNEONOBE DAIYONKOONITUKI DAINARU NANSHOKUO
SIMESITARUO MOTTEWAGAHOOWA RYOOTAISIOSITE KOKUMUCHOOKANNI
TAISI DAITOORYOONO SHOOKAINIYORI NISSICHOKUSETU KOOSHOOKAISI
SERARURUBAWAI WAHEINO SHOOKAISHATARU BEIKOKUGAIZEN ENSHOOKOO-
IO KEIZOKUSENTO SURUWAHEIWA SEIRITUOBOOGAI SURUMONONISITE
SONOTAIDONI MUJUNARUKOTOWO SITEKISI BEIKOKUSEIFUNO HANSEIOYO-
OSEI SESEMETARE ET _____ BEIKOKUSEIFUWA EIGOORAN WOYOBI
JUUKEIDAIHYOO TOKYOOGTSURU TOKOROARI JUITIGATU NIJUNIHI
KOKUMUCHOOKANWA RYOOTAISINI TAISI NANBUFUTUIN YORINOTEPPEI
NOMINITEWA MINAMITAIHEIYOO HOOMENNO KYUUHAKUSERU JOOSEIO
KANWASURUNI TARAZUTO SURUMUNE NARABINI DAITOORYOONO IWAYURU
NISSIKANNO SHOOKAIWA JIKIIMADA JUKUSEZUTO SIKOOSURUMUNEO
NOBETARI BEIKOKUSEIFUWA SONOGOMO ZENKI SHODAIHYOO KYOOGIOKAS-
ANE ORITARUGA NIJUROKUHI KOKUMUCHOOKANWA RYOOTAISINITAISI
NIJUUHINO WAGATEIANNI TUITEWASINCHOO KENKYUUOKUWAE KANKEIKOKU-
TOMO KYOOGISERUMO IKANNAGARA DOOISIGATASI TOJEKONOGONO
KOOSHOONO KISOANTOSITE TAIYOO SANOGOTOKIANWO TEISHUTUSERI
SUNAWATI (ITI) NITIBEI SOOGOKANNI OITEJISSAINI TEKIMOOSUBEKI
KONPONTEKI GENSOKUTOSITE SEIJIKANKEINI OITEWAZENJUTUNO
YONGENSOKUO SAIJUTUSERUGA TADASONOUTI DAIYONTENWO FUNSOONOBO-
OSI OYOBI HEIWATEKI KAIKETUNARABINI HEIWATEKI HOOHOOWOYOBI
TETUZUKINIYORU KOKUSAIJOOSEI KAIZENNOTAME KOKUSAIKYOORYOKU
OYOBI KOKUSAICHOOTEI JUNKYONO GENSOKUTO ARATAME KEIZAIKANKEI-
NI OITEWASHUTOSITE ZENKISEIJITEKI GENSOKUNO DAISAN TUUSHOOJO-
ONO KIKAIKINTOO OYOBI BYOODOOTAIGUUNO GENSOKUOFUENSI N (NI)
NITIBEIRYOOKOKUSEIFUNOTORUBEKI SOTITOSITE (I) NITIBEIRYOOKOKU
SEIFUWA EIKOKUORANDA SINASOBUEETO TAITOTOMONI TAHENTEKI
FUKASIN JOOYAKUNO TEIKETUNITUTOMU (RO) NITIBEIRYOOKOKU
SEIFUWA NIHON BEIKOKUEIKOKU SINAORANDA TAIKOKU SEIFUTONO
AIDANIFUTUINNO RYOODOSHUKENWO SONCHOOSI FUTUINNO RYOODOSHUKEN-
NGA KYOOISARURU BAWAIHITUYOO NARUSOTINIKANSI SOKUJI KYOOGIS-
UBEKI KYOOTEINO TEIKETUNITUTOMU MIGIKYOOTEI TEIKETUKOKUWA
FUTINNIOKERU BOOEKIOYOBI KEIZAIKANKEINI OITE TOKUKEITAIGUUO
HAIJOSI BYOODOONO GENSOKUKAKUHONI TUTOMU (HA) NIHONSEIFUWA
SINAOYOBI FUTUINYORI ISSAINOGUNTAIO (RIKUKAIKUU OYOBIKEISATU)
TESSHUUSUBESI (NI) RYOOKOKUSEIFUWA JUUKAIS_____ NOZOKUIKANA-
RU SEIKENWOMO GUNJITEKI SEIJITEKI KEIZAITEKINT SIJISEZU
(HO) RYOOKOKUSEIFUWA SINANIOKERU TIGAIHOOKEN (SOKAIOYOBI

0224 CL
12275KCS.

JVJ 0230 SKED - PAGE 3 S 8 DEC 41 5721

DANHIGITEISHONI MOTOZUKU KENRIOFUKUMU) WOHOOKISI TAKOKUNIMO
DOOYOONOSOTIO SHOOYOOSUBESI (HE) RYOOKOKUSEIFUWA GOKEITEKI
SAIKEIKOKU TAIGUUOYOBI TUUSHOOSHOOHEKI TEIGENNO SHUGINI
MOTOZUKU TUUSHOOJOOYAKU TEIKETUO SHOOGISUBESI (KIITOWA JIYUUH-
INMOKUNI OKU) (JIBINNI TUZUKU) PARA.

NM TU DE JVJ VA.

```
                                          0235 GL
                                          12275KCS.
```

Exhibit #15: Message from Commander-in-Chief Asiatic Fleet (CINCAF) to Washington informing them of British intercept of the two "Winds" instructional messages.

CINCAF Intelligence Report, 281430, 28 November 1941. PHH, Part 17, 2660.

Note at bottom of the copy is the typewritten note indicating that a copy of the message had been delivered to Captain Safford.

The note was delivered by "DW" or Donald W. Wigle, Station "C" (Cheltenham, MD) radioman in charge of Station "C" at the time of Pearl Harbor.

OPNAV-ANX-2 **NAVAL MESSAGE**		NAVY DEPARTMENT	COPY

DRAFTER	EXTENSION NUMBER 2027	ADDRESSES	PRECEDENCE
From CINCAF	FOR ACTION	OPNAV	OP / PRIORITY / ROUTINE / DEFERRED
Released by			
Date 28 NOVEMBER 1941			
TOR Coderoom	INFORMATION	COMSIXTEEN CINCPAC COMFOURTEEN	OP / PRIORITY / ROUTINE / DEFERRED
Decoded by P R WHITE			
Paraphrased by			

TEXT 281430

~~ULTRA~~   ~~ULTRA~~

FOLLOWING TOKYO TO NET INTERCEPT TRANSLATION RECEIVED FROM SINGAPORE X IF DIPLOMATIC RELATIONS ARE ON VERGE OF BEING SEVERED FOLLOWING WORDS <u>REPEATED FIVE TIMES AT BEGINNING AND END OF ORDINARY TOKYO NEWS BROADCASTS</u> * WILL HAVE SIGNIFICANCE AS FOLLOWS X HIGASHI HIGASHI JAPANESE AMERICAN X KITA KITA RUSSIA X NISHI NISHI ENGLAND INCLUDING OCCUPATION OF THAI OR INVASION OF MALAYA AND NEI XX ON JAPANESE LANGUAGE FOREIGN NEWS BROADCASTS THE FOLLOWING SENTENCES REPEATED TWICE IN THE MIDDLE AND TWICE AT THE END OF BROADCASTS WILL BE USED XX AMERICA HIGASHI NO KAZE KUMORI XX ENGLAND X NISHI NO KAZE HARE X UNQUOTE X BRITISH AND COMSIXTEEN MONITORING ABOVE BROADCASTS

*THIS IS IN MORSE CODE

ACTION	
20-G	LFS
20-GX	LPW?
20-GY	LWP

~~RI-SECRET-RI~~

IMPORTANT.—The information contained herein is not to be reproduced or referred to in any manner which may disclose its source

COPY DELIVERED TO CAPT SAFFORD, OP-20-N
31 MARCH 1944   D.W.

CERTIFIED TO BE A TRUE COPY /S/F.C.ALEXANDER, LT COMDR USNR

Exhibit #16: Intercepted version of "Stop" message (Japanese message number 2409). Intercept by Station "S," Bainbridge Island on 27 November 1941.

Transmittal message numbers (Japanese) 511, (San Francisco), 518 (SF), 520 (SF), and 523 (Washington, D.C.).

Washington received Nos. 512, 517, and 521. San Francisco received No. 524. Pages 4506 – 4513, and 4522 – 4524.

The third and fourth parts of the message, Washington nos. 521 and 524 (SF nos. 520 and 524) were sent in reverse order. In other words, part four of the message was sent before part three.

RG 38, Entry 1040 (CNSG Library), Box 156, "Diplomatic Intercept."

```
                IAB                    S 27 NOV 41        4506
```

511 SCDE TOKYO 87 27 930S JG

RIYOJI SANFRANCISCO

DAIQU HQFSK BYHBD UUTDY GOTLN UMGYU ACJCD AIHUW ZDUZL VGWOQ
DRJGR ODJUY JNQYH ABYGT XEMZX GTWTE LXFUU YJWKW WWZDF BJDKG
FBZMQ XZFNK DBUJY HTCJM HHZDB ZCNNK ZIPCK ENXIN WHWYB QMQBK
PRGUX JBJJL NBTGK WOCAG ZGDGO BYCCZ PHICC XJHTG CCCVE CAGGT
HKDNN MMUTZ TUJSY HZYTM HGGFC PKJKX FOCGK XQXXC JUZKF DUMKH
QXQJX CFBBT FIIHV XQYHQ HOTRT RZWCX ZXAHG MFTNG WUMQH EEUNR
MZXUD PEMLQ LENRZ LGJLK QEJBJ BDVJJ HKNIP FBFQP IAZUD JNZAW
CLBCF EHZBK ZDHDB LBBNZ TUAWX WQVUK GSWWZ XRELK SCGYY DJCNE
DYXBA MCPKN 79999 TAKAO
                        TOGO.

                                                    1240 S GL
                                                    9160

        SF DE JAB   S 27 NOV 41   4507

512 SCDE TOKYO 87 27 930S JG

KOSHI WASHINGTONDC

DAIQU HQFSK......

            (SAME TEXT AS OUR #4506)

                                                    1241 GL
                                                    9160

DE TOKYO 93 27 1025S JG

RIYOJI SANFRANCISCO

DAIQU HQFWK BYHBD RFOCJ RBMGW JDHAW TEKIL MNPZN ZYFNK JOAWK
IRFXC RTFSW FWDOX GEHZH QOJDU OCXTZ WAOZB CPLPK NNOSJ CUCPF
MTLOC INVYO IEORC TFVOS OSHNA OCCQW BFRUV CJTWS LFEWH ZKORB
IDJFE GGTPH OKBGV GTWEV DFUZL OQWAA POZMB DMRBZ CRUBN XNCFL
JMOPL ZMWEI VCLMG TCBNC ZJVON OJFNH XOPXP TNLGP

1346 S GL
9160

SF DE JAB   S 27 NOV 41

518 RIYOJI P2/43

GDZPO MSBPW JBJUR LMBYW OPCYA FCCHV WPBZI KGKCN YTWSC WKQKC
UWJWZ PLXTK SYYCO XGFGS UUIBO AWNPP PXQDB FEUBM OJNFN ZXVAH
MAFZS IMCOK FKRUC FVHGB PMWZE PWKJT WCDWQ TKJEF BGROV WDBGD
NOUJF ZURBO GCKCP CDVJL UXNJN GTJME PKFFH WGDCY NKLOK IIHRZ
85555 TAKAO
        TOGO.

1347 S GL
9160

SF DE JAB   S 27 NOV 41

TOKYO
520 SCDE/ 118 27 1110S JG

RIYOJI SANFRANCISCO

DAIQU HQFJK BYHBD NBQNC SVMOD JKCPC NFEOT KPBRW NFHPW BBWCO
HCMNT KMOUA VFPOV GLYNC POVVO CCSGR WRWGJ IDLJS YPAFO IUWNW
KKMVI XOUOT SRWFS TJLZV CVBMW BGUNO ZUFVW ODOYR WBORY ZWNKR
OLZWI CBZDO QOWTC FDUCN OBOPZ NARCN WSYNS OQKIP WBIQW MCNCU
ORVUO BANOR ENKVW KRCCU RBGPE ZSPCE JBONC WWPXW

                                                    1432 G GL
                                                    9160

SF DE JAB   S 27 NOV 41   4512

520 RIYOJI P2/68

RNCIA WZCNG WXOOO POAHN CNGUW PSTCE YRWYW OYBLL HSRRM QWYRQ
BETUR AGAPA LDUUN NNONX REZBB VMEBZ OCVWP OGCPO GICZR IEDBV
THCWB OEWRW NCOWM DWYRU ORFOD ORUBT PCPZD FNVIO RCUWN FOARF
KWBZR ONENY BOUVB WVNPY HDGYU WIICC AAMPP IRWBW GKVFM ZVGRO
WBBFN YUODO JYPHZ PBUYF BMSXA FOPAN JRCPO OMJWQ NNBON OCTBO
PNVJN CPYJO OSNCP RAPER BHOOI WBOBI UARHI AHWPY NJPFU NOLOP
XBRGN BSBNH POPCL FVTNO RWUQK 11000 TAKAO
                                                    TOGO.

                                                    1434 S GL
                                                    9160

SF DE JAB   S 27 NOV 41   4513

521 SCDE TOKYO 120 27 1120S JG

DE TOKYO 93 27 1155S JG

KOSHI WASHINGTONDC

DAIQU HQFNK BYHBD FLVAN IFNBK RESOI RQIFW SRWWO EHZLC WPTNG
SHPOP OPCMP SEERF SEIOK PPQIU JUMYJ WIHJO PTVZI XGQIH GSZYQ
POXJR RMGVW AJIWA PMIRY LWQZZ MPHJM SAZSW BBLJN FNGPO PWQUG
GOKPZ VKIGE YARWB OBWUW YOZXH AGNGT OKWNC NCNTO GOGJT BCKWH
AAWEG CBBOX MQORQ PUEIE YSOZA BSZLD FIKTW UXNAZ

1557 S GL
9160

SF DE JAB   S 27 NOV 41   4523

523 KOSHI P2/43

IOFAP TXCCQ CUCOW PRTVS NWNNP NHGGF CGMDR WRZGO BRBPL OJOWV
SRCAM DWDWT OBSPB TCTII ISFEL DRWBW RKVSN OUTFW WNGIV CHNOU
FXNTD UGUJB IIZFL ZBOQC PGNOC OCOPA UHRDW WLKNR CPISR ZCPCP
CNCAG CFSYK BBCPV SQDFC IMNII WWJDA GCOYE KECOL WZIFJ AUTAB
75555 TAKAO
        TOGO.

1600 S GL
9160

SF DE JAB   S 27 NOV 41   4524

524 SCDE TOKYO 93 27 1155S JG
RIYOJI SANFRANCISCO

Exhibit #17: Stencils of decrypted version of message #2409. (4 pages)

All pages contain key listed for 27 November in kanji numerals. Pages 2-4 also have key in Arabic numerals.

Key reads 12-4-7-13-9-1-19-6-8-17-2-16-11-3-15-18-14-10-5.

CCH Series XII.S, Box 22

十二	十	七	十三	九	一	九	六	八	七	二	十六	十一	三	五	七	四	十	五
X		E	I	C				IV	C	J			X	B		H	2	11
C		N	I	C	U	K	Y		D	B/G			U	N			D	13
J		X	H	2	U	S	H	2	A	D/G			D	2		K	F	15
U		I	V#	P	T	C	T	J	A	I ✓			P	T	2	D	B	16
2		N	2	H	D	G	C	L	W	H	J		O	E	U	X	N	J	17
K	G	W	Q	I	Y		J	N	C	U	J		D	M	A	G	N	D	18
E	M	H	Y	C		Y	M	B	L	W	H		J	L	W	T	M	K	19
D	F	W	H	C		P	H	T	B	Z	K	F	U	Q	X	T	W	M	G	18
U	M	T	Y	Q	X		J	H	G	C	D	N	C	Y	L	W	T	U	F	18
M	N	B	H	J	G	C	Z	K	F	U	I		P	J	E	R	E	T	B
K	G	Q	O	H	I	N	D	W	E	Z	P	K	N	N	V	L	Z	2
H	W	M	T	T	L	E	B	O	H	L	F	J	Q	R	U	X	T	M
2	U	Q	R	G	T	L	D	Z	C	Z	V	B	K	Y	3	K	E	U	Q
X	H	B	T	C	L	N	Y	C	A	B	G	F	X	H	L	G	U	J	X
Q	Q	K	R	C	U	X	N	G	K	W	Q	E	A	G	S	U	5	Z
J	H	P	Z	C	M	B	N	Z	O	R	O	B	J	W	Y	F
X	E	R	W	V	B	A	K	G	D	Q	I	C	Y	L	W	J	H	N
C	E	G	C	E	Y	M	Z	D	H	D	A	G	G	K	Z	W	Z	K
F	U	N	C	X	U	C	I	G	D	R	Z	K	T	Q	X	K	Y	D
B	N	X	Z	A	A	P	P	B	J	U	X	X	E	R	W	J	B
B	R	G	X	G	C	K	C	B	L	G	D	Q	E	J	E	W	M	U
T	M	B	A	G	J	N	K	Y	B	R	J	X	M	B	L	W	H	J
E	Z	J	H	T

酉	七	圭	九	一	十二	六	八	七	二	十一	エ	三	十二	六	四	十	五	
	Z	N	C				W	M	M			Q	J			G	F	11
	K	Y	R	R	J	H			N	C	N		D	E			M	13
	O	I	U	F	M	N		C	P	O	L		B	Z		T	T	15
	R	W	B	O	E	A	V	D	Z	K			F	U	Z	C	L	16
	B	S	N	C	P	O	D	W	N	F		W	E	R	W	B	O	17
C	I	C	X	J	K	C	F	Q	Z	K		F	U	B	A	N	C	18
O	D	W	N		F	C	U	T	Y	R		W	B	O	O	Z	I	19
X	J	K	C		F	Q	Z	K	F	U	G	D	M	G	Z	Z	N	18
G	F	Q	F		H	W	L	J	N	C	P	O	O	C	B	J	V	18
F	E	H	L	R	W	B	O	E	K	F	G	X	J	K	C	V	Y	19
G	G	C	J	B	G	F	Q	F	J	U	D	G	N	C	P	O	Q	
S	G	U	M	M	D	R	W	B	O	H	Z	E	F	P	L	N	I	
U	T	W	O	G	C	U	A	G	A	G	P	H	N	C	P	O	E	
U	P	J	P	W	Y	V	A	R	W	R	Q	Z	Z	D	K	J	O	
I	H	W	L	J	N	C	P	O	K	P	M	H	X	V	N	F	R	
B	O	Z	Z	D	K	J	O	V	I	M	H	Q	V	J	N	N	C	
O	K	P	M	H	L	T	Z	W	R	W	B	O	A	L	O	H	T	
A	B	L	W	A	O	W	M	D	F	Z	P	J	H	U	S	X	F	
W	G	X	E	W	K	S	B	B	X	E	W	D	M	X	J	O	V	
N	V	T	I	T	I	L	D	G	C	P	J	U	A	N	C	P	O	
P	G	K	V	E	I	F	M	D	R	W	B	O	F	J	U	X	S	
P	T	S	C	K	H	E	R	N	T	K	J	C	Z	N	C	P	O	
P	W	Y	L	I	R	W	B	O	F	J	U	X	S	G	P	T	S	
X	E	Y	M	L	Z	H	Z	U	S	T	R	T	I	T				

	12	14	7	13	9	1	19	6	8	17	2	16	11	3	15	18	4	10	5
	⊥	+⑩	x	≡	π	−	÷π	x	∧	+x	=	+li	+=	=	+2	+∧	⑩	+	2
1	P		O	U	1					M	H	U				I	R	W	B
2	O		Z O		A	N	N	C			R	O	U			I	A		G
3	G		K	R	W	B	O	B		J	W	D	N		C	P		O	U
4	I		!	F	Z	Q	L	Z	R	W	B	O				C	E	N	Y	N
5	C		P	O	C	N	O	D	C	Q	B	J		V	A	R	N	B	O
6	Z	K	W	D	N	C	P	O	C	N	W	Y		V	A	B	K	L	Z
7	R	W	B	O	G		X	Q	U	N	C	P		O	M	H	K	L	U
8	I	B	I	R	W		B	O	R	B	O	H	N	C	P	O	M	H	F
9	E	Z	Q	U	X		R	W	B	O	H	Z	N	C	P	O	V	S	V
10	D	R W	B	O	S	G	T	G	N	C	P	O S	H	I	L	R	W		
11	B	O	M	T	O	V	N	C	P	O	M	B	N	G	R	W	X	R	O
12	V	N	C	P	O	M	B	F	E	C	N	U	X	R W	B	O	M	D	
13	T	E	N	C	P	O	S	D	Z	T	T	Y	R W	B	O	U	Q	O	
14	H	N	C	P	O	M	B	U	S	B	K	F	E	R	W	B	O	W	Y
15	C	Y	U	Z	A	J	N	C	P	O	M	B	Z	W	G	I	T	Y	R
16	W	B	O	D	H	K	H	N	C	P	O	M	B	G	K	U	S	R	W
17	B	O	R	F	N	C	P	O	E	N	U	S	B	J	V	A	R	W	B
18	O	U	V	N	C	P	O	B J	V A R	X	V	I	F	R	W	B	O		
19	E	V	U	V	N	C	P	O	B	J	V	A	M	D	M	H	F	E	R
20	E W	B	O	I	G	N	C	P	O	N	F	F	E	L	Z	I	S	T	Y
21	R	W	B	O	U	F	L	Z	N	C	P	P O	B	J	V	A	T	U	Z
22	W	V A	R	W	E	F	N	C	P	O	O	Z	S	G	H J	R	W		
23	N	N	C	P	O	V	A	W	Y	V	A	O	Y	R W	L	A	N		
24	C	P	O	U	S	T	T	R	W	J	G	N	C	P	O	P	Z	G	K
25	O	Y	R	W	T	K	N	C	P	O	L	J	V	A	W	Y	V	A	R
26	W	H	E	N	C	P	O	N	X	O	Y	R	W	F	B	N	C	P	O
27	M	D	N	F	E	B	R	W	S	N	C	P	O	B	J	V	A	L	
28	D	G	K	O	R	W	S	R	N	C	P	Q	I	F	P	B	L	Z	
29	W	Y	V	A	R	W	U	Y	N	C	P	Q	G	U	N	F	M	D	W
30		U	W	R	N	Q	N	C	P	O	O	C	W	Y	U	W	U	I	
31	R	W	K	F	Y	F	K	S											

Exhibit #18: Translation worksheets (W.S.) #818-821 (5 pages) of message #2409.

CCH Series XII.S, Box 22.

```
XE  IC  NC  JX  BH  ZC  NI  CU  KY  DB  GU  ND  JX  HZ
KPJJC   IP  JI  KYOKUMU  PA  KU  NO  SAI  HI  JŌ  JI  TAI
US  AZ  AD  GD  ZK  FU  IV  PT  CJ  JA  TV  PT  ZD  BZ
NI  TAISHO  SURU TŪSIN     HŌHŌ  SITE  SAI  HŌHŌ NIGU  IN
NZ  HO  GC  LW  HJ  OE  UX  NJ  KG  WQ  IY  YJ  NC  UJ
MEI     O  SHI  YŌ SURU  TO SERU  NI    RYŌ TI  PINO  TH SIMO
DM  AG  ND  FM  HY  CY  MB  LW  HJ  LW  TM  KD  FW  HC
MIGI WA  JŪ RAN  SEIMEI (W) SHI  YŌ SHI     TEAT    TSU ZURU
DH  TB  ZK  FU  QX  WM  GU  TY  QX  JH  GC  DN  CY  LW
TEKI NARU TŪSIN BUN ( HI RA BUN )  U  SARU SEI(SU)  SHI
TU  FM  NB  HJ  GC  ZK  FU  IP  JF  UE  TB  KG  QO  HI
KE RAN NAI YŌ  O  TŪSIN  SEN BETU MING NARU  NI  TUKI
ND  WE  ZP  KN  NV  LZ  ZH  WM  TT  TE  BO  HL  FJ  QR
JŌ  I  KAN NAKI O  KI SERA  ( SAKU SEI / )    NITION GUN
                   NETAGI
UX  TM  QU  QR  GL  DZ  CZ  VB  KY  ZK  FU  QX  MB  TC
TO  U.S.S.R. AN SHŌ TUTU SEKI  ]  NO TŪSIN BUN (W)O Kata
NY  CA  BG  FX  HL  GU  JX  QQ  KR  CU  XN  GK  WQ  FA
15   du   ZUTE MYTE [  HI  JI KATA OYOBI KU BI  TA  RYŌ  SYOKI SEI
GS  US  ZJ  HP  ZC  MB  NZ  ZO  PO  BJ  WY  YF  XE  RW
    NI KINAN ZAI KIN (W)O MEI    SURU  S  T  O  P  ende
VB  AK  GD  QI  CY  LW  JH  NC  EG  CE  YM  ZD  HD  AG
   ( NO    SURU GARI TO (SI) SHI )  P     JAPAN NIKO DENPO WA
GK  ZJ  ZK  FU  UX  CU  CI  GD  RZ  KT  QX  KY  DB  NX
TA  NO  TŪSIN TO  KP  BE GU SURU  TYU DEN BUN NO SAI HŌ
ZA  AP  PO  BJ  UX  XE  RW  TB  BR  JX  GC  KC  BL  GD
NI  SUI GNI S.  TO  P    NARI MON JI  O  SŌ NYŪ SURU
QE  JE  WM  UT  MB  AG  JN  KY  BR  JX  MB  LW  HJ  FZ
MONO TUSU ( SURA  (W) RI NO MON JI  IWO SHI YŌ SEZU
JH  (T                    
    )
```

LZ	NC	WM	MQ	JG	FM	KY	RR	JH	NC	ND	FM	BO	TU	FM
KI	P	(IKA	2	KAN	NO	HYŌ	)	P	JŪ	KAN	(·)	FE	RAN	

NC	PO	LB	ZT	TY	RW	BO	EA	VD	ZK	FU	ZC	LW	BS	NC
P	sfull	ARI	MU	RA	full	(·)	AN	FŌ	TŪSIN	NIN	SHI	SEKI	T	

PO	DW	NF	WE	RW	BO	OC	IC	XJ	KC	FQ	ZK	FU	BA	NC
sfull	A	SA	I	full	(·)	RADIO		HŌ	SŌ	NITE	TŪSIN	SE	JŌ	T

PO	DW	NF	CU	TY	RW	BO	OZ	IC	XJ	KC	FQ	ZK	FU	GD
sfull	A	SA	KU	RA	full	(·)	HŌ		HŌ	SŌ	NITE	TŪSIN	SURU	

MG	ZZ	NY	GF	QF	HW	LJ	NC	PO	OC	BJ	VA	FE	HL	RW
NI	TYŌI	TYŌ	SYU	SE	YO	P	sfull	A	S	I	KA	L		

BO	EK	FG	XJ	KC	VY	TG	GC	JB	GF	QF	JU	DG	NC	PO
(·)	KAI	GAI	HŌ	SŌ	BŌ		O	NITE	TYŌ	SYU	FU	NŌ	P	sfull

OC	SG	UM	MD	RW	BO	HZ	EF	PL	NI	CU	TW	OG	CU	AG
A	Z	SIKUMA	full	(·)	TAI	NICHI	ATU	RA	KU	MASU		KU	WA	

AG	PH	NC	PO	EH	UP	JP	WY	VA	RW	BO	ZZ	DK	JO	VI
WA	RU	P	sfull	E	DO	GU	T	I	full	(·)	HININ	(GE)	ZUNGI	(SURU)

HW	LJ	NC	PO	KP	MH	XV	NF	RW	BO	ZZ	DK	JO	VI	MH
BESHI	YO	P	sfull	HA	NA	BUSA	full	(·)	HININ	(GE)	ZUNGI	(SURU)	NI	

QV	UN	NC	PO	KP	MH	LT	ZW	RW	BO	AL	OH	TB	AB	LW
RE	RI	P	sfull	HA	NA	ZO	NO	full	(·)	TENTŌ	NIRU		SHI	

AO	WM	DF	ZP	JH	US	XF	ZW	GX	EW	KS	BB	XE	WD	MX
SIN	(RIYŌSI	KAN)	NI	WIGA		NO	KENEKI	(GOGU	SURU)	IP I		NO	TAME	

JO	VI	NV	TI	TI	LD	GC	PJ	UA	NC	PO	KP	GK	VE	IF
ZUNGI	(SURU)	O	SU	SU	MEI	O	KARE	TASI	P	sfull	HA	TA	KE	

MD	RW	BO	FJ	UX	SG	PT	SC	KH	ER	NT	KJ	CZ	NC	PO
MA	full	(·)	NIHON	TO			TIRU	KOKU	KŌ	DAN	ZETU	SEKI	P	sfull

KP	WY	LI	RW	BO	FJ	UX	SG	PT	SC	XE	YM	LZ	HZ	US
HA	T	TORI	full	(·)	NIHON	TO			TIRU	KANKEI	KI	TAI	I	

TR	TI	IT												
KIN	SU													

(820)

-P	PO	GU	SG	VA	QQ	RW	BO	FJ	QR	UX	SG	PT	QR	GL
spell	HI	Z	I	KATA	spell	(.)	NIHIA	KUN	TV				RON	SHI

DZ	HW	JN	NC	PO	VU	BJ	VA	ZW	RW	BO	FJ	UX	SG	PT
TOTU	SE	RI	P	spell	HI	S	I	NO	spell	(.)	NIHIA	TO		

AG	MY	DO	IP	US	WE	JN	PG	LB	NC	PO	WE	IS	TY	IJ
WA	ZEN	MEN	SEN	NI	I	RI	TOTU	ARI	P	spell	I	BA	RA	HI F

RW	BO	OC	OH	ZW	HZ	EF	KH	ER	NT	KJ	KY	JX	LZ	XA
spell	(.)	KIMIQ PORU	NO TAI	MEN	KOKU	KO	DAN	ZEN	NO	JI	KI	YOTEI		

EW	BJ	YM	NC	PO	WE	MH	KL	LZ	RW	BO	SG	PT	RW	HI
KAI DEN ARITA(SI)	P	spell	I	NA	F.A	KI	spell	(.)					NO	KEN

KS	AN	CZ	IF	NC	PO	VA	IV	VA	FE	AG	RW	BO	SG	PT
SERI TARI	YA	P	spell	I	SH	I	KA	WA	spell	(.)				

ZW	HI	TKS	AN	CZ	NC	PO	FE	IV	VA	AG	II	RW	BO	SG
NO KEN		SERI TARI	P	spell	KA	SHA	I	WA	FI	spell	(.)			

PT	QA	IV	SZ	BJ	GS	GC	EK	LW	TI	NC	PO	CQ	IS	IF
NITAGI				ITDI	O KAI	SHI	SU	P	spell	KO	BA	YA		

FE	AG	RW	BO	SG	PT	KH	DX	ZW	CE	YM	CE	ZB	KR	SG
KA WA	spell	(.)				KOKU	ZIN	NO	JAPAN		NYU RIKU	YUBI	TOKA	

XP	MR	GL	AG	LA	DB	SI	LW	ZH	NC	PO	CQ	DP	MD	RW
RIKUSHI	WA	1	SAI	TEI	SHI	SEPA RETA(y)	P	spell	KO	DA	MA	spell		

BO	FJ	NC	PO	CQ	UI	IF	MD	RW	BO	IJ	NC	PO	CQ	IF
(.)	NY	P	spell	KO	MI	YA	MA	spell	(.)	SIWA	P	spell	KO	YI

MH	II	RW	BO	XR	AF	NC	PO	CU	XN	GK	RW	BO	TM	QU
NA	AI	spell	(.)			P	spell	KU	BO	TA	spell	(.)	H.S.S.R	

NC	PO	CU	JN	IS	TY	RW	BO	QI	TG	NC	PO	CU	TI	ZW
P	spell	KU	RI	BA	RA	spell	(.)			P	spell	KU	SU	NO

LZ	LZ	RW	BI	FA	PT	NC	PO	MD	WY	UW	GK	US	RW	BO
KI	NI	spell	NE	GERMANY	P	spell	MA	T	U	TA	NI	spell	(.)	

OC	MA	WY	UW
ITALY			

PO	UI	MH	UI	RW	BO	ZO	AN	NC	PO	UI	AG	GK	RW	BO
spell	MI	NA	MI	spell	(·)			P	spell	MI	WA	TA	spell	(·)

BJ	WD	NC	PO	UI	IF	ZQ	LZ	RW	BO	CE	NY	NC	PO	CN
CANADA	P	spell	MI	YA	ZA	K	spell	(·)	MEXICO	P	spell	MO

OD	CQ	BJ	VA	RW	BO	ZK	WD	NC	PO	CN	WY	VA	BK	LZ
RO	KO	S	I	spell	(·)	BRAZIL	P	spell	MO	T	I	ZU	KI

RW	BO	GX	QO	NC	PO	MH	KL	UI	BI	RW	BO	RB	OH	NC
spell	(·)	PANAMA	P	spell	NA	PA	MI	NE	spell	(·)	ARGENTINA	P

PO	MH	FE	ZQ	UX	RW	BO	HZ	NC	PO	VS	VD	RW	BO	SG
spell	NA	KA	ZA	TO	spell	(·)	TAI	P	spell	NAN	PO	spell	(·)	FR,I

TG	NC	PO	SI	II	RW	BO	MT	OV	NC	PO	MB	NG	RW	XR
P	spell	TEI	I	spell	(·)	NETHER LANDS,E.T	P	spell	(N)	FA	spell	BU

OV	NC	PO	MB	FE	CN	UX	RW	BO	MD	TE	NC	PO	SD	ZT
P	spell	(W)O	KA	MO	TO	spell	(·)	MA	REI	P	spell	OKU	M

TY	RW	BO	UQ	OH	NC	PO	MB	US	BK	FE	RW	BO	WY	CY
RA	end spell	(·)	AUSTRALIA	P	spell	(W)O	NI	ZU	KA	end spell	NANSEI

UZ	AJ	NC	PO	MB	ZW	GI	TY	RW	BO	DH	KH	NC	PO	MB
REN	PO	P	spell	(W)O	NO	DE	RA	spell	(·)	TEISI	K	P	spell	(W)

GK	US	RW	BO	RF	NC	PO	EN	US	BJ	VA	RW	BO	UV	NC
TA	NI	spell	(·)	P	spell	O	NI	S	I	spell	(·)	NON	P

PO	BJ	VR	XV	IF	RW	BO	EV	UV	NC	PO	BJ	VA	MD	MH
spell	S	MITO (NE)	BU	YA	spell	(·)	RAI	NEN	P	spell	S	I	MA	NA

FE	RW	BO	IG	NC	PO	NF	FE	LZ	IS	TY	RW	BO	UF	LZ
KA	spell	(·)	NEN	P	spell	SH	KA	KI	BA	RA	spell	(·)	TU	KI

NC	PO	BJ	VA	TU	ZW	VA	RW	EF	NC	PO	OZ	SG	HJ	RW
P	spell	S	I	AE	NO	I	spell	NICHI	P	spell	KO	Z	YO	spell

NN	NC	PO	VA	WY	VA	OY	RW	LA	NC	PO	US	TT	RW	JG
TOKI	P	spell	I	T	I	RO	spell	I	P	spell	NI	SI	spell	2

NC	PO	PZ	GK	OY	RW	TK	NC	PO	LJ	VA	WY	VA	RW	HE
P	spell	SAN	TA	RO	spell	3	P	spell	YO	I	T	I	spell	4

NC	PO	NX	OY	RW	FB	NC	PO	MD	NF	EB	RW	WS	NC	PO
P	spell	GO	RO	spell	5	P	spell	MA	SA	RO	spell	6	P	spell

BJ	VA	LD	GK	OY	RW	SR	NC	PO	IF	PB	LZ	WY	VA	RW
S	I		TA	RO		7	P		YA			T	I	
UY	NC	PO	GU	NF	MD	WY	UW	RW	NQ	NC	PO	OC	WY	UW
8	P		HI	SA	MA	T	U		9	P		A	T	U
UI	RW	KF	YF	KS										
MI		O	O	W										

Exhibit #19: Translation of Japanese diplomatic message No. 2409, Tokyo to Washington, 27 November 1941.

SIS 25609, JD-1: 6985. Known both as the "hidden word" or "STOP" message. (4 pages)

Tokyo to Washington, 27 November 1941, SIS 25609. RG 457, Entry 9032, Box 301, Multinational Diplomatic Translations.

SECRET

From: Tokyo
To : Washington
27 November 1941
(J19)

Circular #2409 (In 4 parts, complete)

Rio de Janeiro to Santiago as Circular #324.

(Washington sent to Ottawa, Mexico City, Bogota, Caracas, Havana, Panama, New York, and New Orleans as unnumbered message.)

(Part 1)

   Handle as Chief of Office routing.

   With international relations becoming more strained, the following emergency system of despatches, using INGO DENPO (hidden word, or misleading language telegrams) is placed in effect. Please study this carefully.

   Make up a table with the left column containing the code words and the right the corresponding plain (decoded) text. Please see that there is no mistake in transcribin this.

   EXAMPLE: A message meaning:

   "Japan and U.S.S.R. military have clashed", will read:

   "HIJIKATA and KUBOTA, clerks, have both been ordered to your embassy on 15th (begin spell) S T O P (end spell)."

   In order to distinguish these cables from others, the English word S T O P will be added at the end as an indicator. (The Japanese word "OWARI" (end) will not be used.)

(Part 2)

Code Word	Meaning
ARIMURA	Code communications prohibited.
ASAI	Communications will be by radio broadcasts.
ASAKURA	Will communicate by radio broadcast. You are directed to listen carefully.
ASIKAGA	Reception of overseas broadcast Impossible due to interference.

5609
6985

SECRET (continued) (Y) Navy Trans. 12-2-41 (7)

SECRET   COPY

(PART 2)
CODE WORD   MEANING

ARIMURA   Code communications prohibited.

ASAI   Communications will be by radio broadcasts

ASAKURA   Will communicate by radio bradcast.
                   You are directed to listen carefully.

ASIKAGA   Reception of overseas broadcast
                   Impossible due to interference.

AZUMA   Pressure on Japan increasing continually

EDOGUTI   Prepare for evacuation

HANABUSA   Preparations for evaciation have been
                   completed.

HANAZONO (?)   Prepare to entrust Embassy property to
                   suitable foreign envoy (on consul) there.

HATAKEYAMA   Relations between Japan and ...
                   ... (blank) .....have been severed.

HATTORI   Relations between Japan and ...
                   ... (blank) ... are not in accordance
                   with expectation.

PART 3)

HIZIKATA   Japan's and ... (blank) ... military
                   forces have cleashed.

HOSINO   Japan and ... (blank) ... are entering
                   a full fledged general war.

IBARAGI   Communicate to us probable date of breakin
                   off of relations between Japan and the
                   country to which you are accredited.

INAGAKI   Have you - - ? - the ... (blank) ... Matte

ISHIKAWA   I have - -?- the ...(blank)..matter.

KASHIWAGI   We are commencing military action
                   against ...(blank)...

KOBAYAKAWA   Stop issuing all entrance and transient
                   visas to Japan, to persons of ...(blank)..
                   nationality.

(PART 3) Con't

CODE WORD	MEANING
KODAMA	Japan
KOMIYAMA	China
KOYANAGI	England
KUBOTA	U.S.S.R.
KURIBARA	France (?)
KUSUNOKI	Germany
MATUTANI	Italy

(PART 4)

CODE WORD	MEANING
MINAMI	U.S.A
MIWATA	Canada
MIYAZAKI	Mexico
MOROKOSI	Brazil
MOTIZUKI	Panama
NAGAMINE	Argentina
NAKAZATO	Thailand
NANGO	French Indo-China
NEGI (?)	Netherlands East-Indies
OGAWA	Burma (?)
OKAMOTO	Malaya
OKUMURA	Australia
ONIZUKA	Union of South Africa (?)
ONODERA	Enemy country
OTANI	? (Possibly: friendly, or allied country)
ONISI	Year
SIMANAKA	Day (?)

-3-

SECRET   COPY

(PART 4) con't.

CODE WORD	MEANING
SAKAKIBARA	Tsuki) Month
SIGENOI	(Kō) Paragraph
SANZYŌ	(Toki) Time
ITIRŌ	1
NISAKU	2
SANTARŌ	3
YOITI	4
GORŌ	5
MASAROKU	6
SIMETARŌ	7
YASOKITI	8
HISAMATU	9
ATUMI	0

SIS 25609

JD-1: 6985   (Y) Navy Trans. 12-2-41 (7)

Exhibit #20: Example of telegram sent from Japanese consulate, Honolulu, Kita Nagao, to the Japanese Foreign Ministry (Gaimudaijin), 13 November 1941, encrypted in J-19. Telegram, Kita to Gaimudaijin, Tokyo, 13 November 1941.

NARA, RG 38, Box 167, Folder 5830/69, "Pearl Harbor Investigation: Winds msgs." (3 of 3)

Mackay Radio RADIOGRAM
THE INTERNATIONAL SYSTEM

- Full Rate
- Code Rate (CDE)
- Preferred Rate (LC)
- Radio Letter (NLT)
- Urgent Rate

CHECK
Receiver's Number

Send the following Message Full Rate unless otherwise checked subject to the terms on back hereof, which are hereby agreed

CDE   Honolulu   322

GAIMUDAIJIN TOKYO

BP121 QRBBC   J-19

MMDQI	GYCXO	IZXEW	CDUTR	ICWLL	UHBOI	BBZYU	TDLBE	EGVUA	PYLHE
JBXGD	EUHTH	ZPFNE	THLVY	YUCZU	SLTGI	CXZPN	KLBLE	YQCXV	KZKVV
UQZOX	OHLNQ	SFOOJ	ISSDY	BMPWT	HSGXD	HXSZW	LUHNK	OZAEI	CKZSI
RGHLL	XUULT	IUXDU	NXJWV	MQAZP	YTSLW	JRDVM	TMBUR	TRTMV	NNGBH
KFTZQ	BUWVX	UEYGN	ORTPR	XYFDP	GEYRM	LTOQJ	YLHVI	OUGZO	BACAU
QVQOG	DLWZE	LSZFV	XJMXV	FAQUR	WLOFJ	XVANW	LWKFY	AHGSJ	LMKTJ
KUXJC	GHNNV	ELTEG	RTLGU	UHWKK	UNKXM	HYNDW	BYTTH	XKDGX	ZBWVG
ATMMM	WSIVN	AETTV	PZCAS	YVCXA	NJLHU	UDULG	FUYEZ	ZXEBQ	FCRJW
WYFBI	VQJBR	CISRA	MXVJK	WUZQH	CNBKA	YEDVW	BYPDA	DZWPK	87777
BBRBV									

KITA

Exhibit #21: Translation of Japanese diplomatic message No. 118, Tokyo to Honolulu, 28 November 1941.

SIS 25859, JD-1: 7157, Translated 7 December 1941.

Pearl Harbor Hearings (hereafter "PHH"), Part 37: 668.

SECRET

From: Tokyo (Togo)
To: Honolulu
November 28, 1941
J19 (Priority)

#118. Re your #232[a].

To be handled in government code.

Anticipating the possibility of ordinary telegraphic communication being severed when we are about to face the worst of situations, these broadcasts are intended to serve as a means of informing the diplomats in the country concerned of that situation without the use of the usual telegraphic channels. Do not destroy the codes without regard to the actual situation in your locality, but retain them as long as the situation there permits and until the final stage is entered into.

a - Not available.

b - S.I.S. #25432 in which Tokyo sends a circular giving hidden-meaning words which will be broadcast in the event that code communication is cut off.

Exhibit #22: Federal Communications Commission (FCC) Exhibits, Certification of Secretary FCC, dated 8/18/44, with attachments." (5 pages)

Attachment 2 is "Message intercepted by FCC on 12/4/41."

Attachment 3 is message intercepted by FCC on 12/5/41.

NARA, RG 80, 167EE, Box 122, (JCC) Exhibit 142. (5 pages)

TOP SECRET   SECRET

                         UNITED STATES OF AMERICA

                       Federal Communications Commission

                                           Washington, D. C.,
                                           August 18, 1944

   I hereby certify that the attached are true copies of documents

described as follows:

   Document No. 1 is a true copy of the weather messages which Major
   Wesley T. Guest (now Colonel), U.S. Army Signal Corps, requested
   the Commission's monitors to be on the lookout for in Tokyo broadcasts and to advise Colonel Bratton, Army Military Intelligence,
   if any such message was intercepted. This request was made on
   November 28, 1941 at approximately 2140 GMT.

   Document No. 2 is a true copy of a weather message from Tokyo
   station JVW3, intercepted by Commission monitors at approximately
   2200 GMT, December 4, 1941, which at 9:05 p.m. EST, December 4,
   1941, having been unable to contact Colonel Bratton's office,
   was telephoned to Lieutenant Brotherhood, 20-G, Watch Officer,
   Navy Department, who stated that he was authorized to accept messages of interest to Colonel Bratton's office.

   Document No. 3 is a true copy of a weather message from Tokyo
   station JVW3, intercepted by Commission monitors at 2130 GMT,
   December 5, 1941, which was telephoned to Colonel Bratton at
   his residence at 7:50 p.m. EST, December 5, 1941.

   Document No. 4 is a true copy of two weather messages intercepted by Commission monitors from Tokyo stations JLG 4 and JZJ
   between 0002 and 0035 GMT, December 8, 1941, and telephoned to
   Lt. Colonel C. C. Dusenbury, U.S. Army Service Corps, at the request of Colonel Bratton's office at approximately 8 p.m. EST,
   December 7, 1941. Document No. 4 also contains the Romaji version of these messages.

on file in this Commission, and that I am the proper custodian of the
same.

                                 IN WITNESS WHEREOF, I have hereunto set
                                 my hand, and caused the seal of the
                                 Federal Communications Commission to
          (Seal)   be affixed, this twenty-first day of
                                 August, 1944.

                                                T. J. Slowie
                                                 Secretary

                        S E C R E T
                                                            TOP SECRET

3 (a)

DOCUMENT NO. 1

GROUP ONE IS EAST WIND RAIN

GROUP TWO IS NORTH WIND CLOUDY AND

GROUP THREE IS WEST WIND CLEAR STOP

GROUPS REPEATED TWICE IN MIDDLE AND AT END OF BROADCAST

The above are the weather messages Major Wesley T. Guest requested the Commission to monitor on November 28, 1941.

3 (b)

DOCUMENT NO. 2

TOKYO TODAY NORTH WIND SLIGHTLY STRONGER MAY BECOME CLOUDY TONIGHT TOMORROW SLIGHTLY CLOUDY AND FINE WEATHER

KANAGAWA PREFECTURE TODAY NORTH WIND CLOUDY FROM AFTERNOON MORE CLOUDS

CHIBA PREFECTURE TODAY NORTH WIND CLEAR MAY BECOME SLIGHTLY CLOUDY OCEAN SURFACE CALM

Weather message from station JVW3 transmitted at approximately 2200 GMT, December 4, 1941.

3 (c)

SECRET

DOCUMENT NO. 3

TODAY NORTH WIND MORNING CLOUDY AFTERNOON CLEAR BEGIN CLOUDY EVENING. TOMORROW NORTH WIND AND LATER FROM SOUTH. (repeated 3 times)

Weather message from Tokyo station JVW3 transmitted at approximately 2130 gmt December 5, 1941.

3 (d)

SECRET

DOCUMENT NO. 4

English

THIS IS IN THE MIDDLE OF THE NEWS
BUT TODAY, SPECIALLY AT THIS POINT
I WILL GIVE THE WEATHER FORECAST:
    WEST WIND, CLEAR
    WEST WIND, CLEAR

THIS IS IN THE MIDDLE OF THE NEWS
BUT TODAY, AT THIS POINT SPECIALLY
I WILL GIVE THE WEATHER FORECAST:
    WEST WIND, CLEAR
    WEST WIND, CLEAR

Romaji

NYUSU NO TOCHU DE GOZAIMASU GA
HONJITSU WA TOKU NI KOKO DE
TENKI YOHO WO MOSHIAGE MASU
    NISHI NO KAZE HARE
    NISHI NO KAZE HARE

NYUSU NO TOCHU DE GOZAIMASU GA
KYO WA KOKO DE TOKU NI
TENKI YOHO WO MOSHIAGE MASU
    NISHI NO KAZE HARE
    NISHI NO KAZE HARE

Above are the two weather messages from Tokyo stations JLG4 and JZJ transmitted by them between 0002 and 0035 GMT December 8, 1941.

SECRET

Exhibit #23: FCC translation worksheets for Japanese "weather broadcasts" of 4, 5, and 8 December 1941.

There are two worksheets for 8 December of broadcasts heard at 0002 (GMT) and 0458 (GMT).

NARA, RG 173, Entry 180, Box 5, "Personal Papers of George Sterling." (4 pages)

No. 3.

続いて天気豫報。東京地区
今日は北の風やゝ強く日晴で一時は曇る事が
あります。今晩も明日も北の風で晴天勝ちになる
神奈川 今日は北の風で晴勝ちで午後から
時々雲が多くなる事があります
千葉市。今日は北の風（雨）曇りとなる
海上はやゝ波が・・・

SECRET

ROMAJI

     TSUZUITE TENKI YOHO ... TOKYO CHIKU KYO WA KITA NO KAZE YAYA TSUYOKU HARE DE ICHIJI WA KUMORU KOTO GA ARIMASU. KOMBAN MO MYONICHI MO KITA NO KAZE DE SEITENGACHI NI NARU.
KANAGAWA KYO WA KITA NO KAZE DE HAREGACHI DE GOGO KARA TOKIDOKI KUMO GA OKU NARU KOTO GA ARIMASU.
CHIBA SHI. KYO WA KITA NO KAZE (AME - not clear) KUMORI TO NARU. KAIJO WA YAYA NAMI GA . . .

Translation

     Weather forecast next. Tokyo region. North wind rather strong, clear, may become cloudy temporarily (at times). Tonight and tomorrow, north wind, will be clear most of the time. (Above repeated)
Kanagawa - north wind today, clear. In the afternoon occasionally clouds will increase.
Chiba. (city of) North wind today. (Rain) cloudy. On the sea there will be waves ...

CALL JVW3　GMT 2153-2230　FREQ 11725KC　DATE 12/4/41　RECORD # T4233 N01526　STATION PONDA

No. 6

ROMAJI

    TOKYO FUKIN NO TENKI YOHO WO MOSHI AGEMASU.
KYO WA TOHOKU NO KAZE DE ASA NO UCHI WA KUMORI, NITCHU WA HAREMASU.
SHIKASHI, YUGATA KARA MATA KUMO GA OKU NARIMASU.

    MYONICHI WA KITA NO KAZE, NOCHI MINAMI NO KAZE TO TSUTAETE ORIMASU.

Translation

    Next is the weather forecast for the Tokyo vicinity. Today it is northeast wind. During the morning it will be cloudy becoming clear during the day. However, from this evening, clouds will increase again.

    It has been reported that tomorrow it will be north wind but later south wind.

CALL	GMT	FREQ	DATE	RECORD #	STATION
JVW3	2116-2147	11725	12/5/41	14306 N01522	PONDA

No. 1 [Japanese handwritten text]

Romaji

HONJITSU WA TOKU NI KOKO DE TENKI YOHO WO MOOSHIAGEMASU.

Nishi No Kaze hare

TRANSLATION

Today, especially at this point, we will give the weather forcast.

West wind, clear.(repeat)

CALL	GMT	FREQ	DATE	RECORD #	STATION
JLG4	0002-0035	15105 KC	12/8/41	14191 NO 1600	PONDA

No. 7

ROMAJI

NYUSU NO TOCHU DE GOZAI MASU GA KOKO DE TENKI YOHO WO MOSHI AGEMASU. NISHI NO KAZE HARE, NISHI NO KAZE HARE, NISHI NO KAZE HARE.

Translation

In the midst of the news broadcast I will now give the weather forecast. West wind clear (repeated three times.....trans)

CALL	GMT	FREQ	DATE	RECORD #		STATION
JZJ	0458-0532	11800	12/8/41	14205	NO.1608	PONDA

Exhibit #24: FCC Logs, Radio Intelligence Division, Night Watch Log 28 November - 8 December 1941.

RG 80, Entry 167EE, Box 122, Exhibit 142A (5 pages)

Ex 142A

Dec. 5, 1941

Mr. Sterling:

At 7.45 p.m. Mr. Carter called in from Portland with the following information:

JVW3 2130G

TODAY NORTH WIND MORNING CLOUDY AFTERNOON CLEAR BEGIN CLOUDY EVENING. TOMORROW NORTH WIND AND LATER FROM SOUTH.
(the above was repeated three times)

JVW3 sent a time signal at 2200G and then:

I WILL NOW GIVE YOU THE WEATHER REPORT (nothing further, carrier on but no modulation - evidently cutoff in Tokyo)

REMARKS BY CARTER;
They are getting a more complete picture of the operations now and it is evident that at 2130G the Tokyo weather is transmitted and at 2200G the Tokyo weather and weather for other prefectures. Reception is getting better and estimate efficiency on this assignment has increased approximately twenty-five percent.

------------------- F I N I -------------------

Foned Col. Bratton and gave him the message at 7:50 p.m.

Remarks by Col. Bratton:

Results still negative but am pleased to receive the negative results as it means that we have that much more time. The information desired will occur in the middle of a program and possibly will be repeated at frequent intervals. (Asked Col. Bratton if I should communicate the information to Portland- concerning the fact that the desired data will be in the middle of a program.) No. I will have a conference with Lt. Col. Dusenberg in the morning and will contact Mr. Sterling in that regard.

------------------- -F-I-N-I- -------------------

DE

FEDERAL COMMUNICATIONS COMMISSION

SECTION OF MAIL AND FILES

FROM

TO

RADIO INTELLIGENCE

DIVISION

(The following handwritten)

Night Watch Log

Nov. 24th to Dec. 8th
1941

RETURN THIS FILE
PROMPTLY

DE

PAPERS ARE NOT TO BE
REMOVED FROM
THE FILE

Nov. 24, 1941	1.	At 6:55 PM the Supervisor of the Coast Guard Radio Station at Alexandria, Va. telephoned to report that W9WGI was causing serious interference to their circuit on 4050 kcs. Requested Supervisor to inform this office immediately if the interference was again heard. (No further reports from CG up to midnight)
Nov. 25, 1941		At 9:10 the Supervisor of SA-P telephoned in from Jackson, Miss. requesting information relative to the resignation of Henry Gantt, an operator at SA-10. (Memo. re: conversation placed on Mr. Sterling's desk.)
Nov. 26, 1941		Handled routine correspondence and traffic.
Nov. 27, 1941		At 6:20 pm Monitoring Officer Cave of NA-9 called in regard to Wash. Case 4001 and 4002. Mr. McIntosh gave Cave the information requested.
Nov. 28, 1941		At 7:55, the Major Guest telephoned in requesting Mr. Sterling's home phone number. Gave him the requested information. At 8:00 pm long distance operator called on Na. 2995 stating that Portland, Oregon was calling and desired to contact Mr. Sterling. Informed operator that Mr. Sterling was not here but that he could be reached at his home Evergreen 278. At 10:20 Mr. Sterling called giving instructions he wished passed on to Mr. Norman, Mr. North and Miss Perry.
Nov. 29, 1941		Handled routine correspondence and traffic.

Dec. 1
1. 5:05 P.M. Monitoring Officer CA-8 (Bairiey) telephoned to report that Ferguson (Wash. 3423) original informant, has moved out of neighborhood where original key clicks had been heard and requested further instructions. Told Bairiey to contact Officer House of Auburn Police for further information. Also contact Ferguson at his new address for detailed description of signals he had heard previously.

2. At 5:45 P.M. telephoned Col. Bratton. Gave him a message per Mr. Sterling's instructions.

3. 9:05 P.M. telephoned Mr. Sterling re verification of frequencies for Portland.

4. 9:30 P.M. Monitoring Officer Duncan SA-5 telephoned from Tallahassee, Fla. stating he had heard unlicensed station JUMP (Wash. 3930) and probably could have complete evidence of unlicensed operation within two days. He stated that the subject was undoubtedly using a phonograph oscillator. Duncan requested information as to whether he should remain in Tallahassee or return to St. Augustine and work on some in-active alleged subversive cases. Informed Duncan to remain in Tallahassee two more days and endeavor to complete his evidence on Wash. 3930.

5. 9:45 P.M. sent TWX to Portland confirming frequencies.

Dec. 2
1. At 7:35 P.M. long distance operator called on Na 2995 asking for Mr. Sterling. Operator stated that Portland, Ore. was calling. Informed her that Mr. Sterling was not here but that he could be contacted at his home in Baltimore, Evergreen 278.

Dec. 3
1. 6:15 P.M. received TWX from GS-P relative to NDA cases.

2. 6:25 P.M. telephoned Mr. Peterson for information concerning NDA cases.

3. 6:43 TWX to GS-P containing instructions relative to NDA cases.

4. 7:15 P.M. long distance operator of Portland, Ore. called on NA 2995 for Mr. Sterling. Informed her that Mr. Sterling was not in office at present but that I would try to contact him.

5. 7:20 called Lafayette Bowling Alley and had them page Mr. Sterling. They reported that Mr. Sterling had already departed.

6. 7:45 P.M. Mr. Sterling called this office and directed me to take message from Mr. Carter at Portland, Ore.

7. 7:52 P.M. contacted Mr. Carter at Portland, Ore. and obtained message for Mr. Sterling.

8. 7:55 P.M. telephoned Col. Bratton at his home and delivered a message in accordance with Mr. Sterling's instructions.

9. 8:37 P.M. Mr. Sterling called this office and contents of message from Portland, Ore. was read to him.

Dec. 4
1. 6:55 P.M. called Mr. Norman at his home in reference to message from GS-P concerning Mr. McKinney. Mr. Norman advised that no further action was necessary.

2. 8:12 P.M. received a message from Mr. Carter at Portland, Ore.

3. 8:25 P.M. unable to contact Lt. Col. Dusenburg either at the War Dept. or at his home.

4. 8:40 P.M. telephoned Mr. Sterling requesting instructions relative to a message from Mr. Carter.

5. 8:45 P.M. called ONI watch officer at Navy Dept. to ascertain if he was permitted to accept messages of interest to Col. Bratton's office. The officer in charge stated that he was not certain but that he would inquire and call me back.

6. 9:05 P.M. Lt. Brotherhood 20-G Watch Officer Navy Dept. telephoned to state that he was authorized to accept message in question. Gave Lt. Brotherhood the message from Mr. Carter.

7. 9:32 P.M. Lt. Brotherhood called to inquire if any other reference to weather was made previously in program intercepted by Portland. Informed him that no other reference was made.

Dec. 5.
1. 7:45 P.M. Mr. Carter called in from Portland, Ore. with a message.

2. 7:50 P.M. telephoned Col. Bratton at his residence and repeated the message from Mr. Carter.

3. 11:05 P.M. Monitoring Officer Dunphey of CA-6 telephoned in requesting information on Wash. Case 3259. Informed Dunphey would try to get the information for him in the morning.

Dec. 6.
1. Handled routine correspondence and traffic.

Dec. 8.
1. 6:15 AM Mr. Dunphey called in, no results. Told him take six hours off, then assume duties for six hours, then eight hours off, alternating with Baltimore Unit.

8:00 A.M.
2. /Mr. Meriwether called in, no results. Told him to remain on job until noon when CA-6 unit would take over. Informed him to take over watch again at 6:00 P.M.

3. 8:50 A.M. NA-3 called re Washington Case 3722, off air. Mac gave him some important bearing and/or intercept assignment.

4. 12:00 Noon. Mr. Meriwether and Mr. Blum at office. One will take 6:00 P.M. to Mid., the other 6:00 A.M. to Noon, sandwiched with Falls Church.

5. 12:10 P.M. Mr. Berle of State Department called - Wanted Mr. Fly, finally got Mr. Fly.

Exhibit #25: Translation of Japanese diplomatic message No. 2444, Tokyo to Washington, 1 December 1941.

SIS 25606, JD-1: 6984.
Translated 1 December 1941.

NARA, RG 457, Entry 9032, Box 301, "Multi-national Diplomatic Translations"

From: Tokyo
To : Washington
1 December 1941
(Purple)

Circular #2444

The four offices in London, Hongkong, Singapore and Manila have been instructed to abandon the use of the code machines and to dispose of them. The machine in Batavia has been returned to Japan. Regardless of the contents of my Circular message #2447*, the U.S. (office) retains the machines and the machine codes.

Please relay to France, Germany, Italy, and Turkey from Switzerland; and to Brazil, Argentina, and Mexico from Washington.

*Not available.

25606

Exhibit #26: Translations of Japanese diplomatic message No. 2445,

Tokyo to Havana, 2 December 1941,
SIS 25879, translated 8 December 1941;
and message No. 2447, Bern to Ankara,

SIS 25837, JD-1: 7125,
translated 6 December 1941.

NARA, RG 457, Entry 9032, Box 301,
"Multi-national DiplomaticTranslations."

From: Tokyo (Togo)
To: Havana
December 2, 1941
J19-K9

Circular #2445   Strictly secret.

Take great pains that this does not leak out.

You are to take the following measures immediately:

1. With the exception of one copy of the O^a and L^b code, you are to burn all telegraph codes (this includes the code books for communication between the three departments and the code books for Army and Navy communication.

2. As soon as you have completed this operation, wire the one word Haruna.

3. Burn all secret documents and the work sheets on this message.

4. Be especially careful not to arouse the suspicion of those on the outside. Confidential documents are all to be given the same handling.

The above is preparatory to an emergency situation and is for your information alone. Remain calm ―― ―― ――.

Also sent to Ottawa, Vancouver, Panama, Los Angeles, Honolulu, Seattle and Portland.

a - PA-K2 system.
b - LA system.

ARMY   25879   SECRET   Trans. 12/8/41 (3)

SECRET

From: Bern (Mitani)
To: Ankara
December 2, 1941
J-19

(Tokyo Circular #2447)

Orders have been issued to our diplomatic officials in North America (including Manila), Canada, Panama, Cuba, the South Seas (including Timor), Singora, Chiengmai, and to all our officials in British (including our Embassy in London) and Netherlands territory to inform me immediately upon the burning of all their telegraphic codes except one copy of Oite and "L".

Relay from Berlin to Lisbon, Helsinki, Budapest and Vienna; Relay from Rome to Bucharest, ---; relay from Berne to Vichy, Ankara, Lisbon, Madrid; relay from Rio to Buenos Aires, Lima, Santiago, ---, Mexico, Panama, Bogota; relay from Bangkok to Hanoi, Saigon; relay from Canton to Haihow, ---.

ARMY   SECRET   Trans. 12/8/41 (S)

Exhibit #27: Translation of Japanese diplomatic message No. 867,

Tokyo to Washington, 2 December 1941.

SIS 25640, JD-1: 7017.
Translated 3 December 1941.

NARA, RG 457, Entry 9032, Box 301, "Multi-national Diplomatic Translations."

From: Tokyo
To : Washington
(Purple)
2 December, 1941

#867   REVISED TRANSLATION

1. Please destroy by burning all of the codes you have in your office, with the exception of one copy each of the codes being used in conjunction with the machine, the O code (Oite code) and the abbreviation code (L). (This includes other Ministries' codes which you may have in your office).

2. Also in the case of the code machine itself, one set is to be destroyed*.

3. Upon completing the above, transmit the one word HARUNA.

4. Use your discretion in disposing of all text of messages to and from your office, as well as other secret papers.

5. Destroy by burning all of the codes brought to your office by telegraphic courier Kosaka. (Consequently, you need not pursue the instructions contained in my msg #860**, regarding getting in touch with Mexico.)

* It was not previously known that Washington had more than one code machine. However, the following would indicate they held at least two:
   (a) Paragraph 2 directs "one set" (Hitokumi) be destroyed.
   (b) Paragraph 1 directs retention of 1 set of machine code keys.
   (c) On 3 December, the day after this "destruction" order, there was normal volume both ways in machine traffic.

** (Dated 1 December) JD-1: 6941 (SIS #25550) Have courier Kosaka, now enroute Brazil to Washington, return to Japan in the Tatsuta Maru leaving Los Angeles the 25th. If he cannot go to Mexico as planned, communicate with Mexico to arrange the business he was to attend to.

JD-1: 7017   (See SIS #25640 for Army translation)   Navy Trans. 12-3-41

Exhibit #28: Translation of Japanese diplomatic message No. 2461,

Tokyo to (Circular), 3 December 1941.

SIS 25855, JD-1: 7123.
Translated 6 December 1941.

NARA, RG 457, Entry 9032, Box 301, "Multi-national Diplomatic Translation."

From: Tokyo.
To : - - (Circular).
3 December 1941
(PA-K2)

Circular #2461

    Secret.

    Please keep the code list (INGO HIKAE)*
(including those in connection with broadcasts) until the last
moment, and if by any chance you have already destroyed them
they will have to be resent to you, so please notify us of this
fact immediately.

    This message is as a precaution.

*"Hidden Word" code to be used in plain Japanese language messages.

Exhibit #29: Listing of HARUNA messages from Japanese diplomatic facilities acknowledging the destruction of codes (2 pages). Read columns: Originator of message, "file date" (date of message), intercept date and time, date and method intercept was sent to Washington (note mail, air, or courier), date received at SIS, Washington, and remarks that contain source of intercept with station message number. [*The notations "PLG3," next to Batavia and "PMA," next to Soerabaja, are the callsigns of the Netherlands East Indies commercial radio stations that actually received the message from Tokyo. This use of local radio facilities was not uncommon.*]

Page two is copy of intercepted cable from the Japanese diplomatic facility located in Hollywood, CA, to Tokyo. Source is SRH-415 "Haruna Messages from Various Japanese Offices Abroad Signaling Destruction of Codes, December 1941."

Orig	Filed date time	Intcpt date tm	Mailed	Rcvd SIS	Remarks
DUBLIN	12/6 1040A	None		12/12(?)	May stopped by censor
WASHINGTON	? 819P	12/7 0121G	12/8 mail	12/10 907A	Stn 1 23956
SO. TCKHLA	12/7(?) 530P	1810G	12/8 Air	12/17 1236P(?)	Stn 5 013667
CHICAGO	12/6 1109A	12/6 1722G	12/6 Air	12/8 1108A	Stn 2 16142
OTTAWA	12/4 257P	12/4 2050G	12/5 Air	12/6 1025A	Stn 2-16020
SEATTLE	12/4 951S	12/4 1850	12/5 Courier	12/5 917A	Stn 7-54146
S. FRAN	12/4 659P	12/4 0342	12/6 AIR	12/8 1109A	Stn 2-16048
SEATTLE	12/4 951S	12/4 1901	12/5 AIR	12/6 1025A	Stn 2 16017
HAVANA	12/2 1811	12/3 0050	12/3 Courier	12/3 920A	Stn 7 53838
HOLLYWOOD	12/2 802P	12/3 0446	12/4 AIR	12/5 952A	Stn 2 15932
PORTLAND ORE	12/3 1215P	12/3 2033	12/4 AIR	12/6 1024A	Stn 2 15949
PORTLAND ORE	12/3 1215P	12/3 2030	12/4 Courier	12/4 ?	Stn 7 54003
NEW ORLEANS	12/2 517P	12/3 0016	12/3 Courier	12/3 920A	Stn 7 53840
NEW ORLEANS	12/2 511P	12/3 0005	12/3 AIR	12/4 1031A	Stn 2 15908
NEW ORLEANS	12/2 511P	12/3 0041	12/3 Courier	12/3 920A	Stn 7 53891
PLG 3 BATAVIA MENADA	12/3 419S	1123	12/3 Air	?	Stn 5 013322
PYA SOERABAJA	12/3 545	12/3 0610	12/3 Air	?	Stn 5 013315
B.C. VANCOUVER	12/2 546P	12/3 0302	12/4 AIR	12/5 952A	Stn 2 15922
PANAMA	12/2 342P	12/2 2151	12/3 AIR	12/4 1031A	Stn 2 15893
NEW YORK	12/2 507P	12/2 2348	12/3 AIR	12/4 1031A	Stn 2 15903
NEW YORK	12/2 507P	12/2 2355	12/3 Courier	12/3 920A	Stn 7 53834

HARUNA MSGS

STATION 2   3 DECEMBER 1941

HOLLYWOODCALIF

GAIMUDAIJIN TOKYO

HARUNA

NAKAUCHI

0446/8E

15932

Exhibit #30: WDGS G-2 message of 5 December 1941 to G-2 Hawaii Department instructing General Fielder's office to contact Commander Joseph Rochefort via Fourteenth Naval District "regarding weather message."

NARA Box 457, Entry 9032, B1369, Folder 4217.

STANDARD FORM No. 14A
APPROVED BY THE PRESIDENT
MARCH 10, 1926

FROM: WAR DEPARTMENT
Date: DEC 5 1941
BUREAU:
For the Acting A. C. of S., G-2

Colonel, G. S. C.,
Executive Officer, G-2.

TELEGRAM

OFFICIAL BUSINESS—GOVERNMENT RATES

SENT NO. 519, 12/5

December 5, 1941.

#519

ASSISTANT CHIEF OF STAFF HEADQUARTERS
G2 HAWAIIAN DEPARTMENT
HONOLULU TERRITORY HAWAII

CONTACT COMMANDER ROCHEFORT IMMEDIATELY THRU COMMANDANT FOURTEEN

NAVAL DISTRICT REGARDING BROADCASTS FROM TOKYO REFERENCE WEATHER

I certify that this message is on
official business and necessary   MILES
for the public service.

Colonel, G.S.C.
Executive Officer, G-2

SECRET CABLEGRAM   **SECRET**
las

DECLASSIFIED
Authority WWD963016
By IT NARA Date 6-7-06

Exhibit #31: Translation by Office of Naval Intelligence of news program broadcast by station "JZI," 8 December 1941 (Japanese time) on 9535 kilocycles. This translation was provided to the Honolulu offices of the Federal Bureau of Investigation and the Federal Communications Commission on 15 December 1941 (7 pages). "Winds" message, "West Wind Clear," appears on pages 3 and 5 of the transcript. Pearl Harbor Exhibit 142D, Federal Communications Commission,

NARA, RG 80, Entry 167EE, Box 120; also in PHH, Part 18: 3325-3329 (7 pages)

November 14, 1945

MEMORANDUM TO MR. GESELL:

The attached communication was received by me from my Supervisor in Hawaii on November 14, 1945. I am furnishing it for your information.

In passing, I would like to add that the Hawaiian staff of the Radio Intelligence Division was not authorized by the War Department to participate in the weather intercept.

G. E. Sterling
Assistant Chief Engineer

Attachment

FEDERAL COMMUNICATIONS COMMISSION
Engineering Department
Radio Intelligence Division
November 7, 1945

COPY

Address reply to:
609 Stangenwald Building
Honolulu 1, T. H.

**PERSONAL AND
CONFIDENTIAL**

VIA CLIPPER AIRMAIL

Mr. George E. Sterling
Chief, Radio Intelligence Division
Federal Communications Commission
Washington 25, D. C.

Dear Mr. Sterling:

I have read with interest the extracts from the Army and Navy Pearl Harbor boards. I agree with you that the Army's statement to the effect that, "On December 7 a number of illegal radio stations interfered with the radio operations of the Army." is the result of ignorance and lack of understanding on the part of Army personnel concerned. I should like to know the exact basis for the statement. I assume that something more than the general allegation was made.

There have been numerous references in the newspapers lately to the coded Japanese weather message which was to reveal their plans. In reading through the translations of Japanese news broadcasts recorded at HA-P and translated by the O.N.I., Honolulu, I came across the following with which you are probably familiar. However, since it differs considerably from the current news stories and may be in addition to the "Weather Message" referred to, I am repeating it for your information. This translation was made from recordings of the JZI Japanese language broadcast on 9535 kc. for December 8, 1941, Japan time. The translation included a report of the Japanese attacks for the day (December 8, Japan time, being December 7, Honolulu time) and, therefore, the "Weather Forecast" followed rather than preceded the Pearl Harbor attack. The O.N.I. translator inserted the following in parentheses between news items: "(Here a weather forecast was made--as far as I can recollect, no such weather forecast has ever been made before. His exact words were: "Allow me to especially make a weather forecast at this time--'West wind, clear'". Since these broadcasts are also heard by the Japanese Navy it may be some sort of code.)" It will be noted that the O.N.I. translator was apparently unaware of any previous search for such a forecast. The same weather forecast was repeated later in the December 8 broadcast.

The translations made by the O.N.I. were furnished this office and the F.B.I. by messenger. We did not receive the translations for December 8 until December 15, 1941. As a matter of fact, I believe that the translations for December 3, 4, 5, 6, 7 and 8 were all received from the O.N.I. on December 15. This was not an unusual delay since translations had generally been received from a week to two weeks after the date of the broadcast.

Present indications are, according to the newspapers, that the Senate House Committee which is investigating the Pearl Harbor attack will not visit Hawaii for sometime.

Sincerely yours,
/s/ Lee R. Dawson

Station JZI Program
Date 12/8/41 (Japan Time)
Frequency 9535 Kilocycles

With our army and navy entering in a state of war with England and America at dawn of the 8th, an Imperial declaration of war against England and America was announced. Our army and navy, hence, has entered in a state of war with England and America. In regard to this, the Imperial army and navy headquarters at 6 am on the 8th announced that our army and navy entered a state of war with England and America in the Western Pacific at dawn today, the 8th. At the same time, the brilliant achievements of our armed forces, too, were announced by the Imperial Army and Navy headquarters, as follows: (1) Our Imperial Navy at dawn today, the 8th made a death-defying raid upon the American naval and air strength in the Hawaiian area. (2) Our Imperial Navy at dawn today sank the British gunboat ....(sounded like Petrol) and captured the American Gunboat ....(sounded like Nico) at Shanghai. (3) Our Imperial Navy at dawn today raided Singapore and achieved great results. (4) Our Imperial Navy at dawn today bombed enemy military establishments at Davao, Wake and Guam. (5) Our Imperial Army, upon entering into a state of war at dawn today, attacked Hongkong. (6) Our Imperial Army, cooperating closely with our Imperial Navy, undertook a landing operation in Malaya at dawn today and is obtaining great results.

Furthermore, according to a Domei dispatch from the front, our imperial air force at eight this morning carried out its first raid on Hongkong and returned safely back to their base. Immediately afterwards, a second raid reportedly was carried out.

Then, a Domei dispatch from Honolulu reported that our naval air force raided Honolulu at 7 am Hawaiian time, which is 3:05 am Japan time.

According to an announcement made by the White House, the casualty inflicted by our air force's raid was very great and the oil storage tanks on Guam, which is presently being besieged by our Imperial Navy, are throwing up large amounts of smoke.

A British gunboat was sunk and an American gunboat was captured. This news was announced by the Imperial headquarters, but according to the announcement made by the headquarters of our fleet in China waters at 9 am today, the 8th, our Commander-in-Chief of the fleet in the China waters sent his staff officers to the British Gunboat Picadelli (phonetic) and the American Gunboat Wills (phonetic), respectively, immediately after our country entered in a state of war at 5:40 am and requested them to surrender for the peace and order of Shanghai. Since the British gunboat refused to surrender, we were compelled to sink it. The American gunboat was captured with............. Thus read the announcement.

-1-

Our Imperial army is repulsing the British troops which have invaded Thailand. In regard to this, our embassy in Bangkok made the following announcement at 4 am today: For a long time, we have been expecting the British troops to invade the southern part of Thailand and, as expected, they began to cross the Malayan border early this morning. To preserve the peace of the Southern Pacific and protect the independence of Thailand, our government immediately started a negotiation with Thailand and, at the same time, started an attack against the British troops, which are being presently wiped out. Thus was the statement announced by our embassy in Thailand.

The next is a Domei despatch from Shanghai. Since dawn today, Shanghai has been in a state of war and to maintain the peace and order within the International Concession, our army and navy detachments made a special penetration. At the same time, the following announcement was made in the names of the high commanders of our army and navy in Shanghai: The Japanese troops have been reinforced within the international concession, but what the aim of the Japanese troops is to maintain the peace and order, and prosperity of the international settlement. The Japanese troops have no hostile feeling against the residents carrying on rightful occupations within the concession.

Our imperial army has disarmed the American marines stationed in North China. In regard to this, a Domei despatch from Peking reported that our imperial army this morning issued an ultimatum to disarm to the 200 American marines stationed in Tientsin, Peking and Tsingtao (?) and since each accepted this ultimatum, the disarming of the marines was carried out at 1 pm today.

Today, his majesty, the Emperor, released an Imperial decree to our Imperial Army and Navy, as follows: "Since the outbreak of the China incident, my army and navy have stoically fought for over four years to punish the bad and in spite of their great achievements, the war has not been quelled yet. After considering the past and seeing the England and America's claims are scandalous, I attempted to make my government settle the situation peacefully. In spite of this, not only did England and America show no sincerity to consider peace, but instead strengthened their military and economic coercion in an attempt to make our country yield. Hence, to protect our country's existence and self-defense and establish lasting peace in East Asia, I have decided to declare war against England and America. Having faith in your loyalty and bravery, I look forward to the accomplishment of our ultimate aim and the upholding of our national glory".

In reply to this Imperial decree, War Minister Tojo and Navy Minister Shimada respectfully made the following reply: Your subjects, Hideki and Shigetaro, respectfully reply. WE cannot help but be deeply impressed on receiving such a glorious (?) decree and we, subjects, promise to cooperate solidly and exert our utmost effort and thus expect to respond to your will. On behalf of the government and the Army and Navy, we, Hideki and Shigetaro, your subjects, respectfully make this reply. December 8, 1941.

                        (Signed) Hideki Tojo, Minister of War.
                        Shigetaro Shinada, Minister of Navy.

Since our Army and Navy has started a war against England and America in the Western Pacific at dawn today, our Government at 7 am today held an emergency session of the cabinet at the premier's residence. Outside of Foreign Minister Togo, all the cabinet ministers were present. Firstly, Minister of Navy Shimada reported the developments of war against England and America and based on this report, the course to be taken by the government was decided, whereupon Premier Tojo called on the Emperor and reported the decision.

According to a Domei dispatch from Washington, Foreign Minister Togo reported by order Envoys Kurusu and Nomura to call on Secretary of State Hull at 1:00 P.M. on the 7th, 3:30 A.M. of the 8th Japan time, and present our government's official reply to the American note of the 26th. At the same time, Foreign Minister Togo invited American Ambassador to Japan, Grew, to his official residence at 7:30 A.M. today and handed him an official note similar to the one handed to Secretary of State Hull. Immediately afterwards at 7:45 A.M., he invited British Ambassador to Japan, Craigie and explained to him the text of this reply.

Immediately after our loyal Army and Navy had entered a state of war with England and America at dawn today, it was decided to break off diplomatic relations with both countries and enter a state of war. Consequently, our government at 11:45 A.M. today declared war against England and America. At the same time, an order for the convocation of a two days special session of the Diet on the 15th was issued. At the emergency session urgent bills of appropriations and other nature will be presented and, at the same time, the governments policy to cope with the unprecedented emergency is expected to be explained by Premier Tojo and other ministers.

(Here a weather forecast was made as far as I can recollect, no such weather forecast has ever been made before. His exact words were "Allow me to especially make a weather forecast at this time, 'West wind, clear'." Since these broadcasts are also heard by the Japanese Navy, it may be some sort of code.)

At 8:30 A.M. today, our government made the Foreign Ministry announce the results of the Japanese-American negotiation and the Japanese-American notes. The announcement made clear the real facts of the effort exerted by our government till the very last minute to preserve the peace of the Pacific. Japan's note to America was an official reply to America's note of the 26th and notified the fact no settlement can be expected even if the negotiation were to be continued. It actually was a final notice to America, and within it, our country made public to the world the reason for declaring the war. It is as follows: That America's principles adhered to in the Japanese-American negotiation are idealistic and her proposal, for example, is absolete and ignores the realities of East Asia. That England and America's economic oppression is more mean than armed resistance. That the imperialistic exploitation of England and America has been the root of disorder in East Asia. That the continuation of aid to Chungking absolutely cannot be ignored by our country. That England and America, scheming with the other hostile nations, are intensifying their action to make Japan and China fight each other, but our country is............ Taking these five points up, our country's fairness was made clear to the world.

Now, let me give you the text of the Foreign Ministry's announcement. From the standpoint of settling the Pacific problems peacefully and thus contributing toward world peace, our government has carried on negotiations with America ever since the middle of last April. At first, a proposal was made by America, but, just at that time, the joint defense of French Indo-China was concluded. Then, England and America, cooperating with each other, took action to strengthen their economic oppression. Hence, Premier Konoye sent a message to President Roosevelt in August to urge America to reconsider her action. However, America, adhering to her claims for the abrogation of the Japanese-German-Italian Alliance, the withdrawal of Japanese troops stationed in China and the matter of international trade without discrimination, totally rejected our claim. Of course, these demands cannot be accepted by our country. As a result, our country hurriedly dispatched Envoy Kurusu to America and bearing patience upon patience, our country continued the negotiation with a conciliatory attitude. However, America, adhering to her principles, which are counter to the realities of East Asia, assumed an attitude to ignore our claim and effort. At the same time, England, Chungking, Dutch East Indies and Australia renewed their effort to strengthen their anti-Japanese preparation. Hence, the Japanese-American negotiation finally reached a critical state. Besides, the situation surrounding our country became such as to leave no room for optimism. Since it became clear that America absolutely has no intention to continue the negotiation, our government sent a memorandum as of the 7th to the American Government and made her attitude clear. The developments of the Japanese-American negotiation announced by the Foreign Ministry were as follows: Our country's desire to establish the East Asia mutual prosperity sphere and contribute toward world peace has been trampled by the world war fever and the challenging threats of England and America. America, mobilizing 10,000,000 soldiers and setting up a two-ocean navy of 3,500,000 men, has intensified her unjust scheme to make the world her own. Even in the recent Japanese-American negotiation, they attempted to oppress our country with an arrogant attitude of being not even afraid of God, and as an attitude toward the leader of East Asia, it was too much to ignore. In spite of this, our country, hoping for America's consideration to the very end together with our people, continued to remain calm. However, today, the war of the

-4-

Pacific has been brought about by America and England. It should be definitely stated at this time that President Roosevelt and Premier Churchill has undertaken the Pacific war without consideration of the war's havoc on humanity as one of their program for the domination of the world. In the course of the four and a half years of the China incident, each and every Japanese has shed tears of indignation against England and America's wicked hostile attitude, but has remained patient for the sake of the peace of the Pacific as well as the world. This patience, today has reached its limit. The time has come to rise unitedly and risk the fate of the nation for the cause of righteousness.

At dawn today, December 8, the announcement of the Imperial Army and Navy headquarters to the effect that our Imperial Army and Navy will enter a state of war against American and British forces in the Western Pacific at dawn today was made public throughout our country through the radios and newspapers. Every one throughout the country has now further strengthened their determination that the inevitable has at last come and instantaneously, our peace loving idea has been transformed into a determination to punish the evil and cut off the sinister hands of the outrageously wicked England and America. Today, the sky over Japan was clear and devoid of even a speck of cloud and under this blue sky, which seemed to be congratulating the promising future of Japan, who has risen to fight for the establishment of a new order of East Asia as well as of the world just like the brilliant rays of the sun, our excellent air force, as an indication of our strong air defense, is flying about everywhere! When I received this report that war on the Pacific had broken out, I hurried to my............and on my way, I saw reflected upon the passers-by as well as those working, a hereto unseen expression of seriousness. Then with the issuing of the Imperial decree declaring war at 11:45 A.M., the nation's determination to march forward and support the emperor's will gushed forth. Not long afterwards, Premier Tojo's confident determination of our country was announced over the radio, and, at the same time, the achievements of our Navy, which is carrying on operations against American and British forces from Malaya to Honolulu with an overflowing amount of power as though the Pacific were too small, were reported throughout the nation. Hence, the confidence and spirit to rise against England and America and to secure Asia as the haven of the Asiatic race through the establishment of a new order of the world has been made to flare up within the heart of the people.

The next is a Domei despatch of the 8th from Stockholm, which states that according to a Reuter's despatch of the 7th from Washington, official sources in Washington believe that Germany will declare war against America in the next 24 hours.

At this time, let me again make a weather forecast "West wind, clear". (Repeated this forecast).

Now, let us broadcast to you the talk of Major General Yoshizumi,

Exhibit #32: Intercepted "hidden word" (or Stop) message, Japanese serial #92494, sent on morning of 7 December 1941 by Japanese Foreign Ministry to several stations. "Jap Msgs, October - December 1941,"

RG 38, Entry CNSG Library, Box 156; also in PHH, Part 37:729.

```
SF DE JAH                    S 7 DEC 41                    5651
   621 S TOKYO 19 7 850S JG
   KOSHI PANAMA
   URGENT 92494 KOYANAGI RIJIYORI SEIRINOTUGOO ARUNITUKI
   HATTORI MINAMI KINENBUNKO SETURITU KIKINO KYOKAINGAKU
   SIKYUU DENPOO ARITAS$ STOP -- TOGO'


         XX                                  1205 S JP
                                             7630
   S 387/7 850S GR20
   OBESE OVALS RPWMO RFNMO RTJMO RWFMO GNOME



     SF DE JAH                    S 7 DEC 41               5652
     622 S TOKYO 19 7 850S JG KOSHI HAVANA
     623 S TOKYO 19 7 850S JG RIYOJI HONOLULU
     624 S TOKYO 19 7 850 JG RIYOJI NEWYORK
     625 S TOKYO 22 7 850S JG JAPANESE CONSUL VANCOUVER
     626 S TOKYO 22 7 850S JG JAPANESE MINISTER OTTAWAONT
        ( SAME TEXT AND SIGN AS OUR NR5651 )


     SF DE JAH                    S 7 DEC 41               5653
     627 S TOKYO 19 7 850S JG RIYOJI SANFRANCISCO
     628 S TOKYO 19 7 850S JG RIYOJI PORTLANDORE
     629 S TOKYO 19 7 850S JG RIYOJI SEATTLE
     630 S TOKYO 19 7 850S JG RIYOJI NEWORLEANSLA
     631 S TOKYO 19 7 850S JG RIYOJI CHICAGOILL
     632 S TOKYO 19 7 850S JG RIYOJI LOSANGELESCAL
        ( SAME TEXT AND SIGN AS OUR NR5651)

                                                  1243 JP
                                                  7630
```

Exhibit #33: Corrected translation of the 7 December 1941 "hidden word" message.

Exhibit No. 142, NARA, RG 80, Entry 167EE, Box 120; PHH, Part 37: 3321

From: Tokyo
To: (Circular telegram)
7 December 1941
(Plain Japanese language using code names)

Circular #2494

    Relations between Japan and England are not in accordance with expectation.

Note: The above is the translation furnished the President and other high officials at 1100 (EST) on Dec. 7, 1941. In the rush to get it out, one code word was overlooked. The correct translation reads as follows:
"Relations between Japan and the following countries are not in accordance with expectation: England, United States."
This omission, which was not discovered until January, 1944, does not appreciably change the information that was available at 1100 (EST) on Dec. 7, 1941.

Note: The Army translation of Circular #2494 (supplied in March, 1944) is as follows:
"Relations between Japan and ————————are approaching a crisis (on the verge of danger): England, United States."

Note: See JD #6985.

JD-1:7148   SECRET   (M)   Navy Trans.   7 December 1941 (STT)

Exhibit #34: Message from War Department, Office of the Chief Signal Officer, Signal Intelligence Service, to monitoring stations in the Philippines, the Territory of Hawaii, and the Presidio, requesting all "Japanese clear messages ending with English word Quote STOP Quote."

CCH Series XII.S, Box 22.

FROM: WAR DEPARTMENT
OCSigO, Signal Intelligenc[e]
R.W. Minckler, Lt.Col., Signal Corps

TELEGRAM
OFFICIAL BUSINESS—GOVERNMENT RATES

PRIORITY - SECRET

DECEMBER 7, 1941

734 ~~SIGNALS MANILA PI~~
530 ~~FORT SHAFTER~~ TH
403 PRESIDIO OF SAN FRANCISCO CALIF

SEND TO WAR BY PRIORITY ENCIPHERED RADIO ALL JAPANESE CLEAR MESSAGES ENDING WITH ENGLISH WORD QUOTE STOP UNQUOTE SPELLED REPEAT QUOTE STO[P] UNQUOTE SPELLED COPIED SINCE NOVEMBER TWENTYSEVEN AND HEREAFTER

COLTON ACTING

SENT NO 734 to Manila, 12/7
SENT NO: 530 to Hawaii, 12/7
SENT NO. 403 to Pres. of S.F. 12/7

SECRET

Exhibit #35: U.S. Navy Technical Mission to Japan, Interrogation No. 11; Personnel Interrogated: Mr. Shinroku Tanomogi, 30 November 1945.

NARA, RG 457, Entry 9032, Box 1369, Folder 4217, "Pearl Harbor Investigation and Miscellaneous Material."

Also, see PHH: Part 18, 3310.

- COPY -

U. S. NAVAL TECHNICAL MISSION TO JAPAN

INTERROGATION NO.   11   PLACE: FLTLOSCAP
                          DATE: 30 November 1945

Subject: Radio Tokyo Broadcast December 8.

Personnel Interrogated: Mr. Shinroku Tanomogi, Head of Overseas Department of Japan Radio Broadcasting Corporation in December 1941; presently member of the Diet and secretary to the Minister of Transportation.

Interrogator: Captain Peyton Harrison, USNR

Interpreter: Lt. (jg) Stanley E. Sprague, USNR.

Summary:

    Mr. Tanomogi, as head of the Overseas Department, was in charge of programs, including news programs, beamed to foreign countries. All news releases were controlled or "censored" by the Information Bureau of the Cabinet, the Communications Bureau of the Communications Ministry, and the General Staff.

    Mr. Tanomogi was usually on duty at Radio Tokyo every other night. He was on duty the night of December 7 (Tokyo Time) and stated that the regular schedule of programs was broadcast. At about 0400 on December 8, he received a telephone call from the Information Bureau informing him that Japan was at war and that scheduled programs would have to be re-arranged and preparations made for broadcasting important government communiques. An official of the Information Bureau arrived at Radio Tokyo early on the morning of December 8 to work out details with Tanomogi's staff. Tanomogi remained at Radio Tokyo until about 1800 of December 8. He stated that they broadcast only what was given them by Domei News or by the Information Bureau. "All news was official government news".

    Mr. Tanomogi was asked if he remembered the "east wind rain" weather report broadcast about 1500 on December 8. He replied that he was not listening to the broadcasts at that particular hour, but that he had a vague recollection of some such announcement being broadcast among the releases abruptly ordered for transmission that day by the Information Bureau.

    Mr. Tanomogi was handed a copy of Drew Pearson's article in the Honolulu Star-Bulletin of November 9, 1945. He stated that he would have known of it if a message such as that described as being broadcast December 4 had been transmitted and that he had no recollection at all of any "east wind rain" report or any similar phrase being broadcast prior to December 8.

- COPY -

Incl: 3

Exhibit #36: Message, Department of State to American embassy London, United Kingdom (with note for repeats to the American embassy, The Hague, Netherlands, and the American legation, Canberra, Australia) relaying request from the Joint Congressional Committee for information concerning monitoring of Japanese broadcasts by the radio intelligence services of all three countries of the "Winds" message at any time prior to and including the date of the attack on Pearl Harbor.

NARA, RG 59, Department of State, 6 November 1945. 711.94/11-645, 1945-49 Central Decimal File. (4 pages)

TELEGRAM SENT

Department of State

Washington, November 6, 1945

SECRET
RELEASE PROCEDURE

AMEMBASSY
LONDON

DEPT has received from Congressional Joint Committee on the Investigation of the Pearl Harbor Attack a communication essential portion of which reads as follows:

"Under date of November 19, 1941, Japan advised its representatives abroad that if danger arose of a breach of diplomatic relations with the United States, or Russia or the British, and the cutting off of other means of international communications, an emergency system for warning Japanese diplomatic representatives of impending break in diplomatic relations would be used, by adding in the middle of the daily Japanese language short wave news broadcast the following:

"(1) In case Japan-United States relations were in danger, the words Higashi No Kazeame (East Wind Rain).
"(2) In case of Japan-Russian relations in danger, the words Kitanokaze Kumori (North Wind Cloudy).
"(3) In

TELEGRAM SENT

Department of State

Washington,

-2-

"(3) In case Japan-British relations in danger, the words Nishi No Kaze Hare (West Wind Clear).

this signal to be given in the middle and at the end of the broadcast as a weather forecast, 'each sentence to be repeated twice'. This arrangement also said, 'When this is heard, please destroy all code papers, etc.'

"At the same time, on November 19, 1941, the Japanese sent further notice to its representatives that when their diplomatic relations with the United States, Russia or the British were in danger, there would be added at the beginning and at the end of Japanese general intelligence broadcasts words as follows:

"(1) If it were Japan-United States relations, the word 'Higashi'.
"(2) If it were Japan-Russia relations, the word 'Kita'.
"(3) If it were Japan-British relations (including Thai, Malaya, and Nei), the word 'Nishi'.

these words to be repeated five times at the beginning and end of the broadcast.

"The

TELEGRAM SENT

Department of State

Washington,

-3-

"The Joint Congressional Committee Investigating the Attack on Pearl Harbor of December 7, 1941 are trying to ascertain whether any broadcasts under this system were monitored and overheard, either by the United States or by Australia, the Dutch East Indies or the British, and, if so, on what day and at what time such a broadcast was overheard, and if so the text of the broadcast, and whether either of the three nations mentioned, having overheard the broadcast, advised the United States of the fact. We are particularly interested in the period from November 27th to December 7th inclusive, and suggest that the inquiry first cover that period and then, if time permits, work back to November 19, 1941."

Please make urgent inquiry of GOVT to which you are accredited in regard to matters indicated in foregoing and report results promptly by telegram at earliest possible moment.

Byrnes

- 4 -

CODE ROOM: Please repeat to American Embassy, The Hague as Department's 125 and to American Legation, Canberra, as Department's 113.

SA:B:VJ   U   BC   NOE   S/CR

Exhibit #37: Message, American legation, Canberra, Australia, to Department of State, 16 November 1945, in response to State cable of 6 November 1945.

NARA, RG 59, Department of State, 16 November 1945. 711.94/11-1645, 1945-49 Central Decimal File.

DEPARTMENT OF STATE

INCOMING TELEGRAM

DIVISION OF CENTRAL SERVICES TELEGRAPH SECTION

ACTION: SA
INFO:
S
U
C
A -D
SA
EUR

AMN-1803-Z
This telegram must be paraphrased before being communicated to anyone other than a Government Agency. (RESTRICTED)

Canberra

Dated November 16, 1945

Rec'd 6:11 a.m., 16th

Secretary of State

Washington

168, November 16, 3 p.m.

External Affairs states exhaustive search by monitoring service of its records has revealed nothing (Dept's 113 November 6, 5 p.m.) However they state that they may have missed code signals since their monitoring service at that time only followed trends and did not take down Japanese broadcasts verbatim.

MINTER

DM

RESTRICTED

Exhibit #38: Messages from American embassy, The Hague, Netherlands, 5 December and 6 December 1945, and 26 January 1946, in response to State cable of 6 November 1945.

NARA, RG 59, Department of State, 5 and 6 December 1945, and 26 January 1946. 711.94/12-545, 711.94/12-645, and 711.94/1-2646, 1945-49 Central Decimal File. (3 pages)

DIVISION OF
CENTRAL SERVICES
TELEGRAPH SECTION

ACTION COPY

DEPARTMENT OF STATE

INCOMING TELEGRAM

ACTION: SA/B
INFO:
S
U   EG-R
C   Paraphrase before com-
EUR   municating to anyone
DC/R-1

1530

The Hague

Dated December 5, 1945

Rec'd 11:32 a.m., 5th

SECRET

Secretary of State

    Washington

US URGENT

271, December 5, 11 a.m.

FONOFF states that up to present (REDEPTEL 125, November 6 and 169, December 4) careful search of archives and inquiries of competent authorities have produced negative results but that matter will be pursued further.

                              HORNBECK

EDA

SECRET

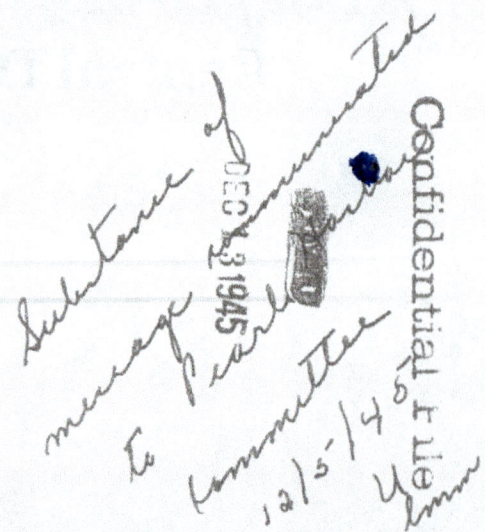

DIVISION OF
CENTRAL SERVICES
TELEGRAPH SECTION

DEPARTMENT OF STATE

INCOMING TELEGRAM

ACTION COPY

ACTION: EUR
INFO:
S
U
C
SA/B
DC/R-1

WHC-II
Paraphrase before communicating to anyone.

SECRET

2219
The Hague
Dated December 6, 1945
Rec'd 10:36 p.m., 6th

Secretary of State
Washington

273, December 6, 4 p.m.

Foreign Office states that while search is being continued, (EMBTEL 271, December 5 and REDEPTEL 173, December 5) it does not expect positive results as far as Netherlands is concerned; that Govt Netherlands East Indies has been approached but has furnished no report as yet-we assume due chaotic conditions that territory, and that Embassy will be informed if and when information is forthcoming or when all possibilities of search are considered exhausted.

HORNBECK

WMB
SECRET

DIVISION OF
CENTRAL SERVICES
TELEGRAPH SECTION

DEPARTMENT OF STATE

INCOMING TELEGRAM

ACTION COPY

ACTION: EUR

INFO:
S
U   RKB-O
C   Paraphrase before com-
FE   municating to anyone.
A-D
DC/R   SECRET

9760

The Hague

Dated January 26, 1946

Rec'd 1:12 p.m., 27th

Secretary of State

Washington

105, January 26, Noon

Embassy has received note from Foreign Office dated January 24 stating that prior to Jap invasion Netherlands East Indies all reports monitoring Jap broadcasts had been destroyed (REDEPTEL 125, November 6 and EMBTEL 273, December 6, 1945); that this applies to Netherlands Indies Government archives as well, and that for this reason Foreign Office regrets inability to furnish information which Congressional Joint Committee investigating attack on Pearl Harbor has requested.

Copy of note by air pouch.

HORNBECK

WMB
SECRET

Exhibit #39: Messages from American embassy, London, United Kingdom, 4 December and 15 December 1945 and 31 January 1946, in response to State cable of 6 November 1945.

NARA, RG 59, Department of State, 4 and 16 December 1945 and 31 January 1946. 711.94/12-445, 711.94/12-1545, and 711.94/1-3146, 1945-49 Central Decimal File. (3 pages)

DIVISION OF
CENTRAL SERVICES
TELEGRAPH SECTION

ACTION COPY

DEPARTMENT OF STATE

INCOMING TELEGRAM

ACTION-EUR
INFO:
S   AMM-C
U   Paraphrase before com-
C   municating to anyone.
SA/B
DC/R-1

SECRET

1217

London

Dated December 4, 1945

Rec'd 4:45 p.m.

Secretary of State

Washington

US URGENT

NIACT 12721, December 4, 9 p.m.

We have just learned from FONOFF that although their inquiries not yet complete there is no present evidence of receipt of any "wind" message prior to morning of Dec 8, 1941, day after Pearl Harbor attack. (REDEPTS 9745 Nov 6 and 10493, Dec 4). FONOFF states a Jap broadcast containing code messages was relayed from Hongkong to Singapore and received at Singapore six hours after Pearl Harbor attack. Jap code text not yet available. We will press FONOFF for further details if desired.

WINANT

NPS
SECRET

711.94/12-445

DIVISION OF
CENTRAL SERVICES
TELEGRAPH SECTION

ACTION COPY

DEPARTMENT OF STATE
INCOMING TELEGRAM

ACTION: EUR
INFO:
S
U
C
SA/B
DC/R

JWM P
Paraphrase before communicating to anyone.

SECRET

5545

London

Dated December 15, 1956

Rec'd 7:26 p.m., 15th

Secretary of State

Washington

13161, December 15, 2 p.m.

We talked this morning with Foulds Jap expert in FONOFF regarding "WINDS" messages. (REDEPTS 10544, December 5). He was in FONOFF just previous to and at time of Pearl Harbor and states that from his personal knowledge no such messages were received prior to December 8, 1941. FONOFF is still investigating but has yet no information which would alter that contained in Embassy's 12721.

WINANT

DU

SECRET

711.94/12-1545

DEC 18 1945

Confidential File

DIVISION OF
CENTRAL SERVICES
TELEGRAPH SECTION

DEPARTMENT OF STATE

INCOMING TELEGRAM

ACTION COPY

ACTION: UR
INFO:
S
U
C
A-D
SA/D
DC/R

EOC -P
Paraphrase before communicating to anyone.

SECRET

11281
London
Dated January 31, 1946
Rec'd 4:20 p.m.

Secretary of State,
    Washington.

1183, January 31, 4 p.m.

Foreign Office officials state investigation (Dept's 960, Jan 28, 8 p.m.) has drawn complete blank and they see no point in investigating further.

                                WINANT

DM

SECRET

711.94/1-3146

Confidential File

Exhibit #40: Captain Laurance Safford's Statement before the Joint Congressional Committee (JCC). (24 pages)

NARA, RG38, Box 166, "Folders on the Winds Message," Folder 5830/69 (1 of 3), "Statement Regarding Winds Message," by Captain L.F. Safford Before the Joint Committee on the Investigation of the Pearl Harbor Attack.

Composed on 25 January 1946, Safford delivered this statement before the JCC on 1 February 1946.

STATEMENT REGARDING WINDS MESSAGE
BY
CAPTAIN L. F. SAFFORD, U. S. NAVY

BEFORE THE

JOINT COMMITTEE ON THE

INVESTIGATION OF THE PEARL HARBOR ATTACK

S. CON. RES. 27

25 January 1946

STATEMENT REGARDING WINDS MESSAGE
by
Captain L. F. Safford, USN

PREVIEW

There was a Winds Message. It meant War--and we knew it meant War. By the best estimate that can be made from my recollection and the circumstantial evidence now available, the "Winds Message" was part of a Japanese Overseas "News" Broadcast from Station JAP (Tokyo) on 11980 kilocycles beginning at 1330 Greenwich Civil Time on Thursday, December 4, 1941. This time corresponded to 10:30 p.m. Tokyo time and 8:30 a.m. Washington time, December 4, 1941. The broadcast was probably in Japanese Morse code, and was originally written in the Kata-Kana form of written, plain-language Japanese. It was intercepted by the U.S. Navy at the big radio receiving station at Cheltenham, Maryland, which serves the Navy Department. It was recorded on a special typewriter, developed by the Navy, which types the Roman-letter equivalents of the Japanese characters. The Winds Message broadcast was forwarded to the Navy Department by TWX (teletypewriter exchange) from the teletype-transmitter in the "Intercept" receiving room at Cheltenham to "WA91," the page-printer located beside the GY Watch Officer's desk, in the Navy Department Communication Intelligence Unit under my command. I saw the Winds Message typed in page form on yellow teletype paper, with the translation written below. I immediately forwarded this message to my Commanding Officer (Rear Admiral Leigh Noyes, USN), thus fully discharging my responsibility in the matter.

PREPARATIONS FOR INTERCEPTION

There are various sources of the so-called "Winds Code," two of which have already been introduced as evidence: Tokyo Circular 2353 on page 154 of Exhibit No. 1 and Tokyo Circular 2354 on page 155 of Exhibit No. 1. The most important source was Commander-in-Chief Asiatic Fleet secret dispatch 281430 of November 28, 1941, addressed for information to the Commander-in-Chief Pacific Fleet and Commandant 14th Naval District--thus letting them in on the secret. I had taken no action personally on the first tip-off (Tokyo Circular 2354), because I was still awaiting the instruction of higher authority. CINCAF 281430 together with Tokyo Circular 2353 and other collateral intercept information apparently made an impression upon the Director of Naval Intelligence, for he immediately sent word to me, through the Director of Naval Communications, that he wished the Communication Intelligence Organization to make every attempt to intercept any message sent in accordance with the Winds Codes. It was a request from Admiral Wilkinson and an order from Admiral Noyes. I hastened to comply, with the secondary motive that it would be a feather in our cap if the Navy got it and our sister service didn't.

Just about the time I received Admiral Wilkinson's request, I was shown Tokyo to Washington Serial 843, dated November 27, 1941, prescribing a "schedule of (Tokyo News) Broadcasts," which gave me something tangible to work with as well as giving added meaning to the Winds Code. The "November 29 deadline" indicated that the Winds Code might be used to notify overseas officials as to things which would "automatically begin to happen." Tokyo Circulars 2353 and 2354 blueprinted what this action would be. Tokyo Serial 843 implied that such notification would be made. After a conference with my subordinates, I drafted a summary of Tokyo Serial 843

-2-

(or had Kramer do it for me), had it coded in the COPEK system, and released it myself at 6 p.m. (Washington time) on November 28, 1941. This secret message was transmitted "Priority" to the Commandants of the 14th and 16th Naval Districts for action, and to the Commander-in-Chief Pacific Fleet and Asiatic Fleet for information, and may be identified as OPNAV 282301. This took care of our overseas Communication Intelligence Units: they now had all the available technical information on the subject. I know that they monitored the Tokyo Voice Broadcasts; I also know that Corregidor monitored the Tokyo Morse Broadcasts; in fact, Corregidor and Heeia went beyond their instructions and guarded the Tokyo Broadcasts 24 hours a day. Captain Rochefort and Commander Lietwiler can verify this.

I discussed the situation with Commander Welker, in charge of the intercept and direction-finder stations, and with Chief Radioman Lewis, his technical assistant. Our prospects for interception looked somewhat dubious. We were not encouraged when a day or two later Washington and Rio objected to the new frequency assignments and Rome complained about the poor quality of the Tokyo Voice Broadcasts.

I would like to digress long enough to invite the attention of the Committee to the fact that OPNAV 282301 is not included in the "Basic Exhibit of Dispatches" (Exhibit No. 37), and that Tokyo Serial 843 (JD-1 #6899: SIS #25446) is not included in the "Intercepted Japanese Diplomatic Messages" (Exhibit No. 1). Three other relevant intercepts not appearing in Exhibit No. 1 are also of interest at this point, namely:

Washington to Tokyo Serial 1197 of November 27, 1941 (JD-1 #6908: SIS #25476
Rio to Tokyo Serial 482 of November 30, 1941 (JD-1 #6982: SIS #25571)
Rome to Tokyo Serial 768 of November 29, 1941 (JD-1 #6981: SIS #25604).

These 5 documents should be introduced as evidence for purposes of record.

Welker, Lewis and I agreed that 5160 kilocycles would probably come in nicely at Manila and at Pearl Harbor. Station JHL was of too low power to reach the greater distances to the continental United States. 9430 kilocycles appeared a bit high for a night frequency in winter, as far as the West Coast was concerned. There did not seem to be a remote possibility of the 11980 kilocycles and 12265 kilocycles being heard by any station in the Pacific Ocean or along either shore at the time of day scheduled. Nevertheless, we decided to have Bainbridge Island monitor the Tokyo Morse Code Broadcasts on the chance that the times given in Tokyo Serial 843 might not be given in Tokyo time or the schedules could be heard because of freak conditions. We did not order Bainbridge Island to monitor the Tokyo Voice Broadcasts because its two sound recorders were guarding the two ends of the Tokyo - San Francisco radio telephone circuit. Our estimates for Bainbridge Island were closely realized: excellent receivability at the wrong time of day and almost a complete "black-out" of reception/during the period on the higher frequencies scheduled for the Winds Message broadcast.

We agreed that the best chance of intercepting the listed schedules (other than those on 5160 kilocycles) was on the East Coast of the United States. During the winter months the East Coast had good reception of Tokyo during the few hours included in the schedules. Our best bet was Cheltenham, which had been guarding the MAM (Tokyo) Broadcasts to Japanese Merchant Vessels, so we had up-to-the-minute data on the receivability of Tokyo. According to my memory we decided to play safe and have all East Coast intercept stations monitor the Tokyo Broadcasts. We agreed it would be impossible to hear Voice Broadcasts from Tokyo on the East Coast and therefore did not attempt it. We did not order Guam or Imperial Beach (California) to monitor any of the Tokyo broadcast schedules.

Commander Welker or I sent TWX messages directing the intercept stations at Bainbridge Island (Washington) and at Cheltenham (Maryland) to monitor the schedules given in Tokyo Serial 843 as first priority and to forward all plain-language Japanese intercepts on these schedules to the Navy Department by teletype. We may have sent these instructions to other stations also. We did not want English or coded messages--only written Japanese. We gave the same instructions to both stations, and sent them out immediately after releasing the previously-mentioned OPNAV 282301.

I have confirmation of the above orders plus knowledge of existing receiving conditions in the monthly reports from Cheltenham, Winter Harbor and Bainbridge Island, extracts from which are quoted below:

Station "M" (Cheltenham) - Operations - November 1941

 Receiving conditions throughout the month were very good on all frequencies. Atmospheric disturbances have been at a minimum. Orders received from OP-20-GX at 2315 (GCT) November 28, via teletype to give highest priority to various broadcasts at designated Japanese broadcast stations. These schedules were covered and found to be press broadcasts sent in both Kana and English. Log sheets were forwarded to OP-20-GX daily with regular traffic files.

Station "M" (Cheltenham) - Operations - December 1941

 Receiving conditions during the month were fair to good on all frequencies. At 2300, 7 December 1941, telephone orders received from OP-20-GX to drop the Tokyo JJC/MAM schedules and assignments; continued watch for Orange activity.

Station "W" (Winter Harbor) - Operations - December 1941

 Receiving Conditions in General. Daily attempts were made to intercept Tokyo and Osaka channels employed to Europe, but only on a few occasions was any intercept possible.

Station "S" (Bainbridge Island) - Operations - November 1941

During the month of November a sharp increase has been noticed in the amount of message traffic sent on the Kana General Information Broadcasts. Where before we seldom averaged more than one or two such messages monthly, it is now not unusual for two or three such messages to appear daily. These messages are sent in both number code and Kana.

On 28 November, a directive was received by TWX from Op-20-GX which called for coverage of the following stations at times specified, with priority transmission of intercepted material by TWX. Times listed were given as PST. Because the use of PST time designation is unusual, we asked for a verification, but were told that time zone was uncertain and verification was not possible.

PST	(GCT)	STATION	FREQUENCY
0100	(0900)	JVJ	12275
0130	(0930)	JUO	9430
0200	(1000)	JVJ	12275
0300	(1100)	JHL	5160
0400	(1200)	JHL	5160
0500	(1300)	JHL	5160
0530	(1330)	JHP	11980

Since the time zone indicated was not certain we were faced with the possibility that the time could be either GCT, PST, zone -9, or even a combination of these. As soon as the directive was received we started copying all broadcasts of this same type which were readable at "S". We found that in some cases other stations were tied in with the Stations listed in the original directive, and that although we could not copy the station listed we could copy the cornetted channel carrying the same broadcast. The stations and times that we can copy are listed below. Time used is GCT.

GCT	STATION	FREQUENCY	CORNETTED WITH
0000	JVJ	12275	JUP
0030	JUD	15880	JVJ/JAU2
0100	JUD	15880	JVJ
0130	JVJ	12275	
0200	JVJ	12275	
0230	JVJ	12275	JUP/JUD
0300	JVJ	12275	JUD
0330	JVJ	12275	JUD
0400	JVJ	12275	
0430	JVJ	12275	
0500	JVJ	12275	JUD
1300	JHL	5160	
2200	JVJ	12275	
2300	JVJ	12275	
2330	JVJ	12275	

In addition to the stations previously named, the Winds Message was monitored for at the following localities, to my personal knowledge:

Heeia, T. H.	(U.S. Navy)	Voice only
Corregidor, P.I.	(U.S. Navy)	Voice and Morse
Singapore	(British Intelligence)	-?-
Australia	(Australian Intelligence)	-?-
Java	(NEI Intelligence)	-?-

Intercept stations in Canada, England, and China probably watched for it too. And, of course, the Japanese diplomatic and consular stations listened for the Winds Message themselves on their own receiving sets.

On December 1, 1941, I was shown the translation of Tokyo Circular 2444 (Exhibit No. 1 - page 209), advising that London, Hongkong, Singapore and Manila had been ordered to destroy their code machines, and instructing Washington to retain its machine regardless of other instructions. The significance of the Winds Message now became very clear to me and I began to take the matter most seriously. So did Colonel Sadtler, over in the War Department. The only means by which Tokyo could announce its decisions of peace or war to its overseas diplomatic representatives who had destroyed their regular codes was by means of the emergency Winds Code. This applied to London and the Far East but not to Washington. Higher authority in the War and Navy Departments likewise took a greatly increased interest in the Winds Message, and began heckling me as to the possibility of having missed it. I instituted a daily check of the incoming teletype messages to see that our intercept stations were doing as much as could be expected of them.

One evening, about December 1, 1941, I drove out to Station "M" at Cheltenham, Maryland, and remained until about midnight. The primary purpose of my visit was to inspect the new landline telegraph for direction-finder control which had been completed at Cheltenham and the Navy Department, which was scheduled to be placed in service on December 1, 1941, but which had been delayed by installation difficulties at some of the outlying stations. I made a personal check of the Winds Message watch and, as I recall, found that Chief Radioman Wigle was monitoring the Tokyo News Broadcasts 24 hours a day and had assigned qualified Kana operators to this duty. I have further documentary proof that Cheltenham was monitoring the Tokyo broadcasts in the fact that between 1200 and 1500 GCT, on December 6, 1941, Cheltenham intercepted and forwarded to the Navy Department Tokyo Serials 902-2 and 904, plus two other messages. This is entered in the GY log for December 6, 1941: Items Nos. 6609, 6610, 6618, and 6619. These messages were transmitted by Station JAH (Tokyo) to San Francisco on 7630 kilocycles. The Tokyo - San Francisco circuit was not a regular Cheltenham assignment.

I may summarize the preparations for interception by stating that the United States Navy listened for the Winds Message at Cheltenham, Maryland, and did everything that it possibly could to intercept it elsewhere, and that the other Services did all that they considered reasonable.

INTERCEPTION

There is no basis for assuming that the Winds Message had to be sent on a Voice Broadcast. In 1941, the Japanese Government was sending out "General Information Broadcasts" as well as "Domei News" to its Diplomatic and Consular Officials in foreign lands. This was partly to give speedier service, partly to permit use of the Japanese Morse Code and the Kata-Kana form of written Japanese, and partly to be independent of foreign communication systems in emergency. Each office had its own Japanese radio operator and its own short-wave receiving set. We knew it. The United States Government was doing the same thing itself, with a Navy radio operator serving at each post. The German Government was doing likewise but was a bit ahead of us, with machine reception. We used to "sample" these broadcasts periodically until the F.C.C.'s Foreign Broadcast Intelligence Service came into existence and relieved the U.S. Navy of this duty. I wish to reiterate that neither Japan, the United States, nor Germany was dependent on Voice broadcasts for direct communication from the seat of government to overseas officials. The radio schedules listed in Tokyo Serial 843 were in Morse (i.e., dot-and-dash) code exclusively: either Japanese Morse, International Morse, or both. We expected that the Winds Message would be sent in Morse Code--and it was. If the Winds Message had been sent on a Voice broadcast the U.S. Navy would have missed it, unless it came on a schedule receivable at Pearl Harbor or Corregidor.

The original documents giving details of the interception of the Winds Message are not available. Therefore it is necessary to reconstruct the situation from circumstantial evidence and by process of elimination. Collateral information has been plotted or recorded on a single sheet, a reduced-size photograph of which is appended. This graph tells the story better than words and shows just what actually happened. It should convince the most skeptical. As I have previously testified, the frequency, distances, and time of day were such that the Winds Message could be heard on the East Coasts of the United States and Canada, while it was a physical impossibility for it to be heard (except under freak conditions) on the West Coast of the United States and Canada, Pearl Harbor, Manila, Java, and Singapore. Everything checks perfectly: there is no element of doubt as to conditions of radio wave propagation.

The Winds Message could be heard also in the North Atlantic Ocean, British Isles, and Western Europe, but it could not be heard in Burma, Australia, or in Rio de Janeiro. It was sent on the so-called "European Schedule" of Tokyo's big foreign broadcasting station "J-A-P" and was intended for London. We knew that the Japanese Ambassador in London had destroyed his secret codes three days previously: this was the only way that Tokyo could get news to him/ secretly. Reception or non-reception at other points was irrelevant. Tokyo knew full well, before the Winds Message was sent, that it probably would not be received in Washington or in Rio. That was immaterial--the Winds Message was intended for London. Our ability to intercept it was due partly to good luck, partly to my foresight, and partly to the high quality of the Navy operators and receiving apparatus at Cheltenham.

The Winds Message broadcast was forwarded by teletype (TWX) from Cheltenham to the Navy Department (Op-20-GY) shortly before 9:00 a.m. on December 4, 1941. Kramer distinctly recalls that the Winds Message was shown to him by the GY Watch Officer after 8:30 a.m. on that date. It was my recollection, as stated in previous testimony, that I had first seen the Winds Message a little after eight a.m. on December 4, 1941. The Winds Message broadcast was about 200 words long, with the code words prescribed in Tokyo Circular 2353 appearing in the middle of the message, whereas we had expected to find the code words of Tokyo Circular 2354 in a Morse broadcast. All three "code words" were used, but the expression meaning "North Wind Cloudy" was in the negative form.

When I first saw the Winds Message, it had already been translated by Lieutenant Commander Kramer, in charge of the Translation Section of the Navy Department Communication Intelligence Unit. Kramer had underscored all three "code phrases" on the original incoming teletype sheet. Below the printed message was written in pencil or colored crayon in Kramer's handwriting, the following free translations:

> "War with England (including NEI, etc.)
> War with the U.S.
> Peace with Russia."

I am not sure of the order; but it was the same as in the broadcast and I think England appeared first. I think Kramer used "U.S." rather than "United States." It is possible that the words "No war," instead of "Peace," were used to describe Japan's intentions with regards to Russia.

"This is _it_!" said Kramer as he handed me the Winds Message. This was the broadcast we had strained every nerve to intercept. This was the feather in our cap. This was the tip-off which would prevent the U.S. Pacific Fleet being surprised at Pearl Harbor the way the Russians had been surprised at Port Arthur. This was what the Navy Communication Intelligence had been preparing for since its establishment in 1924-- War with Japan!

DISTRIBUTION

I immediately sent the original of the Winds Message up to the Director of Naval Communications (Rear Admiral Noyes) by one of the officers serving under me and told him to deliver this paper to Admiral Noyes in person, to track him down and not take "no" for an answer, and if he could not find him in a reasonable time to let me know. I did not explain the nature or significance of the Winds Message to this officer. In a few minutes I received a report to the effect that the message had been delivered.

It is my recollection that Kramer and I knew at the time that Admiral Noyes had telephoned the substance of the Winds Message to the War Department, to the "Magic" distribution list in the Navy Department, and to the Naval Aide to the President. For that reason, no immediate distribution of the smooth translation of the Winds Message was made in the Navy Department. The six or seven copies for the Army were rushed over to the War Department as rapidly as possible: here the Navy's responsibility ended. The individual smooth translations for authorized Navy Department officials and the White House were distributed at noon on December 4, 1941, in accordance with standard operating procedure. I have no reason for believing that the Army failed to make a prompt distribution of its translations of the Winds Message.

I am thoroughly satisfied in my own mind that Admiral Noyes telephoned to everyone on his list without delay: I cannot bring myself to imagine otherwise. There is some question as to whether the Admiral was understood, but this only shows the unreliability of telephone messages. Any misunderstanding of what Admiral Noyes said was of negligible effect because written translations of the Winds Message were distributed within

2 or 3 hours of his telephone calls. In fact it was not until 1944 that any suggestion or criticism was offered that any official on the "Magic" distribution list - Navy, Army, State Department, or White House - had not been notified that the Winds Message had been received or that the Winds Message had been translated in any terms other than War and Peace.

My final verification of the fact that the Winds Message translation was typed and distributed lies in the fact that about December 15, 1941, I saw a copy of it in the special folder of messages which were being assembled for Admiral Noyes to present to the Roberts Commission. I checked these over with Kramer for completeness as well as for the elimination of irrelevant material. Kramer told me in 1944 that he had shown Assistant Secretary Forrestal a special set of Pre-Pearl Harbor messages about December 10, 1941, when Secretary Knox was making his personal investigation at Pearl Harbor, and that he discussed those messages with Mr. Forrestal for about two hours. This set of messages was apparently the basis and possibly the identical file that was given Admiral Noyes and shown to the Roberts Commission via Admiral Wilkinson. This was the last time I saw the Winds Message. I believe that the translation of the Winds Message was given the JD-1 Serial number of 7001, because this number is missing and unaccounted for, and comes within the range of messages translated on December 3 and 4, 1941.

The distribution of the Winds Message was the responsibility of Naval Intelligence and not Naval Communications. I had no responsibility in the matter after forwarding the original message to Admiral Noyes and after checking Kramer's "folder" to see that the messages were presented in a logical and understandable order.

ACTION TAKEN AS A DIRECT RESULT OF THE WINDS MESSAGE

About an hour after I had sent the original Winds Message up to Admiral Noyes I received a call from him on the inter-phone to the effect that we ought to tell Guam to burn their excess codes and ciphers. I replied that I was in full agreement but there were other odds and ends to be taken care of, and that I would have some messages ready for his approval by noon.

As a direct result of the Winds Message and other contemporaneous information from intercepted Japanese messages, I prepared the following secret messages:

OPNAV 041754 (Priority) - Not yet introduced as evidence

OPNAV 042000 (Priority) - Not yet introduced as evidence.

OPNAV 042017 (Deferred) - Page 44 of Exhibit No. 37.

OPNAV 042018 (Deferred) - Not yet introduced as evidence.

OPNAV 042019 (Deferred) - Not yet introduced as evidence.

I took four of these messages up to Admiral Noyes' office, cleared them through the Assistant Director of Naval Communications (Captain Joseph R. Redman) and made an appointment to see the Admiral with his secretary, as per office instruction. I was called to his office shortly before 3:00 p.m.

OPNAV 041754 was a correction to a previous Priority message, and was sent in response to a Priority service message requesting verification of the last four groups of OPNAV 040343 (page 43 of Exhibit No. 37). I released this message myself during the noon hour to save time.

OPNAV Priority 042000 for action of CINCPAC, CINCAF, COM 16, COM 14, Guam and Samoa, made a "new Intelligence" cipher effective immediately and directed the immediate destruction of the old cipher by Guam and Samoa. This message was released by Admiral Noyes himself, and is the most

-16-

important of the five which were sent on this occasion because the precedence did give some idea of urgency.

OPNAV Deferred 042017, for action of Guam and for information of CINCPAC, CINCAF, COM 14 and COM 16 was sent in the new cipher made effective by OPNAV 042000. It directed Guam to destroy excess cryptographic aids and other secret matter. This message was rewritten by Admiral Noyes and was released by Admiral Ingersoll. My original wording was much stronger than the message actually sent, because I had directed the destruction of everything except the system in which sent and the current edition of the Direction Finder Code. However, I was not trying to use this message as the vehicle for a war warning as I had the day before in OPNAV 031855 (page 41, Exhibit No. 37). I was just trying to insure that Guam "stripped ship" before a Japanese Commando-raid from Saipan, 100 miles away, captured a complete allowance of codes and ciphers, a matter for which I was officially responsible. Admiral Noyes made no mention of a war warning when he directed me to prepare this message and I feel sure he did not have any such warning in mind when he toned down my original draft. This message had to be sent "for Information" to CINCPAC, and others, as notification that Guam's allowance of codes and ciphers was being reduced, and as a reminder to Guam to notify the addressees what systems would be available for its future communications. This message was sent DEFERRED to insure that OPNAV 042000 would arrive well in advance and thus avoid confusion and unnecessary messages at this critical time.

OPNAV 042018 and OPNAV 042019 are not important except that they help establish the date the Winds Message was intercepted and the time and date that the unsent warning message, prepared by Commander McCollum, was seen by me.

EVALUATION OF THE WINDS MESSAGE

Evaluation of the Winds Message was not based on JD-1 #6850 and #6875 alone. CINCAF 281430 gave much stronger translations of Tokyo Circulars 2353 and 2354, which dispelled any doubt as to whether or not WAR was meant by the literal translation:

"Japan - (blank) relations are in danger."

This message contained official British translation furnished by Singapore, from which I quote:

"NISHI NISHI ENGLAND <u>INCLUDING OCCUPATION OF THAI OR INVASION OF MALAY AND N.E.I.</u>"

That means war, no matter how worded. No one disputed this British translation in November-December, 1941: in fact our own translation was considered consistent with it.

Two confirmations of the British translation came from the official Netherlands East Indies Government translations of Tokyo Circulars 2353 and 2354. Colonel Thorpe, the Senior Army Intelligence Officer in Java, sent an official message via the Navy addressed to General Miles, the Chief of Army Intelligence in Washington, which is a matter of record in previous Pearl Harbor investigations. This message may be identified as Alusna Batavia 031030 dated December 3, 1941. I quote from this message:

"FROM THORPE FOR MILES WAR DEPT. CODE INTERCEPT: -
JAPAN WILL NOTIFY HER CONSULS OF <u>WAR DECISION</u> IN HER
FOREIGN BROADCASTS AS WEATHER REPORT AT END.
- EAST WIND RAIN UNITED STATES;
- NORTH WIND CLOUDY RUSSIA;
- WEST WIND CLEAR ENGLAND <u>WITH ATTACK ON THAILAND MALAY AND DUTCH EAST INDIES</u>."

Copies of this message were circulated in the Navy Department, and the Chief of Naval Operations was indicated as receiving a copy.

Consul General Foote, our Senior Diplomatic Representative in the Netherlands East Indies, on December 4, 1941 (Java time), which is December 3, 1941 (Washington time), sent a similar message to the Secretary of State, from which I quote:

"WHEN CRISIS LEADING TO WORST ARISES FOLLOWING WILL BE BROADCAST AT END WEATHER REPORTS:
- ONE EAST WIND RAIN <u>WAR WITH UNITED STATES</u>,
- TWO NORTH WIND CLOUDY <u>WAR WITH RUSSIA</u>,
- THREE WEST WIND CLEAR <u>WAR WITH BRITAIN INCLUDING ATTACK ON THAILAND OR MALAYA AND DUTCH INDIES</u>.

- -

WHEN THREAT OF CRISIS EXISTS FOLLOWING WILL BE USED FIVE TIMES IN TEXTS OF GENERAL REPORTS AND RADIO BROADCASTS:
- ONE HIGASHI EAST AMERICA,
- TWO KITA NORTH RUSSIA,
- THREE NISHI WEST BRITAIN <u>WITH ADVANCE INTO THAILAND AND ATTACK ON MALAYA AND DUTCH INDIES</u>.

This message was received in the State Department at 9:19 a.m. on December 4, 1941 (Washington time). Copies were forwarded to the War and Navy Departments by the State Department Liaison Officer, Mr. Orme Wilson. They were given a wide circulation in the Navy Department.

My own evaluation of the foregoing, on December 4, 1941, was about as follows:

(A) The Basic Japanese War Plan was divided into 3 categories or provided for 3 contingencies, any or all of which might be followed, namely:

    (1) War with the United States

    (2) War with Russia

    (3) War with England including the invasion of Thailand and the capture of Malaya and the Dutch East Indies.

(B) The Winds Message gave us the answer in all 3 cases: Affirmative for the 1st and 3rd categories, and Negative for the 2nd.

(C) The Winds Message was probably a "Signal of Execute" of some sort.

The "Signal of Execute" theory received strong confirmation from a secret message received from the Philippines in the early afternoon of December 4, 1941. This message informed us that the Japanese Navy had introduced a new cipher system for its so-called "Operations Code" at 0600 GCT that date. This time was $7\frac{1}{2}$ hours before the Winds Message was broadcast. I might add that there was only one J-A-P European broadcast per day, so the times coincided as closely as possible. I would like to add also that my subordinates on Corregidor spotted and reported this change only nine hours after it was made. The message may be identified as Commandant 16th Naval District Priority 041502 dated December 4, 1941, and was addressed to Naval Operations and the Commandant 14th Naval District but not to the Commander-in-Chief, U.S. Pacific Fleet. So far as I know, this message has not been introduced as evidence before any previous investigation of the Pearl Harbor disaster. In fact, this is the first time it has ever been mentioned except to Admiral Hart. The unusual hour and unusual date at which the Japanese Navy changed its "Operations Code," combined with the Winds Message and other collateral information available in the Navy Department, made this message highly significant as the probable "Signal of Execute" to the Japanese Navy. Up till now the Winds Message has had to bear a double burden in my testimony.

As I have previously testified, we expected that if the Japanese did suddenly attack the United States this attack would come on a week-end or national holiday. In fact, a warning message to this effect had been sent out in April, 1941 (page 1 of Exhibit No. 37). The War Department over-emphasized the imminence of War as forecast by the "November 29, deadline" and predicted that the Japanese would strike during the week-end of November 29-30, 1941. The Navy Department estimated the situation more accurately - the Japanese armada which had been concentrating for the Southern Invasion was too far from any conceivable objective to give serious consideration to this date. Also the covering Naval forces were not yet deployed and other signs indicated that the U. S. Army estimate was a bit premature.

-21-

The next week-end, December 6-7, 1941, was just the reverse. The Winds Message and the change of the Naval Operations Code came in the middle of the week: 2 days to Saturday and 3 days to Sunday. It was unthinkable that the Japanese would surrender their hopes of surprise by delaying until the week-end of December 13-14, 1941. This was not crystal gazing or "intuition"—it was just the plain, common sense acceptance of a self-evident proposition. Colonel Sadtler saw it, and so did Captain Joseph R. Redman, U.S.N.—according to Colonel Sadtler's testimony in 1944, before the Army Board of Investigation. The Japanese were going to start the war on Saturday, December 6, 1941, or Sunday, December 7, 1941. The War and Navy Departments had been given 72 hours' advance notification of the attack on Pearl Harbor by the Japanese themselves.

- FINIS -

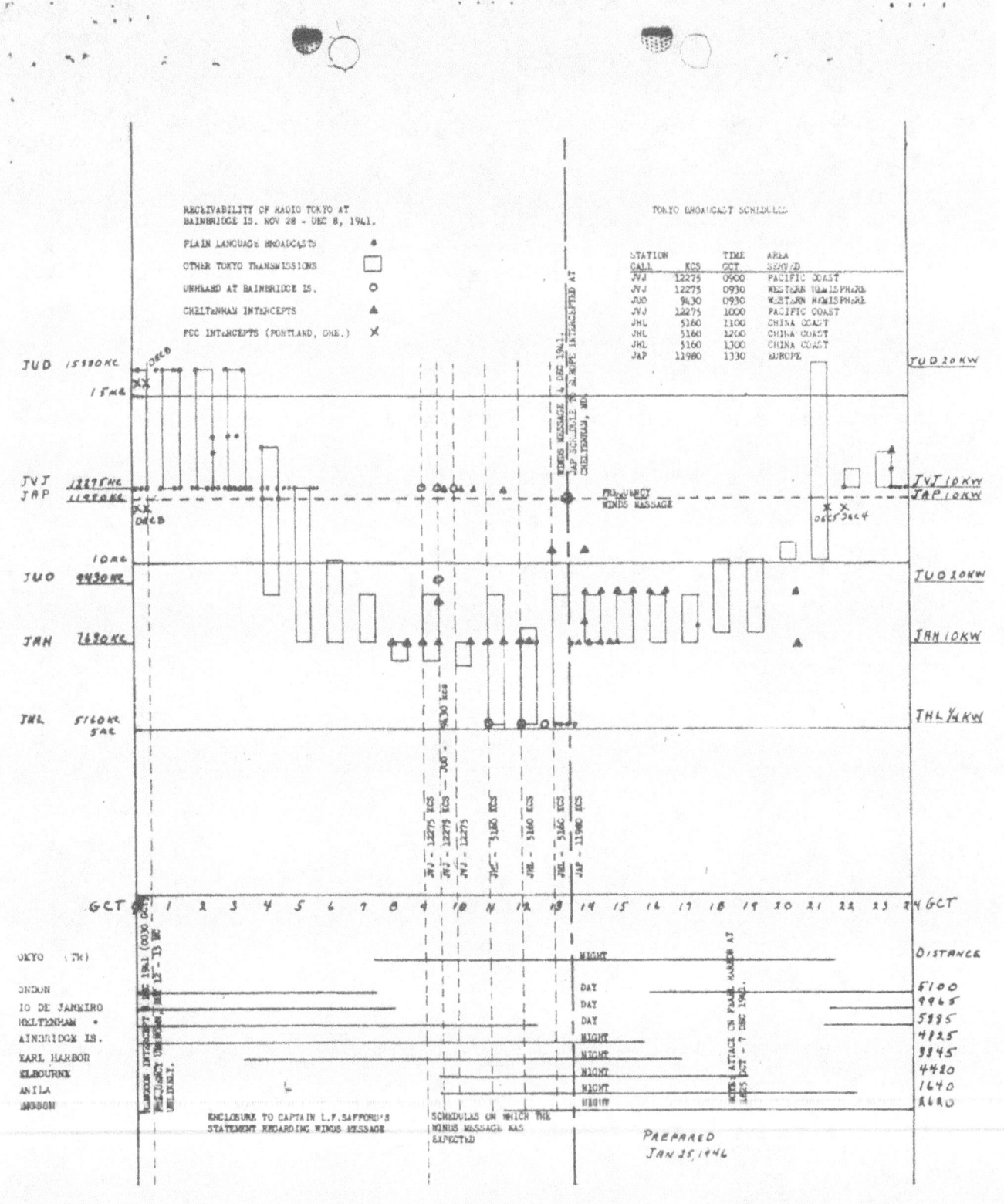

Exhibit #41: Letter from Captain Laurance Safford to Commander Alwin Kramer, 22 December 1943 that includes reference to "Weather report" or "Winds message." (2 pages) "Safford-Kramer Letter[s],"

NARA, RG 80, Pearl Harbor Liaison Office, Entry 167A, Box 4; PHH, Part 8: 3698

NAVY DEPARTMENT
OFFICE OF THE CHIEF OF NAVAL OPERATIONS
WASHINGTON

22 December 1943

My dear Kramer-San:

I am preparing a secret paper covering events which took place the early part of December, 1941. I am getting all the help that I can from Linn and from such records as are still available. My memory is bad as to ~~the very newest~~ details, which is the reason for preparing this memorandum, and I have forgotten or am very vague as to certain things which I clearly recalled a year ago. I am writing to you to ask you to help me as far as you may be able to do so.

I realize that your reply will have to be censored and therefore you must be guarded as to what you state. Also, I am phrasing my questions very carefully, in the event that my letter might fall into unauthorized hands. I am saving a copy of my letter so it will be merely necessary to give the question number and a brief answer, which should not disclose anything to an outsider.

With reference to events on December 6, 1941:

1. What time did you see Mr. R. that evening and show him the papers?
2. Was Mr. H. there or was he called in, or did you see him first and go over to Mr. R. with him?
3. What time did you see Admiral S. that evening and show him the papers?
4. If answer to 3 is negative, how and when was Admiral S. first informed?
5. How and when was Admiral W. first informed?
6. Linn remembers that you stayed till after 1 a.m. What time did you leave the Navy Building and go home?

With reference to events on December 7, 1941:

7. What time did you get down to the Navy Building the next morning? (Brotherhood said it was sometime after 0700.)
8. What time did you see Mr. R. that morning and show him the new papers?
9. Was Mr. H. there or was he called in?
10. My check shows you had Part 14 plus another paper setting the conference time at 1 p.m. Do you recall taking any other papers with you, and can you give me a hint as to their contents?
11. Were Mr. K. and Mr. S. called in that morning or were they notified in any way?
12. How long did you stay with Mr. R.?
13. When did you see Admiral S. that morning?
14. With reference to a certain conference held that morning, do you know who attended it and how long it lasted?

With regards to what happened afterwards:

15. Did you ever tell Admiral W. what you told me?
16. Or McCollum, or anyone else?
17. When did Admiral W. first see or learn about ~~these~~ *Part 14 and other* papers?
18. We can't find the original "Weather Report" (sent on Dec. 5th) and its translation. What became of it?
19. Can you offer any pertinent remarks?

Things seem running ~~a little~~ better out at the Annex now that Wright is here. I think he has done a marvelous job of creating order out of chaos, but his task is by no means finished.

I hope you are enjoying the balmy climate of Hawaii. I certainly think that you, personally, have benefited by the change of duty.

Please give my regards to Dyer, Huckins, Williams, and the others.

With best wishes for the Holidays,

Sincerely,

L. F. Safford,
Captain, U. S. Navy.

Commander A. D. Kramer, U.S.N.,
Fourteenth Naval District,
Pearl Harbor, T.H.

Exhibit #42: Letter in response from Kramer to Safford, 28 December 1943. (2 pages) "Safford-Kramer Letter[s],"

NARA, RG 80, Pearl Harbor Liaison Office, Entry 167A, Box 4; also PHH, Part 8:3699-3700.

JOINT

INTELLIGENCE CENTER
PACIFIC OCEAN AREAS
Commandant, Navy 128
c/o Fleet Post Office
San Francisco, Calif.

28 December 1943

MEMORANDUM FOR: Capt. SAFFORD

1510 First indications of arrival
2100 Completed. Left after phoning to locate Adm B., Adm. T.,
    Col. B. of M.I.D., Adm. W., etc.

    1.   Did not, personally, but left with one of Adm. B's ass'ts in the situation room on Penn Ave. with positive instructions re-urgency (to be delivered at once). He was entertaining at the time, but I learned later in the evening he had seen it.

    2.   No, on all counts. Army was taking care of that and I know only that he knew of it by 2230 (see item 9) and possibly had seen it c/o Col. B. by then.

    3.   Did not. (See items 4 and 5).

    4.   Believe Item 5 phoned that eve (see next). Possibly Adm. T did too. I know he saw it as soon as he reached office next A.M. (about 0900).

    5.   At 2105 by phone to his home where he was entertaining Adm. B and others, told him what I planned to do. His chief concern was getting it to Item 1 and 2, which are covered above. Arrived at his home at 2320 where he, and Adm. B also, saw it and were informed re-others, particularly Item 1. I don't recall whether B then phoned re-Item 1 to check delivery or not. Believe at this time Item 5 phoned 3.

    6.   Left Item 5 place about 0030, stopped by, then proceeded.

    7.   About 0730.

    8.   Did not personally, but left first batch about 0945, 2nd about 1100 at Item 8 house, c/o Adm. B.

    9.   No; at his office. Item 11 (first one) was shown it at his home about 2200 previous night and he made a number of phone calls including Item 2. Meeting was then arranged for Item 2, 11 (both) and others at Item 2 office at 10:00 A.M. where I was instructed to be with it and anything else. Meeting held at 1000 as scheduled and new items (1st batch) delivered together with old. Col. B. was on hand there too for Item 11 (second).

JOINT

INTELLIGENCE CENTER
PACIFIC OCEAN AREAS
Commandant, Navy 128
c/o Fleet Post Office
San Francisco, Calif.

10. (a) I don't recall precisely how our friends numbers run in the hundreds (or thousands) but in units from about 02 to 09 or 10.

(b) The first few of these, NOT including first sentence last half this item, were on hand by 0900 and were completed and being delivered at 0945 (to Item 8) and 1000 (see Items 9 above). Item 5, 3, T, and others got them about 0930 at a meeting being held in Item 9 office.

(c) On returning about 1020 from Item 9 office the remainder of #02-10 were arriving, including this item, i.e., 1st sentence last half, and also quotes in Item 19. These were delivered to all hands, including Items 11 (both) at Item 2 office by 1100 with my comments to Item 11 (first one) on how the hour tied with the sun, and moves in progress, elsewhere.

11. Yes. See 9 and 10 above.

12. Did not. See 8 above.

13. About 0900 at his office with others, and left night before matters. 1st batch of new given about 0940, 2nd about 1045 (all this was not personal but via his senior aide because of meeting in progress. They were passed in to him promptly however.)

14. There were 2 I know of, and I believe another c/o Col. B. The one in Item 9 above was at least 1½ hours. Another started about 0900 with 10, 11, 12, 16, 20, and others there, lasting to 1130 that I know of, and probably later.

15-16. Reference obscure. Would you clarify? If re-general security (i.e. lack) late in spring, yes!

17. See Items 13 and 14 above.

18. The first one of the " " was not as indicated in parentheses, but as indicated in Item 10-c above. It went into Z files. GL should have it now unless it was among files turned over to Army.

19. For the most part covered above, until Item 15 (16) is clarified.

Exhibit #43: Safford's coded letter to Kramer, 22 January 1944. (4 pages) With Safford's associated private code listing. (2 pages)

NARA, RG 80, Pearl Harbor Liaison Office, Entry 167A, Box 4; also PHH, Part 8: 3700, 3703-4.

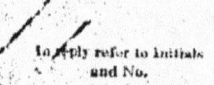

NAVY DEPARTMENT
OFFICE OF THE CHIEF OF NAVAL OPERATIONS
WASHINGTON

22 January 1944

My dear Kramer-san:

Thanks for your very prompt reply. I did not receive your Dec. 28th letter till Jan. 17th, and had almost given up hopes. What a break for you, as well as the cause, to be ordered to Admiral Halsey's staff. I can see the hand of Providence in it.

I am sending by separate cover (air mail) a condensation code to use. If you want to add to it, use numbers #151-#200 inclusive. I would like to hold it down to a single sheet of paper. I am also sending by ordinary mail a copy of #35 and a clipping to give to #42 at some auspicious occasion. You will understand this letter better when they arrive.

With regard to taking #42 into confidence, wait patiently for the proper moment, and then shoot the works. Tell him everything he will listen to and show him whatever documentary proof you may have. Use your own judgment and don't force the issue. Do as good a job as you did on #136 and #137. In my opinion the proper moment for disclosure would be any of the following:

    (a) #42 is detached from Sopac;
    (b) # 5 is detached from Sopac;
    (c) #10 is detached from Sopac;
    (d) # 9 calls on #42 or #10;
    (e) #18 calls on #42 or #10;
    (f) #42 discusses #31 or attack on #92 in your presence;
    (g) #42 asks you the reason for the alleged failure of 20-G to know what was going on;
    (h) #137 (plus 3 years);
    (i) #6 visits #42;
    (j) #42 visits #6.

Be prudent and be patient. I am just beginning to get things lined-up on this end. No one in #15 can be trusted. Premature action would only tip off the people who framed #31 and #32, and will also get #8 and #10 into very serious trouble. Yet we must have the backing, the rank, and the prestige afforded by #42. Tell #42 that I knew #31 was a scapegoat from the start, but I did not suspect that he was victim of a frame-up until about #114 (plus 2 years), could not confirm it until #132 (plus 2 years), and did not have absolute proof until about Jan. 18, 1944. #8 has overwhelming proof of the guilt of #15 and #65 plus a list of about fifteen reliable witnesses.

Please answer the following questions by Item No.:

20. Re your Item #2, is Col. B. #59?

21. What or whose job in the Navy did Col. B.'s job correspond to?

22. Do you know what Army officers were notified or shown the papers by Col. B., and when?

In amplification of my Items #15 and #16:

    I recall your telling me that you saw #3 about 0900 (EST) on #137.
    He looked at the papers and exclaimed, "My God! This means War!"
    You said, "Admiral, it has meant war for the past three months."
    #3 continued, "I must get word to #31," and picked up a message blank.
    Then another idea entered his mind, and he said, "Does #53 know of this?"
    You replied, "Most of it was sent over to his office last night. This last part (#77) was sent over ten minutes ago and should be on the General's desk by now."
    #3 dropped the message blank and reached for the telephone.

(End of your tale.)

23. Can you verify or correct the foregoing?

24. Did #3 get #53 on the telephone and what did he say?

25. Were there any other witnesses? If so, who?

26. Did you tell #9 or #5, or anyone else?
(Be sure to tell Admiral Halsey - when the time comes.)

27. Re your Item #15 and #16. What do you mean by "general security" (i.e. lack) late in spring? Was it the Chicago Tribune leak after Midway? Incidentally, tell the full story of this to #42 and explain that #5 tried to stop the prosecution and attending publicity but #24 insisted (to give publicity to himself and to #25) and was backed up by #29 and #28.

28. Do you know if any of the following were called as witnesses by #36?
    (a) #5
    (b) #9
    (c) #10
    (d) #6

29. Were the JD files in CZ custody or any messages from these files ever submitted to #36?

30. Were #5, #9, #10, or anyone else, cautioned or warned, or instructed **not** to ever mention the events of #136 and #137 or the investigations conducted by #36? In this connection, I am sending you #35 by ordinary ship's mail. I will comment on it in further correspondence.

31. Do you know when and how #53 first got the news of #75 and #76, and what action he took?

32. Same for #77 and #78.

33. Re my #14. I meant the conference on #137 between #3 and #53 which resulted in #89. I did not know of the other conferences and am delighted to learn of them. Can you add any names to those already given by you for:

34. The one in #2 office?

35. The one in #3 office?

36. The one "c/o Col. B."?

37. The one between #3 and #53?

38. How much does #9 know?

39. Will #9 come through willingly?

40. What is your estimate of #5 in this respect?

41. Will he talk for #42?

42. What about #6?

Comment

With regard to the quotes of my Item 18 and your Items 18 and 10(c), you were describing #80, of which we have copies of the original and its translation in the CZ files. This was sent and received on #137. I was asking about #74 which was broadcast at 0430 (GCT) on #134 or #135. (Not sure of exact date.) It was heard by "L" and "M" and sent in by teletype. It was unheard by "S", "H", and "C", who listened for it. (I have this from the Station "S" files, plus statements of #19 and #20.) This message (in Morse) included the words - "Higashi no kazeame. Nishi no kaze hare. (Negative form of kita no kaze kumori.)" The warning was not sent in the manner prescribed by #72 or #73, but was a mixture. The GY watch officer was not sure of it so he called you and you came in early and verified it. Murray recalls it and so do I. Either you or

Brotherhood (?) were waiting in my office when I came in that morning and said, "Here it is!" We had been waiting a week for it and Station "S" had been forwarding reams of P/L messages by teletype.

As a result of #74, #9 prepared #90 - which was a very long message ending up with the translation and significance of the warning in #74. I read the message in #7's office and was witness to the discussion of it between #7 and #5. I took for granted that #90 would be sent and did not know otherwise until #132 (plus 2 years). I believe that I told you about this message and stated that it had been sent. Anyway, I was living in a fool's paradise from #134 to #137. I learned from #19 that #9 knew #90 had not been sent (#19 was informed by #9 at #92).

More Questions

43. Do you recall #74?

44. Did you know any or all of the circumstances of #90, how much, and when did you learn it?

45. When did #9 learn that #90 had not been released?

46. Do you know who blocked #90 or refused to release it? (#5 was pushing it but apparently did not feel he had the authority to release it himself.)

47. Can you throw any other light on the subject?

- - - - - - - - - - - - -

One final word - I do not know how well you know #18. I have known him for 18 years. He can be trusted and will come through for us. Get in touch with him out there if you can.

Well, this is about enough for one installment. Please give my best regards to any of my friends that you may run into out there.

Sincerely,

L. F. Safford,
Captain, U.S. Navy.

Commander Alwin D. Kramer, U.S.N.,
COMSOPAC Staff,
c/o F.P.O., San Francisco, Calif.

SECRET   January 21, 1944

AIR-MAIL CODE FOR PERSONAL CORRESPONDENCE

#1	-	Mr. Roosevelt	: #51	-
#2	-	Mr. Hull	: #52	-
#3	-	Ad. S. Stark	: #53	- Gen. Marshall
#4	-	Ad. I. Ingersoll	: #54	- Deputy Chief of Staff
#5	-	Ad. W. Wilkinson	: #55	- D.M.I.
#6	-	Ad. T. Turner	: #56	- D.M.P.
#7	-	Ad. N.	: #57	- C.S.O. (Gen. O.)
#8	-	Safford	: #58	- Minckler
#9	-	McCollum	: #59	- Bratton (?)
#10	-	Kramer	: #60	- Dowd
#11	-	Mr. Knox (#11-first)	: #61	- Mr. Stimson (#11-last)
#12	-	Linn	: #62	- Rowlett
#13	-		: #63	- Adjutant General
#14	-		: #64	- Chief of Air Corps
#15	-	Opnav	: #65	- General Staff
#16	-	Nav. Intell.	: #66	- M.I.D.
#17	-	Nav. Comm.	: #67	- Signal Corps
#18	-	Rochefort	: #68	-
#19	-	Wright	: #69	- J-19
#20	-	Dyer	: #70	- Machine
#21	-	Huckins	: #71	- Minor System
#22	-	Holtwick	: #72	- Circular #2353 (Sets up #74)
#23	-	Mason	: #73	- Circular #2354 (Sets up #74)
#24	-	Big Jit	: #74	- General Intelligence Broadcast containing false "Weather Report"
#25	-	Little Jit	:	
#26	-	Wenger	: #75	- Serial #901 (Sets up #902)
#27	-	Goggins	: #76	- Serial #902 (1-13) (The Works)
#28	-	Ad. King	: #77	- Serial #902 (14) (The Finale)
#29	-	Ad. Horne	: #78	- Serial #907 (1:00 p.m.)
#30	-	Ad. Nimitz	: #79	- Circular #2409 (Sets up #80)
#31	-	Ad. Kimmel	: #80	- Circular #2494 (PL code msg.)
#32	-	Gen. Short	: #81	- Tokyo Circular #
#33	-	Ad. Bloch	: #82	- Tokyo-Washington Serial #
#34	-	Ad. Hart	: #83	- Washington-Tokyo Serial #
#35	-	Roberts Report	: #84	- Tokyo-Berlin Serial #
#36	-	Roberts Commission	: #85	- Tokyo-Hsinking Serial #
#37	-	Chief Justice Roberts	: #86	- Hsinking-Hongkong Serial #
#38	-	Ad. Standley	: #87	- Message sent on date indicated
#39	-	Ad. Reeves	: #88	- Message indicated by following ref. No.
#40	-	Gen. McCoy	: #89	- *
#41	-	Gen. McNarney	: #90	- **
#42	-	Admiral Halsey	: #91	- Washington
#43	-	Ad. Beardall	: #92	- Pearl Harbor
#44	-	White House Aide	: #93	- Guadalcanal
#45	-	Aide to CNO	: #94	- London
#46	-	CincAF	: #95	- Corregidor
#47	-	Com 16	: #96	- Singapore
#48	-	Comsopac	: #97	- Melbourne
#49	-	Cincpac	: #98	- Tokyo
#50	-	Com 14	: #99	- Berlin
			: #100	- Rome

* Message described in par. 50 (Page 9-XI) of #35
** Message to #31 originated by #9 on #134 (or #135) but never released.

(over)

SECRET

```
#101 -  xxxxxxx
#102 -  xxxxxx
#103 -  xxxxxxx
#104 -  Nomura
#105 -  Kurusu
#106 -  Gen. Umedzu (Hsinking)
#107 -  Jap. Prime Minister
#108 -  Gaimudaijin
#109 -  The Son of Heaven
#110 -
#111 -  Oct. 16, 1941
#112 -  Nov. 6, 1941
#113 -  Nov. 14, 1941
#114 -  Nov. 15, 1941
#115 -  Nov. 16, 1941
#116 -  Nov. 17, 1941
#117 -  Nov. 18, 1941
#118 -  Nov. 19, 1941
#119 -  Nov. 20, 1941
#120 -  Nov. 21, 1941
#121 -  Nov. 22, 1941
#122 -  Nov. 23, 1941
#123 -  Nov. 24, 1941
#124 -  Nov. 25, 1941
#125 -  Nov. 26, 1941
#126 -  Nov. 27, 1941
#127 -  Nov. 28, 1941
#128 -  Nov. 29, 1941
#129 -  Nov. 30, 1941
#130 -
#131 -  Dec. 1, 1941
#132 -  Dec. 2, 1941
#133 -  Dec. 3, 1941
#134 -  Dec. 4, 1941
#135 -  Dec. 5, 1941
#136 -  Dec. 6, 1941
#137 -  Dec. 7, 1941
#138 -  1325 (EST) Dec. 7, 1941
```

Exhibit #44: Letter, Admiral Husband Kimmel to Admiral William Halsey, 18 March 1944,

Pearl Harbor Exhibit 150,

NARA, RG 80, Entry 167EE, Box 120; also NARA, RG 38, CNSG Library, Box 166, Folder 5830/69, "Pearl Harbor Investigation: Winds msgs."

EXHIBIT 150

C O P Y

280 Bronxville Road
Bronxville, New York
18 March 1944

Admiral William F. Halsey, U.S.Navy
Commander South Pacific Fleet
c/o Fleet Post Office
San Francisco, California

Dear Bill,

You have on your staff Commander A.D. Kramer, U.S.N., who was on duty in the Communications Office in the Navy Department at the time of the attack on Pearl harbor and for some time prior to that date. I believe he has knowledge of facts and incidents which occured in the navy Department hwich are of interest and value to me. Will you please obtain from him an affidavit and ask him if he will supply me with a copy. I will assure him that I will make no use of the affidavit without his permission so long as he is alive. If he does not wish to supply me with a copy of the affidavit, I would appreciate it very much if he will make the affidavit, put it in a secure place and inform me when I can obtain it.

There was a message received in the Navy Department on December 4th or 5th, 1941, which came to be called the "winds Message". I should like to know:

What station first received the Winds Message?

What date was it received in Washington?

When was it deciphered, translated, decoded and delivered to responsible officials in Washington?

What officials in Washington saw the translation of the Winds message and when?

What was the substance of the information contained in the Winds Message?

What Action towards notification of Field Commanders of contents of message and implications thereof was taken?

There was a note delivered by the Japanese Ambassador to Mr. Hull on 7 December 1941.

When were the first 13 parts of this message received, decoded and delivered to responsible officials in Washington?

Admiral William F. Halsey, USNAVY   18 March 1944

What officials in Washington received translations of the first 13 parts of this message and when did each receive them?

When was the 14th part of the message received, decoded and delivered?

What officials in Washington received translations of the 14th part of this message and when did each received it?

What action was recommended by you or anyone else of which you have knowledge?

There was a message directing the Japanese Ambassador to deliver a note to Secretary Hull in person at 1:00 P.M. Easteren Standard Time on 7 December 1941.

When was this message received in the Navy Department?

What agency decoded the message and when was decoding completed?

What agency translated the message and when was the translation delivered to the Navy Department.?

What officials in Washington received translations of this message and when did each received it?

What action was taken as a result of this message?

When Commander Kramer delivered this message to Mr. Knox a memorandum pointing out that 1:00 P.M. Eastern Stadard Time was sunrise in Honolulu and midnight in Manila and that the whole thing meant sunrise air raid in Pearl Harbor within a few minutes after the delivery of the Japanese note.

Will you please have Commander Kramer answer all of the fore-going questions of which he has knowledge and put them in the form of an affidavit and also request him to include in his affidavit any other matters of which he may have first-hand knowledge. I shall be very grateful to him for this matter will be of considerable interest and value to me.

My kindest regards to you always Bill.

Most Sincerely yours,

/s/ H. E. Kimmel.

Exhibit #45: Memorandum, 8 November 1945, Subject: "JD-7001, Special Studies Covering," and attachment showing distribution of "JD" serial numbers 6998 through 7022 (2 pages).

**Exhibit 142B, RG 80,
Pearl Harbor Liaison Office,
Entry 167EE, Box 120.**

6 (A)

8 November 1945

Subj: JD-1: 7001, special studies concerning

1. In an effort to locate JD-1: 7001 the following sources have been exhaustively studied:

       a. numerical file of JD-1 #'s.
       b. chronological file of Japanese Diplomatic translations.
       c. the "Japanese diplomatic traffic log" for 1941.
       d. old GZ card index of Japanese diplomatic traffic, under Tokyo circulars and Tokyo-Washington circuit.

2. A special study of Jd-1 #'s was made to determine the relationship between the date of the message, the date of translation of the message, and the JD-1 #. The results of this study are attached to this memo.

3. From this study it would appear that JD-1: 7001, if such number was assigned to a translation, was for a message dated 28 November 1941, translated on either 12-2-41 or 12-3-41 by the Army. As all of the JD-1 #'s on both sides of JD-1: 7001 were translated on either 2 December 1941 it seems reasonably certain that the message was dated on or prior to 3 December 1941.

4. Throughout the JD-1 numerical file there are incidents of cancelled numbers. The reasons for some of these cancellations are not given: others are given as follows: "duplicate of message previously numbered", "additional part of message already assigned a number", and "number skipped by mistake".

5. In October 1944 and on 14 May 1945 Lieut. Comdr. G. E. Boone called Col. Rowlett at Arlington Hall and secured from him the following information concerning the Army numbering system in 1941: Occasionally numbers were cancelled, but there was no indication given of the reason for the cancellation, by whom it was made, nor by whom it was authorized. He stated that there were other cases of numbers cancelled in the 1941 file.

/s/ Sally T. Lightle,

/t/ Sally T. Lightle,
Lieut., USNR.

	JD-1 #	DATE OF MESSAGE	DATE OF TRANSLATION	ARMY OR NAVY TRANS.
	6998	22 Nov 1941	12-2-41	A
	6999	27 Nov 1941	12-2-41	N
	7000	28 Nov 1941	12-3-41	A
	7001	---------- ---	-----	-
	7002	28 Nov 1941	12-3-41	A
	7003	28 Nov 1941	12-2-41	A
	7004	28 Nov 1941	12-3-41	A
	7005	28 Nov 1941	12-3-41	A
	7006	29 Nov 1941	12-3-41	N
	7007	29 Nov 1941	12-2-41	N
	7008	29 Nov 1941	12-2-41	N
	7009	29 Nov 1941	12-2-41	N
	7010	29 Nov 1941	12-2-41	N
	7011	29 Nov 1941	12-2-41	N
	7012	1 Dec 1941	12-3-41	N
	7013	1 Dec 1941	12-2-41	N
	7014	2 Dec 1941	12-3-41	A
	7015	2 Dec 1941	12-3-41	A
	7016	3 Dec 1941	12-3-41	N
	7017	2 Dec 1941	12-3-41	A N (revision)
	7018	3 Dec 1941	12-3-41	N
	7019	3 Dec 1941	12-3-41	N
	7020	3 Dec 1941	12-3-41	N
	7021	2 Dec 1941	12-3-41	A
III	7022	2 Oct 1941	12-4-41	A

**Exhibit #46: Morio Tateno Interview
(3 pages), 30 June 1961,**

**RG 38, CNSG Library, Box 166,
Folder 5830/69, "Winds Msgs"**

C O P Y

June 30, 1961

Memo to Wade Bingham

From: Kenneth Ishii

Subject: Morio Tateno Interview. (re. Yoshikawa story).

    I called on Morio Tateno today (June 30) at the Japan Broadcasting Corporation (NHK). Tateno, Vice-Director of the Commentators' Section, was referred to me by a friend of mine (Mr. Miino) at NHK whom I thought might know something about the weather reports said to have been made from Radio Tokyo (NHK's station name) around the time of Pearl Harbor.

    Tateno's main points were: (1) that he himself broadcast a weather report on Radio Tokyo's shortwave network at the hour Yoshikawa says he tuned in, and (2) that the weather report he read was "West wind, clear," not "East wind, rain" which is what Yoshikawa claims he heard.

    We started off by going through Tateno's routine on that day. At the time he was an announcer assigned to the Domestic News Section and concurrently handled shortwave Japanese newscasts for the Overseas Section. He recalled his shift was from 1800 dec. 7 to 1000 dec. 8 (Japan time). He worked the domestic news side until midnight. At midnight the Japanese-language overseas newscasts began -- every hour on the hour up through four a.m. The newscasts, Tateno recalled, lasted ten minutes.

    On this particular night, Tateno was told at first to be ready to deliver a special weather report on the 0200 overseas news. But there was a delay (Tateno was not told why), and he was not given the report xxxxxxxxx until just before 0300. Tateno received his instructions from the Chief of the Overseas Section (a Shinnojo Sawada, now believed to be in the advertising business).

    About midway in the 0300 newscast, Tateno said he read these words: "We now bring you a special weather forecast. West wind, clear." he read this twice -- and twice again on the 0400 newscast.

    With regards to Yoshikawa's own recollection (set forth in his article, "Top Secret Assignment", U.S. Naval Institute Proceedings, Dec. 1960) that the words were "East wind, rain," Tateno strongly defends himself. "Yoshikawa is obviously wrong," he said. "I myself made the broadcast, and I clearly remember what I said."

    Yoshikawa writes that while at breakfast at 0755 at the Honolulu Consulate-General he heard the first bomb fall on Pearl Harbor, after which Consul-General Kita hurriedly in "and we silently listened to the 8 o'clock news on Radio Tokyo. It was a broadcast of routine news, except that inserted in the narration was a single phrase, twice repeated, which told us that the Imperial Japanese Navy had attacked Pearl Harbor." Eight o'clock on December 7 in Honolulu was 0300 December 8 in tokyo when Tateno went on the air with his first reading of the weather message. This should dispel any doubts

COPY

that the message was actually broadcast, despite the apparent failure of the U.S. to pick it up.

Yoshikawa writes that "East wind, rain" stood for war with the U.S., while "North wind, cloudy" would have meant war with Russia, and "West wind, Clear" war with Britain. By this reckoning, Tateno was informing his listeners that Japan and Britain were at war. Actually, Japan declared war simultaneously against both the U.S. and Britain: both countries are named in the war declaration. Thus -- again by Yoshikawa's reckoning -- Tateno should have read two messages, "West wind, clear"

k.1s 1 / morio tateno interview - 2

and "East wind, rain." as the primary source, Tateno's word obviously carries more weight. It is my personal observation, as a Japanese who himself served in his country's armed forces during the war, that given a choice, a Japanese officer would select "West wind, clear." It suggests a bright, auspicious start, especially desirable because of the enormity of the undertaking. One recalls that during the Russo-Japanese war, Admiral Haihachiro Togo issued a similarly optimistic weather report (his was real) prior to engaging the Russian fleet in a battle that to this day stands as the greatest naval victory in Japanese history.

Tateno himself had no knowledge of the meaning of the weather report. But it could guess it was an important code message. He told me: "we never broadcast weather reports on overseas news programs, so I knew something was up." He stressed that 0300 and 0400 on December 8 were the ONLY times that a weather report was read on an overseas Japanese language newscast from Radio Tokyo (or on any other Japanese overseas broadcast): that no such reports were ever read before December 8 or after that date. If necessary, confirmation or denial of this can probably be obtained from other NHK sources. Overseas newscasts were not taped, so there is no recorded evidence. However, Tateno indicated willingness to do a re-broadcast of the weather message if C'S desired.

A point to note is that when Tateno volunteered the information about the 0300 and 0400 broadcasts, I had not yet told him about Yoshikawa's claim to haveing heard the weather message at 0800 Honolulu time. It was not until later that we figured out that 0300 in Tokyo was 0800 in Hawaii.

I asked Tateno, "Do you know where the orders to read the weather message came from?" He replied he presumed that Imperial General Headquarters gave them direct to Overseas Section Chief Sawada.

After the 0400 broadcast, Tateno went back to the domestic news side. Domestic newscasts started at 0600. Tateno says that although he read the 0600 domestic news, it was not until 1700 that he was given the Imperial General Headquarters announcement of Japan's declaration of war to broadcast. Tateno recalled the announcement itself listed 0600 as the release time. The delay in getting it on the air was the subject of inquiry at the International

- 2 -

C O P Y

Military Tribunal for the Far East before which Tateno was brought to testify. He told me: "Actually, I was already in the studio waiting for seven o'clock when the war declaration was rushed to me. Imperial General Headquarters telephoned the text of the declaration at the last minute to the Domestic News Section. Junnosuka Tanaka (Now Chief of NHK's Broadcasting Station at Mito City) took it down and personally brought it to me. I led off the newscast with the declaration. I read it twice."

Tateno ended his shift at 1000 but he said he stayed at work until noon because of the rush of work attending the outbreak of hostilities.

Exhibit #47: Memorandum to Carter W. Clarke from William F. Friedman, 19 September 1944 (2 pages). Selected pages from handwritten notes of meeting with Captain Safford (5 pages) numbered 11, 12, 15, and 16.

NARA, RG 457, Entry 9032, Box 1360, Folder 4217, "Pearl Harbor Investigation and Miscellaneous Material."

19 September 1944

MEMORANDUM FOR COLONEL CLARKE:

Capt. Safford told me the following in a conference with him on the afternoon of 17 September in his office:

The Winds execute message came in during the night of 3-4 December 1941, Washington time, and was first seen by him at about 0800 4 December. A smooth translation was made and a special distribution in advance of the regular noon distribution was made at 0900, 4 December.

The Winds execute message, according to him, was not intercepted by any of their stations except one on the east coast. The logs of all of their intercept stations with the exception of the log of the station at Bainbridge Island have been destroyed, so that the log of whatever station on the east coast it was which actually intercepted the Winds execute message is not available. Safford says that the Winds execute message took the form of an insertion within a regular news broadcast from Tokyo in Morse code and in the Japanese language in Romaji, and that it not only had the words indicating a break in relations between Japan and England and the United States but it also contained a negative for a break in relations between Japan and the U.S.S.R. Apparently, according to Safford, the Japanese mixed both of the codes, the one in circular 2353 and the one in circular 2354 (Army 25392 and 25432) in their haste or confusion.

Safford says that, realizing the meaning of the Winds execute message, he prepared messages to their various overseas stations with regard to the destruction of cryptographic aids at points exposed to possible capture by the Japanese, and these messages went out at about 1500, Washington time, 4 December 1941, as released by Adm. Noyes and Adm. Ingersol. Safford further said that Commander McCullom also took action by drafting a warning message, about 500 words long, in which he summarized the events from the first of July, giving the translation and meaning of the Winds execute message and including other corroborative information of recent date, and he ended his message with a specific warning that "war is imminent." Safford said that he read the message and that the warning was complete, clear and forceful. McCullom took the message to Adm. Wilkinson, who in turn consulted with Adm. Noyes. The latter was of the opinion that to send such a message would be an insult to the intelligence of the Commander-in-Chief. Safford said, and I presume that he was present because he quoted verbatim the following as being a statement by Adm. Wilkinson to Adm. Noyes: "I do not agree with you. Adm. Kimmel is a very busy man and he may not see the picture as clearly as you and I do. I think it only fair to the Commander-in-Chief that he be given this warning, and I intend to send it if I can get it released by the front office." Safford said that Wilkinson left immediately after the conference to see Adm. Ingersol or Adm. Stark and to try to get their approval to release the message. Safford further stated that he thought the message had been sent but did not discover until November 1943 that this was not the case and that the message had never been sent.

History of Top Secret Message, Army No. 25850

With reference to the foregoing message, Capt. Safford told me the following at the same conference: The message came in to OP20GX between four and five o'clock on the morning of 7 December, Washington time, it having been intercepted at about three o'clock that morning at Station S, Bainbridge Island, and sent in by teletype. The message was deciphered immediately in OP20G, where there was a lot of traffic awaiting translation. Lt. Brotherhood, who was coming off watch at seven o'clock in the morning, and Lt. Pering, who was relieving him, both say that Message No. 907 was delivered to the SIS for translation, it being in a batch together with Nos. 905, 906, 908, 909 and 910, all marked "urgent."

No. 907 was sent back, translated by SIS, to Navy and reached OP20G at about 10:20 a.m. When Commander Kramer saw it he immediately made another trip to take this message around to the various interested people, Adm. Stark, The White House, the State Department and Sec. Knox. Safford says that he doesn't know if the following note was appended to all of these copies, but to the copy which Kramer delivered to Sec. Knox at about eleven o'clock, Washington time, was appended the following note by Kramer: "One p.m., Washington time, is approximately midnight at Manila and sunrise at Honolulu. The message means a surprise air raid on Pearl Harbor this morning."

William F. Friedman
WILLIAM F. FRIEDMAN

①

2353 — Original int — Bainbridge — 19th fwded by Tpletype
[J-19 key for this one recovered by Singapore.
Passed to Wash by Len on 24 Nov 41.]
not able to read them when rec'd on 19th
2354 — Same applies
Mrs McCarthy + Mrs Burr were the only
two working on them — as no urgency

                                  on 28 Nov
Navy sent out msgs to all int stations to teletype
in all plain lang from Tokyo — East Coast
stations as well as Bainbridge. Give priority
    ↑ in trans   Time   Sta   Freq
as per   0100   JVS
Tokyo 8-13   0130   JUO
27 Nov 1941   0200   JVJ
JD1-6899   0300   JHL   We sent msgs to int. stns
                    0400   JHL   — Dec 41
                    0500   JHL
                    0530   JHP

On 27 Nov notified to record Transpacific — San F Tokyo
radiophone circuit + mail all records by air mail
to 20GX.

On 3 Dec Navy read directive to cover SF Int'national
Circuits to Tokyo in add to reg assgn + fwd all
p.l. JG tfc to WA91 via TWX (in add to Code tfc already
    so to Teletype   being sent)

All log sheets from Sta S obtained but it did not
get winds execute msge. Safford believes one of them East.
Coast int sta got winds execute msge but when
tried find out which one, found logs of all 4
stations had been destroyed. Orig int. also
still missing.

Transcription of Handwritten Notes by William F. Friedman, 17 September 1944.

NOTE: Missing text (words and letters) are enclosed with brackets '['. Original underlines and cross-outs are retained. Original brackets are in bold face ']'.

Page 1

2353 – Original int[ercept] – Bainbridge – 19th f[or]w[ar]ded by teletype
    [J-19 key for this one recovered by Singapore.
    Passed to Wash[ington] by L[on]d[o]n on 24 Nov 41.]
    Not able to read then when rec'd [received] on 19th
2354 – Same applies
    Mrs. McCantley and Miss Burr were the only
    two working on them – as no urgency

(as per Tokyo 843 27 Nov 1941 JD1-6899) Navy sent out on 28 Nov to all its stations to teletype in all plain lang[uage] from Tokyo - East Coast
stations as well as Bainbridge. Give priority
in trans[missions]

Time	Sta[tion]	Freq[uency]	
0100	JVJ		
0130	JUO		
0200	JVJ		
0300	JHL		We sent msges to int stns
0400	JH		2 Dec 41
0500	JHL		
530	JHP		

On 27 Nov Notified to record Transpacific - San F[rancisco] Tokyo
    radiotelephone circuit & mail all records by air mail
    to [OP] 20GX
On 3 Dec Navy rec[eived] directive to cover SF International
circuit to Tokyo in add[ition] to reg[ular] assign[ment] & f[or]w[ar]d all
p.l. [plain language] JG [Japanese Government] TFC [traffic] to WA9I [OP-20 G teletype address] via TWX (in add[ition] to code TFC already being sent)

All log sheets from Sta[tion] S (Bainbridge) obtained but it did not
Get winds execute msge. Safford believes one of their East
Coast int[ercept] sta[tions] got winds execute msge but when
 tried [to] find out which one, found logs of all 4
stations had been destroyed. Orig[inal] int[ercept] also
still missing.

② check w/ Safford

Safford says Winds Ex msge came in on 4 Dec. It was during the night (3-4) Dec 41 Wash time & was 1st seen by him at about 0500 - 4 Dec. Smooth trans was made & spl distrib made about 0900 4 Dec — in addn of reg distrib at noon. He prepared msges of destr of crypto aids at points exposed to cap by Jap. These went out as released by Adm Noyes + Adm Ingersoll. They went out about 1500 Wash time 4 Dec. (filing time). McCollum also took action in a warning msge about 1300 wds long, summar events from July, gave int & mean'g Winds ex msge, also other corrob of recent date & end with specific warning War is imminent. Warning was complete clear & forceful — masterpiece. Wilkinson, who was resp but junior, sent to Noyes for comment. Noyes said Think it won't to Nutell of C in Chief, Wilk said I do not agree with you. Adm K is very busy man & he may not see this as clearly as you & I do. I think it only fair to C in C that he be given this warning & I intend to send it if I can get it released by the Front Office. Wilk left immed after to give msge to R Adm Ing for his app'l & ref to Adm Stark. Safford thought msge had been sent but didn't disc until Nov #3 that it had not been sent.

★ Safford: msge in Morse, Romaji, Had negative Kita, positive Hygashi & positive Nishi. Apparently Japs mixed both codes.

* Safford says Winds ex[ecute] msge came in on 4 Dec
& as result was during the night 3-4 Dec 41
Wash[ington] time & was 1st seen by him at about
0800 - 4 Dec. SP Smooth trans[lation] was made &
sp[ecial] distrib[ution] made about 0900 4 Dec in addition
to reg[ular] distrib[ution] at noon.|| He prepared msges
of distr[ibution] of crypto[graphic] at points exposed to
cap[ture] by Jap[anese]. These went out as released
by Ad[miral] Noyes & Ad[miral] Ingersoll. They went
out about 1500 Wash[ington] time 4 Dec. (filing
time). McCollum also took action in a
warning msge about 500 w[or]ds long, summary [izing?]
events from July 1, giv[es] tr[anslation] & mean[ing] of Winds
ex[ecute] msge, also other corrob[oration] of recent date
& end with specific warning war is imminent.
Warning was complete clear & forceful - masterpiece
Wilkinson who was respon[sible] but junior sub[ordinate] to Noyes
for comment??? Noyes said think it insult to
intell[igence] of C[ommander] in Chief [Pacific Fleet]. Wilk[inson] said I do not agree
with you. Adm[iral] K[immel] is very busy man & he may not
see pic[ture] as clearly as you & I do. I think it
only fair to C[ommander] in C[hief] that he be given this warning
& I intend to send it if I can get it released by
the front office !! Wilk[inson] left immed[iately] after to
give msge to R[ear] Adm[iral] Ing[ersoll] for his app[roval] or ref[er] to
Adm Stark. Safford thought msge had been
sent but didn't disc[over] until Nov [19]43 that it
had not been sent.

* Safford: Msge in Morse, Romaji. Had negative Kita,
positive Higashi & postive Nishi. Apparently Jap[ane]s[e]
mixed both codes.

(3)

~~H. ????~~ told Safford that McCullow was positive attack would come sunrise Sunday morning + went to Stark at 9:00 a.m. Sunday morning to beg him to send warning msge. Stark refused. & McC told this to Rochefort & Wright when McC was passing thru Honolulu. Either Wright or Roch told Safford

Tokyo No. 901 very impt — SIS 25838
                SIS 25850 (to deliver text to Sec State at 1:00 p.m. 7th)
Re " No. 907 — Came in bet 4-5 a.m. OP20GX
Int at Bain about 3 AM + sent in to TT ype. End copy
reached telegraph off at Dupont C about 7 am
that morn. Msge decoded immed + zo G. Both
Brotherhood who was coming off watch + Boring
who was coming on, say msge was delivered to
SIS for translation. 905, 6, 7, 8, 9, + 910 all
marked "urgent" were sent over from tt at same
time. Boring remembers he took these over — Watch
changed at 7 a.m. + ust got msges cleaned up
ready for translation.

1st half of 902 came in by TT from Bain at about
11:30 a.m. on 6 Dec. Wash time. Boring was on watch
+ checked up with SIS — who was closing (Sat p.m.) so
Navy took msges + began working on it. About 3pm
rest of 902 less pt 14 came in + Kramer got back
to Dept + he immed called up SIS + asked for
help. (Schukraft) There were people on duty
in SIS but on their own time. Got Rowlett at
3:30. Got Doud back, two girls (1 crypt + 1 typist)
R took some facts out himself. Finn came

Page 3

? H---di-wash [unclear text] told Safford that McCollum was positive
attack would come sunrise Sunday morning & went
to Stark at 9:00 AM Sunday morning to beg him
to send warning msge. Stark refused. [McC told
this to Rochefort or Wright when McC was passing
thru Honolulu. Either Wright or Roch[efort] told Safford.]

Tokyo No. 901 very impt[important] == SIS 25838

.....rest of page discusses fourteen-part message sent by Japan 6-7 December. Not relevant to Winds message...

Safford - East Coast Sta - all Stns
Comm to Wash by TT - Records of
previous destroyed but later verified by mail
Cheltenham & Winter Harbor
old destroyed
Copies of Sta comp. lost
" sent in to Dept can't be
loc + S thinks they were
destroyed by new Comers
all in a mess. Chased out old
timers & it was mess.

6 diff witnesses have testified re W_ex.
                    april
Told Hart --- put one E Coast Stns &
logs bee destr.   In morse code but
in form prescribed for voice.

Safford – East Coast Sta[tions] – All st[ation]s
Comm.[unicated] to Wash[ington] by T[ele]T[ype].
Records of TT trans[lations] destroyed but later verified
by mail Cheltenham & Winter harbor
all destroyed
Copies of Sta[tion] comp[word unclear] dest[royed]
   " " sent in to Dep[artmen]t can't be
     loc[ated] and G [??] thinks they were
     destroyed by new Comers
     All in a mess. Chased out old
     timers & it was mess.

\===========/

6 diff[erent] witnesses have testified re W[inds]
Ex[ecute] Told Hart in April .ut[first letter unclear] one
E[ast] Coast st[ation]s &
logs been destr[oyed]. In Morse code but
in form prescribed for voice.

Lt. W. H. Davis — Asst Watch O - 6-7
Lt Cmdr. Pering — Watch O   "
   Neither of them ever heard of Winds
Executed

—

Rochefort says Fielder never came to him
   re Winds Code
Says might have gone to see Lt Cmdr.
E. T. Layton (F. Intell.) but R doesn't
know. Wright says he does not
think Fielder came to see Layton

—

Committee didn't ask Poch anything re
Winds. Understanding was not to
be questioned re any top secret matters

Lt. W.H. Davis – Asst Watch O[fficer] – 6-7 Dec
    Lt. Cmdr. Pering – Watch O[fficer]
    Neither of them ever heard of Winds
    Execute

=

Rochefort says Fielder never came to him
    Re Winds Code
Says might have gone to see Lt. Cmdr.
    E.T. Layton (F[leet] Intell[igence]) but
    R[ochefort] doesn't know. Wright says he does
    not think Fielder came to see Layton.

    Committee didn't ask Roch[efort] anything re
    Winds. Understanding was not to
    be quest[ioned] re any Top secret matters.

Exhibit #48: Operator log for station "M," 2 December 1941 with notation by Ralph Briggs. *"Below Comments added on 12/5/60. I, Ralph T. Briggs, new on duty at NAVSECGRUDET [Naval Security Group Detachment] as OINC, duly note that all transmissions intercepted by me between 0500 and 1300 on the above date are missing from these files & that these intercepts contained the 'Winds message warning code'. My operator sign was 'RT' & these intercepts were made at station M. 'RT' "* –

Naval Security Group, SRH-051. Interview with Mr. Ralph T. Briggs on 13 Jan 1977. Also reproduced in John Toland, *Infamy: Pearl Harbor and its Aftermath.* (New York: Berkeley, 1983)

```
                                              M 2 DEC 41
                                              OPR-RS
FROM   REMARKS                                TIME
                                              0402
                                              12430E
    RS OFF TO (RT)
        COPY PRESS SKDS HR ON(SEE             0500
                       OTHER LOGS)            12275
    RT OFF TO SE                              1300
```

Below Comments added on 12/5/60

I, RALPH T. BRIGGS, NOW ON DUTY AT A NAVSECGAUDET AS OINC, duly NOTE that all transmissions intercepted by me between 0500 thru 1300 on the above date are missing from these files & that these intercepts contained the "Winds message warning Code. My operation sign was RT

RT

Exhibit #49: Message of 3 November 1945 describing the destruction of Cheltenham station logs and intercepts in December 1942.

RG 38, CNSG Library, Box 166 Folder 5830/69, "Pearl Harbor Investigations: Winds msgs" (Folders 1 of 3)

NAVAL MESSAGE — NAVY DEPARTMENT

R1 38054

FROM: SUPRADSTA PT LYAUTEY
DATE: 8 NOV 46
DECODED BY: EVENSEN

FOR ACTION: OP-20-G
ADDRESSEES: OPOPOP

SABAK 082034

UPON SECURING CHELTENHAM INTERCEPT ACTIVITIES LATTER PART DECEMBER 1942 ALL STATION LOGS AND INTERCEPTS DISPOSED OF BY BURNING. YOUR 071655. MATERIAL DESTROYED IN ACCORDANCE WITH STANDING INSTRUCTIONS THAT TIME.

071655: FOR RAD ELEC LEWIS. WHAT DISPOSITION WAS MADE OF CHELTENHAM COPIES OF OPERATORS LOGS AND INTERCEPTS FOR PERIOD IMMEDIATELY PRECEEDING PEARL HARBOR AND IN ACCORDANCE WITH WHAT ORDERS.

ACTION G3   INFO: G
                         G-1
                         G-5 ✓
                         G-6
                         G-L
                         GW
                         GCDO

F16 "Disp P.H. docs."

SECRET

Make original only. Deliver to Code Room Watch Officer in person. (See Art. 76 (4) NAVREGS.)
OPNAV 19-67

DECLASSIFIED
Authority 003003
By NARA Date 11/6/07

Exhibit #50: Operator log for station "M," 2 December 1941, without notation by Ralph Briggs.

RG 38, CNSG Library, Box 167, Folder 5830/77, "Pearl Harbor Investigations: Info Rqts by Capt Safford, 1946-1947."

M 2 DEC 41
OPR-RS

```
TO   FROM  REMARKS                                        TIME
 JQE  DE  JBQH  QRJ CUL                                    0402
                                                          12430E
           RS OFF TO RT.
 ON  JVJ/JUP COPY PRESS SKDS HR ON(SEE                     0500
                             OTHER LOGS)                  12275
           RT OFF TO SE                                    1300
           ....JJC 13640 UNHEARD...EKB ON
           10230 JUST AUDIBLE SENDING NRS-
           UNABLE TO COPY.....                             1301
```

Exhibit #51: Message from Chief of Intelligence (COIS), Singapore, received in London on 8 December 1941 (0113Z), reporting intercept by site at Hong Kong that "severance of Japanese relations? admitted imminent."

RG 80, Entry 167CC, Box 92, Clausen Investigation Exhibits.

COPY

SECRET   MESSAGE   IN

From: C.O.I.S. Singapore.   Date 8.12.41.
                                                   Received: 0113

                    Naval Cypher (D) by W/T

Addressed Admiralty (for D. of N.I.) Navy Board Melbourne.
          Navy Board Wellington. S.O. (I) Hong Kong.
          N.S.H.Q. Ottawa.

          AIDAC

     Information received at 2010Z 7th by Hong Kong that severance
of Japanese relations ? admitted imminent.

                                        2912Z/7

D.N.I. (4)
O.I.C. (3)
D.S.D. 9
File X

Exhibit #52: Cable from British Secret Intelligence Service (S.I.S.) representative in Manila, Commonwealth of the Philippines to S.I.S. representative, Honolulu, Territory of Hawaii, 3 December 1941,

Record Group 80, Entry 167CC, Box 92, "Exhibit 1," item "q," Clausen Investigation Exhibits.

Urgent cable received from Manila night of Dec. 3, 1941

We have received considerable intelligence confirming following developments in Indo-China:

A. 1. Accelerated Japanese preparation of air fields and railways.

2. Arrival since Nov. 10 of additional 100,000 repeat 100,000 troops and considerable quantities fighters, medium bombers, tanks and guns (75 mm).

B. Estimates of specific quantities have already been telegraphed Washington Nov. 21 by American Military Intelligence here.

C. Our considered opinion concludes that Japan invisages early hostilities with Britain and U. S. Japan does not repeat not intend to attack Russia at present but will act in South.

You may inform Chiefs of American Military and Naval Intelligence Honolulu.

cc. Col. Bicknell
Mr. Shivers
Capt. Mayfield

Exhibit #53: British government response (GC&CS #11279), 31 August 1946, to Colonel Clausen inquiry regarding Wilkinson 3 December 1941 cable from Manila.

RH 80, Entry 167CC, Box 92, "Exhibit 1," item "r," Clausen Investigation Exhibits

TOP SECRET ULTRA

From London, 31st August 1945

ULTRA   IMPORTANT

GOR 682 from GCCS 11279

Following from C.S.S. for Jones.

<u>A.</u> Colonel Wilkinson, who was stationed at Manila and is now with 48000 and temporarily in U.K., was recently approached by Lieutenant Colonel H. C. Clausen, of Judge Advocate General's Department U.S. Army, in connection with investigation of General Short and Admiral Kimmel for Pearl Harbour disaster. He carried credentials from Secretary of War.

<u>B.</u> He brought copies of 2 telegrams from Manila to Honolulu, of November 26th and December 2nd, which were as follows:

1. "November 26th, 1941. Most Immediate.
   Secret Source (usually reliable) reports:
   (a) Japanese will attack Krakow Isthmus from sea on December 1st without any ultimatum or declaration of break with a view getting between Bangkok and Singapore.

   (b) Attacking forces will proceed direct from Hainan and Formosa. Main landing point to be in Songkhla area valuation for above is number 3 repeat 3 (i.e., only about 55 to 60 per cent probable accuracy). American military and naval intelligence Manila informed."

2. "December 2nd, 1941. Most Immediate.

   (a) We have received considerable intelligence confirming following developments in Indo-China:
      (I) Accelerated Japanese preparation of airfields and railways.
      (II) Arrival since November 10th of additional 100,000 repeat 100,000 troops and considerable quantities fighters medium bombers tanks and guns (75 mm).

   (b) Estimates of specific quantities have already been telegraphed to Washington November 21st by American Military Intelligence here.

TOP SECRET ULTRA

(c) Our considered opinion concludes that Japan envisages early hostilities with Britain and United States. Japan does not repeat not intend attack Russia at present but will act in south. You may inform Chiefs of American Military and Naval Intelligence Honolulu."

C. Colonel C. anxious to know basic source of para C. of telegram of December 2nd, and in particular, whether this was in "special" category. In point of fact, para C. was based on a B.J. Wilkinson was unaware of source and passed information to Honolulu as he appreciated that I possessed no direct communications.

D. As far as can be judged, the earlier information was based on agents reports, but Clausen only pressing for origin of para C.

E. You should consult with G-2, as security Ultra at stake if this evidence made public.

Exibit #54: Multinational Diplomatic Translation #25783 (Japanese serial #839), Tokyo to Hsinking, 1 December 1941.

RG 457, Entry 9032, Box 301.

From: Tokyo.
To : Hsinking.
1 December 1941
(Purple)

#893

- - - - - - - -In the event that Manchuria participates in the war - - - - in view of various circumstances it is our policy to cause Manchuria to participate in the war in which event Manchuria will take the same steps toward England and America that this country will take in case war breaks out.

A summary follows:

1. American and British consular officials and offices will not be recognized as having special rights. Their business will be stopped (the sending of code telegrams and the use of short wave radio will be forbidden). However it is desired that the treatment accorded them after the suspension of business be comparable to that which Japan accords to consular officials of enemy countries resident in Japan.

2. The treatment accorded to British and American public property, private property, and to the citizens themselves shall be comparable to that accorded by Japan.

3. British and American requests to third powers to look after their consular offices and interests will not be recognized.

However the legal administrative steps taken by Manchoukuo shall be equitable and shall correspond to the measures taken by Japan.

4. The treatment accorded Russians resident in Manchoukuo shall conform to the provisions of the Japanese-Soviet neutrality pact. Great care shall be exercised not to antagonize Russia.

25783

Exhibit #55: Telegram from Walter Foote, U.S. Consulate General, Bandeong, Batvia, Netherlands, East Indies, 4 December 1941, to Secretary of State Cordell Hull.

It reports gist of two Japanese diplomatic messages(likely retransmissions of Japanese messages, serial Nos. 2353 and 2354) containing instructions for Japanese diplomats to monitor for news broadcasts with special weather phrases or words, which are open code messages for them to destroy holdings of cryptographic material and secret papers.
The two messages were intercepted, decrypted, and translated by the Dutch cryptologic unit, Kamer-14.

NARA CP, RG 59,
Decimal Files 711.94 1945-49.
Also reproduced in PHH, Part 17:32.

TELEGRAM RECEIVED

BF
This telegram must be closely paraphrased before being communicated to anyone. (SC)

Batavia

Dated December 4, 1941
FROM
Rec'd. 9:19 a.m.

Secretary of State,
Washington.

220, December 4, 10 a.m.

War Department at Bandoeng claims intercepted and decoded following from Ministry Foreign Affairs Tokyo:

"When crisis leading to worst arises following will be broadcast at end weather reports: one east wind rain war with United States, two north wind cloudy war with Russia, three west wind clear war with Britain including attack on Thailand or Malaya and Dutch Indies. If spoken twice burn codes and secret papers."

Same re following from Japanese Ambassador Bangkok to Consul General Batavia:

"When threat of crises exists following will be used five times in texts of general reports and radio broadcasts: one Higashi east America, two Kita North Russia, three Nishi west Britain with advance into Thailand and attack on Malaya and Dutch Indies."

Thorpe and Slawson cabled the above to War Department. I attach little or no importance to it and view it with some suspicion. Such have been common since 1936.

FOOTE

HSM

Exhibit #56: True form or matrix (stencil) of message #. 2353, 19 November 1941.

NARA RG 80, PHLO, Entry 167A, "Office Reference ("Subject) Files, 1932-1946."
Winds Code, Station "W" to Witnesses.
Folder: Winds Code - Misc Material

	8	17	12	4	5	18		19	7	11	9	4	1	6	16	13	15		
1	X						E	I	C					N		C	S		
2	T				W	Y	N		Y	K	Y	E		S	N	I	C		
3	U				K	Y	M		T	A	N	W	E	N	F	D	B		
4	T	H	Z		W		I		X	H	Z	U	S	G	K	I			
5	Y	I	O		W	V	M	T	G	S	W	U	Y	K	U	Q	E		
6	Q	X	F	U	X		K	Z	R	S	K	H	S	C	F	W	A	O	A
7	D	C	E	C	Y		S	I	L	W	B	S	B	N	F	K	X	F	Z
8	W	L	U	G	S		X	E	Y	M	L	Z	F	F	N	U	S	T	R	G
9	D	U	Q	E	Q	X	G	F	H	E	K	F	G	X	J	K	C	K	Y
10	P	E	I	Y	Z	T	V	E	F	J	N	X	N	A	I	I	X	Z	W	M
11	S	Z	P	K	R	D	B	N	X	A	E	N	E	L	Z	L	J	X	J
12	C	T	N	C	L	A	B	O	T	M	W	D	X	E	Y	M	K	Y	U
13	Q	E	Q	X	G	H	L	G	U	O	M	L	W	K	Y	F	E	X	
14	D	W	L	D	V	B	N	C	N	G	B	O	E	F	P	B	X	E	Y
15	M	Z	W	U	Q	E	Q	X	G	H	L	V	M	K	Y	F	E	X	D
16	C	U	C	N	J	N	N	B	N	C	T	K	B	C	O	C	X	P	X
17	E	Y	M	K	Y	U	Q	E	Q	N	M	H	L	H	Z	N	B	A	O
18	M	S	B	L	M	D	Q	V	M	O	V	B	M	T	O	V	E	R	C
19	X	N	V	E	A	X	P	Z	T	V	B	H	L	Z	A	L	W	K	Y
20	F	E	X	D	K	P	Q	V	V	B	N	C	N	V	J	G	N	P	Q
21	O	A	F	U	F	X	E	E	Q	X	J	K	C	G	G	B	V	U	X
22	N	J	F	X	D	M	M	G	R	A	N	D	B	O	A	D	B	E	R
23	V	T	M	K	D	A	D	J	B	G	Q	N	C	N	U	D	M	A	G
24	V	P	U	S	B	D	Z	K	-	B	U	X	Z	H	M				

DATE 19 NH 1941 MSG. NO. Circ 2353
FROM Tokio TO Washington
K-10 Form Period 11-20 November 1941 Good for __ columns

Glossary of Terms and Abbreviations

ABC-	American-British Commonwealth Staff Agreement or American, British, Canadian Military Agreement (March 1941)
AN	*angoo or angoo koodo*
BAMS	broadcast to Allied merchant ships
CAST	covername for the USN cryptologic site in the Philippines
CINCAF	Commander-in-Chief Asiatic Fleet
CINCPAC	Commander-in-Chief Pacific Fleet
COM-14	Commander, 14th Naval District (Territory of Hawaii)
COM-16	Commander, 16th Naval District (Philippines)
COMINT	communications intelligence
CNO	Chief of Naval Operations
ACNO	Assistant Chief of Naval Operations
DNC	Director of Naval Communications (OP-20)
FCC	Federal Communications Commission
FECB	Far East Combined Bureau
FO	Foreign Office (UK)
G-1	staff element in charge of personnel
G-2	staff element in charge of military intelligence
GMT	Greenwich Mean Time
GC&CS	Government Code & Cypher School (UK)
"GY"	Element of Op-20-G charged with cryptanalysis and decryption
"GZ"	Element of OP-20-G charged with translation and code recovery
HYPO	covername for the USN cryptologic site at Pearl Harbor, T.H.
"J-series"	designator for Japanese diplomatic cryptographic systems.
JCC	Joint Congressional Committee
"JD-"	prefix for serialized translations of Japanese diplomatic messages
"JN-"	prefix for serialized translations of Japanese naval messages
KHz	kilohertz
MAM	Japanese merchant ship broadcast
MI	military intelligence (G-2)
MNDT	multi-national diplomatic translation
MS	monitoring station
NARA	National Archives and Records Adminsitration
NEGAT	covername for the USN cryptologic facility in Washington, D.C.
NSA	National Security Agency
NSG	Naval Security Group
OCSigO	Office of the Chief Signal Officer (US Army)
ONI	Office of Naval Intelligence (OP-16)
OP-16	Director of Naval Communications
OP-20-G	Division of Naval Communications charged with naval cryptology and cryptography
OPNAV	The support staff for the Chief of Naval Operations
ORANGE	Covername for the M-2 Japanese cipher machine for naval attachés; combatant "color" assigned to Japan
PHH	Pearl Harbor hearings
PHR	Pearl Harbor report
PT&T	post, telephone, and telegraph
PURPLE	Covername for the Japanese diplomatic cipher machine in use after 1940
RED	Covername for the Japanese diplomatic cipher machine in use from 1936 to 1940.
RG	Record Group
SIS	Signals Intelligence Service
SRH	Special Research History
SRNA	Designator for translations of Japanese naval attachés
TWX	leased teletype

WDGS War Department, General Staff
WPL War Plan
WRNS Women's Royal Navy Service
W.S. Work Sheet
"X-day" Japanese designator for the start of its offensive – 8 December (Tokyo), 7 December (Washington, Honolulu)

Sources and Selected Bibliography

National Archives and Records Administration and National Security Agency

RG 38, Records of the Chief of Naval Operations, Commander Naval Security Group, CNSG Library.

RG 80, Records of the Secretary of the Navy, Pearl Harbor Liaison Office.

RG 128.3 Records of Joint Committees, 51st - 98th Congresses, 1890-1984.

RG 173, Records of the Federal Communications Commission.

RG 457, Records of the National Security Agency/Central Security Service, Historical Cryptographic Collection

Center for Cryptologic History, National Security Agency, Fort George G. Meade, MD, Historical Collection Series XII.S

Private Archival Collections

The Laurance Safford Collection, National Cryptologic Museum Foundation, Fort George G. Meade, Maryland.

Papers of Admiral Husband E. Kimmel, American Heritage Center, University of Wyoming, Laramie, WY.

Hearings and Government Publications

Hearings before the Joint Committee on the Investigation of the Pearl Harbor Attack. Congress of the United States, Seventy-Ninth Congress. Pursuant to Senate Concurrent Resolution No. 27 Authorizing an Investigation of the Attack on Pearl Harbor on December 7, 1941, and events and Circumstances Relating Thereto (Washington: United States Government Printing Office, 1946), 39 Volumes

The United States Department of Defense, *The "Magic" Background to Pearl Harbor* (Washington: USGPO, 1980), 8 Volumes.

National Security Agency, Special Research History (SRH) 051, "Interview with Mr. Ralph T. Briggs, 3 January 1977," 11 May 1980

————————, SRH-115, "United States Army Investigations into the Handling of Certain Communications Prior to the Attack on Pearl Harbor, 1944-1945," 19 February 1981

————————, SRH-118, "Incidental Exhibits Re: Pearl Harbor Investigations (MIS/WDGS), 15 April 1981

————————, SRH-125, "Certain Aspects of "MAGIC" in the Cryptological Background of the Various Official Investigations into the Pearl Harbor Attack," by William F. Friedman, 22 May 1981.

Military Intelligence Service, War Department, General Staff, SRH-128, "Study of Pearl Harbor Hearings," 23 January 1947.

————————-, SRH-177, "Interrogation of Japanese Concerning Broadcast of the 'Winds Execute Message', October – November 1945," 16 July 1982

————————-, SRH-210, "Collection of Papers Related to the 'Winds Execute Message', United States Navy 1945," 22 November 1983

————————-, SRH-233, "U.S. Navy Director of Naval Communications Memoranda on the

Congressional Investigations of the Attack on Pearl Harbor," 23 March 1983

—————————-, SRH-407, " Collection of Memoranda by the Signal Security Agency (SSA) re: 'Winds Execute Message', September 1944" 16 June 1992

—————————-, SRH-415, "Haruna Messages from Various Japanese Offices Abroad Signaling Destruction of Codes, December 1941," 23 February 1993.

Shaw, H.L. Captain, *History of H.M.S. Anderson*. 24 May 1946. United Kingdom Public Record Office (The National Archives) HW 4/25

Selected Bibliography

Aldrich, Richard J., *Intelligence and the War Against Japan*. Cambridge: Cambridge University Press, 2000

Bartlett, Bruce R. *Cover-up: The Politics of Pearl Harbor, 1941-1946*. New Rochelle: Arlington House Publishers, 1978

Budiansky, Stephen, *Battle of Wits: The Complete Story of Codebreaking in World War II*. New York: The Free Press, 2000

Clark, Ronald, *The Man Who Broke Purple*. Boston: Little Brown & Company, 1977

Clausen, Henry C., and Bruce Lee, *Pearl Harbor: Final Judgment*. New York: Crown Publishers, 1992

Costello, John. *The Pacific War, 1941-1945*. New York: Quill Books, 1981

Dallek, Robert, *Franklin D. Roosevelt and American Foreign Policy, 1932-1945*. Oxford & New York: Oxford University Press, 1979

Gannon, Michael, *Pearl Harbor Betrayed: The True Story of a Man and a Nation Under Attack*. New York: John Macrae Books, 2001

Herzog, James H., *Closing the Door*. Annapolis, MD: Naval Institute Press, 1973

Homes, W.J., *Double-Edged Secrets*. Annapolis, MD: Naval Institute Press, 1979

Kahn, David, *The Codebreakers: The Story of Secret Writing*. New York: MacMillan Company, 1967

Keiichiro Komatsu, *The Origins of the Pacific War and the Importance of 'Magic'*. New York: St Martin's Press, 1999

Layton, Admiral Edwin T., (with Roger Pinneau and John Costello), *And I Was There: Pearl Harbor and Midway – Breaking the Secrets*. New York: William Morrow and Co., 1985

Lewin, Ronald, *The American Magic. Codes, Ciphers and the Defeat of Japan*. New York: Penguin Books, 1983

Morison, Samuel Eliot, *History of United States Naval Operations in World War II: The Rising Sun in the Pacific, 1931-April 1942*. Volume III, Boston, MA: Little, Brown and Company, 1975

Parker, Frederick D., *Pearl Harbor Revisited: United States Navy Communications Intelligence, 1924-1941*. Fort George G. Meade, MD: Center for Cryptologic History, 1994

Persico, Joseph E., *Roosevelt's Secret War. FDR and World War II Espionage*. New York: Random House, 2001

Prange, Gordon, *Pearl Harbor: the Verdict of History*. New York: McGraw-Hill, 1986

Rowlett, Frank B., *The Story of Magic: Memoirs of an American Cryptologic Pioneer*. Laguna Hills CA: Aegean Park Press, 1998

Rusbridger, James, and Eric Nave, *Betrayal at Pearl Harbor: How Churchill Lured Roosevelt into World War II*. New York: Summit Books, 1991

Smith, Michael, *The Emperor's Codes. Bletchley Park and the Breaking of Japan's Secret Ciphers*. New York: Bantam Press, 2000

Smith, Stanley, *Investigations of the Attack on Pearl Harbor. Index to Government Hearings*. New York: Greenwood Press, 1990

Stafford, David, *Roosevelt and Churchill, Men of Secrets*. Woodstock and New York: The Overlook Press, 1999

Stinnett, Robert, *Day of Deceit: The Truth about FDR and Pearl Harbor*. New York: The Free Press, 2000

Theobald, Rear Admiral Robert, USN, *The Final Secret of Pearl Harbor: The Washington Contribution to the Japanese Attacks*. New York: The Devin-Adair Company, 1954

Toland, John, *Infamy: Pearl Harbor and its Aftermath*. New York: Berkeley, 1983

Van Der Rhoer, Edward, *Deadly Magic*. New York: Charles Scribner's Sons, 1978

Victor, George, *The Pearl Harbor Myth: Rethinking the Unthinkable*. Washington, D.C: Potomac Books, 2007

Wohlstetter, Roberta, *Pearl Harbor: Warning and Decision*. Stanford: Stanford University Press, 1962

INDEX

A

American Black Chamber (ABC), 6-7
Army Pearl Harbor Board, 59, 61-62, 70-72
Asiatic Fleet, United States, 26, 30

B

Bainbridge Island, Washington (Station S), 2, 10, 13, 19, 24, 35
    intercept of Hidden Word message, 44-46
    intercept of Winds instructions, 15-16, 38-39
    tasked to intercept Winds Execute, 33, 67-68
Broadcast to Allied Merchant Ships (BAMS), 85-86
Bandung (Netherlands East Indies), 10, 23
Barkley, Alben, 62
Batavia (Netherlands East Indies), 26-27, 30, 41, 50
Bicknell, George W., 44
Bissell, Clayton, 61, 65, 74-75, 90
Bratton, Rufus, 35-38, 43-44, 46-47, 65, 75
Briggs, Ralph, 2, 85-88, 92
Brotherhood, Francis M., 2, 37, 57, 69, 76
Bryant, H. L., 65, 74, 77

C

Cage. *See* general cryptography: stencil.
CAST (Corregidor Island), 33, 35-36
Cheltenham, Maryland, monitoring station, 57, 63, 65
    Briggs, 85-88
    destruction of records, 75-76
    intercept tasking, 67-69
Chief of Naval Operations (CNO), 32, 44, 55-56, 62
    sends warning message, 64, 71-72
China, 1-5, 11-13
CIU. *See* Communications Intelligence Unit.
Clarke, Carter W., 58
    interview of William Friedman, 61
    report of General Marshall order to destroy records, 58, 61, 75, 77
Clarke Investigation, 25, 58-61, 67, 75
Clausen, Henry C., 2, 61
Clausen Investigation, vii, 59-61
    attitude to Safford, 77
    suspected British intercept of Winds messages, 82-84
CNO. *See* Chief of Naval Operations.
communications (Japanese)
    cable, 6, 40-41
    diplomatic net, 16, 23, 40
    merchant ship broadcast (MAM), 68, 86-87
    Morse code, 37, 40, 69
    commercial and government broadcast stations, 40, 81
    Ippa Joho, 26
    JAH, 45
    JAP, 63-64, 68-69
    JAV, 33
    JHL, 32-33
    JUO, 32-33
    JUP, 33
    JVJ, 32-33, 36
    JVW3, 36, 38
Communications Intelligence Unit, Hawaii (CIU), 34, 44
Costello, John, 100
cryptography (general) 3-6
    covered or hidden code, xiv
    enciphered code, xv, 5, 9
    indicator, xvi, 15, 18-19, 23-24
    key, 5, 15, 18-21, 23-25
    matrix, 18-19
    stencil, 19, 24-5
    substitution cipher, 4-5, 17, 21

supencryption, 21, 23
transposition cipher xv, 5, 17
cryptography (non-Japanese)
    ADFGVX system, 21, 28
    Enigma cipher machine, 10, 13, 54
    Kryha machine, 4
cryptography (Japanese) 4-5
    Ciphers:
        K-5, 17-19, 23
        K-6, 17
        K-7, 17
        K-8, 17
        K-9, 17
        K-10, 17-19
        Q-1, 18
    Diplomatic systems:
        J-11, 17
        J-12, 17
        J-14, 17
        J-15, 17
        J-16 (Matsu), 16-21, 23, 27-28
        J-17 (Hagi), 17, 19, 23
        J-18 (Sakura), 17, 23
        J-19 (Fuji), 15-17, 19-20, 23-24, 38
        J-22, 97
        LA, 4, 24, 42-43, 97
        PA-K2, 19, 24, 38, 42-43, 97
        Purple machine, 1, 5, 10, 31, 65
            decryption of, 8-9, 21, 24, 54, 57
            destruction of, 41-42
            status, 15, 17
            used to encrypt, J-18 23
        Red machine, 4-5, 8-9, 12, 16
    Naval systems:
        AD, 5
        AN Code, 9, 10
        AN-1 Code, 54, 64, 97
        B Code, 5
        Black, 5
        Blue Code, 5, 9
        IKA machine, 5
        JN-25 (general), 6, 9, 10-11, 64
        JN-25A, 54
        JN-25B, 54
        Red Code, 5

D

Department of State (U.S.), 2, 6-7, 27, 34, 71, 82
Department of War (U.S.), 6, 58-59, 61, 63, 71
Director of Naval Communications (DNC, OP-20), 32-33, 37
Domei, 33
Driscoll, Agnes Meyer, 9, 53-54
Dusenberg, Carlisle, 47

E

Enigma. *See* cryptography (non-Japanese).

F

Far East Combined Bureau (FECB), 10, 30, 36, 82-83, 92
Federal Bureau of Investigation (FBI), 35
Federal Communications Commission (FCC),
    capabilities, 34-35
        Hears West Wind Clear, 47-8, 80-81, 83, 86, 88
        Intercept stations, 35, 47, 81
        monitors Wind message, 35, 44
        Radio Intelligence Division (RID), 34-35, 49
        reports false winds messages, 36-38, 64, 69, 73
FECB. *See* Far East Combined Bureau.
Foote, Walter, 2, 27, 82
Forrestal, James, 61, 64
Fort Monmouth, 8, 13, 34
French Indochina, 1, 11, 31, 46, 84
Friedman, William F., 1, 7, 20, 54, 65,
    Friedman and Safford, 57-58, 61, 75
    reaction to J-19, 22-23
    revised Winds translations, 25-26

G

G-2 (U.S. Army intelligence), 35, 37, 46, 55, 58, 60, 75
Gaimusho, 4, 15, 23, 27, 31-32, 42, 70
Gearhart, Bertrand, 79
Gerow, Leonard T., 38, 43
Government Code & Cypher School (GC&CS), 10
Great Britain, 1, 3, 6, 10-12, 25-26, 80-83, 95, 98

H

Halsey, William, 56, 79, 81
Hart, Thomas, 32-33
Hart Inquiry, 2, 32-33, 59, 68-72, 74-75, 78
Haruna message, 42, 50, 95
Hasso (codeword), 42
Hawaii, 10, 13
Hewitt, H. Kent, 58-59
Hewitt Inquiry, 58-62, 64, 66, 68-70, 73-75, 77-78, 82
hidden word (Ingo Denpo) or Stop message, 38-46, 56, 73, 78-79, 83, 95-96
Hinoki. *See* cryptography (Japanese): Purple machine
Hong Kong, 10, 12, 36, 41, 82-3
Hull, Cordell, 2, 31, 46-47, 51, 56
Hurt, John, 7, 25
HYPO, 34, 44, 97

I

indicator. *See* general cryptography.
Ingersoll, Royal E., 2, 44

J

J-Series. *See* cryptography (Japanese).
Japan 4-6, 9-12, 22, 34, 40, 56, 59, 61
    Broadcast Corporation, 80-81
    destruction of papers 25, 27
    embassies 42
    strategy, pre-war 95
Joint Congressional Committee (Pearl Harbor hearings), 53, 62-63, 66-67, 77, 82

K

Kahn, David, 54, 100
Kamer-14, 10, 14, 26
Keefe, Frank, 79
Kido Butai (Pearl Harbor Striking Force), 12, 98
Kimmel, Husband, 34, 44, 55-56, 60, 76-77, 79-80
Knox, Henry, 31, 56, 59, 64
Konoye, Fumimaro, 11-12
Kramer, Alwin, 36-37, 59, 62, 68-70
    changing testimony, 69, 73-79, 98
    letters to Safford, 56-57, 66, 70
    Stop message, 45-46
    Winds translation, 63-64
Kurusu, Saburo, 31, 47

L

Layton, Edwin, 34, 36, 49
Linn, George W., 76

M

Magic, 20-21, 44, 60-61, 63-64, 71, 79, 88
Marshall, George C., 31, 38, 46, 65-66, 75, 99
    purported destruction of Winds message, 58, 61, 65, 75
Mauborgne, Joseph, 22-23
Mayfield, Irving, 34, 39
McCollum, Arthur, 36-37, 44, 55, 57, 64-65, 72-73, 76, 78-79, 88
Miles, Sherman, 37, 43-44
Missing translation (#7001), 55, 58, 64, 71, 75
Mori tap, 79, 91
Morse code, 26, 32-33, 35, 46, 57, 63, 67, 85
Murray, A. A., 57, 65, 69

N

Naval Court of Inquiry, 59, 62, 68-69, 71, 77-79
Naval Security Group, 85, 92
Nave, Eric, 26, 29
Netherlands, 1, 10-11, 25-26, 41-42, 48, 68, 82
Netherlands East Indies (NEI), 1, 10, 68, 82
Nomura, Kichisaburo, 31, 46-48
Noyes, Leigh, 32, 35, 37-38, 44, 57, 60, 63-65

O

Olmstead, Dawson, 65, 74
Office of Naval Intelligence (ONI, OP-16), 32-33, 35-36, 47, 58, 63-63, 72
OP-20-G, 29, 35-36, 41-42, 45, 85, 87, 89, 92
    early codebreaking, 9-10, 13, 96
    J-19, 15, 24-27
    OP-20-GX, 33, 39
    OP-20-GY, 37-38, 63-65, 68-69, 78, 82
    Safford and, 53-55
    and Winds message, 71-73, 76
    working with SIS, 21-22
OPNAV (Chief of Operations staff), 32-33, 36, 56, 71, 74
Orange (Japan), 3, 5

P

Pacific Fleet, United States, 1, 3-4, 11
Parke, L. W., 74
Pearl Harbor, 1, 6, 9, 16, 20, 74, 85-86, 95
    espionage against, 49, 81, 98
    hearings on, 44, 53, 58-59, 61-62, 66
    Japanese planning against, 11-12, 97-98
    vulnerability to attack, 3-4
    warnings to, 55-56, 63-64, 72, 96
    Winds message and, 82-83, 88, 100
Pettigrew, Moses, 75
Portland, Oregon, FCC monitoring station, 35, 47
Post Telephone & Telegraph (PT&T), 40

Purple machine. *See* cryptography (Japanese): diplomatic.

R

Radio Corporation of America (RCA), 15, 41, 45
Radio Intelligence Division (RID). *See* Federal Communications Commission.
Rainbow Plans (U.S.), 5, 10
Red machine. *See* cryptography (Japanese): diplomatic.
Roberts Commission, 48, 55, 58, 62, 64, 78-79, 89
Rochefort, Joseph, 9, 34, 44, 53, 75
Roosevelt, Franklin D., 2, 4, 11-12, 31, 46, 53, 58, 63, 71, 76, 85, 87-88, 93, 96
Rowlett, Frank B., 1-2, 4, 11-12, 15, 2023, 27-28, 53-54, 65

S

Sadtler, Otis K., 1, 34, 37-38, 58-59, 61, 65, 75
Safford, Laurance F., 9, 22, 24, 32-33, 95, 98-100
    affidavit, 54, 56, 67-73, 75-76, 78, 79
    Congressional assessment, of 77, 99
    early career, 53-54
    letters to Kramer, 54, 58, 66, 68, 78-81
    list of personnel who knew of Winds message, 65, 74-75, 88
    missing records, 55, 58, 67, 72, 75-76, 85-87
    testimony before Pearl Harbor hearings:
        Army Pearl Harbor Board, 59-61, 70-71
        Hart Inquiry, 59, 75
        Hewitt Inquiry, 61-62
        Joint Congressional Hearings, 62-66
        Naval Board of Inquiry, 59-60
Schukraft, Robert E., 34, 37
Secret Intelligence Service, MI-6, United Kingdom (S.I.S.), 83-84
Short, Walter C., 56, 58, 78
Signals Intelligence Service, US Army (S.I.S.), 1, 7-9, 12-13, 20-22, 25, 34, 37, 39, 42

S.I.S. *See* Secret Intelligence Service; Signals Intelligence Service.
Sonnett, John F., 64, 74
Spadling, Isaac (Ike), 58, 61, 75
Station S *See* Bainbridge Island
Stark, Harold R., 31, 60, 62, 65
State Department, *See* Department of State
stencil. *See* cryptography (general).
Sterling, George, 34-36, 38, 49
Stimson, Henry L., 7, 31, 56, 61, 83-4

T

Tanomogi, Shinroku, 81-82
Tateno, Mori, 81-82
Togo, Shigenori, 15
Toland, John, 54, 86, 89-90, 92, 100
TWX (leased commercial teleprinter), 55, 63, 67, 78
Turner, Richmond K., 38, 65, 72-3

W

War Department, *See* Department of War
War Plans (WPL)
    WPL 13, 10
    WPL 46, 10
Washington Naval Conference, 3, 6
Welker, George W., 65, 67-68, 73-74, 77
Western Union, 15
Wigle, D.W., 68, 85, 87
Wilkinson, Theodore S., 32, 35, 57, 65, 72-73, 84
Winds Message, 16
    Actual Winds message, 46-48
    Execute message, 31-32, 34-38, 41, 43-44, 46, 53, 55-80, 82-88
    false messages, 36-38, 64, 69, 73
    Message # 2353, 24-25, 96
    Message #2354, 15, 25-27, 96
    missing records, 55-56
    phrases, 27, 31-38, 46
        Higashi No Kaze Ame 25, 37, 57, 78, 85
        Kita No Kaze Kumori 25, 36-37
        Nishi No Kaze Hare 25, 47
    Safford testimony and, 55-80
    search for, 31-32, 53, 55-56, 66-67, 76-77, 80, 83
    set up messages, 24-25, 27, 30-32, 34, 95
    words, 27, 33, 40, 42
        Nishi 25-26
        Kita 25-26
        Higashi 25-26
Winter Harbor, Maine, monitoring station, 55, 57, 67-8

X

X-day, 98

Y

Yamamoto, Isoroku, 11
Yardley, Herbert O. 6, 7, 12-13
Yoshikawa, Takeo, 81